W9-DBE-683

BUILDING A COMMUNITY OF CITIZENS

*Civil Society in
the 21st Century*

Edited by

Don E. Eberly

UNIVERSITY
PRESS OF
AMERICA

Lanham • New York • London

THE
COMMONWEALTH
FOUNDATION
for Public Policy Alternatives

Copyright © 1994 by
The Commonwealth Foundation

University Press of America®, Inc.
4720 Boston Way
Lanham, Maryland 20706

3 Henrietta Street
London WC2E 8LU England

Copublished by arrangement with
The Commonwealth Foundation

Library of Congress Cataloging-in-Publication Data

Building a community of citizens : civil society in the 21st century /
edited by Don E. Eberly.
p.   cm.
Includes bibliographical references.
1. Citizenship—United States.   2. Civil society—United States.
3. Civics.   4. Political participation—United States.   5. United
States—Politics and government.   I. Eberly, Don E.
JK1759.B888   1994   320.4973—dc20   94–22687 CIP

ISBN 0–8191–9613–4 (cloth : alk. paper)
ISBN 0–8191–9614–2 (pbk. : alk. paper)

Dedication

This book is dedicated to my children, Preston, Caroline, and Margaret, three remarkable sources of joy and optimism, as well as to the kids of America, in the hope that the ideas presented here and the actions they inspire will make their world, and their children's world just a little bit more humane and promising.

Contents

Preface

Today Americans face momentous challenges and change at a dizzying pace. Pollster George Gallup has described the profound shifts in American society as a "great historical tidal wave--a set of monumental political, social and economic impulses, which are carrying us relentlessly toward a rendezvous with the future."

Suddenly, Americans are turning inward and asking fresh questions: What is the state of our values and democratic institutions? Can the country that is the birthplace of modern liberty remain a world leader if current trends continue? As old belief systems collapse, new paradigms and priorities emerge seeking to determine the social and political contours of the 21st century.

In September 1863, Abraham Lincoln dedicated a cemetery to young soldiers who gave the full measure of devotion in the war. The question Lincoln asked on that solemn occasion is the question that devoted citizens and leaders must ask anew today: "Can this nation, or any nation so conceived and so dedicated, long endure?"

Many are taking a fresh look at the content of our nation's character and are sensing that America is once again facing a threat -- this time from within. The 20th century's reigning dialectical materialism produced not only a failed totalitarian experiment: it produced in the democratic and secular west a moral apathy and indifference that has left society aimless and rudderless.

America's greatest weaknesses lie in the civic, cultural, moral realm where government solutions are often deficient and unworkable. David Blankenhorn of the Institute for American Values speaks of an American "social recession" and a "cultural regression" that has serious consequences for America's future. He says, "there is a declining sense of civic obligation, a lowering of trust in social institutions, a diminution of caring for one another in society, along with the increase of a range of personal pathologies," among which he includes declining mental health, crime, teen suicide, and an assortment of personal maladies.

This book is a call for a cultural and civic renaissance in America. The battle to restore the basic ideas and values of the American experiment will be profoundly different than previous conflicts and challenges Americans have faced.   Mapping the task starts with difficult questions. What foundations exist to provide for the restoration of badly weakened public institutions and civil society? How can urgently needed reforms be advanced in a political process dominated by interests strongly resistant to reform? How can basic American philosophical principles be strengthened without simply advancing ideologies that compete for power?   How can one restore a culture, along with its institutions and professions, without resorting to statism and demagoguery?

Our political life and public discourse are in trouble. People perceive much of government to be an incompetent and costly failure and consider politics remote and disconnected.   Politics has evolved into a highly calibrated business in which a fairly permanent governing class is both the producer and consumer of what takes place.   The public, not surprisingly, sees politicians as serving their own purposes, more prone to create than solve crises, and less likely to supply real solutions for improving the quality of life.

Men and women of principle must move to restore lost integrity in our nation's political and governmental institutions while also candidly admitting to the limitations of politics to renew American life.   Public cynicism is rooted in the fact that while government has underperformed, politics has been oversold. Political agendas of both the Left and Right have been dramatically exaggerated as sources of national renewal. Creating the good society is neither easy nor simple: it requires improving our public life--strengthening both personal and civic virtue--not just cleaning up our political institutions.

The wisest use of public platforms would be to summon forth from the people a new resolve to strengthen civil society, particularly the institutions of family and community upon which it rests.   Public leaders should communicate more candidly that they and their initiatives are not the answer: that if we are going to save families, make our neighborhoods friendly and safe, and restore such lost virtues as honesty and civility, then we, the people, must do it. Politicians cannot recreate lost community, only citizens can, but their honest words and mediating influence could certainly steer society in this direction. Politics restored to its proper and unpretentious place in society might return hope to Americans seeking to live in a society less splintered by race, class, and divisive politics.

Politics, as we know it, injures more than it renews and heals society. Central to renewed balance is the restoration of a fuller, broader, older concept of citizenship. Harry Boyte, author of *Commonwealth: A Return to Citizen Politics*, and contributor to this volume, says it is time to stop complaining about public problems and start rebuilding the quality of our public life. It is time, he says, to reinvent citizenship: not a sentimentalized version, but a social covenant involving hard work and sacrifice. Whatever government does or does not do, the job of restoration and renewal will fall heavily to citizens.

Those serious about restoring citizenship will accept that problems do exist for individuals that sometimes require public help. Many barriers to citizenship and self-sufficiency do exist, and for many poor Americans the lack of meaningful opportunity is real. Still, renewal based upon a revival of citizenship will recognize that barriers to opportunity are as frequently inward as they are external to the individual. At no time in American history was there opportunity plentiful enough that the path to self-sufficiency was assured or easy for most citizens.

In the end, resuscitating an older, fuller concept of citizenship requires that individuals must be seen as capable of self-government by both themselves and their leaders. Indeed, responsibility must be made the cornerstone of America's basic social contract. There is scant hope for change based upon top-down strategies, impersonal theories, or simply a new round of programmatic reforms. Citizens must take responsibility for nourishing institutions, imparting character, and rediscovering timeless wisdom for daily life. America's expert class has asserted too great hegemony over much of American life, robbing individuals of their status as true citizens.

The duties of citizenship are carried out in the context of associational life, not just through participation in politics. This is civil society, the realm in which Americans conduct most of their lives and which supplies a form of participation that is most meaningful and satisfying. The strength and authority of such institutions as family, church and synagogue, neighborhoods and voluntary associations, have been steadily weakened in America by both a driving individualism in the culture and from pressures by well-meaning but intrusive public policies.

Only through the commitments of millions of Americans can this vital voluntary sector be maintained and reinvigorated. Americans themselves will have to resist the steady loss of civic autonomy by fortifying local associations and institutions against assaults from the culture and the state. There is little hope of creating genuine community without curbing both individualism and bureaucratization.

The family, in particular, must be held up as the only genuine foundation for real community, meaningful human bonds, and social sympathy and continuity. Once again, it will fall to individual Americans to confront family disintegration. Like so many topics, the debate over family has become too politicized. Family is not a conservative or liberal idea; it is both. It conserves positive habits and the capacity for self regulation, and it assures true human progress in a liberal society. Thus responsible conservatives and liberals should abandon attempts to harness the family to partisan agendas, and undertake joint social ventures to achieve family restoration in the sphere of civil society. Whatever else family debates include, they must have as their primary objective the restoration of the basic unit of the family. Everything else is secondary.

America has no choice but to deal with the contest between diversity and a common culture. It has long been assumed that America is held together by the preservation of a unique American creed. America's public philosophy is one that embraces racial and ethnic diversity, yet seeks to assimilate all into a shared sense of destiny based upon the ideals of progress, equality, optimism, and opportunity. This public philosophy embodies a shared vision for the common good. It is not the *E Pluribus* without the *Unum*. It calls on Americans to honor and respect America's ethnic mosaic through a well-moderated pluralism, yet also issues a call to transcend the particulars of race, class and religion to find strength in common civic and democratic values.

Finding continued American progress in the midst of a multi-cultural society will require a revisitation of foundational principles. Abraham Lincoln stated that all of the political sentiments he possessed emanated from one single rich source: the Declaration of Independence, which read "We hold these truths to be self-evident, that all men are created equal, that they are endowed by their Creator with certain unalienable Rights, that among these are Life, Liberty and the pursuit of Happiness." If this basic creed was sufficient to guide a nation's passage through our most perilous and bloody conflict, it is certainly adequate to repair the fractured civil order of a nation at peace at home and abroad.

So, how can we rebuild confidence in schools, restore neighborhood integrity and mobilize citizens to restore lost community? What is needed to rebuild civil society, diminish individualism and restore self restraint and civility? These are the questions to which the contributors to this volume have given serious consideration.   And they join the editor in urging the reader to search for his or her own application of the civic vision embraced throughout this volume, at whatever level of influence, in every community of America.

Acknowledgments

I am extremely grateful for the exceptional staff work of Cliff Frick, Communications Director at The Commonwealth Foundation, who helped guide the book to completion; intern Scott Bishop whose superb organizational skills and eye for quality improved the volume considerably; and Deb Strubel, whose technical editing assistance made the project enjoyable and manageable.

I am further indebted to each of the outstanding contributors to this volume. Many of them are friends and I am convinced they represent some of the most innovative thinking in America on the concerns addressed in this volume. Each author is contributing, in his or her own unique voice, to the project of strengthening citizenship, renewing our democratic life, and repairing the institutions of civil society.

I am especially indebted to those thinkers on the American scene at present who, while diverse in their politics, are united in their vision for a renewed civil society. Namely, Amitai Etzioni of the Communitarian movement, Bill Bennett, former Secretary of Education and author of *Book of Virtues*, David Blankenhorn of the Institute for American Values, Bill Galston, Domestic Policy Adviser to the President, and Michael Novak of the American Enterprise Institute. These are among the pioneers who are leading the way to a new framework for seeing America's social problems, and are sources of inspiration to both the editor and many who have contributed to this volume.

Finally, I wish to thank the University Press of America for believing that this project would result in a volume deserving broad circulation.

Introduction

The Quest for a Civil Society

Don E. Eberly

We are all recognizing that the kinds of rationalistic, scientific, technical, organizational responses to human needs in the past several centuries are not sufficient to respond to people's deeper yearnings, their spiritual desires, and the way they treat one another.

First Lady Hillary Rodham Clinton[1]

There has to be some core of shared values. Of all the ingredients of community this is the most important. The values may be reflected in written laws and rules, in a shared framework of meaning, in unwritten customs, in a shared vision of what constitutes the common good and the future.

Common Cause Founder, John W. Gardner[2]

The alternative to the naked public square is the reconstitution of civil society in America. And what is "civil society?" Civil society is the achievement of a genuine pluralism in which creeds are intelligibly in conflict.

Conservative think tank President George Weigel[3]

The communitarian perspective recognizes that the preservation of individual liberty depends on the active maintenance of the institutions of civil society where citizens learn respect for others as well as self-respect; where we acquire a lively sense of our personal and civic responsibilities, along with an appreciation of our own rights and the rights of others; where we develop the skills of self-government as well as the habit of governing ourselves, and learn to serve others--not just self.

From the Communitarian Platform[4]

We are increasingly living in a political society at the expense of a civil society. The challenge... is to stand up for the principles of a civil society-- one based on voluntarism--while standing in the midst of a statist conflagration... the level of taxation is the measure of our failure to civilize our society.

Libertarian advocate, Edward H. Crane, President, The Cato Institute[5]

The American political party that best gives life and breath and amplitude to civil society will not only thrive in the twenty-first century. It will win popular gratitude and it will govern.

Catholic theologian Michael Novak[6]

There seems to be a great deal of agreement, from conservatives to liberals, about the need to improve civil society. Despite this seeming consensus across the political spectrum, however, the search for a humane, civil, and well-ordered society remains elusive as the 21st century approaches. As the title suggests, this volume explores the condition of America's civic and democratic life and seeks a foundation for progress in the 21st century.

America is in the midst of social convulsions at home and global change of a scale, velocity, and uncertainty that futurists say may be unprecedented in human experience. In the midst of a surging economy, large majorities from virtually every sector of society worry that something very basic has gone wrong at the core of society, something that cannot be measured in the traditional terms of Gross National Product (GNP) growth rates and unemployment figures. Public worries increasingly concern cultural indicators, such as rising teen pregnancy, violence, and declining Scholastic Achievement Test (SAT) scores, factors as important to national advancement as a growing economy.

But even this social data reveals only the measurable indicators of societal regression. The quality of life is more and more shaped by unmeasurable things that have weakened, like basic civility and manners. Many report finding life coarser, their culture cruder, the public debate angrier, and the treatment of individuals less respectful than when they grew up. There is a sense that Americans have become shortsighted and selfish, obsessed with rights and entitlements, and that quality, excellence, and commitment to work have all waned.

The mood is peculiar in light of the nation's successes. For one, America presently stands taller than perhaps any nation in history. By defeating the forces of totalitarianism, the United States occupies the position of undisputed heavyweight: the only true military and economic superpower. America is still the most coveted destination for immigrants; it is exporting more goods and services than any nation in history; it is employing more of its population than ever; and its technological genius is still unmatched around the world. In sum, it is the richest, mightiest, and most magnetic of any nation on the globe.

For decades during the cold war, the need for a well-defined identity and moral purpose was reinforced as America led a unified democratic front against Communism. Her core principles needed little further articulation. That the East-West conflict and the national resolve it produced held things in equilibrium cannot be denied. With the East-West conflict gone, however, America no longer leads out of necessity. If it is to continue to lead other nations, it will do so less out of moral necessity and more by moral example.

The entire world is free to decide which sociopolitical system to adopt. America is increasingly being judged globally, not by its military prowess, but by social conditions at home. It is humbling for the world's richest industrial nation to have a poverty rate twice that of any other industrial nation and to be singled out by international agencies as a world leader in child poverty and youth homicides.

While no ideology appears to compete today with the dominance and increasing popularity of democratic capitalism as the best system to satisfy human aspirations, the picture is by no means that simple. The factors leading to human conflict that have reemerged around the globe, and even at home, in recent years are the ancient forces of race, ethnicity, religion, and nationalism. They represent some of the most vexing fissures that have marked the human landscape from the beginning of time and are the kind that democracies have proven weak to manage.

Democratic capitalism has vindicated itself in surviving repeated challenges in the 20th century, whether depression at home or ideological challenge abroad. But how sufficient is economic advancement, many are asking, if our schools do not function, if crime defies control, and if children have lost their innocence in an adversarial culture of violence and banality? When a society becomes completely indifferent to the need to safeguard its own children from harm and lets one in four fall into poverty, it risks losing its status as a world leader.

Voicing worry about the status of American society involves risk. One can easily be tagged a pessimist, a declinist, or a nostalgist. Such talk seems out of place in America for the simple reason that we have always been an optimistic nation; pessimism is almost unAmerican. Social historians have described America as a country that fundamentally lacks a tragic sense.

The United States has always passed through difficult transitions with unbroken resolve, confident that our civilization stands above the immutable laws of history which seem to assure that nations wane as surely as they wax. Americans have been reminded again and again by their leaders that, come what may, we are a people of destiny; economic prosperity at home and privileged status in the world are assured almost as a matter of birthright. But growing numbers of American leaders are apparently taking exception to this American "exceptionalism." In fact, some fear that if our internal vulnerabilities are left unattended, we may succumb to those laws of history America has defied for over two centuries. Unlike some of her European counterparts, countries held together by racial or ethnic homogeneity, long histories, or strong ancestry, the United States is held together by a set of ideas and values. The glue that holds the United States together is of the kind that, with neglect, could grow fragile.

As we near the end of a century and a millennium, America is entering a collective search for its national soul. The country is in the midst of profound changes in demographics, technology, and the structure of society. The great projects that stirred nationalist spirits in the past-- whether settling frontiers, defeating international communism, or launching "great societies"--have either been accomplished or were tried and failed.

The debate for the balance of this decade, and perhaps well into the next century, will focus on a modern paradox: how can a society that has produced more freedom and prosperity than any other in history, and has been so generous in its distribution, also increasingly lead the world in so many categories of social pathology? Many realize that politics alone has not effected what Americans prize the most--a humane and civilized society. Neither the welfare state nor a surging capitalism has solved many of society's persistent problems; in fact, each has contributed in its own way to the corrosion of civil society and its institutions. When the mediating structures of society--families, churches, communities, and voluntary associations--are weakened to the breaking point, individuals are increasingly left isolated and vulnerable within an ever expanding state. Neither the conservative mantra of "more markets" nor the liberal song of stronger "safety nets" in an expanded state has proven adequate.

Forces of modernity, more than politics, have produced much of society's fragmentation and rootlessness. Social thinkers have long recognized the precariousness of society. The magnetic forces of cooperation and solidarity can quickly be replaced by the centrifugal tendency to abandon attachment and obligation. These pressures have been particularly acute during our era, a time sociologist Daniel Bell has characterized as "a rage against order" because of its steady undermining of voluntary institutions and restraints.

THE SEARCH FOR NORMATIVE VALUES

America, the undisputed military and economic leader of the globe, shows every sign of being under immense social strain, as evidenced by her cities, her schools, her families, and her youth, problems which seem largely unaffected by changes in politics or the national economy. Many observers argue that the crisis that has come to former totalitarian countries may come to the liberal West as well. Futurist Richard Eckersley attributes social disintegration throughout the West to a failure to provide a sense of "meaning, belonging and purpose in our lives as well as a framework of values. Robbed of a broader meaning to our lives, we have entered an era of often pathological self-preoccupation."[7]

What happens to the society that has been severed from its underpinnings, in which faith, culture, and politics have become fragmented and devoid of meaning and citizens have lost a shared basis for a common life together? The result is the loss of community, a declining social order, the erosion of trust in authority, and the increased assertion of human passion through power rather than reasoned judgment.

As sociologist Peter Berger has said, excessive relativism produces a painful sense of impermanence and uncertainty. When relativism reaches a certain intensity, "absolutism becomes very attractive again" as people "seek liberation from relativism."[8] For growing numbers throughout the Western world, the desperate search for meaning and belonging ends in the total subjugation of the self in fanatical nationalism and fundamentalism.

Liberal scholar John Gardner states starkly: "Without the continuity of shared values that community provides, freedom cannot survive.

Undifferentiated masses never have and never will preserve freedom against usurping powers." The answer, according to Gardner, is to strengthen the intermediary structures of society in order to close the gap between the individual and state and fortify families and communities which are the ground-level generators and preservers of values and ethical systems.[9]

The challenge is to restore an ordered freedom and to resist abuses of either freedom or order. Some have used freedom to advance a radical expressive individualism that completely dismisses concern for the moral ecology of society. Conversely, the abusive reach for order has made its debut in growing cases of warrantless searches, vigilantism, and the National Guard being summoned to police urban housing projects.

This project of restoring an ordered freedom will require shoring up personal and civic values and treating the stress fractures on the institutions of civil society. If America suffers from a poverty of spirit, it suffers even more from a loss of language to address declining public life and common values. The language embodying the concepts of personal and public virtue has been eradicated. Traditionalist scholar John Howard has documented the broad segment of vocabulary along with the concepts they embodied that have simply been rendered obsolete on American soil. Modesty, decency, probity, rectitude, honor, politeness, virtue, magnanimity, and propriety are words that--along with their opposites such as shame and disgrace--have disappeared from current use. "They don't even enter into the calculus of public discussion and decision-making."[10]

Perhaps words like probity and rectitude bespoke the mentality of an era that is now gone forever and one to which few would prefer to return if given the choice. But they were words that conferred approval or disapproval on behavior that was thought good or bad for a healthy society. And they embodied respect for others.

The language of the latter 20th century, by contrast, treats personal and civic virtue as though they are purely private concerns. The language of public life is the dialect of the quantifiable, the rational, the scientific, and the technical--language of calculation and control but not language of values and meaning. It is a dialect that suits well the designers and managers of the paradigm of the present age.

Americans of good will who seek escape from the sterility of modern secular society are handicapped by the absence of a shared framework for discussing core American values. While secularism has not supplied public life in America with a sense of meaning and purpose, sectarianism has framed spiritual restoration largely in terms of politics and power. Secularists and sectarians alike have come to understand and explain social reality in the context of power and, thus, resist attempts to transcend politics and to find common ground in building a better, less political society.

The emergence of religious and ideological wars in America only points to the collapse of the American public philosophy. In reality, Americanism is a matter of the mind and heart. G. K. Chesterton said that America was built upon a unique "creed," a creed so dominant that it was set forth "with dogmatic and even theological lucidity" in our founding documents.

Nations are said to live by their myths. What binds America together are the ideas that live on--its myths, its history, and its still unfolding story. Is there an American creed around which Americans can unify in the late 20th century, or will centrifugal forces continue to gain strength? What are the myths and stories of America as a land of imagination and opportunity? What informs our attitudes and shapes our political sentiments? Is there an American memory that stretches, as Abraham Lincoln said, like a "mystical chord" from "every patriot grave and battlefield to every heart and hearthstone in America?" Or have Americans, as is often alleged, become self-absorbed, animated mostly by the promise of more rights and entitlements than calls to civic duty?

The anxiety about the current rush to debunk the myths that nurture a nation come from across the political spectrum. Conservative Reagan speechwriter Peggy Noonan decries the "compulsive skepticism" of the modern mind that only feeds cynicism. Liberal scholar Arthur Schlesinger Jr. worries that "the historic idea of a unifying American identity is now in peril in many arenas--in our politics, our voluntary organizations, our churches, our language." He believes the end result will be "the fragmentation, resegregation and tribalization of American life."[11] Free societies must be replenished with things that classical philosophers would describe as "pre-political," those things that are more important than and prior to politics and economics. Given the nature of our dilemma, America appears to be entering one of those phases again.

Even though the visible signs continue to point to social balkanization, a new paradigm which will draw people in from across the political spectrum is slowly being born. The ancient Greek word paradigm means a new model, or framework for how we "see" problems in society. And so it is with the paradigm that is emerging: it is being constructed almost entirely on the basis of how Americans and their leaders choose to see and understand root causes of America's social and democratic problems. People are not moving so much to the Left or to the Right as they are moving out of old categories and old ways of looking at problems. Civic renewal is a different enterprise than winning elections for one's ideological or partisan point of view.

We may assume that in the century immediately ahead, the forces for synthesis will gain strength and steadily compete with the forces of polarization. Growing numbers will turn away from the false choices that are so frequently presented in fragmented, ideologically driven politics: extreme moralism versus extreme secularism, feminism versus traditionalism, individualism versus communitarianism, and so on.

When the realization emerges that what America needs, above all else, is civic revitalization, then growing numbers will also come to accept that what America does not need a lot more of what is currently being offered in public debate--more capitalism or anti-capitalism, more political Left or political Right, more government or less government. Americans can afford to be partial on all of these points, as are many contributors to this volume, and still conclude that what America really needs is an all-fronts mobilization of individuals to improve the social and moral infrastructure of America.

Chief among the objectives of this movement will be forging a new consensus on the basic values upon which a free society rests. Citizens and leaders from all sectors of society will be needed to rebuild American greatness around the tripod of character, community, and culture.

The task will be difficult. It will, of necessity, involve a debate about values: a debate which can either divide or unify, attract or repel, depending upon whether the antagonists in that debate have in mind forging a new American public philosophy or simply winning partisan squabbles.

The debate about values is not about single issues, or even predominantly about legislative conflicts. Declining values either cause or compound some of society's most pressing problems--its litigiousness, its runaway entitlements, its special interest politics, and its insatiable demand for new rights. But legislative correction alone will do little to change the deeper cultural roots.

By definition, asserting values cannot be confused with a call to simply assert power. Attempts to restore declining cultural values and order through power often only provoke and exacerbate the conflict. The American renewal movement that is coming will not focus predominantly on political ideology or partisanship for the simple reason that neither is capable of social regeneration, and both often undermine it.

The objective of ethical renewal is the renewal of people and their social institutions, not just government. It will require reasserting certain core values, which will necessitate doing away with a radical, ethical pluralism which holds that no ideal is superior to another and that building the good society can be done without any basic agreement on the rules. This project will not be accomplished through the heavy-handed power of the state, but through voluntary value-shaping institutions of America.

America needs a new venue for discussing values, one less dominated by partisan politicians, and a new language, more civic and less sectarian, more civil and less belligerent. Anxiety about public and private morality runs across the political spectrum, and there is much at stake for everyone, regardless of religion or ideology. The debate concerns the kind of society all Americans, conservative or liberal, live in.

Since this volume is about the renewal of community, of citizenship, and of civil society, some definition of concepts is imperative.

WHAT IS COMMUNITY?

Man is a social creature by nature and is dependent upon society for satisfying his basic needs. The citizen in a liberal society is one who can rise above purely private calculation that comes with competitive individualism and can dwell cooperatively in community.

Politics has done little to call Americans to higher ends than material striving or the pursuit of rights. Neither of today's competing political philosophies of liberal egalitarianism or conservative libertarianism present a framework for human progress outside of man as an autonomous, rights-bearing consumer. One envisions man as the bearer of ever multiplying legal rights; the other pictures man mostly as a consumer in an unfettered marketplace. In neither framework is the individual encumbered with a duty to serve something one would call society. American society has invented more rights and provided more consumer choices than any in human history. But neither legal rights nor consumer opportunities are sufficient by themselves to hold a society together.

The alternative to rights-based individualism is what Michael Sandel describes as the "classical republican tradition" in which private interests are "subordinated to the public good and in which community life takes precedence over individual pursuits."[12] The classical republican tradition offers a vision for the individual operating, not just in competition with others or in conflict with the state, but in relationship to community.

Periodically, the American tide turns against individualism's excesses. Guardians of the American experiment, from the Founding on, were conscious of the need to balance untrammeled self-interest with the solicitation of virtue. It is not from the benevolence of the butcher, the brewer, or the baker which we can thank for our dinner, as Adam Smith said, but from their regard for their own interest. But the pursuit of interest alone does little to ensure that one's dinner will be enjoyed in a society of safety and civility.

Alexis de Tocqueville, the Frenchman who traveled the United States in 1833, is broadly regarded as one of the most astute observers of America's unique social and political culture. This book offers ample evidence that Tocqueville's keen analysis of America's problems of democracy is being enlisted once more, as repeated references are made to his writing throughout this work. Chapter Six, by Edward Schwartz, is committed exclusively to applying Tocqueville's analysis to understanding American society.

Tocqueville noted the creative tension in American society that exists between the power of self-interest and the pull of the public interest. He said Americans tended to explain almost all the actions of their lives by "the principle of self-interest rightly understood." An enlightened regard for themselves constantly prompted them, according to Tocqueville, "to assist one another" and to be willing "to sacrifice a portion of their time and property to the welfare of the state."

This was American self-interest, enlightened and pragmatic, in a full and unique display. Self-interest develops continents and fuels enormous energies toward industrial and technological innovation. The impulse to rise above the narrow pursuit of private interests is equally important to preserve well-ordered human society in which the fruits of one's labor can be enjoyed. Today, as has long been the pattern, new attempts are being made to invent a social philosophy that issues a call to community.

Communitarianism, for example, guided by sociologists Robert Bellah and Amitai Etzioni, is moving to erect a new sociopolitical framework that would be, in Bellah's words, "less trapped in the cliches of rugged individualism" and "more open to an invigorating, fulfilling sense of social responsibility."[13] This is a movement, like those that came before, that is searching for a new social equilibrium. It seeks to provide a greater balance between rights and responsibilities, to establish checks on the deepening impulse toward moral license, and to apply brakes to run-away individualism.

The key to community is understanding its voluntary nature.

Community cannot be ordered through legislation or summoned forth by verbal admonition--it springs from the habits of a people's heart. Calls to community can quickly degenerate into a reach for something that is far removed from, rather than firmly rooted within, the American heritage of civic republicanism. The answer to the excesses of liberal individualism is not coercive communitarianism.

If the concern is repairing social order and moral connectedness, then community is not and cannot be the work of the national government or even massive social movements. Indeed, the idea of creating a national community, as some are prone to suggest, may be a contradiction in terms, particularly on the ultra-pluralistic soil of America.

Rebuilding community cannot be achieved by absorbing the idea of community into the massive organizational structures of modern society. Small indigenous communities face constant threats from the homogenizing power of the large modern organizations. Indeed, it is large omnipresent structures--such as the central state, ideological movements, or the national media culture--along with their totalizing effects on society, that may be the most destructive of community. Each structure, in its own way, presents the paradox of modern individualism: the individual exalted, the individual overshadowed and abandoned.

The tendency in a nation driven to ever greater fragmentation by political interest groups and racial and ethnic subgroups is to resist groupings in the name of asserting a common civil life. Yet, properly understood, these groupings may represent an effort to reconnect atomized individuals. These subcommunities may subordinate the individual to a local voluntary society without wholly submerging him or her in a national community thus, causing further isolation.

If Americans are to build "a community of citizens," as the title recommends, they will have to do so within, not outside of, American philosophical traditions. Rediscovering the American public philosophy will aid in asserting new definitions of the common good without entirely submerging individual or group identity, or absorbing the private sphere into the already overbearing public realm.

The call to community and greater social cohesion in response to rapid and often reckless social change can also degenerate into a nostalgic and reactionary yearning for a lost golden age, one that was perhaps more carefree, harmonious, and virtuous, but also more stratified by race, gender, and class.

Few would seriously want to trade off all of the progress--whether economic, technological, or social--that has been won in recent decades for a return to the 1950s. The need for shared identity and belonging that most Americans now sense will have to be achieved by accommodating, not reversing, the social advances of recent decades. The frontiers of the 1990s will involve a search for improvements in our social life by moderating the excesses of social movements.

WHAT IS CITIZENSHIP?

The defining characteristic of America's unique experiment in democracy is reducible to one core principle: self-government. In early America, the people were considered sovereigns, not subjects, because they were individually self-regulating. When Chesterton spoke of the creed that animated American life he described its core component as the pure classic notion that "no man must aspire to be anything more than a citizen, and that no man shall endure to be anything less."

There was a clear sense among the Founders that the size, scope, and cost of external government was directly and inversely related to the presence of internal self-regulation among the people. Maintaining a capacity for self-government based in an ample supply of individual character, knowledge, and commitment to democratic participation was seen as the most urgent project of democracy's guardians. Anything less than an informed and active citizenry could lead to the abuse of government power. The call to civic action, issued then and periodically since, has also been presented as a direct challenge to the American cult of egoism, individualism, and privatism.

Today's understanding of citizenship is defined almost entirely in terms of political activity, especially voting, as Michael Joyce and several other authors point out in Section One. When politicians appeal to individuals to exercise citizenship, they usually mean "come out and vote for us so we can do something for you."

Empowerment, to use the term of current vogue, is mostly a political term. When used in politics, it is frequently used to build support for legislative action by politicians, policy professionals, and social service providers. It means turning control of the work of public life over to qualified experts who, then, design and launch public programs on an affected group's behalf. Democracy ceases to be about participation and becomes about programs.

To be a citizen is to be socially engaged. David Green, author of *Reinventing Civil Society*, suggests that since the contest between socialism and capitalism is over, advocates of freedom must work to build a new framework he describes as "communal liberalism," which aims to rebuild "a sense of community or solidarity compatible with freedom."[14]   A society strong in communal solidarity is a society rich in citizenship, where common people take it upon themselves to nourish the institutions, habits, and morals upon which a humane society rests. The civic ethic includes meeting human need directly and voluntarily. It means turning acts of benevolence into opportunities to treat the whole man by strengthening the ideals of self-improvement and character development.

This vision for wellness and vitality is one on which free societies depend for progress, yet it is conspicuously absent from much publicly funded and administered charity. Vast resources in both the public and private sectors are now controlled by professional caregivers who exhibit a morbid preoccupation with illness, abuse, and victimization.

The concept of the individual, not as citizen, but as client is now pervasive. The provision of public assistance to tens of millions of Americans is often accompanied by the subtle message that recipients are hopelessly trapped in conditions that require the permanent help of advocates, interest groups, and government workers. It produces a mindset that dwarfs citizenship for poor and non-poor alike. It leaves the poor feeling justified in doing little to reclaim control of their lives and the non-poor feeling no obligation to intervene with neighborly aid.

The language of social action today is not the common language of a caring citizenry but rather the technical jargon of a professionalized therapeutic state. It is the language of programs, policies, and healing through clinically certified experts. Our current public language creates a picture of society in which most institutions except the state are dysfunctional and where human relationships are frequently abusive and, thus, in constant need of trained mediators. When society is motivated less by a vision for wellness and progress than for identifying new forms of disorder, politics is turned into what neighborhood empowerment activist Robert Woodson calls "grievance-based" politics. Citizens are reduced to clients; politicians are reduced to voicing grievance-based claims. The result, Woodson says, is "an inverse relationship between the leader and the people; his success depends on their continued failure."

Too many leaders, activists, and professional caregivers have a vested interest in preserving rather than solving human problems. Many social and political organizations across the political spectrum would face precipitously declining budgets if the individuals, families, and neighborhoods they presume to represent were suddenly restored to strength.

The politics of grievance and victimization have not made Americans any more tolerant, any more compassionate, or any more sensitive to the volatile issues that so quickly erupt into nasty recriminations when social problems become entirely the concern of the political class.

The key ingredient of citizenship is fostering a genuine social sympathy among the people. The real objective of a renewed citizenship would be to reclaim the individual by refusing to delegate the business of public life and public aid entirely to government professionals. Programs would seek to strengthen mediating structures and would view citizenship as the very lifeblood of society. Programs would seek to join the poor and non-poor together as neighbors, volunteers, and partners in community renewal.

Individuals must be restored to full participation in the whole of public life. Whatever government does, or does not do, the job of restoration and renewal will fall heavily to citizens. Citizenship will be restored when people recognize that the reach for political power to solve our deepest social problems has been a Faustian bargain. If empowerment means anything it must mean that individuals, including the family and neighborhood structures that form one's social habitat, are granted greater independence from enlightened bureaucratic caregivers and from the permanent political class that presumes to speak for them.

WHAT IS CIVIL SOCIETY?

Citizenship entails a range of social duties that are carried out through the associational life of a community. Civil society is the realm of volunteer networks and informal associations in which individuals conduct much of their lives.

A well-functioning society is made up of what Edmund Burke called "little platoons;"[15] Emile Durkheim called "the little aggregations;"[16] and Christopher Dawson called the "interpenetrating orders--political, economic, cultural and religious."[17] Each order should possess a considerable amount of independence.

Many of these vital institutions of society have been weakened. Robert Bellah, author of the critically acclaimed book *The Good Society*, points to the collapse of institutions, particularly the family, that nurture and socialize children. In recent years, "the local communities, extended kin groups and religious organizations, as well as the many economic, legal and political functions" which support the family have been sapped of strength and vitality.

The essence of civil society was established most effectively in our own generation by Peter Berger and Richard John Neuhaus in the classic *To Empower People*, which entered the term "mediating structures" into the vernacular. By mediating structures they meant, above all, the institutions such as families, churches and synagogues, voluntary associations, and neighborhoods, that come between the individual and the state. "Mediating structures," they argued "are essential for a vital democratic society."

Public policy, Berger and Neuhaus said, should protect and foster mediating structures and, whenever possible, should "utilize mediating structures for the realization of social purposes."[18] This would result in true empowerment, not just for individuals, but for the institutions and associational networks that are necessary for sustaining individuals in community.

Recently politicians, think tanks, and political interest groups have rediscovered the notion of civil society, and their interest is welcomed. But, it is very doubtful that reconstruction of the civic order will be led by politicians. Says scholar Robert Royal, "Barring a truly great spirit in the White House--someone like Lincoln, who would understand the shape and limits of what the state can do to encourage a healthy civil society--we must look elsewhere for moral and civic reconstruction."[19]

Civil society is not about politics and it is not, according to Royal, about "democratic machinery or the well-managed bureaucratic state. Civil society is precisely a human order that is larger and richer than the state."[20] The institutions that make up civil society thrive in the absence of political encroachments and frequently falter when supplanted by government.

In Chapters Four and Five, generations experts William Strauss and Neil Howe and global trends expert William Van Dusen Wishard investigate the powerful forces--demographic, intellectual, and global--affecting the health of civil society.

WHAT IS CULTURE?

At its deepest level, culture is the values, beliefs, and habits by which individuals order their lives and which are then manifested and mirrored in public life in hundreds of forms, from the condition of our universities to the quality of our prime time television, to the health of our neighborhood institutions, to our civility in public debate. For culture to be culture it must have the effect of civilizing humanity. Webster presents culture as a concept indicating progress, not regress. It is not a term that would be appropriate to use to describe a group of people who are brutal, barbaric, and anarchic.

Culture is the soil in which the seeds of a healthy human society are planted and replanted. The civilizing work of culture is accomplished primarily through the cultivation of character and intellect, and the refinement of aesthetic tastes. It is about our manners and our morals.

In Chapter Two, Heather Higgins attempts to answer the basic question of what, exactly, is American culture. What are the core irreducible commitments that individuals must bring to their collective identity as Americans? What ingredients are required for a culture and society to be functional, and what are those ideals in America? Jeffrey Eisenach, in Chapter Three, attempts to recover an understanding of the core idea of progress as an animating force in society.

Culture may be more determinative of the quality of our common life, and over the long term of our national success, than our public policies, advanced legal system, or vibrant economy. The life of culture is deeper and more important than government because it reflects what individuals value. As Plato said, "Give me the songs of a nation and it matters not who writes its laws." Burke said: "Manners are more important than laws. Upon them, in a great measure, the laws depend."

In addressing the issue of culture on the American continent, one must be especially careful. Unlike cultures having ancient roots such as on the European continent, many find the very thought of an American culture oppressive, old-fashioned, or simply irrelevant. Any attempt to reassert shared values runs against a powerful grain of individualism, which is perhaps the most distinguishing mark of contemporary American culture.

America's acceptance of rampant pluralism militates against attempts to create an undergirding culture or reinforce common values. There appears an almost inbred native resistance to anything monolithic or uniform. American individualism and pluralism run deep and, in recent decades, have become excessive. Americans display a remarkable tolerance for the conflict and disorder that frequently result from a lack of commitment to the common good. Ralph Waldo Emerson described the idea that society would issue a claim on the individual as a conspiracy against "the manhood of every one of its members."

We have a culture, then, with a penchant for negating culture. In America, perhaps like nowhere else, the very definition of freedom means the freedom to be different, the freedom to live by one's own lights, and to find happiness in one's own ethnic identity and cultural experience--in other words, to escape the constraints that often operate on individuals in less dynamic cultures. Rugged individualism and cultural pluralism have not been without their benefits. For centuries, immigrants have come to America seeking escape from cultures that suffocate individual expression and achievement through rigid social stratification. The spirit of adventure and innovation that has animated Americans for centuries drew its strength, not from conformity to a reigning culture, but from throwing off the boundaries of social class and old sociopolitical arrangements, whether mercantilism or state-sponsored religion.

Is a common culture necessary to maintain a liberal civil society? Calls to restore traditional American values are not likely to succeed if what is intended is the denial of freedom to individuals as well as ethnic groups to assert their own uniqueness and escape the boundaries that exist in the countries from which they emigrated. Such an agenda would be neither realistic nor compatible with over 200 years of American experience.

Still, this wholly privatized concept of society can be very destructive of public life. Sociologists dating back to Emile Durkheim have warned about societal disintegration resulting from the erosion of shared beliefs and common purpose. Tocqueville worried about excessive individualism and materialism producing an atomistic society. What Tocqueville was describing was not a society at all, but a collection of individuals living in resistance to the notion of enduring common interests, pursuits, traditions or beliefs that make up a society. Tocqueville predicted "democratic despotism" would result for a society with weakened civic institutions in which the individual stands alone and alongside a powerful state.

EDUCATING FOR A CIVIL SOCIETY

The cultural transmission belt of a free society is education, which probably explains why education policy has become such a battle zone. Education transmits a free society's highest ideals and imparts the knowledge necessary for democratic participation. The ultimate end of education is not simply preparation for competition in a technological world; it is nourishing the habits of virtue and character needed for cooperation in human society.

American public education was forged out of a desire to draw together many separate identities into one national quilt. Its founders constructed it, according to Arthur Schlesinger Jr., as "the great instrument of assimilation" whose purpose was the creation of "a unifying American identity." Today's educational system is paralyzed by the thought of assimilation into Americanism.

Schlesinger maintains that the "militants of ethnicity" now view the main objective of public education, not as assimilation, but "the protection, strengthening, celebration, and perpetuation of ethnic origins and identities." But this separatism, he says, "nourishes prejudices, magnifies differences, and stirs antagonisms."[21]

In the struggle to build student self-esteem and achievement around ethnic identity, the search for shared civic values and common democratic interests can easily be defeated. The late Christopher Lasch argued that the loss of historical continuity in America has created a culture of competitive individualism which is degenerating into a narcissistic preoccupation with self.

Learning respect for the accomplishments of a nation's past is necessary to preserve a society's identity and heritage. The literature of earlier periods emphasizing fortitude, perseverance, and self-control gave way to the pursuit of success and self-fulfillment. The narcissist, says Lasch, lives "only in, and for, the present."

The cumulative effect, according to educator Peter Gibbon, is that our children "are not being raised by exemplary lives and confident schools; nor by high culture, vigilant communities, families, churches and temples, but rather by an all-enveloping enemy culture interested in amusement, titillation, and consumerism."[22]

Schools cannot be blamed for the collapse of other value-shaping institutions, such as the family, nor for an epidemic of ethical relativism that is society-wide. Nevertheless, no movement to strengthen American democracy, civil society, or ethical standards will be effective if it fails to counter the American cult of the unrestricted self.

The pursuit of the moral life requires the pursuit of ends and ideals larger and higher than the subjective self. Teaching the virtuous life is difficult when man is viewed as a completely autonomous decision maker. When morality is contingent, heroic acts and virtuous deeds are not regarded as universally valued services to man but merely as expressions of subjective desires. In Section Two, authors Denis Doyle, Dennis Denenberg, Eric Ebeling, and John Cooper discuss how education can return to forming character, strengthening community, and nourishing good habits of citizenship. Few would suggest that schools return to moral exhortation or to the teaching of religious doctrine. The key is in understanding what is wrong with the false extremes that currently present themselves and to build consensus around values that are still nearly universally held.

Philosopher Alasdair MacIntyre argues that the chief means of moral education in classical societies was storytelling. In classical antiquity, students were tutored by the heroes of ancient Greece and Rome. Storytelling is a lost tradition in the modern era. Lessons meant to encourage moral reasoning often involve perplexing and unresolvable dilemmas. When moral lessons are filled with ambiguities, the suggestion is that all morality is in a state of constant flux. Rather than aiming to strengthen ethical awareness, students are trained in procedural skills in order to arbitrate differences in a moral environment characterized by constant disagreement.

Societies committed to preserving a sense of heroism and the pursuit of virtue do not treat morality as though it consists of endless argument over rules. They do not give children the impression that the pursuit of the moral life is completely subjective, private, and futile. The result of encouraging endless criticism in the name of promoting cultural pluralism is weakened allegiance to any common heritage or shared values.

POLITICS, LAW, AND AMERICA'S PUBLIC DISCOURSE

The Decline of Politics

The state of American democracy, by broad agreement, is not good. It has been a long while since politics was given credit for having made life fundamentally better for Americans. The combined effect of a spiraling national debt, unrestrained entitlements, a failing educational system, and an ineffective criminal justice system has most Americans charging government with extortionate incompetence.

The linkage between citizen participation and decision making in a representative government is indispensable to preserving democratic legitimacy and vitality. In America, that sacred connection between elections and what government does is an ever more tenuous one, making it harder to convince an already cynical public that "every vote counts."

First, there is a deepening realization that political debates have become disconnected from the real life experiences and concerns of ordinary Americans. Debates have turned sterile, repetitive, and, to many citizens, simply irrelevant.

Second, citizens are mostly separated from any meaningful role in shaping the government they are asked to finance. Their role is mostly one of following, not affecting, the formation of major decisions. The manipulation of the electoral process by interest groups, lobbyists, and political professionals has made the process seem remote to ordinary individuals. Liberal Tom Hayden observes:

> The real crisis is the emergence of the special interest state, a permanent, insulated state within the democratic state. It's defining obsession is with immediate interests at the expense of future welfare.

What happens to a democracy when its basic institutions are perceived to lack credibility, even legitimacy? Part of the problem, according to growing numbers of observers, is that our institutions of democracy were not set up to handle the scope of functions and conflicts currently weighing upon it. As currently organized, the American political process can only be seen as inefficient and ineffective because managing public affairs in a society as complex as America's, whose problems are often beyond managing, makes it nearly impossible.

In Chapter 11, I address reasons, beyond the malfeasance of elected officials, why politics inspires so little confidence. Politics cannot possibly meet the expectations it has built up in the people because few politically viable answers exist for the public problems that trouble Americans the most. America's most vexing social problems--illegitimacy, father-absent families, crime and violence--lie largely beyond the capacity of political agendas of either the Left or Right to solve. For the foreseeable future, academic and policy professionals will be asked more frequently to document the failures of public programs than to map believable plans for new ones. The best thing for politics to do is tackle the tough problems that only governments can solve and candidly admit what politics cannot do.

Politics As Governmentalism

Most discussions of politics immediately assume that the object of "political" activity is always to order the affairs of government. The central feature of modern politics is its peculiar preoccupation with simply managing government--tinkering with bureaucracy, adjusting tax codes, and tightening criminal statutes. The ancients viewed politics as a means of improving man's capacity to better himself and to practice self-government. Politics entailed the elevation and ennoblement of man through broader engagement in the life of the polity. Politics was rarely separated from the deeper normative questions regarding the purposes for which citizens lived, individually and corporately. Statecraft meant more than simply advancing individual interests within the realm of government;

in large measure it was soulcraft, to borrow columnist George Will's term. Politics, practiced as soulcraft, concerned itself with the condition of a person's mind and soul, his or her habits of industry, moderation, courage, public spiritedness and capacity for sound democratic judgment--characteristics which republican forms of government were thought to depend upon for survival. It sought not to overwhelm public managers with insoluble problems, but to summon forth from the people a willingness to engage fully in the resolution of public concerns.

In Chapter 12, Colleen Sheehan describes how democratic institutions, including parties, often undermine civic involvement. A political system that has given up on the possibility of individuals governing themselves has lapsed, whether it wants to admit it or not, into some form of paternalistic authoritarianism, be it oligarchy, aristocracy, or simply a benign system of central control in which enlightened public managers are charged with governing a compliant and docile citizenry. Little about politics today seeks to fortify public-spirited citizenship. Politics reinforces a vision of society inhabited by unencumbered private individuals, pampered with promises, fortified with multiplying legal rights, and awash in consumer choices, yet paradoxically, more subject than citizen. Political debates which once entertained public reflection on the higher ends of life in a just and good society have been replaced by politicians reciting their accomplishments in ladling out pork-barrel projects.

The corroding effects of modernity and materialism have eroded the deeper linkages of the citizen and his or her responsibilities to transcendent principles. Politics has lost ground because it is about little more than governmentalism, particularly the crass angling for leverage over the appropriations process. As author Jonathan Rauch laments, today's politicians "have turned every social argument into an argument about government, politics or law. Libertarians, anti-government conservatives and left-liberals disagree on many things, but they are all governmentalists."[23]

Can we find an approach to thinking about ourselves, developing rules for conduct, and reclaiming normative values without ritual deference to the government and its alphabet soup of program offerings? Can individuals and communities be called upon to debate how to govern themselves in any meaningful sense?

Rauch recommends a rather modest experiment that could put the question to the test. He suggests planting the brainiest policy works from the political Left, Right, and Center in a three day conference. They would be asked to address America's social problems with only one basic condition: no one would be permitted to promise a single change in federal or state statutes. At first, they would be unhappy, confused, at a loss. Then, after a while, he predicts, "they will start to think about the very large portion of America that is not the government. They will hatch ideas, some of them possibly good. They will begin to think a bit differently." That, says Rauch, is where the next quarter century begins-- "with the realization that governmentalism has long since reached its limits."[24]

The business of democracy is enabling the people to govern their own lives as well as to draw citizens into the process of shaping public life across a range of functions. The good society can *not* be doled out like just another entitlement; it can *not* be pieced together through programs, or stimulated into existence by more tax cuts. It must be achieved through the cooperative efforts of individual Americans from all walks of life.

Personal Manners and the Public Discourse

If democracy were somehow hoisted upon the examination table and its contents placed under clinical examination, its words would reveal a body riddled with disabling viruses.

In no area are society's extremes of individualism more evident than in its public debate. Rarely is there the faintest reference to any concept of the common good. *Washington Post* columnist William Raspberry describes a process that has moved beyond the normal give and take among various competing sectors and ideologies into "a near-total breakdown of the American society into warring component parts." Raspberry questions whether anyone speaks the language of national interest any more.

Civil society involves the exchange of ideas--even vigorous arguments over competing ideas and values. But to disagree in a civil society requires sharing enough in common to have something to disagree about. According to the late John Courtney Murray:

> The whole premise of the public argument, if it is to be civilized and civilizing, is that consensus is real, that among the people, everything is not in doubt, but that there is a core of agreement, accord, concurrence, acquiescence. We hold certain truths; therefore we can argue about them.

Without this sense of acknowledging the other's humanity, says Murray, debates degenerate into shrill mutterings. Whoever wins, society loses, and "the barbarian is at the gates of the city."[25]

The classical philosophers were concerned about rhetoric and the public discourse. The story of the Roman Empire is a record of one monumental success heaped upon another only to be followed by internal collapse of civilization into disorder. Disorder was fueled in part by the endless polemics that broke out between warring factions during the latter stages of the republic, producing bitter and eventually violent recriminations.

Strong republics are not shaken by bitter polemics and recriminations, but then neither are such tactics necessary if the political and social order is healthy. Public rhetoric is a barometer of a political regime's health and reflects whether society has given way to a tacit state of nature in which individuals and groups are determined to go their own way, come what may.

Thomas Hobbes, a philosopher familiar with the notion of the state of nature, believed a well-ordered society required broadly shared rules of debate. Writing in *Leviathan*, Hobbes established 19 rules, or "natural laws" for preserving peaceful and dignified conduct in debate. These "articles of peace," as they were called, essentially established the "golden rule" of public life--"do not that to another, which thou wouldst not have done to thyself." To Hobbes, the one irreducible requirement for civil public debate was possessing genuine respect for the rights and dignity of one's fellows. Article 10 insisted that "everyone acknowledge another as one's equal by nature." Article 8 admonishes that no practitioner of democracy "by deed, word, countenance, or gesture declare hatred or contempt for others."[26]

Rights, Wrongs, and Responsibilities

The well-ordered civil society and the political society are in dialectical tension. When government becomes the ally of an extreme rights-based individualism cut off from any connection to a higher morality, it is forced to accommodate greater demands for individual legal gains. This restless search for human progress through legal reforms is the very root of the politicized society. When only the law and politics arbitrate human affairs, everything becomes political--even the most basic human relations. What follows is a state that expands radically even as its competence and legitimacy ebb.

The American legal system has developed the tendency to translate every dispute into the language of untrammeled individual entitlement, according to Harvard law professor Mary Ann Glendon. The result is the replacement of substantive constitutional principles for what political scientist Michael Sandel calls a "procedural republic" in which individuals are endowed with rights and entitlements but have little consciousness beyond that.

When any concept of a higher law or any notion of self-evident truths has been destroyed, the only real basis for asserting the inestimable moral worth of all of human life is also extinguished. Without the aid of transcendent principles, morality becomes contingent on human choice, and the human person is subject to the arbitrary whims of democratic majorities.

The result is what Philip Johnson calls "the modernist impasse." When people have concluded that man gets to decide everything on the basis of democratic majorities, people are subjected to "the whims of whoever controls the law-making apparatus."[27] The law degenerates into an arbitrary tool of the politically organized. A right conferred on one group becomes an obligation imposed on another. One person's gain is another's loss. The legal system is forced to find ever more perfect balances and boundaries between conflicting parties and claims. People expect the law to simultaneously confer the right to sexual freedom as well as freedom from sexual assault; to guarantee gender and racial advantage for some and the protection against reverse discrimination for others; to protect the rights of criminal offenders and the rights of those offended; to guard the rights of free speech but initiate new rights against the insult of hateful speech; to defend both the rights of individuals and communities, and so on.

The law has always been expected to strike careful balances in these areas, but never before has it been called on to split conflicting demands with such exasperating precision. This degree of legal harmony and balance is, of course, beyond the capacity of the law and state agencies to achieve. The law begins to resemble a harried referee who has the impossible task of policing a sport that is both choked by rules and overwhelmed by rule infractions. The players of society are reduced to fighting over the rules.

Beyond Left and Right

On the political front, politics is about to yield to new coalitions and new themes emphasizing quality of life in the context of neighborhood. These themes will include a new citizenship that views individuals, not just those speaking for them, as the agents of change and a new localism that aims to expand the capacity of private and public institutions closest to the people to solve problems.

Most solutions are local, which means they are beyond affecting by national ideological movements operating at the top of the political system. Labels are relevant then only to the extent that political ideology is relevant.

The old paradigms of Left and Right are increasingly less useful and more internally conflicted. In Chapter 13, Lawrence Chickering argues that words like "conservative" and "liberal" have come to mean so many conflicting things "that coherent talk about politics has become all but impossible." Liberalism and conservatism each has its freedom and order wing, one emphasizing modernist values of individualism, freedom, and reason, the other emphasizing order, community, and values.

Each distinction is further reduced by its common assumptions and attitudes about government. According to Chickering, "The left and right argue opposite positions from the same basic assumption: that institutional reform--change in the powers and actions of the central government--is necessary to correct all fundamental problems. Liberalism and conservatism alike are preoccupied with the central state. Almost no one, says Chickering, "is concerned with building positive forms of individual and community self-governance."[28] He wonders why there is no greater debate about how to empower individuals in small communities to solve economic and social problems.

If individuals are to be made not subjects but citizens again in small self-governing communities, new institutional arrangements will have to be devised to provide for greater participation in governing.

American politics pays lip service to the ideal that "all politics is local." But the greatest intellectual thought is given, not to the 82,000 subnational units of government, but to the presidency and Congress. The symbol of American democracy has become less the town hall meeting and more the presidential pen. The prize for a successful political party or ideological movement is the presidency or control of Congress.

Federalism

The tendency in modern times is to assume that the more difficult the problem, the more desirable it is to turn to specialists and governmental authorities at a higher and more remote level. The federal government's design still reflects that of the 20th century's architect of central control, Frederick Taylor. The science of public management is inherently oriented toward constructing large central agencies from whence professional systems of command and control can design and implement solutions to problems by way of standardized rule-making. The value of scientific management has supplanted the value of democratic participation. The entire administrative apparatus of the central government is presently designed on the assumption that expert decision makers are more capable of solving social and economic problems than smaller self-governing arrangements.

If democracy is to be defended, perhaps new rule-making arrangements must be devised to enable citizens to articulate their concerns and aspirations and to mediate their conflicting demands in ways that strengthen, not weaken, their participation and sense of connection. As Eugene Hickok argues in Chapter 14, the strengthening of democracy may thus hinge on new forms of federalism which create smaller authority centers for citizens, in greater numbers, and at lower levels of government.

Societies are complex configurations of relationships, and any society as complex and diverse as America's cannot possibly be governed from the top in any meaningful sense. This is particularly true as national self-identity is being slowly weakened by forces above and below the national government: global economics on the one hand, and regional power and local democratic movements on the other.

Governments must keep pace with the economic and technological forces that are shaping society, lest they obstruct progress. What are those forces today? According to futurist Alvin Toffler, they are the pull of power away from the center, political "demassification," and "mosaic democracy."

Although the means for expanding citizen participation exist in the form of decentralization and a rapidly developing electronic technology, the nation's dominant political culture, of both the Left and the Right, fight to keep the focus of debate on centers of authority that are the most remote from the people. Why, in today's world of technology, regional economics, and declining power and legitimacy of central states, does the national government, or even state governments for that matter, continue to monopolize power?

Citizens must be granted greater control over issues and debates, particularly those at the local level. Politics driven from the bottom at the level of community may prove to have a number of advantages for a democracy in search of renewal, providing basic protections are provided for political minorities. For one, local decision making may be more inclined to search for consensus than a national politics of ideological conflict and interest group gridlock.

For another, local participatory democracy may dramatically reduce public cynicism toward a political process that Ross Perot described as "a costly sideshow." And finally, decentralist republicanism might dramatically reduce the cost of government. If resources are not wasted by being passed through multiple levels before arriving at their intended destination, public support for needed public action would be more sustainable.

AMERICAN CIVIL INSTITUTIONS

Societal Fragmentation

In *Habits of the Heart*, communitarian sociologist Robert Bellah mapped the destruction of America's civic life and the weakening of vital institutions that sustain human society such as marriage, family, and religion. Bellah singled out individualism as the source of the disintegration of human relationships into ever more tenuous, fragmented, and distrustful patterns.

The 20th century has witnessed the emergence of the self as the main form of reality and a withdrawal by individuals from the public sphere to pursue purely private ends. What Bellah was describing was the stress fractures of American civil society; the weakening of the very mini-societies that provide order and meaning to human beings. For civil society to be repaired, it must tackle the tough issues: issues of race and ethnicity, the underclass, religion, and marriage and family.

In this section of the book some of America's leading thinkers contribute to mapping strategies for finding common ground and a basis for a civil life together on some of these most vexing issues. In Chapter 15, Barbara Dafoe Whitehead and David Blankenhorn search for a new family framework that offers men and women the possibility of finding a common life together. Glenn Loury looks, in Chapter 16, for solutions that escape the mechanistic theories that seem to dominate public discussion about the urban underclass.

The Role of Religion

Americans remain a deeply and incorrigibly religious people. Yet how religion has or should influence our common life together is a matter of deep confusion and division--between secularists who speak the sterile language of economic entitlement and political rights, and religious movements that refuse to accommodate, in language or methods, democratic pluralism.

For tens of millions of Americans, religion is of paramount importance. Religion concerns the "first things" which inform and shape all other aspects of life. President Clinton publicly acknowledged this when he reaffirmed that "we are a people of faith" and that "religion helps to give our people the character without which a democracy cannot survive."[29]

The work of the spiritual realm entails primarily that of ministering to the conscience and souls of people, and by extension, the soul and conscience of society. A society searching for order plunges into deeper disorder when this harmony is lost. Political scientist David Walsh has said that a civilization is in a state of crisis "not when its order has broken down for one reason or another, but when the attempt to restore the authoritative order of society is itself ineffective and thereby serves only to exacerbate the original problem."[30]

In a free society, the state must be a subsidiary of society--it must be society's servant, not its master. It is equally wrong for either secularists or religious believers to try to master society through the state. The more realistic mission would be to minimize the intrusive powers of the state in society, working to restore the institutions of civil society.

The solution, as presented by William Boxx in Chapter 17, is in rediscovering the notion of subsidiarity, developed by John Courtney Murray. Disharmony has been created in America by the state's secularization of life and the marginalization of religious faith in public life. But disharmony can also be created by religious activism that confuses the legitimate need to restore values with illegitimate attempts to place religious authority over government, and by extension, the populace.

Religion, according to historian Christopher Dawson, serves a higher order and must not obscure or trivialize its mission by letting herself be used "as the instrument of secular power and politics." The idea, according to Dawson, that the spiritual life of society should "be ruled and guided by a political party would have appeared to our ancestors a monstrous absurdity."[31]

This struggle between the secular and sacred has always been settled in favor of properly ordered spheres of influence. In *Democracy in America*, Alexis de Tocqueville was struck both by religion's force in American society as well as the proscribed nature of the realm that religion occupied.

Religion, according to Tocqueville, "retained a greater influence over the souls" of people than any country in the world. Religion's role in the society of the early 1800s was one of nourishing the habits of restraint, industry, and tranquility that were thought necessary to maintain republican institutions. Although religion's influence over manners and morals--the "habits of the heart"--was vast, organized religion maintained a studied distance when it came to political parties and public affairs. In America, said Tocqueville, religion "exercises but little influence upon the laws and upon the details of public opinion; but it directs the customs of community, and, by regulating domestic life, it regulates the state."[32] The clergy, in particular, were careful to preserve the unique and honored station they occupied in society. They eschewed all parties," filled no public appointments, and were "excluded by public opinion" (and by law in several states) from serving in legislatures.[33]

Tocqueville's recorded observations, now over 150 years old, serve as a timely reminder of what is at stake for religious belief when boundaries are confused. Tocqueville observed, "The church cannot share the temporal power of the state without being the object of a portion of that animosity which the latter excites."[34]

The aim of religious believers must be to create a good society by voluntary means, not through political movements seeking legislative solutions to moral and spiritual problems. Such a movement would aim to revitalize culture, not just correct a nation's politics, understanding that culture more shapes, than is shaped by politics.

Leading sociologist Os Guinness hopes for a new American renaissance that introduces Americans again to a public philosophy that would include a commitment to a new civil public discourse and the pursuit of justice for people of all faiths as well as no faith. This philosophy, which Guinness describes in Chapter 18, is a shared vision for the common good. It embraces liberty for individuals, tolerance for America's ethnic mosaic, and a well-moderated pluralism. It finds strength in what Americans have in common. A return to a strong public philosophy can heal a land divided by race, class, religion, and ideology.

A genuinely American public philosophy would attempt to advance a shared vision for the common good, producing a truce of sorts between the reimposers and the removers of religion. Those who discount the importance of our common ideals fail to appreciate their role in making one nation out of many.

PERSPECTIVES ON CIVIL SOCIETY

The final section of this book concludes in much the same fashion as the book started. The authors look at the project of strengthening American civil society from a range of philosophical perspectives: traditionalist--Allan Carlson; communitarian--Roger Connor; libertarian--Doug Bandow; populist--Harry Boyte, and finally a chapter by Elizabeth Lurie which argues for the creation of a new democratic and cultural "center".

The questions that this book ponders may take decades to fully answer: Can the political and civic order be renewed without resort to demagoguery, reaction, or worse, bitter and possibly violent conflict? Can the American spirit of progress based upon optimism, hope, and perseverance be reimparted to a generation more alienated and compulsively skeptical than perhaps any other? Can religious faith serve again to fortify a weakened society without resort to a politicized and sectarian public orthodoxy? Can society curb excessive victim status without forgetting that, for too many, being left behind in the world's most prosperous society can be embittering? Can an authentic appeal be made for private individuals to embrace an American creed, and can a uniquely American sense of identity be restored without canceling out ethnic and religious differences? All Americans of good will are invited to contribute to the resolution of these questions.

ENDNOTES

1. Eleanor Clift, "Interview: I Try to Be Who I Am," *Newsweek,* 28 December 1992, 24.

2. John W. Gardner, *Building Community,* published by the Independent Sector, September 1991, 16.

3. George Weigel, "Christian Conviction and Democratic Etiquette," *First Things* (March 1994): 34.

4. *The Responsive Communitarian Platform: Rights and Responsibilities,* published by The Communitarian Network, 1.

5. Edward H. Crane, "Civil Vs. Political Society," *The Cato Policy Report,* published by the Cato Institute, Spring, 1993.

6. Michael Novak, "The Conservative Momentum," published by the Center

for the American Experiment, June, 1993, 5.

7.   Richard Eckersley, "The West's Deepening Cultural Crisis," *The Futurist*, (November-December 1993): 10.

8.   Peter L. Berger, *A Far Glory: The Quest for Faith in an Age of Continuity* (New York: Free Press, 1992), 45.

9.   Gardner, *Building Community*, 5.

10.   John A. Howard, "A Sure Compass," published by the Rockford Institute, 1992, 6.

11.   Arthur M. Schlesinger, Jr., *The Disuniting of America: Reflections on a Multicultural Society* (New York: W.W. Norton and Company 1992), 17.

12.   Michael Sandel, quoted from John O'Sullivan, *The Loss of Virtue: Moral Confusion and Social Disorder in Britain and America, A National Review Book*, 1992, 86.

13.   Robert Bellah, et al., *The Good Society* (New York: Knopf, 1991), 15.

14.   David G. Green, *Reinventing Civil Society: The Rediscovery of Welfare Without Politics* (London: Institute of Economic Affairs, 1993), 3.

15.   Peter L. Berger and Richard John Neuhaus, *To Empower People: The Role of Mediating Structures in Public Policy* (Washington, D.C.: AEI Press, 1977), 4.

16.   Ibid.

17.   Christopher Dawson, *Beyond Politics* (Freeport, N.Y.: Books For Libraries, 1971), 21.

18.   Peter Berger and Richard John Neuhaus, *To Empower People*, 6.

19.   Robert Royal, "Reinventing The American People," *The American Character*, published by the Ethics and Public Policy Center, No. 6, Fall 1993, 3.

20.   Ibid., 26.

21.   Arthur M. Schlesinger, Jr., *The Disuniting of America*, 17.

22.   Peter H. Gibbon, "In Search of Heroes," *Newsweek*, 18 January 1993, 9.

23.   Jonathan Rauch, "Caesar's Ghost," *Reason Magazine* (May 1993): 55.

24.   Ibid., 57.

25.   John Courtney Murray, *We Hold These Truths: Catholic Reflections on the American Proposition* (New York: Sheed and Ward, 1960), 11-12.

26.   Thomas Hobbes, *Leviathan*, 1651, chapters 14-15.

27.   Philip E. Johnson, "Nihilism and the End of Law," *First Things* (March 1993): 19.

28.   A. Lawrence Chickering, *Beyond Left and Right: Breaking the Political Stalemate* (San Francisco: ICS Press, 1993),159.

29.   Quoted from George Weigel, "Christian Conviction and Democratic Etiquette," 30.

30.   David Walsh, *After Ideology* (San Francisco: Harper, 1990), 18.

31.   Dawson, *Beyond Politics*, 26.

32.   Alexis de Tocqueville, *Democracy in America*, vol. 1 (New York: Vintage Books, 1945), 315.

33.   Ibid., 320.

34.   Ibid., 322.

I. The Transformation of American Civil Society

Chapter 1

Citizenship in the 21st Century: Individual Self-Government

Michael S. Joyce

INTRODUCTION

The word "citizenship" today typically brings to mind political activity of some sort, particularly voting.

The essence of citizenship, or so it seems from the hectoring swarms of voter education and turn-out drives that descend upon us every election year, is to vote faithfully, and perhaps even thoughtfully, after acquainting ourselves with all the policy prescriptions of the various candidates for office. To be a good citizen, in other words, demands that we wade through those mind-numbing charts of policy positions regularly published each election year, which dutifully set candidate X's 17-point plan for reducing the deficit side-by-side with candidate Y's 21-point plan for doing the same.

Citizenship thus understood is necessarily an episodic, infrequent, to say nothing of onerous duty. Its chief purpose seems to be to turn over to supposedly qualified experts the *real* business of public life--namely, designing and launching public programs of all sorts, which will bestow upon the victims of poverty or AIDS or discrimination or some other insidious force the tender mercies of bureaucrats, policy experts, social therapists and others, who claim to be uniquely able to cope with such problems by virtue of professional training.

Once the citizen has voted, in other words, he or she is supposed to get out of the way, and let the experts take over. Small wonder, then, that Americans today feel deeply alienated from the realm of public life, and that citizenship understood as voting holds so little appeal.

A BROADER VIEW OF CITIZENSHIP

The citizenship-as-voting notion can be a profoundly impoverished understanding of that activity. There is another, more traditional, and far more encompassing view--one that regards citizenship as an individual's active participation in that vast realm of human affairs known as *civil society*.

Now, civil society is a far more expansive field for human endeavor than the political sphere. Civil society encompasses *all* the institutions through which individuals express their interests and values, outside of and distinct from government. Thus, it contains our activities in the marketplace, including acquiring private property, holding a job, and earning a living. It embraces what we do as loving members of our families, as students or concerned parents within our schools, as worshipful participants at our churches, and as faithful members of neighborhood associations, clubs, fraternal and sororal lodges, and ethnic and voluntary associations of all sorts.

Citizenly activity within civil society occurs not episodically or infrequently, as with voting, but regularly and constantly, in countless small ways that are so much a part of the texture of our everyday lives that we are almost unaware of them. Every time we attend church, go to a PTA meeting, help a charity drive, or perform faithfully and well a task at work, we are being decent citizens.

In further contrast to voting, which supposedly engages chiefly our abstract reasoning and objective judgment about candidates and policies, citizenship in this larger sense engages the full human being. That is, the institutions of civil society appeal to and sustain our spirit and heart, as much as our mind.

Heart and spirit are nurtured by the songs and fairy tales of home, the lessons of Sunday School, the instruction at school, and the gentle advice and perhaps criticism of a neighbor. These enrich us, create bonds and obligations within us, and demand that we, in turn, teach the lessons, sing the songs, and provide the honest, loving advice and criticism to others.

Through these countless, subtle, daily interactions, our civil institutions give form and substance to the everyday qualities and values without which life itself would be impossible: honesty, perseverance, self-restraint, personal responsibility, and service to others. These institutions act by rewarding us when these values appear, punishing when they do not, and by mercifully and willingly sustaining those who may fall behind, in spite of good-faith efforts to live by civil society's rules. Sound civil institutions ensure that those cherished values are passed on to the next generation, by surrounding the maturing child and young person with constant, quiet messages of reaffirmation and reinforcement.

Through our vast, complex web of civil institutions we grow and develop into complete human beings by learning to suppress our often chaotic and destructive impulses, to express our connectedness and mutual obligation to each other, and to reach beyond ourselves, so to speak, to higher aspirations, reflecting nobler impulses. Those institutions sustain us, but we in turn must sustain them, for without unremitting, steadfast citizenly involvement, they are doomed to wither and die.

OUR FORMER ROBUST SOCIETY

That America was blessed with a robust, vigorous civil society was once understood to be vital to its health and success. Alexis de Tocqueville's *Democracy in America* is, perhaps, the classic expression of wonder and admiration at the incredible energy generated by the vast array of civic institutions spread across the face of our young nation. Everywhere Tocqueville looked in America, he noted, our citizens had formed associations, committees, and clubs to tackle one or another of the problems facing them in this undeveloped wilderness. Through such citizenly activity, Tocqueville believed, Americans expressed and sustained their civil freedom, accomplished an enormous range of tasks, and, most important, developed fully as rooted, connected human beings.

Tocqueville's admiration for the liberty-sustaining, life-affirming energy of civil society, is, of course, by no means shared by our intellectual and cultural elites today. Instead of citizenship as a vigorous, multi-faceted participation in civil society, we are urged to constrict our view of citizenship to the lonely, sporadic act of the isolated voter.

To explain how this came about would require a lengthy discourse on the modern project--that great philosophical enterprise launched by Machiavelli, Hobbes, and Locke, and carried on in various decadent and corrupt forms today. I will not detail that history here.

But it is important to note the main points of contrast. What to Tocqueville appears as a vast, pluralistic upswelling of groups expressing boundless civic energy, appears to our elites to be a wasteful, chaotic, misguided jumble of amateurish groups meddling unwelcomed in social policy.   What to Tocqueville appears as vigorous, coherent, value-affirming civic associations appears to our elites as stultifying, retrograde, rights-violating tyrannies.

THE COLLAPSE OF CIVIL SOCIETY

To such elites, the virtue of the constricted, citizen-as-voter notion is clear. It quietly and neatly lifts the public business, so to speak, out of the messy world of active citizens and civic institutions, shifting it instead into the neat, rational, smoothly humming world of the centralized, professionalized bureaucracies, wherein the elites themselves prevail.

The result is nothing less than the abolition of civil society. The story of civil society's demise is told most eloquently by sociologist Robert Nisbet in his magnificent classic, *The Quest for Community.*

Modernity, Nisbet argues, assails civil society both from below and from above. From below, the authority of family, church, neighborhood, and school is quietly eroded by the proliferation of individual rights of all sorts, especially the right of self-expression--that is, expression of self with utter disregard, or contempt, for civil society. From above, civil institutions are pressured to surrender authority and function to the professional elites of the centralized, bureaucratic state. Caught in a pincers movement between individual rights and the central state, Nisbet noted, the intermediate associations of civil society struggle and languish.

What has been the result of the modern assault on civil society? Look about you, at the vast array of social ills bearing down upon us: the explosion of illegitimate births in the inner cities, the spread of sexually transmitted diseases, the dramatic increase of violent crime in the streets, the rise of drug abuse, the collapse of public education, and the spread of irresponsible personal behavior of all sorts.

What is the common thread? Very simply, the collapse of civil society--the decay of its institutions and values, and the loss of control they once exerted over human behavior.

Is our response to try to strengthen civil society? Of course not. Our elites instead call for more government programs--more bureaucratic experts and professionals to minister to the hurts allegedly inflicted on hapless victims by industrialism, racism, sexism, and so on--in the course taking away yet more authority from citizens and civil institutions.

Thus is set up the vicious cycle so ably described years ago by Nathan Glazer in his splendid essay, "The Limits of Social Policy." As he noted, the expansion of government social policy does not solve problems, it only makes them worse. Government intervention undermines and weakens the authority of the very civil institutions that had kept undesirable behavior within reasonable limits in the first place. Thus as government programs push into a problem area, civil institutions weaken further, and the problem is compounded.

As we approach the end of the 20th century, we may also be nearing the end of this futile cycle. People are increasingly disenchanted with the manifest impotence of government and its utter inability to perform even the most rudimentary duties assigned to it, such as securing our unmolested passage down our own streets.

Other encouraging signs are to be found in recent election returns and surveys of public opinion, which reflect a massive, palpable discontent with all major governing institutions. Consider the success of term limits and tax-and-spending limits in referenda across the nation. Above all, note the immense popularity of Ross Perot's radical, populist call to return government directly to the people. The message is clear: Americans are sick and tired of being treated as if they are incompetent to run their own affairs.

They are sick and tired of being treated as helpless, pathetic victims of social forces that are seemingly beyond their understanding or control.

They are sick and tired of being treated as passive clients by arrogant, paternalistic social scientists, therapists, professionals, and bureaucrats, who claim exclusive right to minister to the hurts inflicted by hostile social forces.

They are sick and tired of supporting the bloated, corrupt, centralized bureaucracies into which our social therapists are organized to ensure that power and accountability flow to them, rather than to the citizens of the United States.

Americans are clearly willing and eager to seize control of their daily lives again--to make critical life choices for themselves based on their own common sense and folk wisdom, to assume once again the status of proud, independent, self-governing citizens intended for them by the Founders, and denied them by today's social service providers and bureaucracies. In short, Americans are ready for what might be called "a new citizenship," which will liberate and empower them.

This impulse toward a new citizenship is, of course, nothing more or less than a return to the older, far more encompassing notion of citizenship that figured so prominently in Tocqueville's teaching. If properly channeled and directed, this impulse may, in fact, lead directly to the resuscitation of civil society--a regeneration of that vast network of vibrant, liberty-sustaining, life-affirming institutions that once covered the face of this nation.

AN AGENDA FOR REVITALIZATION

What sorts of measures will be required if we are to accomplish this revitalization of civil society?

First, we must be prepared once again to treat Americans as genuinely self-governing citizens, willing and able to reassume control of their daily lives and to make critical choices for themselves. Americans must not be dismissed as helpless victims or passive clients.

Second, we must seek to restore the intellectual and cultural legitimacy of citizenly common sense as a way of understanding and solving problems. This suggests an effort to re-establish the dignity of traditional folk wisdom and everyday morality with renewed emphasis on teaching and nurturing personal character--the customary guideposts of everyday life. This will mean taking on intellectually the radical skepticism about such "unscientific" approaches propagated by professional pseudo-scientists eager to preserve their intellectual hegemony.

Third, we must reinvigorate and reempower the traditional local institutions--families, schools, churches, and neighborhoods--that provide training in and room for the exercise of genuine citizenship, that pass on folk wisdom and everyday morality to the next generation, and that cultivate and reinforce personal character. This will require efforts to reform such local institutions for far too often today's churches, schools, and related "mediating structures" have themselves succumbed to the view that Americans are mere clients or consumers of therapeutic social services.

Fourth, we must encourage the dramatic decentralization of power and accountability away from the centralized, bureaucratic, "Nanny state" in Washington, back to the states, localities, and revitalized "mediating structures." We should also strive to refocus moral authority back to such structures, and away from corrupt intellectual and cultural elites in the universities, the media, and elsewhere, who regard traditional mediating structures as benighted purveyors of reactionary prejudices.

Finally, we must be willing to challenge on all fronts the political hegemony of the "helping" and "caring" professionals and bureaucrats who have penetrated so many aspects of our daily lives, and who profit so handsomely from the "Nanny state." We will need to dramatize their status as entrenched, corrupt special interests, more concerned about advancing narrow ideological agendas and protecting political prerogatives than about serving the public. This will require not only traditional approaches like policy research, but more innovative approaches as well. For instance, media and writing projects could capture the vivid, compelling human stories of those who suffer at the hands of paternalistic, arrogant bureaucrats and professionals, and the equally compelling human stories of those who have launched successful grassroots, citizen empowerment projects.

What are the chances of successfully revitalizing civil society through the new citizenship? It is easy to be pessimistic. After all, the entire weight of the modern project seems to be behind the destruction of the independent civil realm.

Tocqueville himself was well aware of the destructive effects that modernity would have on civil institutions. Indeed, his purpose in writing *Democracy in America* was precisely to warn mankind about the impending storm of modernity--to tell us that the old, established institutions of civil society would soon be borne away by the cyclonic winds of modern individualism and the centralized state.

In America, however, he witnessed the remarkable spectacle of hitherto unrelated individuals--complete strangers--coming together to form wholly new forms of civil institutions, in the very teeth of the modern storm. The impulse toward civil association--the yearning for genuine citizenship within civil society--is not so easy to destroy, he seemed to suggest.

World events of the past decade only confirm Tocqueville's hopefulness. No movement ever undertook the eradication of civil society with more zeal or determination than Marxism, that totalitarian perversion of the modern project. And yet beneath the seemingly smoothly humming state bureaucracies of the former Soviet Union and Eastern Europe, there sprouted once again the seeds of civil society--churches, civic associations, unions, dissident groups, free presses. Even as the resolve of the Free World halted Marxism's outward thrust, so from within, Marxism began to decay and crumble, as the nascent institutions of civil society flourished and spread. The liberation of Eastern Europe and the former Soviet Union soon made it apparent that modernity's "final offensive" against civil society had failed utterly.

Let us take heart both from these events, and from Tocqueville's hopeful teachings, as we undertake here in the United States the revitalization of civil society through the new citizenship. There can be no more urgent task than the resuscitation of the civic sphere, which alone makes and genuine citizenship possible.

Chapter 2

Building Blocks of Our American Culture

Heather Richardson Higgins

INTRODUCTION

Americans are different. When traveling abroad Americans are easy to spot. When Americans are asked why they love their country, their answers are different from those given by people of other nationalities: they like the place, or the food, or the culture. We like our way of life, who we are, and what we represent. The American difference derives in part from the fact that we are a nation of transplants and movers, a nation of immigrants and their restless heirs. Being American has not yet become a function of where you are born, or of your parentage, but of your buying into a certain set of ideas that define what it is "to be an American"--ideas that anyone, regardless of ethnicity, religion, or geographic origin can adopt and be just as much an American tomorrow as we are Americans today. Concomitantly, subscribing to the antithesis of those ideas is what makes it possible to be considered "un-American" in a way it would be hard for a Chinese to be un-Chinese or an Italian to be un-Italian.

What are the attitudes Americans hold that define their culture? Where did these ideas come from? Have they held constant since our founding, or have they changed over the years? Do these specific principles make a difference to us, to our economy, to our politics, and to the fabric of our lives? If so, and perhaps most importantly, do we have in place the cultural building blocks that are necessary for a prosperous future?

THE AMERICAN FOUNDING

> In a monarchy each man's desire to do what was right in his own eyes could be restrained by fear or force. In a republic, however, each man must somehow be persuaded to submerge his personal wants into the greater good of the whole . . . A republic was such a delicate polity precisely because it demanded an extraordinary moral character in the people.[1]

Americans embarked on an enormous experiment, something well beyond what even the early Greek republics had attempted. It was an experiment in a form of government which, far more than any other, relied on the character of the people. Historically, republics had been torn apart by faction and internal struggle. So the prospects for success were less than promising.

Republics, by definition, exist for the good of the people. But more than that, for their self-governing authority they rely on order from below, order derived from respect, not fear, of authority. They rely, in short, on virtue, not only private virtue but particularly public virtue (which is itself an extension of private virtue) as the critical factor which would cause individual citizens to constrain their personal wants to the greater good of the commonwealth. Many thought no people could have enough of such virtue to make a republican form of government work, and so many were certain such an experiment would fail.

In some sense then, the American character became both the question and purpose of the American Revolution. Historian Gordon Wood has written:

> The essential question raised in debates Americans had with themselves in 1776 over the wisdom of independence was social: were Americans the stuff republicans were made of?--surely the most important and most sensitive issue in all of the Revolutionary polemics, for it involved not any particular economic advantages or political rights, but rather the kind of people Americans were and wanted to be.[2]

THOMAS JEFFERSON AND HIS VISION

Thomas Jefferson was convinced that Americans as a people did in fact have the necessary character and saw it, as did others, in our confidence, our energy, our youth, and our rusticity. Even more so, perhaps, the potential for success was widely perceived in American industriousness, honesty, frugality, and public spiritedness. Some went so far as to claim that Americans even seemed more intelligent.

Perhaps most important, however, was that America was composed of "outgroups," colonials and provincials looked down upon by England. Jefferson was no exception.

> Jefferson . . . was, in fact, representative of the British provincial who, when he looked at England and Englishmen, saw an insufferable arrogance . . . [W]hen he wrote the Declaration of Independence, he expanded the principle of equality into a grand and sonorous universal principle, an assertion generally regarded as having its roots in the Enlightenment philosophy to which he was devoted. It is common, however, for outgroups quickly to translate their demands for specific recognition into values claimed to have universal validity. Of these, the most cherished is the ideal of the equality of all men, for it is hoped that as the ideal grows in acceptance, the specific degradations inflicted by arrogant majorities and power groups will decline.[3]

The equality to which Jefferson and his contemporaries subscribed was an equality of opportunity, quite unlike the equality of condition, or outcome, that so many assume today. It recognized that men were indeed born with different capacities--even, Jefferson would have argued, different capacities for their innate moral sense[4]--and did not pretend that they could be otherwise without impinging their liberties (by forcing a false leveling). Rather, instead of challenging the reality that some will rise to social or political preeminence, they sought to change the source of that prominence, away from the historical paths of privilege, wealth, and title. Jefferson invoked a *natural* aristocracy, one achievable by all men and based on virtue, temperance, independence, and devotion to the commonwealth. "In a republican system, only talent would matter."[5] America was to be, and has become, a nation where anyone can arrive and "just do it," a land of liberated dreamers and entrepreneurs limited only by the scope of their talents and ambitions.

In emphasizing this natural aristocracy based on virtue, Jefferson moved beyond Locke and his vision of man as an independent individual motivated primarily by a desire for self-preservation, who required the state for no purpose other than to preserve his individual rights and resolve conflicting interests. While Jefferson relied heavily on the tradition of Locke and classical liberalism, he also incorporated aspects of both classical republicanism and social ethics.   Locke had diverged from previous thought by developing an idea of natural rights (life, liberty, property) that did not rely on natural law and revealed religion as necessary precursors, a view which over time developed into a rights-oriented view of human relationships. Lockean ethics therefore are "essentially negative by virtue of their moral imperative to not harm others, to refrain from infringing upon other's rights and freedom, allowing them to pursue their own interests in ways they see fit."[6] Classical social ethics, by contrast, "are positive in the sense that they insist that it is not enough to merely refrain from injuring others; moral action requires an effort to improve others, encouraging the perfection of their souls."[7] Classical ethics move beyond a rights-only view, holding that there are standards that govern consensual relations and calling on us to participate in the community, to volunteer, to "do the right thing." They take us beyond ourselves, and move us beyond the negative and minimal world of not interfering with the rights of other people to the affirmative moral sphere of assisting them.

These seemingly conflicting viewpoints were melded by Jefferson in several ways. First, since Jefferson saw man's nature in the classical republican sense--man as a social being needing both to participate in political life and to achieve economic independence in order to fully realize his human nature--Jefferson found a positive role for government in his republican schema. Where Locke had argued for government only in the negative, that is, as a necessary instrument to preserving individual rights, Jefferson expanded upon Locke, building in a sense of social responsibility, arguing for politics as a vehicle for cultivating man's highest virtues. In Jefferson's view, however, that government must be small and participatory: a classical republic. The existence of that local republic, in turn, would protect individual rights from the tyrannies of centralized government and the elites it would breed.   To paraphrase Richard Hofstadter, the Federalists feared power in the majority, whereas Jefferson feared it anywhere else.

Jefferson was not opposed to elites per se. He had an abiding faith in the individual energy, initiative, and capacity of the American people and thought that from them would rise a natural elite, thereby "replacing the traditional hierarchical society and hereditary aristocracy with a hierarchy of republican regimes and an aristocracy of merit and virtue."[8] To him, the differences were critical "between this natural aristocracy, with its positive effect on society, and the artificial or 'pseudo' aristocracy, founded on wealth and birth without either virtue or talents, and its destructive effects on society."[9]

In addition to, first, the role of small republics and the emphasis on localism as cultivators of virtue, and, second, the idea of a natural aristocracy, Jefferson was concerned with three other ideas which would reverberate through American cultural thought: the need to cultivate our moral capacities, the importance of private property and economic independence, and the necessary role of religion to the ethics of a free society. With regard to the first, he believed that while our moral sense was innate, it needed to be strengthened and refined, a belief which led to his emphasis on the moral value of public education. "Jefferson," according to historian Robert Kelly, "was the original prophet of the American faith in popular education. Education would not only ensure the success of a democratic government, it would equip men to utilize their talents and open the way for the rise of . . .'an aristocracy of virtue and talent'."[10] This hope was a reflection of Jefferson's sophisticated view of the development of ethical conduct: that such conduct is neither wholly innate or up to the individual, on the one hand, nor the responsibility of society, on the other, but that the ethical conduct of individuals was properly the responsibility of both.

Second, Jefferson recognized that property ownership and economic independence were essential to the citizens of a republic. In his *Notes on the State of Virginia,* Jefferson declared: "Dependence begets subservience and venality, suffocates the germ of virtue, and prepares fit tools for the designs of ambition." He saw economic independence as central to public virtue and thus critical to the citizen's qualification for political participation. Economic independence was also the wellspring of the citizen's political power and his bulwark against the corruption of a strong centralized government. This was Jefferson's chief argument against Hamilton and the Federalists, and one which has been repeated again and again through American political life: "For Jefferson, . . . there was a constant struggle between a corrupt centralized government that wished to control all wealth and power (giving it out as patronage to control the masses) and a strong, independent, democratic citizenry capable of ruling itself with wisdom, virtue, and self-respect."[11] Additionally, Jefferson recognized that ownership of property helped generate support for law and order--an essential feature to any functioning republic.

Third, Jefferson was an advocate of religious freedom, not because he was opposed to religion, but precisely because he recognized its importance and was concerned about its institutional corruption. He wrote in *Notes on the State of Virginia*: "Had not the Roman government permitted free inquiry Christianity could never have been introduced. Had not free inquiry been indulged at the era of the reformation, the corruptions of Christianity could not have been purged away. If it be restrained now, the present corruptions will be protected, and new ones encouraged." Jefferson was a moralist who saw Christianity, in particular, as being of paramount importance. Unlike ancient moral philosophy, whose ethics dwelt within the realm of private goodness and well-being, Christian ethics sought to serve "public goodness and well being (i.e., one's duties to others and to society). . . Christ's ethical teachings of love, repentance and forgiveness, of universal brotherhood and charity provided, for Jefferson, 'the most sublime and benevolent code of morals which has ever been offered to man' for his life in society."[12] This ethical outlook, which specified our obligations to one another, was not only essential to the proper ordering of a free society, but was to become one of the key characteristics of American culture--the capacity to love the other, to trust beyond immediate family, to feel responsibility for fellow citizens.

Jefferson's views were not universally held, particularly in the post-revolutionary environment when virtue seemed to go into decline and a new taste for luxury and social elitism took over. The philosophical splits which had been masked by a common interest in defeating the British were now exposed. Even those who had dreamed of America as a "Christian Sparta," who felt our success in the revolution and achievement of independence had been dependent on the moral reformation of the people and God's consequent approbation, began to wonder whether moral instruction was sufficient, whether perhaps institutional reforms were necessary to sustain the type of character necessary to the future success of the Republic. We are used to thinking of the past in terms of the broadly held ideas which defined different eras. And indeed the national ideology of our first American century was Republicanism. But there were serious differences between Americans regarding their conception of what that should mean, who we were, and how we should conduct ourselves.

THE ETHNO-CULTURAL DIVIDE

"The energies shaping public life are emotional as well as rational, cultural as well as economic."[13] The energies Robert Kelly refers to took on new dimensions after the Revolution. Without a common hostility to the British to unite them, Americans fell broadly into two camps: those who saw America as a purer, better England (primarily the Anglicans, Episcopalians, and Quakers) and those who saw America as the antithesis of Britain (essentially the less well-to-do among the Scots, Scots-Irish, Dutch, and Germans).[14] The first group supported urbanization and industrialization. They saw themselves as intellectually sophisticated, culturally superior, more virtuous and upright, and closer to God than most. They tended to be Federalists and were composed of those who saw America as a Christian Sparta and sought to practice a politics of virtue; they believed that for the Republic to survive it needed to be united by a shared way of life through which we would all become more morally pure. They preached the virtues of godly living, self-discipline, industry, self-denial, hard work, and public virtue. But they sought to achieve these habits not only through prescription, but through direct moral, legal, and economic intervention, leading them to support a strong central government.

A second element within the Federalists favored a strong government, though primarily for economic reasons. They wanted mercantilist and protectionist policies, much as England had, to foster domestic industry. They were advocates of modernization and development, and "envisioned an America that was centrally organized, economically activist and commercialized, orderly and obedient to elite leadership."[15]

In contrast to the Federalists' beliefs were those of the Jeffersonian Republicans, who favored rural life and saw themselves as the keepers of country virtue (in contrast to urban corruption), tradition, and a stable, simpler, "natural" way of life. They too were formed of essentially two groups. The southerners, in particular contrast to the puritanic Yankees of New England, emphasized liberty, not moral purity, advocating that life should be lived as a person saw fit. As devotees of Adam Smith, they were suspicious of bankers and merchants (feeling that business tends to conspire with government) and believed that what government there was should be small and inactive. Yet these early libertarians admired the arrogant imperiousness of the gentry, unlike the other more egalitarian strain among the Republicans, who tended to be preoccupied with showing that not being English (which was equated with having wealth, power, and position) did not mean being unequal. Yet they too were followers of Adam Smith and worried about a too-powerful government with ties to business. On the cultural front, they shared the southerners' laissez-faire attitude, primarily in the interest of keeping their own customs.

With time, the names of the parties shifted, though the themes remained largely the same. The Jeffersonian Republicans became the Jacksonian Democrats, the party, by and large, of religious free thinkers who emphasized separation of church and state, cultural laissez-faire, and anti-temperance (composed as they were of Scots-Irish with their whiskey and Germans with their beer). The Federalists became Whigs who emphasized law and order, sober living, steady habits, proper manners, and temperance, while blaming crime and social problems on minorities.

With the arrival of the first significant block of Catholics in the 1850s, however, a substantial realignment took place. Since the Catholics tended to join the Democrats (the party of the "outgroups"), the Scots-Irish, along with the Baptists and Methodists, left the party, first joining the anti-Catholic Know-Nothings party, and then the newly formed Republican party (when the Know-Nothings broke up over the slavery issue). In the long term, that cultural laissez-faire attitude of the Democrats, which caused them to accept slavery, cost them much of their moral credibility. Regarding slavery, Samuel Tilden, leader of the Democratic party, said, "No man has the right or duty to impose his own convictions upon others," and that it was "mere theory which held that 'slavery is a wrong, without reference to any condition of time, place, or circumstances.'"[16] The Republicans' anti-slavery position was not, of course, universally virtuous and morally based. For example, various Republicans were opposed to slavery in the new territories essentially for reasons of economics and race: they desired to save the territories for white settlers and free labor. With time, however, the moral arguments of the abolitionists prevailed, and with the ascendance of the Republicans after the Civil War came the ascendance of their Yankee culture, which emphasized the pursuit of progress through orderly behavior, self-discipline, hard work, and a spirit of enterprise and entrepreneurialism. The idea of "progress" referred to in this chapter is the Aristotelian view of achievement, betterment, and fulfillment of purpose, not the liberal view of progress as something inevitable which leads to perfection.

This "progressivism" became the dominant ideology of the second century of American politics, and within that framework the same nationalist/moralist versus libertarian/egalitarian split continued. Yet despite their differences, between them the parties emphasized those characteristics which are central to American civilization--the importance of personal character and public virtue, an emphasis on individual liberty within a context of transcendant truth, a faith in the entrepreneur and the capacity for progress, a trust for the wisdom of the American people to judge what was best for them. Over time, both sides began to rely increasingly heavily on a stronger national government, the Republicans particularly favoring government intervention to both create jobs and prop up the economy (in the depression of 1890, for example) and to encourage moral reform (the best known example being Prohibition).

With the advent of the New Deal, the Democrats embarked on a redefining course of favoring government intervention; with the War on Poverty and the concurrent focus on "social justice," Democrats too began to use government aggressively to promote their moral and cultural vision. In the last 30 years, moral authority has been largely abdicated by the culture and ceded to the state, the seemingly limitless solution to all our ills. This shift, from reliance on the virtue of the people to a reliance on laws and programs promulgated by government, has been influenced by the unintended implication of the idea of liberty as formulated by John Stuart Mill in the mid-19th century in his radical book, *On Liberty*.

REDEFINING LIBERTY

[W]e are now discovering that absolute liberty also tends to corrupt absolutely. A liberty that is divorced from tradition and convention, from morality and religion, that makes the individual the sole repository and arbiter of all values and puts him in an adversarial relationship to society and the state--such a liberty is a grave peril to liberalism itself.[17]

Until Mill wrote *On Liberty*, a liberty that was authentic was conceived as having properties and qualifications which extended beyond the self. Liberty was not only the way for people to realize their full human potential by practicing the civic virtues and exercising their moral and social sympathies. Liberty was itself in the interest of the commonwealth, for only a free man could achieve the economic independence and voluntary participation in government that would create a necessarily virtuous citizenry. Gertrude Himmelfarb succinctly points out:

No [philosopher] went so far as to propose anything like an absolute, or near-absolute, principle of liberty. Each limited or qualified liberty in a significant respect: liberty of speech, 'but not out of anger, hatred, or a desire to introduce any change in the state on his own authority' (Spinoza); liberty, but only within the law and not for 'opinions contrary to human society, or to those moral rules which are necessary to the preservation of civil society' (Locke); liberty, but not 'unlimited,' consisting 'only in the power of doing what we ought to will, and in not being constrained to do what we ought not to will' (Montesquieu); liberty of speech, but not of action (Kant's 'argue, but obey'), the liberty of the individual as against government, but not against 'public opinion' or 'society' (Jefferson and Paine); freedom, but under conditions of 'order and moderation' (Macaulay); liberty, but not 'without morality, nor morality without faith' (Tocqueville).[18]

Mill's idea of liberty was simple and absolute and thus most appealing: No one has the right to interfere--either with another's political liberty (through political tyranny) or with their personal liberty through social tyranny--unless he has the justification of self-protection.

It sounds good. Who doesn't think that he personally should have no constraints placed upon him--that he can decide for himself what's best? But this proposition faces real problems in the real world.

Mill assumed two things in asserting this unfettered principle of liberty. The first was that since truth was knowable and important, even in a free marketplace of ideas where all ideas and opinions were presented as equally true and equally valuable, truth itself would be evident. The second premise combined an optimistic (though not yet secular) view of human nature with the expectation that "civilization . . . would continue to impose upon individuals the 'eminently artificial discipline' that was the moral corrective to human nature. [Mill] also took for granted that those virtues that had already been acquired, by means of religion, tradition, law, and all the other resources of civilization--would continue to be valued and exercised."[19]

Unfortunately, Mill was wrong. Had modernism not come along, it might have been easier to assert that there is such a thing as truth, and to distinguish what was true from what was in error. But modernism, and its correlative secular view of man, precluded that. The reason is this: there are only two possible views of man. An intentionally simplified explanation can be used for the purposes of this chapter. The Calvinist/Thomist split on the question of the essential goodness of man on the one hand, and the problems of the relationship between secularism and the good (primarily the issues of error and utility) on the other, will not be discussed here.

The first, traditional view, is that we are capable of both good and evil-- in religious terms, we are fallen. Since man is not perfect, the good must originate from some outside source--generally God or natural law. In the secular view, man is good. Man is therefore the arbiter of what is good, and each person's viewpoint is just as valid as the next. The problem with the secular view is that this outlook works only so long as most of society clings to its quaint notion that there are indeed standards of conduct.

Otherwise, once relativism is the norm, all hell breaks loose. If everyone's ideas have equal weight, then the ideas of the nihilists, or the hedonists, or the Nazis, for example, are just as valid as any other, are just as "good," and begin to color what the culture teaches its young and practices itself. George Will has pointed out:

> The preservation of a nation requires a certain minimum moral continuity, because a nation is not just "territory" or "physical locality." A nation is people "associated in agreement with respect to justice". . . [The continuance of that nation] presupposes efforts to predispose rising generations to the "views" and habits and dispositions that underlie institutional arrangements . . . [It is] mistaken to dismiss the possibility that changed patterns of moral choices can have large and intolerable social consequences.[20]

Nihilism or hedonism or Nazism may not, in their genesis, necessarily entail "harm," as specified by Mill's vision of full liberty. But the consequences to society can be real and drastic.

What has happened to Mill's argument for unfettered liberty is this: First, it has taken a cudgel to truth by making error equally worthy of our attention, thus enabling the so-called postmodernists to go a step further by denying "not only absolute truth but contingent, partial, incremental truths. For them absolute liberty is not, as it was for Mill, the precondition of truth; rather it is the precondition for the liberation from truth itself." Second, by undermining truth, we have undermined cultural norms and morals, with grave consequences. By creating this void we have invited the intrusion of law into the vacuum that should be filled by the ethics of the public square and social sanction (e.g., speech codes, or the confusion over definitions of rape). Further, we have eroded much of the moral sensibilities, language, and habits of thought that are the basis for good legislation, as in the travesty of legalizing assisted suicide. And we have deprived citizens, particularly parents, of the cultural support on which they depend for guidance, assistance, and affirmation.

A culture is a living entity--plant it in good soil and it will flourish; plant it where there are few nutrients or even poison, and your results will be vastly different. A culture's soil is the attitudes and values which nourish it. The attitudes and values that predominate in a society will make all the difference to its ultimate success.

WHICH VALUES?

[S]ound laws do not rule people; sound laws help nurture the fabric of assumptions and disciplines by which people rule themselves . . . Democracy subverts itself if it subverts the habits of self-restraint, self-denial and public-spiritedness . . . Warning--the ethos of this society may be harmful to your moral health.[22]

In 1992, Lawrence Harrison wrote a fascinating book, *Who Prospers*, which assessed the various fortunes of nations around the world. What he discovered is that being prosperous is tied fairly directly to holding a certain set of values; having the opposite predisposition tends to be antithetical to success. Many of the poor are not poor because of economics per se, but because they hold, often as will their larger culture, a set of cultural norms that hinder them helping themselves. Culture, he finds, influences "group or national political, economic, and social performance. Culture is a coherent system of values, attitudes, and institutions that influences individual and social behavior in all dimensions of human experience."[23]

Drawing on the work of Argentine scholar Mariano Grondona and his typology of cultural and ideological factors that influence which countries are "development-prone" and which are "development-resistant," Harrison finds a number of factors which reappear with startling consistency. I have compiled and organized many of these factors into a schematic, which is presented as Table 1.[24]

TABLE 1

	Development -- Prone	Development -- Resistant
Religion	Explains and justifies success.	Relieves or explains suffering.
Salvation	Next world, through good works in this world.	Saved by retiring from this world retire from risks and dangers.
Ethical System	Based on responsible self -- interest and mutual respect.	Morality seeks perfection (altruism, self-denial), which exceeds human nature and becomes utopianism.
*"Lesser Virtues"**	Important to responsibility, social identification; contribute to efficiency, smooth relations.	Unimportant; impinge on individual will.

*Lesser values: eg., tidiness, courtesy, punctuality, job well done.

TABLE 1 (continued)

Perfectibility	Goal to work towards, but no expectations will realize. Flaws expected/accepted.	Flaws seized upon by spiritual and political leaders to induce guilt.
Degree of Trust	Respects/has faith in individual. Radius of trust goes beyond family. Leads to egalitarianism and decentralization.	Suspicious of individual. Non-family viewed with indifference/hostility. Tend toward mistrust, authoritarianism, centralization.
Respect for Law	Basis of authority.	Subordinate to or dictated by the authority.
Democracy	Inevitable; consolidates pluralism, dissolves authoritarianism.	Window dressing for new forms of authoritarianism.
Wealth	Created as product of human effort, initiative. Economy viewed as positive -- sum game.	A natural or physical resource that exists; question of acquiring/ redistributing. Economy as zero -sum game.
Competition	Positive force, promotes excellence, enriches society.	Form of aggression, nurtures envy, threatens stability and solidarity.
Economic Justice	Demands saving and investment for the benefits of future generation.	Equitable distribution to the current generation.
Labor	Moral, social duty, central form of self expression, satisfaction.	Burden, necessary evil; real pleasure and satisfaction attainable only outside the workplace.
Dissent	Critical to progress, reform, search for truth, encouraging.	Heretical, criminal, threat to stability, solidarity.
Education	Nurtures inquisitiveness, creativity.	Transmits orthodoxy.
Mode of Thought	Pragmatism, rationalism, empiricism, utilitarianism viewed favorably.	Those four viewed as threats; tradition, emotion and chance substitute for rationality.
Time Focus	The future, which can be affected by our behavior.	The past. Future viewed as destiny reflecting fatalistic world view.

TABLE 1 (continued)

World	Setting for action, achievement approached with optimism.	Controlled by irresistable forces (e.g., God, multinationals, international conspiracies); approached with pessimism; survival is goal.
Life	What will I do?	What happens to me?

Certainly the development-prone characteristics are recognizable as part of the dominant American experience, and have been central to our success as a nation. The question, in large part, is whether, going forward, we still hold to the mix of attitudes and assumptions which will make further progress possible.

Some look forward and are understandably worried. Gertrude Himmelfarb writes, "The beasts of modernism have mutated into the beasts of postmodernism--relativism into nihilism, amorality into immorality, irrationality into insanity, sexual deviancy into polymorphous perversity."[25]

Just before his death, Richard Nixon wrote:

From the 1960s on, our laws and our mores have been driven by the cultural conceits that took hold during the heyday of the counterculture, including a denial of personal responsibility and the fantasy that the coercive power of government can produce spiritual uplift, cure poverty, end bigotry, legislate growth and stamp out any number of individual and social inadequacies... We have created a culture in which appallingly large numbers ignore the opportunities offered by work, choosing instead those offered by the interwoven worlds of welfare and crime... What the U.S. needs is... a renewal of its commitment to limited but strong government; economic freedom...; and a moral and cultural system that strengthens the family, personal responsibility and the instincts for civic virtue.[26]

This is the central challenge of a free society: the freer it is, the more its citizenry must rely on both their own self-determination and self-control, as well as a strong supportive community, to provide a responsible approach to self-governance and a community in which peaceful coexistence is achieved. Yet during the last 30 years many Americans have forgotten, or taken for granted, why and how free societies work.

The frequent and wanton disregard for human life (as when children kill each other for sneakers), the increasing evidence of greed and corruption, the persistent levels of poverty and dependency, the diminished acceptance of personal responsibility for the consequences of behavior and the willingness to find excuses for such behavior (as in the Menendez trial), the increasingly poor levels of educational attainment--all indicate that the problems this nation face are not merely economic or political but also cultural and behavioral.

Our behavior reflects our choice of which personal and civic virtues we practice or ignore. Though the virtues are often presented as having opposite characteristics which are "bad," in fact each has a complementary quality--for example, self-restraint and self-expression, or deferred gratification and immediate indulgence--which is not bad in itself, but a reflection of correlative goods. Each, when taken to excess, contains the potential for harm--too much emphasis on frugality and you have Scrooge, too much responsibility and self-denial and you have Ethan Frome. The challenge, then, is the mix, the balance, the need for moderation. The surprising danger is this: by shifting the balance slightly, by emphasizing or denying a particular virtue relative to its corollary--by teaching or minimizing the idea that hard work, for example, is important--is ultimately to teach an entire philosophical world view with dramatic societal implications.

For example, if you teach the value of hard work, a virtue long emphasized in American culture, what does it imply? It implies that hard work is worthwhile and that merit and effort count and will be rewarded; that you, the individual, make a difference to the outcome of your own life; that there is progress and an economy that can grow, that work and competition are good. What, on the other hand, is the subtext when children are told that there is no point to hard work? That luck (position, connections, race, wealth) is what matters; that they should envy those who achieve, because they must have gotten there for some reason other than that they were deserving; that effort and merit are not relevant to improving their lives; that the economy is a zero-sum game of allocation; that work is to be avoided.

What do you imply when you teach that saving and deferred gratification are important? You are saying that the individual is responsible for himself and his future, and indeed responsible for his family and future generations; that investment will be rewarded; that there are things more important than pleasure. If you do not teach this view you transmit the opposite message: that someone other than yourself is responsible for your well-being and that of your family; that there is nothing to be gained by investing or waiting, so you might as well consume now; that there are no interests above your own.

What about public virtue and responsibility to others? They teach us that even beyond family we are equal, and have obligations higher than our personal wants; that we are to take care of our neighbor; that we have a stake in this society. If not taught this view, we do not learn to look beyond ourselves, nor learn that it is we, not the abstract state or someone else, who are our brother's keeper, nor feel a stake in this commonwealth other than what we extract from it.

All the virtues teach us, in short, to grow beyond ourselves, to become more other-regarding, and to strive to improve our lot and that of others. In that rests much of America's idealism.

THE AMERICAN VISION

Throughout America's history, within a framework that perceived there to be an objective understanding of truth, the dominant ideas that were the building blocks of our culture have been two: the idea of our own capacity for progress, and the idea that we are all equal, distinguished only by our talents, merits, and virtues--by what we do with our lives. These are quintessentially American ideas; from them flow liberty, justice, the pursuit of happiness, and all those civic virtues whose renewal we hear called for. We are hearing a cry for those virtues precisely because that notion of progress and that understanding of equality have been undercut by the postmodernist world view, a view which holds that what should be equal are outcomes. It is a view which holds that if our outcomes are different, it is not our fault (nothing is our fault, for we are all good) but the fault of "social forces." It is a view which decries competition and calls for the redistribution of wealth, thereby punishing the creators and making economic growth and progress impossible. It is a view which holds that the individual is not responsible for his own actions, and certainly is not to be judged (justice having as its precondition the idea of personal responsibility for action), but to be shown compassion. It is a view which dismisses the moral, cultural, and spiritual as being wholly subjective and thus left wholly to individual whim. It is a view which is both shortsighted and wrong.

America is a country founded on morality and possibility, a nation where anyone can "just do it," and a land where, in exchange for our freedom, we seek to "do the right thing." In both cases, it is a doing done by individual people, not social forces, done as acts of free will. The choices we make are largely a function of the principles we have been taught, the habits of virtue we have or have not acquired. It is a delicate thing to balance the correlative goods and emphasize the necessary virtues, but it is necessary to our ethos as a nation and our success as a polity. America will need to again recognize, honor, and teach those values and attitudes which will encourage and support virtuous choices. Only in so doing will we provide the necessary building blocks for creating a truly prosperous and civil society in the 21st century.

ENDNOTES

1.   Gordon S. Wood, *The Creation of the American Republic 1776-1787* (New York: Norton & Co., 1979), 68.

2.   Ibid., 93.

3.   Robert Kelly, *The Transatlantic Persuasion* (New York: Knopf, 1969), 104.

4.   Garret Ward Sheldon, *The Political Philosophy of Thomas Jefferson* (Baltimore: Johns Hopkins University Press, 1991), 59. I am indebted to this work in particular for the section on Jefferson and this thought.

5.   Wood, *Creation of the American Republic*, 71.

6.   Sheldon, *Political Philosophy of Jefferson*, 13-14.

7.   Ibid., 14.

8.   Ibid., 17.

9.   Ibid., 80.

10.   Kelly, *Transatlantic Persuasion*, 133.

11.   Sheldon, *Political Philosophy of Jefferson*, 78.

12.   Ibid., 105.

13.   Robert Kelly, *The Cultural Pattern in American Politics* (New York: Knopf, 1979), 7.

14.   Ibid. For a complete discussion of the different ethnic groups and their political, policy, and cultural difference through time in American society, see particularly Chapter IX, "The First Century: The era of Bipolar Politics" to which this section is indebted.

15.   Ibid., 273.

16.   Kelly, *The Transatlantic Persuasion*, 270.

17.   Gertrude Himmelfarb, *On Looking into the Abyss* (New York: Knopf, 1994), 106.

18.   Ibid., 81. I have relied here for the discussion on Mill to Himmelfarb's essay, "Liberty: One Very Simple Principle," and recommend it highly.

19.   Ibid., 86.

20.   George Will, *Statecraft as Soulcraft* (New York: Simon & Schuster, 1983), 78, 79, and 83.

21.   Himmelfarb, *Looking into the Abyss*, 82.

22.   Will, *Statecraft as Soulcraft*, 77, 133, and 135.

23.   Lawrence Harrison, *Who Prospers* (New York: Basic Books, 1992), 9.

24.   Ibid., 11-19.

25.   Himmelfarb, *Looking into the Abyss*, 6.

26.   Richard Nixon in *Time Magazine* (May 2, 1994): 34-35.

Chapter 3

American Civilization and the Idea of Progress

Jeffrey A. Eisenach

INTRODUCTION

Progress. As defined by its greatest modern student, Robert Nisbet, it is the belief that "mankind has advanced in the past . . . is now advancing and will continue to advance through the foreseeable future."

No idea is more American. No idea has played a more central role in the development of Western and, more recently, American civilization. No idea is more important to our collective future. And, no idea has suffered more from the cultural nihilism of the past 30 years than the idea of progress.

Writing in 1980, Nisbet concluded his landmark *History of the Idea of Progress* with a warning:

[A]lthough the dogma of progress held magisterial status during most of Western history, it has obviously fallen to a low and sorely beset status in our century. Its future . . . is cloudy to say the least. One conclusion, though, may be stated confidently: If the idea of progress does die in the West, so will a great deal else that we have long cherished in this civilization.

In the 13 years since Nisbet wrote those words, the decline of progress has continued. One major study of public opinion concluded in 1990 that "Americans resent the present and fear the future," a sentiment echoed by

Daniel Yankelovich, who wrote in the Fall 1992 edition of *Foreign Affairs* that "Voters are coping reasonably well with the present; it is the future they fear."

Or, as Peggy Noonan put it recently, "People don't have faith in America's future anymore."

If America is to prosper as a civilization, the idea of progress--our belief in a better future--must be revived; and, given the idea's robustness over thousands of years, it seems quite likely that it will. Indeed, as discussed at length below there are signs such a revival is underway, and that the rebirth of the idea of progress will be the defining cultural event of our age.

Perhaps, then, we should try to understand it.

PROGRESS VERSUS CHANGE

The idea of progress is, for obvious reasons, associated with the idea of change. But progress is a special case of change: Specifically, progress is "good change."

Consider the graphic below. Both lines shown in the graph represent change. Only one of them, of course, represents progress. The question is: Which one?

Part of the answer lies in what metric we assign to the vertical axis. Are we talking about the number of automobiles produced or out-of-wedlock births? Does the vertical axis represent a "good" or a "bad"?

Figure 1

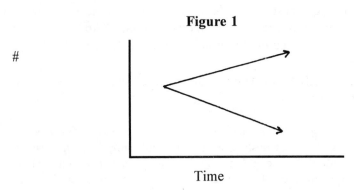

Time

Ah, but you have fallen for the trap--because as you read the paragraph above, you naturally assumed that the number of automobiles produced represented a "good" and "out-of-wedlock births" represented a "bad." Many people would disagree, arguing that we have too many automobiles, or that out-of-wedlock births represent (at least in some cases, viz "Murphy Brown") a positive expression of individual rights.

The point here is this: progress is a heavily value-laden concept, measurable only in terms of an explicit understanding of what is good and evil, right and wrong. "Good change" is progress; "bad change" is decay. Change by itself can never be "our friend." It is either our servant, or it is or our enemy.

Throughout history, progress has had specific connotations and been associated with specific values. Nisbet argues:

> [T]here are at least five major premises to be found in the idea's history from the Greeks to our day: belief in the value of the past; conviction of the nobility, even superiority of Western civilization; acceptance of the worth of economic and technological growth; faith in reason and in the kind of scientific and scholarly knowledge that can come from reason alone; and, finally, belief in the intrinsic importance, the ineffaceable *worth* of life on this earth.

If these five "pillars" have formed the basis for the idea of progress, as Nisbet says, "from the Greeks to our day," and if the idea of progress is indeed to be reborn, we can expect these central premises to be reborn with it. The opposite however, is also true: The renewal of American civilization is inevitably tied to the rebirth of the idea of progress.

PROGRESS AND THE AMERICAN IDEA

Much of what troubles America today can be attributed to the damage done to Nisbet's "five pillars" by what Peter Collier and David Horowitz described as the "Destructive Generation"--the period from the late 1950s through the 1970s when virtually every premise of civilization was challenged.

Scholars from the Left and Right have dissected the resulting decline of American values down to the most minute molecule. From Zbigniew Brezinski's *Out of Control* to William Bennett's *De-Valuing of America*, from Arthur Schlesinger's *Disuniting of America* to Myron Magnet's *The Dream and the Nightmare*, there is no shortage of analysis on either the source or the consequences of that decline.

In their dissection, however, these analyses have tended to ask the wrong question: They have sought to understand what made the patient sick, without understanding what made it healthy in the first place, describing the symptoms and localized causes of "the American disease" but never focusing sufficiently on its relationship to the animus--the motivating mythos--of American civilization.

In this sense, most recent discussions of the American disease pursue an implicit intellectual course consistent with what Thomas Sowell identifies as the "unconstrained vision"--the notion of man's perfectibility. As he explains in *Conflict of Visions:*

> The great evils of the world--war, poverty, and crime, for example--are seen in completely different terms by those with the constrained and the unconstrained visions. If human options are not inherently constrained, then the presence of such repugnant and disastrous phenomenon virtually cries out for explanations--and for solutions. But if the limitations and passions of man himself are at the heart of these painful phenomena, then what requires explanation are the ways in which they have been avoided or minimized. While believers in the unconstrained vision seek the special causes of war, poverty and crime, believers in the constrained vision seek the special causes of peace, wealth, or a law-abiding society.

For America, the "special cause" of success is her mythos, the American idea itself. From John Adams, who wrote that the American Revolution occurred first "in the hearts and minds of the people;" to G. K. Chesterton's words, "America is the only nation in the world founded on a creed;" and Margaret Thatcher's statement, "No other nation has been built upon an idea;", it has always been clear that America's identity transcends geography and ethnicity. As George Santayana wrote, "to be an American is of itself almost a moral condition, an education, and a career."

Michael Vlahos expounds on the concept of a transcendent national mission as a central element of "the American myth":

> Americans still hew, if unconsciously, to their identity as a "New World." Born to a new world of hope, we have been charged with developing a society that will ultimately uplift all humanity. America in our national idea is, and must be, the source of human progress: first as model, but also as agent of world democratic reform. . . . This myth of America as the dynamo of human progress simply cannot be given up. To do so would put at risk the American identity itself.

Today we have gone a step further, doubting not only that America is the "dynamo of human progress" but that the idea of progress itself has merit.

PROGRESS AND THE CIVIC DISCUSSION*

If America is founded on an idea, then American politics can be seen as a means by which we reinterpret the idea over time. As Vlahos explains:

> The idea is the objective of our politics, since it is the idea of America alone that defines and empowers us. The power of the idea means that political groups must seek its legitimacy first. "Ownership" of the idea has always preceded election to office in American politics. . . . The power to reshape the idea is the only real power one can wield in America.

Herman Kahn, the brilliant futurist, understood this well. In his last work of prescience, *The Coming Boom*, published in 1982, Kahn foresaw our current predicament. "The question remains," he wrote, "whether President Reagan--and ultimately his successors--can maintain and build on the opportunities of the present." To do so, he predicted, it would be "important to the coming boom to *reestablish an ideology of progress*" which would "do as much to hasten the coming boom and give it staying power as any single policy maneuver can."

Today it is clear that Reagan's success at "reestablishing an ideology of progress" did not last long beyond his presidency. In retrospect, we can understand why. Reagan's vision of progress was in the *minds* of the American people a vision of America's past. When Reagan spoke of a "shining city on a hill," Americans saw pictures not so much of our future as of a past in which values were clear, government was effective and America was militarily, morally, and economically dominant in the world. If you asked almost any American to describe the "shining city" of which Reagan spoke, the image evoked was of America in the late 1950s.

Ironically, the "shining city of the 1950s" that Americans saw in Reagan's vision was none other than the culmination of the vision laid out by Franklin Roosevelt and the New Deal liberals, a vision expressed, more than in any other single event, in 1939, at the New York City World's

---

*In modern discussions, the term "politics" has come to connote all that is *wrong* with the current political system and has been stripped of any connection with what is *right* with representative democracy. The term "civic discussion" used here refers to America's conversation with itself about the nature of the national myth, a discussion which is most often associated with political campaigns.

Fair, where America's leadership presented a vision of the future explicitly wrapped in the language of progress--"the World of Tomorrow."

It was, naturally, a vision based on the ideology of the New Deal, a combination of state-driven industrial planning and, we sometimes forget, a view of American culture that by today's standards would be labeled "conservative." Writing in a special edition of the *New York Times Magazine* timed to coincide with the opening of the fair, the intelligentsia of the day, consisting of 23 writers including H. G. Wells, Murray Butler, Arthur Compton, Charles Kettering, Henry Wallace, Frances Perkins and Henry Ford, described in great detail the historical underpinnings, economic principles, cultural mores, and practical implications of a world worth striving for. Follow that vision, we were told, and we would create a world full of wonders--of interstate highways, jet airplanes, television sets, and . . . general prosperity.

Jeffrey Hart wrote in his personal evocation of the fair, *From This Moment On*, that it was premised on the idea "that American civilization would matter five thousand years from now . . . indeed, that American civilization (this was the message inside the Perisphere) would be the basis for the world of tomorrow."

At the time, and for many years, that assumption seemed entirely valid. As Alice Goldfarb Williams wrote in her treatment of the 1930s, "the World of Tomorrow, literally constructed on the garbage heap of the past, was not empty metaphor; it echoed too often elsewhere." She concludes, "After a six-year interlude of unparalleled carnage, the World of Tomorrow would begin to unfold." What unfolded, of course, was the 1950s, and the realization of--yes--jet airplanes, interstate highways, television sets . . . and general prosperity: The very same shining city Americans imagined as they listened to Ronald Reagan. The extent to which the 1930s defined the 1950s is at one level not surprising. The leaders of the 1950s were, after all, the very same children who attended, or read about, the 1939-40 fair.

As powerful as that vision was, and as long as it lasted, there can be no doubt that its run is over. For the 110 million Americans born after 1960, it is not even a distant memory, and for nearly all of us, if that vision lives at all today, it lives in black and white reruns of *Leave It To Beaver* and *Father Knows Best* and in yellowing photographs of small children standing with their parents next to cars with large tail fins. It has suffered, as Everett Carll Ladd recently put it, "the worst fate that can befall an idea: It has become quaint."

THE NEXT SHINING CITY

There is no precise way to date the death of the New Deal vision as a motivating symbolic goal. The end of Kennedy's "Camelot" is the date that makes most sense, and scholars like James Q. Wilson and Charles Murray point out most measures of the social pathologies that now dominate our civilization "turned down" beginning in 1963. But there can be no doubt the vision was gone by the early 1970s. Contrast, for example, the optimism of "the World of Tomorrow" with the nihilism of Dartmouth's valedictory address in 1971: "I have made no plans because I have found no plans worth making."

So, for at least 30 years, America has been awaiting a new vision of its future, the next reinterpretation of the American idea. Ronald Reagan came close to offering it--but ultimately, while Reagan changed the world, he did not, in this most fundamental sense, change America.

But history will not be denied. A new American vision of progress is beginning to take shape in the ivory towers of America's think tanks and universities and in grass-roots movements growing up across America. We are about to define for ourselves the next shining city, and to embark on a new journey of pursuit.

America's next shining city will be defined by three facts:

1. William Strauss and Neil Howe make clear in *Generations*, the baby boomers are the most spiritual, moralistic generation since the New Deal.
2. As Everett Carll Ladd demonstrates in his work on "The American Ideology," the boomers' spirituality is consistent with the historical American ideology, which is alive and well--indeed, dominant--in American culture today.
3. It is apparent that the bureaucratic, "welfare state" form of government invented by the New Dealers is obsolete and failing, and that it must be replaced.

The implications of these three facts are profound and pervasive. First, because the boomers believe that values are paramount, they are provoking a much needed reexamination of the moral pillars of American culture. Subplots abound. Multiculturalists, adherents to the value that there are no objective values, attack the Christian Right. New Agers fight both the Christian Right and the multiculturalists, arguing on the one hand that the public square should admit only those spiritual discussions that omit explicit mention of religion, and on the other that we must search for and find objective values. The ideological Left argues for a new Puritanism against smoking, pollution, and pornography, while the ideological Right offers its own brand opposing abortion, promiscuity, and pornography.

Older people of the "Silent Generation" and younger ones of the teen years who find the boomers' fixation on values somewhere between irrelevant and offensive, support "pragmatic" politicians like Perot, worship anti-heroes like Bart Simpson and ridicule with equal disdain Hillary Rodham Clinton's "new politics of meaning" and Pat Robertson's more explicit spiritual message. But these subplots are just that. The central fact is that the boomers are coming to power in every realm of American life, and as they assume the burdens of leadership it is inevitable that they will bring their moralism with them.

The question then raised is whether the boomers will ever find a consensus of belief. Will they ever agree on the metric by which progress will be judged, or will the next two decades be dominated by reruns of Dan Quayle vs. Murphy Brown?

The answer lies in Everett Carll Ladd's work on "The American Ideology." Ladd, the Director of the Roper Center for Public Opinion Research, is perhaps America's leading authority on public opinion and belief. He concludes in a recent article that, "in recent years, even though broad social forces centering around education and electronic communications are shrinking the planet, survey research still shows Americans holding tenaciously and distinctively to the central elements of their founding ideology."

Ladd's point is borne out by the breadth of opposition (from Shelby Steele and Martin Peretz to Lynne Cheney and Thomas Sowell) to multiculturalism, the only major, direct challenge to American ideology left on the planet after the death of communism. The American ideology is much stronger than generally recognized, and it is a good bet that the boomers' quest for a new "politics of meaning" will discover a large common ground within the historical principles of American thought.

The third fact--the increasingly apparent failure of bureaucracy-focused "welfare state" government--creates the prospect for intergenerational cooperation between the two generations that will dominate the next 25 years, the boomers and their pragmatic youngers, the "13'rs."

For the boomers, the failure of the welfare state is a values issue. The poverty, crime, and decadence the welfare state has engendered--children shot in the crossfires or abducted into sexual slavery, abhorrent conditions in public housing, expulsion of *any* sense of right and wrong from the public schools--these unwanted and, for many, unexpected consequences of the welfare state are simply intolerable to a generation that prides itself in doing the right thing. The sense among boomers that they have a *moral* obligation to do something about it is strong, growing, and increasingly coming to dominate both ends of the old Left-Right spectrum.

For the 13'rs, the welfare state is a much simpler matter. It does not work. It kills jobs through high taxes and regulation; it cannot keep the streets (or even our homes) safe from predators; it produces potholes, traffic jams, and bad schools; it costs too much and delivers too little.

In the closing chapters of *Generations*, Strauss and Howe point out that today's generational "constellation" is remarkably similar to the one in place in the 1850s, when a "Silent" generation of compromisers was suddenly replaced by a "Boom-like" generation of idealists willing to die for principle. But our future portends nothing so dark or menacing as America's Civil War. It is far more likely that the generations of our immediate future will find a shared vision of America's next shining city and work together in a new age of American progress.

Yes, it will seem messy as it happens. People for the American Way and the Christian Coalition are not about to lie down together, and the very powerful entrenched coalition that feeds at the welfare state trough will not roll over easily for a new generation of reformers, from Left *or* Right. But the pieces are in place for a new era of American imagination and creation. The future of progress is bright.

Chapter 4

Generational Perspectives on Society: The Millennial Generation

William A. Strauss and Neil Howe

INTRODUCTION

In September of 1988, five- and six-year-old children sported brand-new green-and-yellow coats and ties, blouses and dresses as they arrived for their first day of kindergarten at Washington, D.C.'s Burrville Elementary School. In proposing these standardized clothes, school board member Nate Bush called on parents "to exercise their authority and say, I am the parent, you are the child, and this is a good idea." The contrast could not have been starker between these daffodil-colored younger kids and the older teenage "gangstas" in their colorless "X" jackets, commercial logos, baggy pants, and pump sneakers. The idea caught on. Within three years, 31 D.C. schools encouraged uniforms; many will soon require them. *The Washington Post* editorially praised the growing adult sentiment that "if students dressed alike or conformed to standards of dress they would become more productive, disciplined, law-abiding citizens."

Amid the various dark moods and worsening trends of the 1990s, one very bright spot is heralded by these little kids in green and yellow. They are the vanguard of a new American generation, one destined to be very different from the "Xer" (Atari) babies of the 1960s and what some are calling the "Generation Y" (Nintendo) cohorts from the 1970s. These babies of the 1980s are growing up to be cheerful team-players, worthy of adult protection and praise, as "good" as today's twentysomethings have (fairly or not) been deemed "bad." Not since the 1910s, when today's senior citizens were dressed in Boy Scout brown, have adults seen such advantage in making kids look alike and work together. Not since the early 1900s have older generations moved so quickly to assert greater adult dominion over the world of childhood--and to implant civic virtue in a new crop of youngsters.

What should we call them? Unlike their next-elders, these new kids are the handicrafts of boomers, post-yuppie moralists and fabled perfectionists. The typical 45-year-old parent of today would give a stern middle-aged glare to anyone who dares suggest lining them up behind X and Y as some cabooselike end-of-history "Generation Z." If this generation gets a letter name, make it "A," or "A-plus," or (as today's seniors might put it) "A-OK." Better still, let's dub America's babies of the 1980s and 1990s the *Millennial Generation*, the embodiment of the civic renaissance our nation hopes to achieve as we turn into the new millennium that will define their coming-of-age years and with it their lifetime location in history.

THE CONSTELLATION OF GENERATIONS

While it may be too early to draw their generational boundary just yet, the hoopla around the high school "Class of 2000" suggests that the line should tentatively be drawn between the 1981 and 1982 birth cohorts. As 1995 dawns, America's generational constellation looks like this:

1. 25 million **G.I. Generation** seniors, age 70 on up;
2. 37 million **Silent Generation** nearing old age, 52 to 69;
3. 67 million **Boomers** entering midlife, age 34 to 51;
4. 82 million in the **13th Generation** ("X" and "Y" put together), age 13 to 33;
5. 50 million **Millennial Generation** children, newborn to age 12, with roughly 4.5 million new members born every year.

Do a little math, and you will see that by the year 2001, this Millennial Generation could become the largest in our history. Yet what matters more is *what kind* of generation they are likely to be. All the elements of their parentage, nurture, and situation suggest that Millennials will become America's next example of what we call a "civic" generation. Except in the 19th century, every fourth generation in American history has been of this type. (The most notable other civic types were the Republican Generation of Jefferson and Madison, and the G.I. Generation of

Presidents Kennedy through Bush.) If history follows pattern, today's Millennial children will become the next American generation of team-players, deed-doers, and heroes. They will be protected as children, praised as teens, propelled as young adults, promethean builders in the peak of life, and rewarded elders at the end of life. That is a life cycle quite unlike what 13ers have seen (and, later on, will see) at like age--but very similar to what today's senior citizen "G.I.'s" recall.

How can we say this? Each new generational cohort steps into a society in which certain roles are expected of it. Silent Generation children were expected to be technicians and helpers, Boomers idealists, 13ers pragmatic survivalists. In their respective childhood eras, those were elements in American society that adults (or, in the case of 13ers, the kids themselves) felt were *deficient* in adult society--and, as a corollary, *necessary* in children. What has been missing, and perceived as necessary, as these new Millennial kids have arrived? Civic virtue. Community spirit. Teamwork. Optimism. Positive peer pressure. What are these kids being nurtured to provide? Exactly that.

If neopuritan Boomers get their way, this cohort will graduate from high school marking such a decided trend away from drugs, guns, profanity, and crime that they will be the delight not just of their parents but of the entire nation. This cohort has already been the object of extremely ambitious educational goals. In 1990, the nation's governors set a new agenda demanding a 90 percent high school graduation rate by the year 2000, and President Bush promised that by that year "U.S. students will be first in the world in mathematics and science achievement." Child labor reformers have set the year 2000 as a goal for removing young workers from dangerous and exploitative jobs, and inner-city groups have launched "Project 2000" to provide "young black boys with consistent, positive, and literate black role models" in time for the Millennium.

MILLENNIAL "BABIES ON BOARD"

Propelling this adult mission to craft a civic generation has been palpable (mainly Boomer) disappointment in how the 13ers turned out, and second thoughts about how they were raised. "Save the Next Generation!" shouted the *L.A. Times* after the Rodney King riots. "I'm sorry to say it," observed federal judge Vincent Femia in 1989, "but we've lost a generation of youth to the war on drugs. We have to start with the younger group, concentrate on the kindergartners." The circa 1990 preoccupation with "drugs" reflects a broader anxiety about harms that were done and should not be repeated. In a recent *Atlantic* cover story, Boomer Karl Zinsmeister suggests "preventing young criminals from infecting a class of successors" by "putting the full weight of public protection on the side of babies and schoolchildren." Though "it may be too late to save the 'me first' generation from the folly of the new feudalism," notes former New York mayor Edward Koch (also in 1990), a "new generation" could be provided "the experience of working successfully with others." In one film after another, Boomer directors and screenwriters drew a striking contrast between hardened teens or twentysomethings and cute Millennial "Babies on Board."

First-wave Millennials are riding a powerful crest of protective concern, dating back to the early 1980s, over the American childhood environment. In 1981, the year before the "Class of 2000" was born, a volley of books assaulted adult mistreatment of children through the 13er birth years (*Children Without Childhood, The Disappearance of Childhood, Our Endangered Children, All Grown Up and No Place to Go*). Within the next couple of years, other authors began reconsidering the human consequences of divorce, latchkey households, and value-neutral education. In 1984, two kids-as-devil movies (*Children of the Corn, Firestarter*) flopped at the box office, marking the death of the defining genre on 13er childhood--and the start of a more positive film depiction of children. Through the mid-1980s, studios released several child-as-victim movies (*Raising Arizona, Three Men and a Baby, Baby Boom, For Keeps, She's Having a Baby*). The new cinematic children began helping adults--not, like film 13ers, by sharing parental burdens, but by reminding parents to cope with life more responsibly on their own. From 1986 to 1988, polls reported a tripling in the popularity of "staying home with family." From Jane Pauley's twins to Bruce Willis's Lamaze class to Murphy Brown's sitcom baby, the Boom's media elite reinforced the new interest in infant nurture. Late 1980s babies were declared a "fad" by the *San Francisco Chronicle*, "the new lovers" in the *New York Times*.

The changing tone of the popular culture coincided with the ebbing of the Consciousness Revolution in the early 1980s. First-wave Millennials arrived in an America awash in moral confidence but in institutional disrepair. Some social changes (deferred marriage, smallish dual-income households) became uncontroversial facts of American life, while others ("open" marriages, mind-altering drugs) were rejected. Where 13er parents split apart around the time they watched self-actualizing movies like *Bob and Carol and Ted and Alice*, the Millennials' moms and dads watched *Fatal Attraction* and started turning the numbers around on the rates of divorce (plateauing since the early 1980s), voluntary sterilization (down since the early 1980s), and abortion (plateauing since the early 1980s and down sharply in the early 1990s). A few legislators began criticizing the antichild policy consensus--from unchecked growth in federal borrowing to dwindling health benefits for impoverished mothers.

THIS IS WHERE IT ALL STOPS

As the 1980s passed into the 1990s, the new pro-child politics kept gaining momentum from one year to the next. In 1985, while the Grace Corporation sponsored television public service ads linking the national debt with a crying baby, Congressman John Porter blasted huge budget deficits as "fiscal child abuse." In 1988, *Forbes* magazine ran a cover story entitled "Cry, Baby: The Intergenerational Transfer of Wealth," a new KIDS-PAC lobby was formed around children's interests, and child care surged ahead of foreign policy as the issue of most concern to voters. In 1989, while federal attorneys were filing the first ever lawsuit against apartment units that banned children, George Bush admitted he was "haunted" by the plight of inner-city children and pointed with hope to the straight-arrow example of one crack-house child: seven-year-old Dooney Waters. In 1991, San Francisco voters approved a ballot initiative to guarantee children's programs a fixed percentage of the city's budget-- which, at the time, was well above current funding. In 1992, the nation's Catholic bishops issued a moral appeal to "put children first," 32 community foundations around the U.S. formed an alliance to engage in public advocacy on behalf of foundation, and the United Way set up a nonprofit corporation for the purpose of devoting the next 20 years (the span of a generation) to reverse the "alarming erosion in the well-being of children." In 1993, public fury mounted over the murder (by 13er gangstas) of small children in the nation's inner cities. By 1994, *Washington Post* columnist William Raspberry, who had earlier labeled 13ers a "generation of animals," called for "a crusade for America's children" with the energy and moral righteousness of the old civil rights movement.

The two most recent presidential elections have adopted "Children Come First" themes unlike any the nation has seen since Prohibition. Republican, Democrat, or "Perotista"--all major candidates have started appealing to policies to save children, strengthen nuclear families, and reestablish a new "values" regime (though differences remain on what those values should be). Books like Sylvia Hewlett's *When the Bough*

Breaks shock the nation's conscience about mistreatment of children in much the same way Michael Harrington's *The Other America* did about seniors in the early 1960s. A new communitarian movement has focused heavily on children at the expense of free choices for parents. Welfare reform proposals treat Millennials very differently from 13ers. As the *Post*'s Paul Taylor and David Broder observed, "From statehouses to corporate boardrooms to Congress, a movement is building for greater spending on programs targeted for poor young children--but often at the expense of reduced welfare assistance for their parents and other poor adults." The "only way" to stop the welfare cycle, says Ohio Governor George Voinovich, "is to pick one generation of children, draw a line in the sand, and say to all, 'This is where it stops.'" Congress recently did that in amending Medicaid to cover all poor children under age 18 by the year 2001. (No 13ers need apply.)

As the 1990s began, fortyish Boomers flooded the leadership ranks of the local institutions that dominate a child's world. As they elbowed out the more tolerant fifty and sixtysomething Silent (who had set the tone for 13ers), they set a new no-nonsense tone. "The 60s Generation, Once High on Drugs, Warns Its Children," the *Wall Street Journal* observed of a post-yuppie crowd determined to protect the new children from the social and chemical residue of the euphoric awakening they themselves had launched a quarter century earlier. At school board and PTA meetings, fortyish Boomer parents often chastise the elder Silent for their permissiveness. Where the Silent were inclined to give kids complete information and then let them make up their own minds, Boomers tend to establish firm rules, reinforced by adult supervision and careful attention for any transgressions. In angry answer to suggestions that the answer to drugs lies in more information about them, William Bennett tellingly said of little crack-house Dooney: "This child does not need drug education. That child needs protection, that child needs order, and that child needs love."

At dinner tables around the nation, parents are now telling small children to stay away from drugs, alcohol, AIDS, teen pregnancy, profanity, television ads, unchaperoned gatherings, and socially aggressive dress or manners. Fortyish political candidates are echoing these themes, trying to raise a child generation that will do what they say, not what they did. Increasingly, kids are being nudged out of the cash economy. (Over the last decade, the proportion of child income coming from behavior-based allowances rather than chore earnings has risen steadily.) Meanwhile, Tipper Gore battles lurid rock lyrics, and Michigan's "mother lion" Terry Rakolta campaigns against sex and violence on prime time television, and the Boomer-led Mattel Corporation changes Barbie's doll band from the old "Rockers" to the cleaned-up "Sensations." Grown-up Boomer radicals who once delighted in shocking their own moms and dads started surprising themselves with their own strictly perfectionist approach to child nurturing. In growing numbers, fathers demand "daddy-track" work schedules that allow them more time at home to raise their young children. Garry Trudeau, father to young twins, drew a *Doonesbury* strip that showed a Boomer proudly explaining that he had raised his girl "like an Asian child . . . by teaching her the value of discipline, hard work, and respect for others."

In general, Boomer parents are determined to craft a wholesome environment for their Millennial tots. Where Silent parents of the 1970s had brought 13er kids along to see R-rated movies made *about* them, Boomers of the 1990s started taking their Millennials to see G-rated movies made *for* them. Where the old 13er Willy Wonka-style movies had stressed individualism and differences among kids, the new Boom-produced films (*An American Tail, Oliver and Company, The Land Before Time, The Mighty Ducks, Searching for Bobby Fischer, The Lion King*) stress the civic virtues of equality, optimism, cooperation, and community. Where the Disney animation studios laid off cartoonists during the 13er era, they replenished their staffs during the 1980s. Now they employ more artists than at any time since the 1937 production of Snow White-- and are bopping out new feature-length cartoon movies at a rate that would have been unimaginable in the 1970s. Beyond the cartoon world, Boom scriptwriters are crafting plots with stronger moral lessons and less ambivalent messages about drugs, alcohol, and teenage sex. In sitcoms, parents are becoming less pally and more in charge--making punishments stick, and telling their little minions that they are too young to do this or to know about that. In sharp contrast to the frenetic *Electric Company* and *Zoom* programming of the 13er era, PBS's Barney has proven the popularity of slow-paced and child-friendly shows even when they strike many adults as banal and syrupy in the extreme.

Boomer adults are making similar efforts to take the danger out of the child's daily life. In 1990, New Yorkers expressed deeper anger over nine stray-bullet killings of small children than they had ever felt about the much larger number of murders among 13ers. In the safer suburbs, a wide assortment of new child-safety devices has recently swamped the market-- including the Gerber drawer latches, stove knob covers, furniture corner cushions, toilet locks, I-See-U car mirrors, and Kiddie Kap bicycle helmets (all displayed in a "Perfectly Safe" catalogue). While the 1980s began with states passing laws requiring infant restraints in automobiles, the 1990s started with a Department of Health and Human Services "Healthy Start" infant care program, baby life preservers in commercial airplanes, the nation's first-ever bicycle helmet laws, and a new AAA program of "Safe Playing" reminiscent of the safe streets campaigns when today's seniors were children. Not since the Progressive Era furor over runaway streetcars harming G.I. Generation toddlers (and the Prohibitionists' demand that families be sobered up) have American adults been so determined to guard children from harm.

Nowhere is this more apparent than in shifting recent attitudes about what some 13ers call the "D word": divorce. Parental divorce was a plague that ravaged the 13ers childhood world, especially in the 1970s. If it struck their home, they felt the pain and did not like the splinters it left behind. Whenever it happened to a friend, they watched its blow and feared for their own fates. Now that the 13er child era is over, the studies are in: Children of divorce did less well in school, had more behavioral problems (drug abuse, suicide, violence), and suffered serious loss of parental income, especially among those whose mothers did not remarry. Now, the *Post*'s Paul Taylor perceives a

rally-'round-marriage movement . . . among psychologists who worry about the impact of divorce on children, legal scholars who argue that a children-first policy should be written into divorce law, and marriage counselors who have come to believe that divorce is a cure worse than the disease.

Christopher Lasch, the late chronicler of the "age of narcissism," proposed a constitutional amendment forbidding parents with minor children from divorcing. Recently, as adults have perceived these consequences, divorce rates have plateaued at a level roughly ten percent below their early-1980s peak.

The zeitgeist of the two-career household has also taken a buffeting from the new pro-child consciousness. From 1989 to 1991, the proportion of adults agreeing with the statement "a preschool child is likely to suffer if his or her mother works" rose from 48 to 55 percent--and the proportion of working women who said they would "consider giving up work indefinitely" if they "no longer needed the money" rose from 38 to 56 percent. Meanwhile, employers report that the productivity of working women declines in the late afternoons because of maternal worry about the after school circumstances of their children. While the working mother appears here to stay, other new trends (job-sharing, telecommuting, career sequencing) are reconstructing an adult presence in the preschool and after school child's world.

These recent trends are propelled as much by young 13er parents as by the older Boomers who call more of the shots in community institutions. The 13ers are delaying parenthood even more than Boomers at like age but are showing a greater commitment to making marriages last. The Wirthlin poll shows a yawning "family gap" in attitudes between single 18- to 29-year-olds and those who are married with children. Once 13ers start families, many refuse to mingle careers and kids as did their parents. The 13er moms and dads become profoundly protective of their kids, assertive in their lives, and generous with their time. They widely perceive the two-income family as an economic necessity and the stay-at-home parent (male or female) as an achievement central to their long-term aspirations. Since 1990, while the labor-force participation rate for married women in general has flattened, the rate for married women in their twenties has fallen steeply. In 1993, several NFL players did something unprecedented: They refused to show up for big games on the days they expected their wives to be giving birth. In combination with Boomers, young 13er parents have made moderate-income, suburban-tract "Edge Cities" among the most child-friendly environments in America.

A LOVE FOR OTHER PEOPLE'S CHILDREN

Over the past 15 years, adults of all ages have gradually rediscovered an affection and sense of public responsibility for other people's children. Social historian Barbara Whitehead has perceived that, until recently: "there was a sense that adult self-actualization trumped children's needs. Now, I think the cultural value of parental altruism, of sacrificing for the kids, may be returning." Examples abound. Back in the 1970s, the Boom's "Big Chill" gatherings were all-adult affairs. During the 1980s, they started including babies, then small children, and now bigger children. Back in the 1970s, a parent who tried to enter a restaurant with an infant in a stroller received the scornful glares now reserved for smokers; in the 1990s, they are warmly welcomed. In the middle 1970s, when the child age bracket became the nation's poorest for the first time in U.S. history, the public did not seem to care. By the late 1980s, child poverty was becoming a big deal in the national press--and public loathing of "child abuse" was approaching the level of witchcraft hysteria in hundreds of counties. These days the whole nation anxiously follows the fate of a series of little kids in distress, from "Everybody's Baby" Jessica McClure (saved after being trapped for two days in an abandoned well in

Lubbock, Texas), to two-year-old Tabatha Foster (whose five organ transplants were made possible by $350,000 in public donations), to four-year-old Cecilia Chichan (the sole survivor rescued from a Detroit plane crash).

Across all segments of our society, this new generation of children is being received, and treated, as precious new arrivals. Where the cutting-edge fertility issues of the 13er child era pertained to taking pills or getting surgery to *avoid* having babies, the Millennial era is marked by advances in fertility medicine. In the late 1980s, infertility care and "preemie" (premature infant) care emerged as two of the fastest-growing fields in medicine. In 1970, a two-pound baby had only a five percent chance of living; in 1990, 90 percent survive, at an average cost of over $150,000 per child.

Where 13er kids were best known as latchkeys, throwaways, boomerangs, and other terms implying that adults would just as soon have them disappear, Millennials have come to be perceived as kids whom adults wish to guard with dutiful care. During the two most famous custody battles of recent years, newspaper stories focused less on the parents than on the children--New Jersey's "Baby M" and Virginia's Hilary Morgan. A quarter century ago, such baby stories would have seemed bizarre beyond comprehension. Today they attract intense nationwide concern. Back in the 1970s, an abandoned child was not news, but in the 1992 aftermath of the recent *Home Alone* films, two upper-middle-class Chicagoans who latchkeyed their two children, ages four and nine, during a nine-day Mexican vacation were arrested, jeered, and jailed.

In the Millennial child era, public institutions are viewing children as too high a national priority to trust with the vagaries of incompetent (primarily 13er) young parents. A judge in Washington, D.C., recently sentenced a pregnant first-time drug offender to jail for the explicit reason that her behavior put her unborn child at risk. Where the media once urged parents to allow their 13er children plenty of room for self-discovery, adult society (in the media, legislatures, and courts) is now prodding parents to control the child environment and is enforcing its intention with tough new laws that make parents civilly or criminally liable for their children's misbehavior. Commenting on a new California law that incriminates parents for gang vices committed by children, Ellen Goodman observes that lawmakers have "turned the Bible on its head. . . . They've decided that the sins of the sons shall be visited upon the parents." For the first time in living memory, calls are rising for special orphanages, "academies," and Boys Towns for small children whose parents are deemed socially unfit--places in which William Bennett says children "will be raised and nurtured" under "strong rules and strong principles."

CIVIC VIRTUES

Bennett's *Book of Virtues*, packed with moral messages, provided a clarion call for the teaching of "values," in school and out, to small children--here again, as a corrective for the amoralism Boomer adults see in 13er twentysomethings who had been raised under a more value-neutral regime. In Washington, D.C. and elsewhere, "values-infused curricula" explicitly teach right and wrong. In Texas, many schools declare a "value of the month" which businesses and local police advertise with billboards and storefront signs. "I think there is something profound going on," say Boomers Linda and Richard Eyre, coauthors of *Teaching Your Children Values*, "a backlash to the thinking in the '70s and '80s that families could evolve away from basic values." While their book and Bennett's have risen to the best seller charts, the late 1980s saw a surge in titles like *The Moral Child, Raising Good Children, Bringing Up a Moral Child*, and *Teaching Your Child to Be Kind, Just & Responsible*. By contrast, the cutting-edge titles of the 13er child era were self-help guides and tracts on early-childhood determinism that advised parents to teach children to understand behavioral consequences (and provide latchkey-style "self-help") at very young ages. In books written for children themselves, the new story lines (like Oak Tree's *Value Tales*) focus less on family problems than on family virtues, and the Judy Blume-style, less values-assertive "New Realism" of the 1970s is getting pushed away from younger readers.

As Millennial kids have reached school age, public education has moved not just toward values education, but also toward a "new traditionalism, greater adult assertiveness, and a team approach called "cooperative" or "collaborative learning." Kindergartens have become more academic, and elementary schools are stressing "good works"--an emphasis on helping out with family and neighborhood chores. Sex education has lately centered around calls for continence rather than just the provision of nonjudgmental information. In a series of censorship and search-and-seizure cases, the U.S. Supreme Court reversed a two-decade trend toward student rights and strengthened the hand of school disciplinarians. As Boomers have started controlling public education, PTAs have enjoyed a renaissance, flourishing with new membership and purpose. What Chester Finn calls "a seismic shock" has gripped the adult mood toward education, with sharply increasing support for more homework, longer school days, toughened graduation requirements, greater parental involvement in classrooms, and a standardized curriculum. As funding is cut for programs for "gifted" kids and as "disabled" kids are "mainstreamed," the new emphasis is improving education for "regular kids"--and on making sure all children meet certain standards. The major new challenge against public schools comes not from elite academies but from home schools where stay-at-home parents are investing enormous time in the elementary education of their own children. *No way* will perfectionist Boomer parents let their tots reach age 17 being labeled as "mediocrity" by some national commission, the way 13ers were (fairly or not) back in the early 1980s.

Boom parents have heeded Education Secretary Richard Riley's urging to stop the "hurry-hustle" and "slow down the pace of their lives to help their children." Likewise, parents and teachers have jointly been slowing down the childhood development clock--unlike the Silent, who sped it up. From 1976 through 1988, the proportion of students held back in elementary school jumped by one-third. In 1989, roughly one of every five kindergarten-eligible children were deliberately kept in preschool programs. The sale of Gesell Test materials, used for determining a child's kindergarten readiness, jumped 67 percent between 1984 and 1987. Meanwhile, publishers of children's literature have reversed the 13er-era emphasis on rushing readers to more sophisticated subject matter. Parents now read babylike cloth and cardboard books to Millennial children--books that, when 13ers were little, had to be imported from Europe if they could be found at all. Television watching by children is down (from 1991 to 1992, Nielsen reported a 13 percent decline in Saturday morning cartoon-watching), while periodicals for young children have mushroomed (81 new titles appearing between 1986 and 1991). From sports to nature clubs, children's after school and weekend activities are better organized, structured, and supervised than at any time in memory.

The early 1990s have been marked by what *Time* magazine calls "the Kidding of the American Movies." Where the R rating was the big draw in the 13er child era, producers now are ditching the R for PG-13 or, increasingly, PG. "Nearly extinct this summer are the killer thrillers, with their stark violence, sleazy sex, punk vocabulary--and R ratings" *Time* remarked in 1993. *Time* continued:

> Taking their place is the children's film, in which kids and grownups take reassuring life lessons. . . . Was there ever a bad child in the world--a spiteful, stubborn, domineering sapper of his parents' spirit? There is rarely one in a Hollywood movie, especially this summer, with its flock of

appealing, natural child actors.

Not so long ago, in the 1970s, virtually every (13er) child actor was portrayed as a *Willy Wonka* brat, a *Paper Moon* waif, an *Exorcist* demon, a *Bugsy Malone* proto-adult--or at best a *Kramer vs. Kramer* inconvenience for parents whose minds were elsewhere.

Perhaps no icon better embodies the new slowed-down, cleaned-up Millennial culture than that big purple dinosaur known as Barney. Parents cannot imagine a program more different from the defining 13er child video, the vintage *Sesame Street*. The shift has been from urban to pastoral, New York to Texas, kinetic to lyrical, tough to sweet, individualism to sharing. No longer do monsters come out of garbage cans. And there is no subtext for adults, many of whom (especially non-parents) express irritation at the show National Public Radio has called "wholesome without relief," the *Washington Post* has called "so saccharine it can send adults into hypoglycemic shock." Barney is just the biggest and, maybe, clumsiest of a new round of little kids' marketing and programming that stresses the traditional (note the resurgence in jacks, jump ropes, marbles, and other "nostalgia toys") and the clean (like the tot rap of Chi Ali, M. C. Lyte, and Kris Kross).

Not everyone is pleased with these new directions of American childhood. If the circa 1990 nurturing trends please the Boom, they are in effect a repudiation of the way in which other generations raised their own kids; the Boomer parental prototypes, moreover, have plenty of like-aged critics. Some wonder if the offspring of such families will develop the open-mindedness we now take for granted in children. "What they're learning is that life is black and white," observes columnist Anna Quindlen, without hearing "the long version of answers to life's questions" and without gaining "a measure of empathy and understanding to shade the primary colors of censure." Admitting that today's third and fourth graders "seem more evolved young citizens than we were" at that age, Quindlen sees them assimilating society's "Shalt Nots" about crime, drugs, pollution, and education with disquieting energy and unanimity. *Time*'s John Leo derided the new "competition is out, cooperation is in" attitude toward athletics, describing it as "a New Age approach to sports, drained of fun and skill." Seeing the growing emphasis on fathers (in films like *The Lion King* and movements like the National Fatherhood Initiative), male teachers, and male-only elementary classrooms, 1970s-era feminist crusaders fear for their hard-won triumphs. But the critics are in the minority. Mostly, adults like--no, make that *love*--these new kids.

The facts are starting to support this love. In a recent international survey, U.S. elementary school students placed second in the world (the girls placed first) in reading skills--the sort of finding we never heard during the 13er child era. As the first generation born into a personal computer culture, they come naturally to interactive multimedia technology. Quite unlike 13ers, Millennials are discovering the cyberworld with the help of adults. Before they can learn to become hackers or pirates, they are learning computer privacy, security, and courtesy (thanks in part to Computer Ethics software and videos prepared by the Lawrence Livermore National Laboratory). Today's image of the high-tech child is less of a Dungeons-and-Dragons freak than of a pen pal asking civics questions on Prodigy or CompuServ.

Nowhere is the fledgling Millennial civic virtue on clearer display than with the stunning recent rise in child thrift. According to national surveys, per capita savings rates for four- to 12-year-old children held steady at around 15 percent through 1984, then jumped to 30 percent in the late 1980s--and has now passed 40 percent. Studies are confirming their more savings-oriented ethos, showing little Millennial kids to be less brand-oriented and more value-oriented then teenage 13ers. Children are doing good civic deeds like never before in (Boomer) memory. Says Suzanne Logan, author for *The Kids Can Help*, today's kids are "walking at 1, talking at 2, and volunteering at 3." While some "Eco-Smart" children urge their own parents to give up polluting or smoking, others sleuth around streams and trash piles to track down environmental bandits. Elementary school "Energy Patrols" roam hallways in bright orange jackets and tote official-looking clipboards, in search of broken windows, leaky faucets, open doors, and burned out light bulbs. FBI field offices have started a "Junior G-Men" program through which kids work with an older mentor to study, solve crimes, and earn gold stars. In Washington, D.C., a 12-year-old boy heads the foreign counterintelligence squad, while an 11-year-old girl supervises the terrorism group. "I almost fell off my seat when I heard the kids say 'God Bless America' and 'God Bless the FBI,'" said a local Urban League official. Kids Voting USA, now in a dozen western states, has enabled children to discuss issues, register, campaign, invent slogans and jingles, and vote in mock elections. One study showed 1990 voter participation rates rising by an average of five percent in precincts that had kids' voting programs. "It's created political monsters among Arizona kids," said the head of Phoenix's program. "We couldn't stop them."

Like a generation of Alisan Porters in *Curly Sue*, adults are coming to perceive Millennials as 1990s-era Little Orphan Annies: cheerful, optimistic, team-playing, adorable. And like the angel-winged Anna Paquin in *The Piano*, Millennials are cause, effect, even the *enforcers* of a renaissance in parental values. It is not enough for this child generation itself to be good; its mission in life may be to make other generations *better*. Tellingly, when Pepsi used a small child to introduce its touted new "Gotta Have It" slogan in the 1993 Super Bowl, the campaign bombed. Kids just are not expected to behave that way these days.

THE NEW MILLENNIUM

Today's children show every sign of comprising a generation of *trends*, much as their Boomer parents once had been. The big difference is this: where the Boomer coming-of-age years were marked by worsening trends in every conceivable area of youth life (educational aptitude, crime, substance abuse, suicide, teen pregnancy, civic mores), the Millennial trends are likely to be toward improved education and health care, strengthening families, more adult affection and protection, and a rising sense that youths need a national mission. The last time America had a youth generation whose trends were so uniformly positive was--that is right--when today's senior citizens came of age in the 1920s, 1930s, and 1940s. Recall how, when they reached their late teens, America basked in what is still remembered as "the golden age of the high school"--a time when people of all ages enjoyed the upbeat and unerringly wholesome music and fads of youth.

This generation's future may not be so sunny, of course; a worrisome downside possibility remains. Just ask 13ers who are hitting the economic wall, and sensing the disappearance of the American dream, as they near their 30th birthday. As a group, 13ers are already destined to be the only U.S. generation (aside from the peers of Confederate soldiers) to have a lower lifetime standard-of-living than the generation that came before. If the policy patterns of the last quarter century continue, if public institutions continue to favor seniors at the expense of younger people, the Millennial Generation will also be at risk. America can probably survive the denial of its "dream" to one generation; if the economic plunge strikes the 13th and Millennial Generations both, the consequences could be grave.

A two-decade animus against children cannot reverse itself overnight. Polls still show adults more self-focused than child-focused in behavior, though less so than a decade earlier. Divorce and abortion rates are stuck at high levels, even if they are showing signs of significant decline. Sex, violence, and alcohol and cigarette advertising in the media remain accessible to small children, though the proportion of R-rated films has been falling and the standards for PG ratings have stiffened. American elementary schools are still underfunded and undertalented in comparison with those of other developed nations, but tax revolts against education are cooling off--and public respect for the teaching profession is rising. Child poverty remains stubbornly high (eight times the rate for seniors, when in-kind benefits are counted), enough to convince T. Berry Brazelton that today's children are among the most "desperate . . . and hopeless populations in the world," but the child poverty rate peaked in 1983 and is now gradually declining. Massive federal budget deficits continue, albeit with more evidence of adult guilt over the burdens they will someday impose on today's children. Overall, the arguments of those who stress more values, more structure, and more protection in the child's world are strengthening, from one year to the next, while the arguments of those who disagree are losing ground. Thanks to the parallel efforts of millions of people, America is bringing about a fundamental change in the attitude towards children--and, with it, a change in the national attitude toward the future.

The best reason to be optimistic lies in the self-fulfilling nature of our expectations about today's young people. Hillary Rodham Clinton recently described America's elementary school kids as the "smartest in the world"--a description 13ers never heard political leaders make of them, whatever their age. "Only Eight Years Old," headlined an ad in a 1990 issue of the *Atlantic*, "And *He's* Teaching *Me* About Science!" Ten or 20 years earlier, such an ad would not have appeared--or, if it had, no one would have believed it. In this decade, with Millennial children, people do. Boomer moms and dads are setting out to produce kids who are smart and powerful and dutiful--kids possessed of rational minds, a positive attitude, and selfless team virtue. Someday, Boomers hope, Millennials will build according to great ideals their parents can only envision, act on vital issues their parents can only ponder. These children are not being raised to explore the inner world (Boomers figure they can handle that arena just fine), but instead to achieve and excel at the outer.

Each day, we see dreams and wonders reappear in adult chatter about these little citizens just learning to read, to volunteer, to engage adults in conversation. NASA official Thomas Paine has predicted that "the first Martians are already born and toddling around somewhere here on earth." Others speculate that these smart preschoolers might grow up to be great scientists who can solve the riddle of cancer, great engineers who can protect the environment, and great producers who can put an end to world hunger. The *Arizona Republic* recently asked elementary school students how they expect to improve the world. Their attitude was uniformly upbeat. "We should start now," said an 11-year-old boy. "We can pick up trash. Plant a tree every day. Get groups together." And how do they know they can make a difference? Said young Tracey, "I know it. I just feel it. I believe in myself because my parents and teachers do."

This chapter is based on material presented in *Generations: The History of America's Future* (William Morrow, 1991) by William Strauss and Neil Howe.

Chapter 5

Global Trends Reshaping Civil Society

William Van Dusen Wishard

Power seemed to have outgrown its certitude and to have asserted its freedom
. . . At the rate of progress since 1800, every American who lived into the
year 2000 would know how to control unlimited power. He would think in
complexities unimaginable to an earlier mind.

Henry Adams, 1905

INTRODUCTION

Civil society is a living organism. It is the social expression of
underlying factors that are historic, cultural, psychological, and spiritual.
Civil society is the unseen loom of life which weaves the spirit of a people
together in shared attitudes that form the essential context for self-
government and the peaceful pursuit of common purpose.

When the alignment and balance of the underlying factors shift, the
character and stability of civil society are affected. Traditional concepts
and practices no longer fulfill the function they were assigned. Moral
anarchy and social disruption emerge. Civil society loses its power to
civilize.

That power is recovered only through a new alignment and balance of the underlying factors. This is the precondition for restoring any civil society.

This essay will examine the changing historic context in which civil society exists. While the focus will be on America, reference will be made to a world process, for the factors at work are not unique to the United States; they are global factors affecting Germany, France, Sweden, Great Britain and, to some extent, Asian nations such as Japan. The changes taking place in civil society are but one aspect of a larger transformation that is redefining the context and meaning of human existence.

A WATERSHED OF HISTORY

Civil society in America is being reshaped by the forward rush of events. The historical importance of the 20th century may eventually be that it marked not only the emergence of the quantum and biotech eras, but also the end of the Modern Age and the birth of some new phase of human development.

The Modern Age, which began around 1500, was characterized by the expansion of Europe and the creation of colonial empires; by the rise of the nation-state; by the Newtonian view of the universe and of physical reality; by the printing press and subsequent diffusion of knowledge; by progress defined as the expansion of the scientific and material realms; by the triumph of reason over faith as the defining authority in life; and by an enlarged understanding of liberty. These were the impulses that shaped the Modern Age, and they have now all run their course.

A new set of impulses is shaping the 21st century. America is not simply going through a rough patch, after which life will revert to something we like to think of as normal. The old normalcy is gone. We're passing through a shift from one order of life to another, to nothing less than a state of continuous change.

In an interview with *Fortune*, Jack Welch, Chairman and CEO of General Electric, noted: "People always ask, 'Is the change over? Can we stop now?' You've got to tell them, 'No, it's just begun.' They must come to understand that it is never ending. Leaders must create an atmosphere where people understand that change is a continuing process, not an event."

Welch was talking about GE, but what he said applies to every facet of American life. There is no aspect of human affairs that will escape change in the coming years, and with it, either disappearance, redesign or reformation.

A shift of this consequence creates what Jacques Barzun once termed "dissolving times." Throughout history, Barzun noted, dissolving times have manifested certain characteristics. Such characteristics are once again in evidence:

1. The tendency to blur distinctions of purpose, function, and form
2. A desire to simplify, to return to the innocent beginnings of things
3. The decay of public hope and common purpose
4. The fragmenting of authority, with all its consequences in terms of self government and social order
5. In some quarters, a hatred and repudiation of the past
6. The proliferation of experimental ideas and cultural modes
7. A sense of loss, of decline
8. Institutional collapse as the cohesive force diminishes
9. A rise in general uncertainty about life

This would seem to describe part of the temper of today's America. It is this sense of loss that feeds the "declinist" mentality in some quarters, and elsewhere a sense that events are out of control.

The shift from one historical epoch to another has generally been a process that took at least generations, if not centuries. But the transformation America and the world are experiencing is happening in decades, even in years.

The short-term struggle and pain of adjusting to this shift monopolizes our attention and obscures our long-term vision. Alfred North Whitehead, however, had a sense of that vision: "The greatest advances in civilization," he noted, "are processes which all but destroy the societies in which they occur." *The greatest advance in civilization*--that is what is unfolding, and it will bring with it possibilities that we can now scarcely imagine. It is essential for America to maintain that perspective as we cope with the present and reach for the future.

In the process, the frame of reference within which we have understood civil society, and by which we have understood our journey as a nation is changing, and a new frame of reference is emerging.

SCIENCE'S CHANGING ASSUMPTIONS

We are experiencing an exponential increase in scientific knowledge. Each year, more than 100,000 scientific journals publish the results pouring out of the world's research labs. In the past four decades, science has learned more about how the world and universe work than had been learned in the previous 5,000 years. By the year 2000, the base of scientific knowledge is likely to grow by 200 percent. Fifty years ago we could identify two galaxies. Today we can identify two billion galaxies. We even seem to have made contact with radiation left over from what some scientists consider to be the "Big Bang" which took place perhaps fifteen billion years ago. Thus it appears that we may have established a direct link with the beginnings of time and space.

The assumptions underlying almost 500 years of Western science are yielding to new assumptions. Western scientific enterprise was built on the belief that there is an objective universe which can be explored by methods of scientific inquiry (objectivist assumption); that what is scientifically real must take as its basic data only that which is physically observable and measurable (the positivist assumption); and that scientific description consists in explaining complex phenomena in terms of more elemental events (reductionist assumption).

The new assumptions for the science of the future will be an emphatic departure from many of these assumptions of the past. For example, quantum mechanics suggests that there is no such thing as an "objective experiment"; that the observer affects the outcome. And that consciousness is not the end-product of material evolution; rather, that consciousness was here first. Consciousness may be causal.

Thus we are seeing a shift in our understanding of nature--from solely quantitative relations that are explained by mathematical treatment, to a nature whose essence may be in some realm of reality beyond matter, some expression of reality that flows through the underlying connectivity of all life and events.

Within our own lifetime, science has spawned the mind-numbing technologies that are creating a new context for human enterprise. Technology does not simply augment existing modes of activity. *It changes our perceptions of reality.* A simple example is a change in the way we relate to time. For millennia, people represented time by a circle--first with the sun dial, and then with the clock, both of which suggest a completed totality. The circle represents the cycle of time. Symbolically, the circle also represents the psyche, as well as wholeness. In this sense, the circle has been a basic psychological or spiritual symbol.

But now we have the digital clock, which separates the moment from its relationship to any larger totality. The digital clock is simply time whizzing by, divorced from any greater context. This change especially influences children and how they relate to time. They sense the moment, but not any larger span in which the moment exists.

And so technology alters the underlying meaning of our most basic concepts. It redefines relationships and institutions. It transforms long established social and organizational modes of conducting life.

Thus the institutional structures put in place during one phase of technological development may not suffice when new technologies take over. Corporations recognize this, and scramble to reinvent every aspect of themselves and their operations. Political, educational, and social institutions, however, do not face the same degree of accountability as do corporations, so they have been far slower to adjust to new realities. Restoring America's civil society, however, must include an assessment of how new technologies are altering the human and social contexts within which civil society functions.

THE MEANING OF INFORMATION

The increase in scientific knowledge has fostered a torrent of information that inundates the American mind daily. Consider this: If you were to read the entire Sunday edition of *The New York Times*, you would absorb more information in that one reading than was absorbed in a *lifetime* by the average American living in Thomas Jefferson's day. (On November 13, 1987, *The New York Times* published an edition that was 1,612 pages long and contained over 12,000,000 words.)

The number of books in our leading libraries doubles every 14 years. The local bookstore in Reston, Virginia, carries 100,000 volumes and 5,000 newspapers, magazines or periodicals. Over 12,000 magazines were published in America in 1990, while over the same period, 350,000 new books were published worldwide.

The positive results of all this information are obvious. People's lives have been enriched in countless ways.

But we have yet to find a way of compensating for other less-obvious consequences. For example, psychologists tell us that "information overload" is now a significant cause of mental illness. We have reached a point of what is called "negative information"--so much information that, in some situations, the quality of decisions made actually decreases.

The sheer volume of the data confronting us daily virtually forces a reduction in our span of focus on events. No human brain can begin to comprehend the sum total of the mass-produced data we generate. Thus we lose context and perspective, and with them, a clear sense of the *meaning* of the information we amass. We live in two worlds--the world of data *and* the world of meaning. Meaning requires reflection and time-consuming thought, and at the pace new data is constantly hitting us, time for such thought does not seem to exist. And so the tie between information and human purpose is severed.

In such an environment, the very concept of civil society loses form and focus. For civil society is, in part, an outgrowth of human relationships, and the avalanche of information swamping us every day means that we tend to develop "contacts" rather than human relationships, which are of a deeper quality and character, and can only grow over time.

THE SEARCH FOR NEW INTELLECTUAL THEMES

The major intellectual themes that have driven Western development for well over two centuries have now dried up.

Few people believe in *reason* as an ultimate authority in ordering life. Faith in *the perfectibility of man*--a cornerstone of the Enlightenment--fell victim to the wholesale slaughter of two world wars. *Sociology*, Comte's "science of society," is no longer considered a discipline with laws that can order human affairs. Belief in *utopias* has vanished, at the cost, Zbigniew Brzezinski reminds us, of 77 million lives lost in the 20th century's attempt to build the communist and fascist utopian societies.

Science continues its unabated march, but hardly anyone now believes science will bring us to the promised land. While *capitalism* continues as an economic system--with distinct mutations in different parts of the world--few look to capitalism to provide any larger significance to life.

Modernism has deconstructed. *Postmodernism* has disappeared into a nameless anarchy of styles and attitudes. *Communism* has been buried. *Marxism* has collapsed. *Socialism* is discredited. *Radicalism* has degenerated into spastic anger without any program. *Liberalism*, having won historic gains, now languishes in exhaustion. While *Conservatism* has a political agenda, it still has to find a way to make that agenda be seen as a vision of a highly uncertain future rather than simply a nostalgic relic of the past.

Nationalism--in the 19th century sense of constituting the outer limits of a people's political awareness--is on the wane. What surfaces in places such as Bosnia, Georgia or Tajikistan is not historic nationalism, but an old ethnicity that cries out for a new expression.

Even confidence in *progress,* virtually a Western religion for two centuries, has substantially waned. Indeed, most of the social agenda that constituted the faith in progress has now been enacted into law. Progress has achieved its earlier goals, and it now needs redefinition. The great task now is to save progress from merely a technological interpretation (means), and to redefine it in terms of human needs (ends). Today's human needs are overwhelmingly psychological and spiritual, not material or technological, which is why our historic interpretation of progress is largely irrelevant to our present condition.

Thus it is not surprising that neither major United States political party speaks of progress with any conviction or vision. Politicians speak only of "change" and "solving problems". But the very notion of solving problems suggests that we are confronted with isolated phenomena that will admit to individual solutions; in fact, in every realm of life we are propelled by a continuous process of change demanding constant innovation.

Great intellectual themes carried Western civilization through two of the most progressive--if destabilizing--centuries in history. But the end of the Modern Age and the opening up of a global era now require broader themes to encompass this fresh period of human development. For it should be obvious that if we try to respond to radically new evolutionary circumstances with old thought patterns, no matter how valid such thought patterns may have been in the past, we shall not even be able to understand the new challenges, let alone propose creative responses.

TOWARDS A NEW SYNTHESIS

The demise of the primary themes of the last two centuries has taken place partially because we have effectively reached the end of the Cartesian perspective. Now we are reintegrating the disparate divisions of life into a larger synthesis.

The Cartesian approach did more than break down scientific investigation into its discrete parts. It also separated the whole panorama of existence into segments that, by adherence to immutable laws, so it was believed, could be predicted and controlled. The aspects of reality that could not be reduced to mathematical certainty or be seen as the result of the blind operation of material forces, were treated as mere subjective impressions of the human mind. Insofar as man himself was viewed as a by-product of a vast mechanical order, he was denied the link to any possible spiritual significance. Eventually, scientific determinism, which had been limited to the physical world, was extended to other realms. Thus were born the social sciences of sociology, economics, and psychology.

We have now come to the end of this reductionist theme as a valid perspective of life. We suddenly see that all things are interconnected--a view held in the West from Heraclitus in sixth-century B.C. Greece up to the time of Descartes. It becomes clear that we can only understand one phenomenon if we look at it in relationship to the totality of which it is a part; and that a complete understanding of reality must include subjective phenomena. This view is well understood in the scientific world, but its application to the social and political is only now coming into focus. It is beginning to be understood, for example, in awareness of the relationship between personal character habits and social and fiscal policy. Such an understanding is fundamental to any development of a new civil society.

WESTERN IDEAS GO GLOBAL

Beliefs and institutions that have evolved over centuries in the West are now being absorbed by the rest of the world. The most obvious examples are free economic markets and representative government. But there are others such as the significance of private property, the sanctity of the individual, equality before the law, universal education, social justice, human rights, child labor laws, equality of women, science as an engine of development, and collective bargaining, to name only a few.

While Western nations had centuries to assimilate these ideas, they are being force-fed to Asia and Africa in the time span of a few decades. Whether or not the adoption of Western ideas, not originating in the substrata of the unique Eastern or African psychology, will ultimately have more positive than negative effects remains to be seen.

Whatever the outcome, the power to create technological, economic and social change--or even to know that such change is desirable--is now a global possession. In most civilizations, *continuity* rather than change was the norm throughout history. Only in the 17th century did Western people begin to think about how to effect controlled, intentional change. Now we see massive and constant change taking place simultaneously from India to Mexico, from Egypt to Indonesia. It is a new reality of history. So is the corollary--that what happens on one side of the globe has instant repercussions on the other side. These developments have multiplied world dynamics on an enormous scale, and their repercussions reach to the very core of American life. One obvious example is the global challenge to our economic structure, which has been a foundation of our civil society.

Part of the effect of Western ideas has been the globalization of research, technology, finance, production, and employment. All economies are now a sub-set of a global production system. Electronic products may now include parts from so many countries that it is impossible to identify the place of origin. Companies from New York to California now have their data processing done in Jamaica, India, or South Korea.

As a consequence of this globalization, every nation's control over its economic future is diminishing. Well over 50 percent of the variables affecting the United States economy are outside the control of policy makers in Washington. The Chinese government recently estimated that Beijing can control only about half of the factors affecting China's economy, the fastest-growing economy in the world.

The social, political, and economic beliefs that ascended over time in the West are now creating some wider form of human community.

THE DEFINING POLITICAL AND ECONOMIC FRAMEWORK

Despite the emergence of regional groupings, the nation-state is yielding to the world community as the defining political and economic framework. In this new global community, the number of participants has multiplied, their technical ability to affect each other has vastly grown, and the scope of their purposes has expanded.

As part of this new framework, we see the end of a 450 year period in which the white nations bordering the Atlantic Ocean dominated the world's economic, political, and military affairs. We see the rise of the Pacific Basin as a world economic power. For the first time in modern history, an Asian nation--Japan--has become a greater economic power than any nation in Europe.

We also see this change in the demise of any European nation as a world power. For the first time in five centuries, Europe is not engaged as a formative world force. Rather, Europe has assumed an inward posture, trying to create an economic capability that will permit it to better compete with America and Japan. This inward European posture is having a direct effect on America's own sense of its responsibility and role.

At the same time, nations are searching for some form of supra-national authority. Through the United Nations, countries now jointly intervene in what used to be considered strictly national affairs. In just the past few years, it has happened in Iraq, Somalia, and Bosnia.

Boutros Boutros-Ghali, Secretary General of the United Nations, poses the central issue: "It is undeniable that the centuries-old doctrine of absolute and exclusive sovereignty no longer stands . . . A major intellectual requirement of our time is to rethink the question of sovereignty." This, from a leader of the so-called Third World.

In the process, the very notion of nationhood is being redefined. It is happening everywhere--in Russia, Central Europe, Germany, South Africa, India, Canada, as well as in America.

Before 1960, 80 percent of the immigration to America came from Europe. Since 1960, 80 percent has come from places other than Europe. During the 1980s, more immigrants came to America than any other decade in our history. Roughly 90 percent of all immigration from the less developed to the developed countries comes to the United States.

Miami is now the northernmost city of Latin America. In Dade County, Florida, there are 123 nationalities in the school system. In Chicago, there are more Muslims than Methodists, more Hindus than Presbyterians. In another decade, there will be more Muslims than Jews in America, an historic switch. By the turn of the century, over 50 percent of the new entrants to the American work force will be from what the government classifies as minorities.

By 2025, Spanish may well be the standard language of the majority of ordinary people in southern California, with English as the language of the professional or wealthier class. When today's babies enter their retirement years, white, Anglo-Saxon Americans will be a minority, while Asian-Americans, African-Americans, and Hispanic-Americans will be the majority. America will emerge as the only truly multicultural society in the advanced industrial world.

But even more basic than ethnic composition is a rethinking of the underlying idea of nationhood. Have we now passed the point where the concept of a nation-state dramatically grips the emotions and imagination of a people?

The modern nation-state was born after the Treaty of Westphalia in 1648, and it perhaps reached its apex in the latter part of the 19th century with the emergence of nations such as Germany and Italy. While dozens of new nations have been created since 1945, their formation did not result from the cultural cohesion that brought the 19th century nation into being. Indeed, in Africa, where more new nations have been created in recent decades than anywhere else, tribalism is still a far stronger bond than any adherence to nation.

No one suggests that the nation-state is about to disappear. If only as an administrative necessity, it will continue for a long time to come, albeit possibly in smaller units.

But as a people's awareness and experience expand, so does their collective sense of identification. Early Americans had a fierce adherence to their state. Virginia or Massachusetts meant much more than did the larger concept of the United States. The most distinguished American general of the 19th century, Robert E. Lee, declined the chance to lead his nation in war in order to lead his state.

It might well be that the most intense sense of a distinctly American identity emerged in the period from 1850 to 1950. In terms of identification and belief, and of a "collective soul," that 100 year span may actually have been the true "American Century." Indeed, it should be asked whether today's America is bound together more by mutual interests than by shared convictions.

Since the middle of the 20th century, as jet travel has taken Americans to all parts of the world, and television has created a global nervous system, we have realized that economically, politically, and environmentally our future is bound up with the future of everyone else. The emotional attachment to the concept of nation as a distinct and particular people is buffeted by these realities. When one talks with those in their twenties and early thirties, one discovers that many of them, while glad to be Americans, do not derive their identity from any sense of nationhood. For many, identity comes from being part of a global generation bound together by common cultural tastes and by shared social attitudes.

At the same time, different types of regionalization have taken shape, such as the European Union, the North American Free Trade Agreement, and the Asian Pacific Economic Council nations of the Pacific Rim. Smaller regions include the Cascadia region of the Pacific Northwest and British Columbia; Barcelona, Montpelier, and Toulouse which form the Catalonia region; the Atlantic Arc region of Ireland, Wales, and Brittany; the Basque area and Portugal; the Baltic-North Sea region of Scotland, Scandinavia, Hamburg, and Poland; the Eastern triangle of Prague, Vienna, and Budapest; the Kansai region in Japan including Osaka, Kyoto, and Nara; and the Guangdong region of China.

Then we see the proliferation of countless non-governmental organizations (NGOs) operating on a trans-border basis, technological alliances crossing national boundaries, and giant corporations which are virtually world entities.

The nation-state is gradually yielding authority in two directions; to smaller divisions on some matters, and to larger structures on others.

THE FEMININE IMPULSE

The feminine impulse may be emerging as a defining impulse of the ascending period of history. For example, cooperation rather than confrontation is becoming essential for further development, essential, in fact, for our very survival. The widespread spiritual search, which manifests itself in countless ways, is an expression of the feminine principle.

In terms of Western experience, it might be said that we are entering the third great period of the feminine impulse. The first period was Greece, with its emphasis on philosophy, form, mythology, and beauty. Then came the Roman period with the predominance of conquest, law, order, and construction, which are primarily masculine attributes.

The second feminine period was the Medieval era, epitomized by veneration of the Virgin Mary, by towering Gothic cathedrals and by Dante's *Divine Comedy*. Then came another masculine era, the Modern Age, lasting 500 years. The hallmarks of this era were exploration, conquest, rationalism, the scientific method, and the industrial revolution.

Now we may be entering the third great feminine period. It is exemplified by the collapse of hierarchical structures and the search for more cooperative modes of organizing life, by an increased emphasis on intuition, by a renewed emphasis on *being* rather than *having* and by the feminist movement. This is another watershed of history, for the feminine impulse, as expressed in both men and women, will be a dominant influence in shaping the coming decades, and quite possibly the next century.

PARTNERS WITH NATURE

We have become partners with nature in defining what constitutes a human being. Several years ago, the world heard the story of the woman who had the ovum of her daughter implanted in her womb, and when she gave birth to what turned out to be triplets, she was both their mother and their grandmother.

With genetic engineering, we can determine the characteristics of unborn children--in effect, create *designer children*. Soon we shall have molecular and sub-micron computers implanted into the body and programmed to monitor body functions. We can transfer human traits into animals, and animal traits into humans. We are changing the definition of "humanness."

With "total body prosthesis," we are redefining existence. Cyborgs, part flesh and part mechanical, are already here in the form of artificial body parts. By the end of this decade, every major organ except the brain and the central nervous system will have artificial replacements. Early in the next century we shall see the first human being who has over 50 percent of the volume of his or her body composed of technological implants.

Biotechnology is reformulating the very meaning of life and death. It is raising ethical questions never asked of Moses, Buddha, Christ, or Mohammed.

REDESIGNING GENDER ROLES

We are reinterpreting the respective roles of men and women, roles that were accepted in most cultures for millennia. With this redefinition is coming a rethinking of the family. It is hard to imagine a more elemental shift in the life of a nation. Throughout history, in every civilization, the family has been the primal nourishing agent of life. So our experiments with the family have profound implications for how we train our children in social conduct, for the cohesion and structure of our association as a people, and for the underlying concept of self-government--the family is, or at least has been, the basic unit of all government.

THE MEGA-ISSUE

Eighteen percent--almost one-fifth--of all the people who lived in the past 2,000 years are alive today. It took millions of years to reach the first one billion mark in 1800. The second billion mark was reached in 130 years. Thirty years later we hit the third billion mark. Fourteen years after that we hit the fourth billion mark. The fifth billion was hit in 12 years; and the sixth billion increment will have been reached in an 11 year span (1998).

One consequence, urbanization, means that the mayor of a metropolis such as Mexico City presides over a population greater than the combined populations of Norway, Sweden, and Denmark. The mayor of Los Angeles has a more complex management job than did Henry VIII governing England. The mayor of Chicago presides over a political jurisdiction that, in terms of people, is larger than the political jurisdictions governed by George Washington or Thomas Jefferson.

Europe's population, however, is declining. Only Ireland is reproducing its population. By the turn of the century, none of the 20 largest cities in the world will be in Europe. At some point early in the next century, France and Great Britain will be replaced by South Korea and Morocco on the list of the world's 25 largest nations.

The sheer numbers of people on earth drive almost every issue we face: economic growth; protection of the environment; mass migration; water scarcity; the collapse of religious and ethical traditions; mass starvation and social collapse in Africa. Those same numbers affect the question of civil society in America. Continued legal and illegal immigration from Latin America, China, and Vietnam is only one visible reminder.

THE WILL FOR LIFE?

Concern about earth's environment is not new. Read Socrates' criticism of the defoliation of the hills around Athens to see how long the environment has been a public matter.

We have, however, reached a break-point of history. For thousands of years, the primary question was how to protect people from the ravages of nature. In just our lifetime, that issue has been reversed, and now the essential question is how to protect the environment from the excesses of people. Everyone knows the grim catalogue of crises this reversal has brought. Just three examples: Due to ozone loss, the children in Queensland, Australia, by law, must wear special radiation-protective clothing when going to school. Every day, almost 200 acres' worth of prime topsoil floats past Memphis, Tennessee from Midwest farm erosion. Only about 7,500 tigers remain on the planet, and at current rates of extinction, soon the only tigers left will be those in our zoos and circuses.

What is not greatly appreciated is the profound psychological relevance of our relationship to the ecosystem. At its deepest level, concern about the environment is the human attempt to recapture the organic connection between the individual and nature--a relationship that existed for millions of years before 1850 and America's industrial revolution. Loss of this organic relationship is a significant factor in the change of context in which America's civil society evolved.

Despite the reaction of Americans whose primary perspective is framed by growth statistics and profit margins, the environmental movements, with all their obvious deficiencies, are hopeful indicators. If they could lose the self-righteous stridency which marks some of their efforts, they could be a significant force in restoring a social and psychological equilibrium to 21st century America. For we are faced with the ultimate question--whether humans have the will and wisdom to permit nature to regain and maintain the optimum conditions for life on this planet. Despite significant advances in areas such as pollution control in some American cities, in terms of the human species as a whole, the answer is far from certain.

EXPANDING BORDERS OF IDENTITY

For centuries, national, cultural, ethnic, and psychological boundaries defined a person or a group. Such boundaries helped provide identity.

Now, through global television and easy jet travel, those boundaries are falling, and they no longer constitute the outer limits of a people's identity. While cultural and national groupings still exist, they no longer form a relevant psychological boundary. So the painful question facing each person is: "With whom do I identify? Who is my group? Indeed, does my group even exist as a group any longer?"

The answer, of course, is no; as a separate, isolated, psychologically closed unit, all the groups we've known in the past are being merged with one larger human community. From Alaskan Inuit to New York intellectual, from Southern Baptist fundamentalist to Parisian nihilist, from African villager to Japanese electronics manufacturer, from Muslim fundamentalist to European neo-fascist--what each person is facing is the painful necessity to adjust to the reality of an evolving world community. "East is East, and West is West," but the two *are* meeting, Kipling notwithstanding, in a manner that is causing worldwide cultural and psychological reorientation. One of the great tasks of the 21st century will be to reconcile the extroverted tendency of the West with the introverted propensity of the East.

This collapse of boundaries is one of the primary consequences of space exploration. Seeing the earth from the moon in the 1960s was a seminal event in human history, both scientifically and psychologically. We suddenly saw ourselves as one human unit, without all the national, cultural, or religious beliefs by which we had defined ourselves for centuries.

As George Lucas, creator of the *Star Wars* trilogy put it: "We began to perceive ourselves as a human race, as one world, one little ball of humanity. We had new information with which to go forward. Some people got scared, turned inward, became overwhelmed. Others saw."

Such a development has highlighted the question of personal identity, whether or not we're aware of it as such. "Who am I, and where do I fit into the larger scheme of life?" is an underlying question confronting all of us. Nothing could be more critical to the development of a new civil society than the answers to such questions.

RENEWING THE FOUNDATIONS

We may have arrived at a point where the effects of democracy, industrialization and technology--*taken to their outer limits*--require us to lay new foundations on which a civil society can be erected.

With this thought in mind, consider what Robert Nisbet, in *Twilight of Authority*, has to say:

> [W]hat was present in very substantial measure in the basic works of the founders of political democracy was a respect for such social institutions as property, family, local community, religion, and voluntary association, and for such cultural and social values as objective reason, the discipline of language, self-restraint, the work ethic, and, far from the least, the culture that had taken root in classical civilization and grown, with rare interruptions, ever since. . . The architects of Western democracy were all students of history, and they had every intellectual right to suppose that moral values and social structures which had survived as many vicissitudes and environmental changes as these had over the two and a half millennia of their existence in Western society would go on for at least a few more centuries.
>
> *But in fact they have not.* [Emphasis added]

If Nisbet's appraisal is valid--and there is mounting evidence to support him--then America and the West are faced with a challenge for which there is no precedent in the history of Western civilization. Nisbet's statement merits considerable reflection. He is suggesting that the elements which historically have constituted the foundation and fabric not only of civil society, but of *civilized life*, no longer exist, at least not with enough intensity to control events and to shape the framework of contemporary existence. If this is correct, it is a new departure point in the long story of Western man.

The attributes to which Nisbet refers are not essentially intellectual concepts; they are the fruits of a certain quality of spirit, of a distinctive approach to life, of man's relationship to his fellow man, and even more, of man's relationship to the divine. It is in this sense that civil society, as was suggested at the outset of this essay, is an organic process, and it must grow from the soil of the soul.

TAKING FREEDOM TO A NEW STAGE

Interdependence is becoming the dominant requirement for future progress. In biology and the natural world, the progression of life goes from dependence, to independence, to interdependence. The same holds true of the social and political realms.

Thus we are once again at the forefront of a new political necessity. In the late 18th century, the cutting edge of political experience was a new expression of freedom and independence as defined by the authors of American liberty. Freedom was not a new idea; there had been freedom in other societies at other times. But the early Americans took the understanding of freedom and its requirements to dimensions never before entertained. In that sense, this new expression of freedom and independence was the vanguard of late 18th century political thought and experience.

But today, new developments such as population growth, environmental concerns, and global technological integration, have created a different situation in which independence is no longer at the cutting edge of political necessity. The new imperative is *inter*dependence. Just as the exploration of independence marked the first stages of the American experience, so will the exploration of interdependence mark the initial decades of the coming century.

Acknowledgment of our interdependence as an operating imperative is perhaps one of the most basic requirements of any new expression of civil society.

REVERSING THE ROLE OF CULTURE

For the first time in Western history, we have reversed the primal role of culture. Historically, the function of culture has been to cultivate the higher attributes of life, to encourage the wholeness of personality, and to link the individual with some transcendent vitality. Today, however, culture is accepted as a capricious expression of any human instinct, no matter how base or psychotic, and regardless of its content or effect. Thus we are reaping the results of a culture that acknowledges no hierarchy of values, no intellectual authority, and no social or spiritual tradition. It is a culture that lives for the moment in a chaos of pure sensation.

Goethe described the mission of culture as that of "producing by semblance the sense of some higher reality." Culture, said Matthew Arnold, "is the study of perfection." In this sense, culture has historically been the search for life's highest expressions of truth and beauty. Beauty could be said to be an aesthetic analogue for goodness and perfection, while ugliness might be an analogue for derangement or evil. Part of the function of culture is to help the human soul to discriminate between what is beautiful and ugly, between what is good and evil.

Psychiatrist Erich Neumann believed that the culture of a nation is "determined by the operation within it of an archetypal canon which represents its highest and deepest values, and which organizes its religion, art, festivals and everyday life." Neumann noted that so long as culture is "in a state of balance, the individual is secure in the network of the cultural canon, sustained by its vitality, but held fast." Thus do the "highest and deepest values" of a culture support individual psychic balance, a balance which is the *sine qua non* of any civil society.

During the 20th century, this central purpose of culture has been discarded. Our culture now grants the right of existence to expressions which earlier eras would have considered not only to be senseless, but to be destructive of mental and emotional health and well being. We seem to have arrived at a point described by cultural historian, Christopher Dawson: "When the prophets are silent and society no longer possesses the channel of communication with the divine world, the way to the lower world is still open, and man's frustrated spiritual powers will find their outlet in the unlimited will to power and destruction."

This shift in the function of culture did not start, as some suggest, in the 1960s; it began early in this century. Indeed, Nietzsche had already spotted what was happening in the 1880s when he offered his famous "God is dead" remark. Nietzsche was not saying that the Creator had died. Rather, he was saying that the spiritual impulse that had informed Western civilization for some 1800 years was no longer the inner dynamic of Western culture.

The most famous poem of the 20th century, T.S. Eliot's *The Waste Land*, confirmed Nietzsche's view. Eliot's lines about "the heap of broken images" surely refer to the traditional symbols of Christianity which had lost their primal vitality and significance for so many people. From a psychological view, Eliot seemed to be raising the question of whether modern Western society still had a functioning container--religion--for transcendent phenomena or archetypes. Or, he asked, were we living in the desert and unable to find the source of life-giving water.

In the broadest sense, a distinction can be made between what might be termed a "culture of life," and a "culture of death;" a culture that evokes the fullness of life and elevates the human spirit, and a culture that encourages a darkness of soul, that neutralizes the human spirit.

Most 19th century American culture was a culture of life, that held out the hope and promise of the possible. Most 20th century American culture, while being of the highest technical order, has been a culture of doubt, disillusion, despair, and eventually, nihilism. Nothing quite so well exemplifies this as our lingering fascination with Samuel Beckett's *Waiting For Godot*.

The cultural fashion of the 20th century has been to assert that life has lost its living mystery; that nothing is timeless and enduring; that experience is the touchstone of reality; and that artistic experimentation demands liberation from all inner restraints, moral or otherwise. Despite the vitality and energy that art, literature, and music have exhibited over these decades, artistic expressions informed by these assumptions have resulted in a culture that has fastened on disintegration, rage, and madness.

Against this background, contemporary culture assumes perspective. When we see the suicidal violence on television, when we hear the rage of rap and heavy metal, when we read novels of existential despair, what we're confronted with is the culmination of over 70 years of a culture that has abandoned its historic role of elevating the human spirit, and of reaching into the human soul to evoke nourishing images of life's noblest sensibilities.

Assessing the function and condition of culture is an essential step in the restoration of civil society. As was noted earlier, one aspect of civil society is the balance and alignment of cultural factors. Thus it would seem that a prerequisite of restoring civil society is the creation of a new cultural climate in America, a climate of hope and of possibility, a climate that encourages our young people to reach beyond themselves and grab the edges of a new period of history. Culture must assume again its earlier function--feeding the inner life, and encouraging psychological coherence, which is the foundation of any lasting social order.

THE SPIRITUAL SEARCH

At the heart of civil society is a shared spiritual impulse, and the restoration of civil society in America requires consideration of what has happened to the spiritual life of America in the 20th century, and where we are now in our spiritual journey.

Historians note that for the first time in 2,000 years, the great world religions are seeing a diminishing of their role as the central cohesive force in society. As British historian J.M. Roberts, wrote: "Until our own day, all civilizations had some sort of ordered religious belief at their core. We [Europe and America] are the first great civilization not to be bound together by some common religious conviction." If Roberts' assessment is accurate, much of contemporary America has been separated from its spiritual and psychological roots.

Evidence suggests that such a separation is taking place. We can blame Hollywood for the psychotic themes of our culture, but the fact is that what Hollywood produces is evidently resonating with an inner cleavage in the depths of the American psyche. We readily attribute the violence in our streets to poverty; but individual mayhem and gang warfare are not economic phenomena, and violence is not limited to the so-called poor. Such activity results from a psychological disruption, a disruption which is expressed not only in our streets, but also in our economic life, our politics, our education, our entertainment, and in virtually every facet of contemporary life.

From the psychological point of view, religions are magnificent projections of psychic phenomena. They are systems for psychic healing. Historically the practical function of religion has been to maintain the psychic balance of the individual, thus allowing for peaceful social intercourse to develop.

That America was founded on the spiritual dynamic of Christianity and on the social and moral code of the Judeo tradition is a fact of history. But during two centuries, numerous developments have emerged to alter the way we view our relationship with divine reality.

Such developments would include: the shift from an agricultural to an urban/industrial civilization; creation of a mass society; the emergence of an "intelligentsia," a distinctly intellectual class; the devaluation of language; the devitalization of culture; the emergence of an understanding of the relationship between the conscious and unconscious elements of the self; the gaining of a comprehensive perspective on all the world's religions and myths, and the awareness of numerous commonalties; the recognition of the symbolic and psychological functions of religion; the effects of both affluence and technology on human character and belief; and perhaps most of all, the gaining of god-like powers in understanding and controlling the micro and macro of nature.

Human capability to analyze and manipulate the forces of nature has taken greater steps forward in the 20th century than in all previous history combined. At the same time, our perspectives, our awareness, and our consciousness, have expanded into realms beyond the comprehension of earlier Americans.

It is therefore relevant to ask how 20th century developments have affected our personal relationship to that ultimate reality we call God. As cultures and religions increasingly merge on a global scale--not to mention within America itself--what is the basis of belief? What will give the spiritual dynamic and resonance to a global age that the great religions of the world have given to the relatively isolated human communities of the past?

Such questions in no way suggest that existing spiritual expressions are about to vanish. These questions simply recognize that we are losing the relatively separate contexts in which our religions flowered. So, inevitably, their dynamic of expression must find new forms. It would seem that our relationship to, and expression of that ultimate creative reality is now meant to be experienced in a deeper, broader manner than in earlier eras.

What we are concerned with here may be one of the seminal shifts of history. It may well be that, as a human species, we are moving into a new phase of exploring who and what we are, and why we are here. We are well aware of the scientific, technological, economic, and geopolitical dimensions of this exploration. But another aspect of this exploration could be a fresh experience and expression of the transcendent spontaneity of life.

The first giant wave of expression of the transcendent emerged between the eighth century B.C. and the start of the Christian era. This was the period when the great religions of the world took shape, excepting the Muslim faith which emerged in the seventh century. It was also the stage when consciousness as we now experience it--subjectivity, reflection, purposive and directed thinking, introspection, assimilation, the capacity for willing--evolved. The great religions of the world may well be metaphors by which humankind could experience the mystery, the inexpressible source of this new consciousness. These majestic metaphors have given meaning and anchorage to the human family for over 2,000 years.

But in the past two centuries, and especially in the 20th century, our awareness and our consciousness have taken giant strides forward. So once again our metaphor, our experience of the ineffable, must advance to accommodate our expanded awareness and capabilities. This does not necessarily imply rejection of the spiritual metaphors and disciplines that have served us thus far. But the life of the spirit is dynamic, not static. It must be eternally renewed, and never frozen in time or form. It should continually grow into new expressions that accommodate new stages of human development.

One might well ask what such discussion has to do with the restoration of civil society? Everything; for the life of the spirit is the seedbed of those attributes, suggested in Robert Nisbet's comments mentioned previously, which form civil society's very fabric. All of America's earlier civic forms and institutions were an outgrowth, in some iteration or another, of that spiritual impulse expressed by Christianity. If the forms of civil society have lost their force, it is in no small measure because the spiritual dynamic which gave them birth is no longer as vibrant as it once was. Its energy and vigor have diminished, they have solidified into static form.

Thus it is no wonder that a massive spiritual search is one of the most basic characteristics of America today. It manifests itself in countless ways. Bill Moyers television interviews with Joseph Campbell were part of this search. So is resurgent fundamentalism, which is taking place in all religions worldwide. New Age spirituality is part of this search, as are the turn to Eastern thought and religion, and the rise of cultism in its various forms. A new religion is announced every week in America. Looked at from this perspective, even some drug addiction began as a genuine search for some experience of the "other," something beyond the dictates of the ego. The search is even apparent in *some* of the lyrics of rock music. U2's song *Forty*, for example, was taken verbatim from *Psalm 40*.

It is obviously impossible to predict how this spiritual search will unfold in the coming decades. We are not engaged in a rational, objective process. This is not like starting a new business or civic association. Nor is it a search that has to do with any particular church or religion. *This is the search for a greater expression of life.* It is the attempt of the human soul to relate itself in a fresh way to something beyond the temporal, beyond our current representation of reality. It has been a human impulse from time immemorial, and its steady advance is the on-going hope of humanity.

Clearly there is no formula or blueprint to tell us what to do. In every era, in every region of the world, the evolution of enlarged expressions of life has been evoked by individual men and women. Humanity does not advance as a result of the collective; it advances through individual effort.

The outcome of today's search depends on each one of us and how we probe the depths of our own soul. Is my mind receptive to a wider expression of truth, or is it locked in some set outlook or organized system of thought? In what do I ultimately put my security? What links my inner life with some dimension of eternity? How do I decide what moral criteria will govern my decisions? In all my search for success and happiness, do I take enough time to understand *myself* and the workings of my inner life, a knowledge which is the essential basis of effective action? Do I have some larger faith that enables me to reach forward even in the most painful moments of darkness? Do I take adequate time for *silence* to do its nourishing work in the deeper reaches of my life? What is the quality of my self-discipline, which alone guarantees liberty? How do I find the inner freedom of a creative reality?

These are the critical questions we all must ask. The answers, in due season, will shape a fresh spiritual expression for America. Eventually, such an expression must exhibit form and structure, for while an expanded consciousness may be a primary aspect of a new spiritual expression, it alone cannot yet govern the raw passions of human nature on a planetary scale. Governance of such passions, of the dark shadow that lurks beneath the surface of civilized conduct, has been a primal function of the world's great religions. Such governance is the essential regulating agent of any civil society.

Of all that has been considered in this essay, the question of a fresh expression of spiritual reality is perhaps the most uncertain and unsettling. It goes to the core of who we are and what we believe. It forces us to reconsider the very foundations of our lives, a process that inevitably creates insecurity and resistance. But such a reconsideration is essential if we are to give birth to something new.

SEEDS OF THE FUTURE

This essay has touched only lightly on the fluctuating context in which civil society exists. Everything we have discussed thus far, in one way or another, affects the character and quality of civil society.

We cannot know the shape and tone of the civil society of the future. No one dreamed up the constituents of civil society in earlier America and then set them in place. Rather, people took responsibility, people believed, people built--and out of those efforts emerged what we now look back on as one of the most sublime expressions of collective civil association ever to emanate from the mind of man.

And so it is for us today--to take responsibility, to believe, to build. As we do that, some new form of civil society will emerge. Most likely it will not be similar in shape or scope to what we've known in the past; today's circumstances are so totally different.

The taking of responsibility, the building of new forms is happening in every field of American life. It is perhaps a social law that when old institutions are no longer effective, people find new ways to discharge the functions the old institutions had addressed.

For example, our legal system is overburdened with a thousand pressures. So what happens? A totally new system of settling disputes arises outside the legal system. Alternative Dispute Resolution (ADR) burgeons across the country. ADR operates at every institutional level, from settling multi-million dollar corporate disputes, to mediating neighborhood squabbles or domestic brawls. The state of North Carolina has instituted a pilot project in Asheville where school children are trained in dispute resolution. When a fight breaks out at school, it is the students trained in dispute resolution who mediate the argument. If this Asheville experiment is successful, students in every high school in North Carolina will be given similar training.

This is civil society at work.

For two decades, we've been swamped with reports deploring the condition of primary and secondary education. So what happens? Innovation. Countless experiments in privatization, programs to give students work experience before graduation, increased number of school days, refocusing on core subjects, higher standards, education at home, computer-assisted education, "entrepreneurial education" focused on achieving results, increasing corporate involvement and sponsorship of educational programs, basic training in ethics and responsibility, and interactive communication technologies.

This is civil society at work.

Our cities are struggling under the weight of crime, drugs, out-migration and inadequate tax revenues. So what happens?

In Pasadena, California, a husband and wife pioneer a direct, simple way of developing constructive citizen involvement. This process effectively brings divergent elements of the city together to form new structures to address job training, drug and alcohol abuse, gang violence, and health care for poor children.

The Pasadena process begins by listening to people representative of the total community to learn of their needs and aspirations. Such listening reveals the community to itself, and acts as a catalyst for cooperative ventures to address social needs. Key to the process is a mindset of building on the best qualities of people, of choosing coalition and trust rather than confrontation, and of thinking for the city as a whole rather than for one group or interest. The results are solved problems and new life for Pasadena.

This is civil society at work.

We see a widening public sense of the obsolescence and irrelevance of politics as a habit of mind and a means of progress. The political community in the Western world was the successor to the Church as the major arena of man's hopes and aspirations. But today, we see a sclerosis of politics and governance that is summed up in one phrase--"Gridlock government."

What happens? Initiatives and referenda on the ballot hit an all-time high. Support increases for "direct democracy" that would enable the public to put its stamp on policy without bothering with intermediaries. Backing grows for public approval at the ballot box for any tax increases. Neighborhood groups organize to address every problem from crime in the streets, to education, to recycling, to garbage disposal. "Twentysomethings" organize "Lead . . . or Leave", an effort to get Congress to reduce the federal deficit. The locus of government shifts downwards.

This is civil society at work.

Reports proliferate of the devastating social effects of family collapse. A primary cause of the collapse is the "missing father." The result is 14-year-old girls with babies, 14-year-old boys with guns. Children who cannot define marriage, as they have no experience of married parents. No role model or authority figure in the home for young boys growing up.

The absence of the father may be the single most critical cause of the social breakdown in America. What happens? Citizens from across the country launch The National Fatherhood Initiative, a citizens' effort to change the cultural attitudes about fatherhood in America, and to restore the meaning of, and commitment to fatherhood.

This is civil society at work.

RIDING THE WAVE

And what about the future?

The shape of the future depends on the decisions you and I make today. The only certainty is that it will be uncertain. But then, the people who crossed from Europe to start a new life in an unknown land, the Americans who plunged westward into the unexplored wilderness to settle and build, the astronauts who landed on the moon, all faced almost nothing but uncertainty. America's future has *always* been uncertain, because *life* is uncertain.

Despite the problems and perils of our times, we should take heart that we are living at this moment in history. For, as Arthur Clarke reminds us, every collective human enterprise is like a surf rider, carried forward on the crest of a wave. The wave bearing us has scarcely started its run; those who thought it was already slackening spoke centuries too soon.

How we ride that wave depends on our quality of hope. Hope is not dependent on an expected outcome. It does not rise and fall with the Dow Jones. Hope is the commitment that, whatever the outcome, my life is given to realizing some larger enduring purpose.

This century's most sublime expressions of hope came from men living in the gulag of existence. Bonhoeffer, Djilas, Solzhenitsyn, Frankl, Mihajlov, Havel and countless others, facing the darkness of extinction, came forth with expressions of a hope that is rooted in eternity. Such people were giving voice to man's ultimate freedom--the freedom to decide how I will respond to any external circumstance.

Civil society is not simply the contrived structure of isolated intellect. It is the social expression of a people reaching for some distant horizon; of a people bound together by an unfailing brotherhood and common purpose, who let the everlasting impulse for life draw them forward to higher levels of awareness and achievement.

The shape of civil society may change, but its essence and function are constant. It remains for us to reach as far forward as hope will inspire; to act on the promise and the possibility of the unknown; to construct the edifice of a new time.

Chapter 6

Tocqueville's Democratic Prescription: "Self-Interest: Rightly Understood"

Edward A. Schwartz

INTRODUCTION

Over the past several years, Alexis de Tocqueville's *Democracy in America* has emerged as so pervasive a source of authority for our understanding of the values and institutions of civil society that it must now be considered the premier commentary on America itself. Indeed, contemporary writers all recognize that their own arguments gain legitimacy if they can find justification in even a brief observation of Tocqueville's. For conservatives, there is the Tocqueville who talked about religion and local communities as mediating institutions that are threatened by the bureaucratic state. For liberals, there is the Tocqueville who heralded the rule of law and who understood clearly the role that voluntary associations play in empowering people and promoting responsible citizenship. Radicals have found support in Tocqueville's claim that "self-interest: rightly understood" in America carries with it the obligation that we help one another and make personal sacrifices for the good of the community.

As useful as borrowing these specific passages from Tocqueville may be in advancing particular points of view, however, they obscure our understanding of what he himself believed. The pieces of *Democracy in*

America are so brilliant that they sometimes make it hard for us to grasp the whole, but there is an underlying thesis behind them.   When Tocqueville tells us that it is "customs" that bind the nation together, not laws, he is warning us to remain attentive to the public role of private institutions, not the other way around.   Voluntary associations, in turn, provided for Tocqueville not an alternative to political participation, but a means toward making it effective.   "Self-interest: rightly understood," finally, required not merely that we permit the government to sponsor programs to improve communities and support the poor, but that we help one another--in our own communities and in society as a whole.

In short, Tocqueville's primary concern for America was that civil society would continue to reinforce and strengthen the ideals of democracy.   "Checks and balances" within the government would not be enough.   Religion and a "spirit of township" were needed to promote cooperation among people who might otherwise tear each other apart. Voluntary associations were needed to create an essential link between citizens and the state.   The principle of "self-interest: rightly understood" that he found in America was essential in cultivating a moral environment in which free individuals would decide to work together.

The precise guidance that we should seek from Tocqueville today, then, ought to reflect these basic concerns.   What role *should* private institutions play in a democracy?   Which values are essential to encouraging responsible citizenship?   Tocqueville's answers to these questions become clear when we examine what he had to say about religion and townships in shaping values, about the role of voluntary associations in empowering people, and about the principle of "self-interest: rightly understood" in promoting cooperation in society as a whole.

RELIGION FACILITATES LIBERTY THROUGH RESPECT

"Religion in America takes no direct part in the government of society," Tocqueville acknowledged, "but it must be regarded as the first of their political institutions; for if it does not impart a taste for freedom, it facilitates the use of it."   His point was that religious liberty was crucial not only in protecting churches, but in preserving the spirit of mutual respect that citizens in a democracy had to share.   "The revolutionists of America," he noted, "are obliged to profess an ostensible respect for Christian morality and equity. . . . Heretofore no one in the United States has dared advance the maxim that everything is permissible for the interests of society . . . .Thus, while the law permits the Americans to do what they please, religion prevents them from conceiving, and forbids them to commit, what is rash or unjust."[1]

Tocqueville was even prepared to argue that the Catholic Church reinforced democracy, despite the hierarchy of its structure. "In the Catholic Church," he observed, "the religious community is composed of only two elements: the priest and the people. The priest alone rises above the rank of the flock, all below him are equal"(300). Everyone in the church--the "wise and ignorant," the "man of genius and the vulgar crowd," the "strong and the weak"--was subject to the same doctrine. Catholicism, thus, confounded "all the distinctions of society at the foot of the same altar," and as a consequence, "no class of men is more naturally disposed than the Catholics to transfer the doctrine of equality of condition into the political world" (304).

For Tocqueville, religion was important in America not so much because it shaped our private beliefs--attitudes toward faith, observance, sexuality-- but because it strengthened the civic values that we shared. "Despotism may govern without faith, "he argued, "but liberty cannot. Religion . . . is much more needed in democratic republics than in any others. How is it possible that society should escape destruction if the moral tie is not strengthened in proportion as the political tie is relaxed?" (307). In America, he was pleased to report, most citizens felt the same way.

TOWNSHIPS PROVIDE PRACTICAL EXERCISES IN COOPERATION

If Americans needed religion to foster an ethic of cooperation, local townships would have to reinforce it. This was the significance of the "spirit of township in New England." "The native of New England," he observed, "is attached to his township because it is independent and free: his co-operation in its affairs ensures his attachment to its interests; the well-being it affords secures his affection; and its welfare is the aim of his ambition and of his future exertions" (68). This ethic was hardly what later became known as "state's rights" or the "not-in-my-backyard" ethic that has emerged in recent years. Quite the opposite. Tocqueville insisted that the sense of belonging and significance that people felt in their own communities rendered them more disposed to act in behalf of the country. It was in the townships, in effect, where a citizen would "collect clear practical notions on the nature of his duties and the extent of his rights" (68).

It would be through "public associations" that citizens would seek to advance both their interests and their values in the larger society. Today, "voluntary associations" are generally thought of as social groups--civic organizations, fraternal societies, non-profit groups of various descriptions. These were certainly included in Tocqueville's definition of the term. "Americans of all ages, all conditions, and all dispositions," he noted, "constantly form associations. They have not only commercial and manufacturing companies in which all take part, but associations of a thousand other kinds . . . . The Americans make associations to give entertainments, to found seminaries, to build inns, to construct churches, to diffuse books, to send missionaries to the antipodes; in this manner they found hospitals, prisons, and schools" (106).

Yet the significance of even these associations lay in the ways in which they encouraged people to act together. "Among democratic nations," he noted, "all the citizens are independent and feeble; they can do hardly anything by themselves; and none of them can oblige his fellow men to lend him their assistance. They all, therefore, become powerless if they do not learn voluntarily to help one another" (107).

ASSOCIATIONS SUPPORT PRINCIPLES OF DEMOCRACY

Nor did Tocqueville see involvement in "civil associations" as an alternative to participating in politics. Indeed, he argued that, "civil associations . . . facilitate political associations," and "political association singularly strengthens and improves associations for civil purposes" (115). Moreover, the larger and more politically powerful the group, the more likely would people want to join it. "Citizens who are individually powerless," he pointed out, "do not very clearly anticipate the strength that they may acquire by uniting together; hence it must be shown to them to be understood. Hence it is often easier to collect a multitude for a public purpose than a few persons; a thousand citizens do not see what interest they have in combining together; ten thousand will be perfectly aware of it" (116).

All of this served to strengthen popular support for the principles of democracy itself. Years earlier, in defending the Constitution, James Madison had warned in *The Federalist Papers* that the tendency of people to form "factions" threatened liberty so severely that we needed a complex national government to prevent any one of them from taking control.[2] For Tocqueville, many of these "factions" actually promoted commitment to democracy by demanding tolerance and mutual respect from their members. When Americans, "meet together in large numbers," he noted, they "converse, they listen to one another, and they are mutually stimulated to all sorts of undertakings." In the process, they "transfer to civil life the notions they have thus acquired and make them subservient to a thousand purposes." Thus, he concluded, "it is by the enjoyment of a dangerous freedom that the Americans learn the art of rendering the dangers of freedom less formidable" (119).

Ultimately, Tocqueville concluded, the combined impact of religion, townships, and voluntary associations inculcated Americans with an ethic of "self-interest: rightly understood" that bound us to each other and to the larger society. On the basis of this principle, Americans would "show with complacency how an enlightened regard for themselves constantly prompts them to assist one another and inclines them willingly to sacrifice a portion of their time and property to the welfare of the state" (122).

THE VALUE OF SELF-SACRIFICE

This picture of Americans in the 1830s "sacrificing their time" to the "welfare of the state" may come as a surprise to those today who believe that individual liberty and *laissez-faire* capitalism were the hallmarks of our early history. Yet Tocqueville was quite clear that a 19th century American knew "when to sacrifice some of his private interests to save the rest." Indeed, while the principle of self-interest: rightly understood produced "no great acts of self-sacrifice," it did suggest "daily small acts of self-denial" (123). Given that such an ethic was relatively easy to preserve, it was respected by most Americans as the only proper basis for mutual coexistence.

Clearly, Tocqueville's image of civil society in America in the 1830s is radically different from the way in which we think about it today. Where religion appears only to shape private behavior now, Tocqueville saw it as reinforcing the principle of equality that Americans were supposed to share as citizens. The "spirit of township" in modern America conjures images of suburban enclaves where the middle class protects its property against "undesirables." The "spirit of township" in Tocqueville's America was the ethic that encouraged people to participate in their communities and as a whole. Voluntary associations today are congenial centers of social intercourse and good works--George Bush's "thousand points of light." For Tocqueville, they were the instruments of empowerment. "Self-interest" today defines how we advance our own interests in competition with one another. For Tocqueville, "self-interest: rightly understood" shaped how Americans advanced their concerns in cooperation with one another. Every aspect of civil society that we think of as being part of a "private sector" today was, for Tocqueville, an expression of the democratic system that America was trying to build.

THE DANGER OF SELF-CENTERED DESPOTISM

Only by properly understanding these elements of Tocqueville's civic idealism can we appreciate his concerns about what would happen if we abandoned them. Indeed, his observations offer little solace to partisans on either side of our current political spectrum. Conservatives who like to recite his chilling critique of the bureaucratic state ignore his equally powerful indictment of the "aristocracy of manufactures" that was emerging under industrial capitalism. Liberals and socialists, in turn, have had to come to terms with Tocqueville's formulation of "despotism" that looks suspiciously like the welfare state. What Tocqueville really believed, it appears, was that America would remain free only if we sustained an ongoing commitment to principles of equality and democracy and preserved the *local* institutions through which people might apply them to their daily lives.

It was small business--not large corporations--that would permit democracy to coexist with private enterprise. "What astonishes me about the United States," he noted, "is not so much the marvelous grandeur of some undertakings as the innumerable multitude of small ones . . . Americans make immense progress in productive industry because they all devote themselves to it at once" (157). Because so many individuals had started businesses, however, did not mean that "rugged individualism" was their creed. Private development coexisted with "immense public works executed by a nation which contains, so to speak, no rich men" (156). Like the spirit of township itself, free enterprise was a cause in which, "the poorest as well as the most opulent members of the commonwealth are ready to combine their efforts" (157).

All of this would disintegrate, however, if the division of labor between managers and workers eventually created an insurmountable gap between them. Tocqueville saw this as a real possibility. As the national thirst for "manufactured commodities" grew, "every day more men of great opulence and education" would open "large establishments" and by a "strict division of labor" seek "to meet the fresh demands which are made on all sides." There would be no genuine relationship between management and labor in such companies. "The manufacturer asks nothing of the workman but his labor; the workman expects nothing from him but his wages" (160).

The effect on both would be devastating. Workers would become less equal on the job even as consumer goods would make them more alike in the community. Such a system, he noted, "first impoverishes and debases the men who serve it and then abandons them to be supported by the charity of the public." Owners and managers, in turn, would gain the power of an aristocracy with none of the traditional values associated with it. Indeed, since "it applies exclusively to the manufactures and to some manufacturing callings, it is a monstrous exception in the general aspect of society." An aristocracy "thus constituted," he concluded, "can exert no great hold upon those whom it employs, and even if it succeeds in retaining them at one moment, they escape the next; it knows not how to will, and it cannot act." Eventually, such an aristocracy would end up being "one of the harshest that ever existed in the world," but if ever "permanent inequality of conditions and aristocracy again penetrates into the world, it may be predicted that this is the gate by which they will enter" (159-161).

Tocqueville was equally concerned, however, about the sort of government that might be needed to regulate a society organized in this way. As is widely recognized, his comments on "What Sort of Despotism Democratic Nations Have to Fear" were astonishing, given that the system that he described would not take shape for decades. As civil society became mass society, Tocqueville warned, it would spawn, "a multitude of men, all equal and alike, incessantly endeavoring to procure the petty and paltry pleasures with which they glut their lives. Each of them, living apart, is as a stranger to the fate of all the rest; his children and his private friends constitute to him the whole of mankind" (318).

All of this would lead to a pervasive, bureaucratic state. While preserving the "outward forms of freedom" and the "sovereignty of the people," it would stand as an "immense and tutelary power . . . absolute, minute, regular, provident, and mild." Such a state would take it upon itself to secure our "gratifications" and "watch over our fate." It would "cover the surface of society with a network of small complicated rules, minute and uniform, through which the most original minds and the most energetic characters cannot penetrate, to rise about the crowd." Ultimately, "the will of man" would not be "shattered, but softened, bent, and guided." "Such a power does not destroy;" Tocqueville warned, "but it prevents existence; it does not tyrannize, but it compresses, enervates, extinguishes, and stupefies a people, till each nation is reduced to nothing better than a flock of timid and industrious animals, of which the government is the shepherd" (318-319).   Needless to say, this was hardly an adequate response to the "aristocracy of manufactures"--or to anything else that might threaten the country in the future.

THE TOCQUEVILLEAN SOLUTION

What, then, were the Tocquevillean "solutions" to the problems that he saw? How can we apply them today? One must move carefully here, since he did not provide us with a simple program, nor was that even his intent. He came to America to observe, not proselytize, and his audience was Europe as much as the United States. As the demand for democracy was spreading throughout the continent, he wanted to offer a report on how it was doing in its new home. There was no "quick-fix" provided here to remedy the defects of its major institutions.

Nonetheless, the central concerns of Tocqueville that we have reviewed here suggest the major institutions that he thought had to be preserved. One, clearly, was religion. Religious principles, he insisted, lay at the heart of our highest democratic ideals.   A second was the local community, where people would know and support one another. The third establishment was the civil and political associations that enabled people to gain strength through collective action.   These were the primary institutions that we had to protect, if we wanted to maintain democracy. We may measure our distance from Tocqueville--and, perhaps, democracy itself--in the cavalier way that we handle these three foundations.

The public discussion of religion and politics today boils down to the religious Right arguing that everyone should convert to Christianity against the secular Left insisting that any mention of religion in politics violates the First Amendment. Tocqueville took an entirely different view. He was quite comfortable with the notion that the clergy had to avoid direct political involvement and that "every man" in America "is allowed freely to take that road which he thinks will lead him to heaven" (418). Yet as we have noted, he saw in the religious doctrine that we are all equal in the eyes of God the essential foundation of the principle that we are all equal in the community as well and that we, therefore, need one another.

This is hardly the main principle that modern conservatives want us to associate with religion--with their insistence that if each of us just went to church and lived right we would *not* need one another. It has also struck at least this graduate from the 1960s, however, that liberals and radicals-- who have marched with ministers for Civil Rights, sheltered anti-war activists in church sanctuaries, and fought for a world in which we are all "brothers and sisters" under the skin--ought themselves recognize the religious foundation of these civic ideals, which they clearly do not. Tocqueville's concern for preserving strong local communities has largely been lost as well. To be sure, the "search for community" is a major pastime today, in salons, on computer bulletin boards, and in a number of urban neighborhoods. The bus ride that Bill Clinton and Al Gore took through America's small towns in 1992 struck a responsive chord with all of us and lent great energy to their campaign. Clinton himself speaks eloquently about restoring a "spirit of community" in America.

Yet "community" in Tocqueville's America was not just a "spirit," it was a reality which millions of Americans shared. It unfolded in real places where people lived over time and gained strength through their association with one another. To build community in America meant preserving these real places. Commerce had to remain decentralized. Politics had to remain participatory. We had to reward those who chose to stay and not just make it easy for people to move.

Above all, we had to recognize that genuine community meant more than just living next door to one another. A "native of New England," Tocqueville explained, "takes a part in every occurrence in the place; he practices the art of government in the small sphere within his reach; he accustoms himself to those forms without which liberty can only advance by revolutions; he imbibes their spirit; he acquires taste for order, comprehends the balance of powers; and collects clear practical notions on the nature of his duties and the extent of his rights" (68). We may properly ask whether any such spirit exists in the townships of America today, or whether its restoration is a matter of serious concern to anyone.

Finally, we may note the steady erosion of the civil and political associations that Tocqueville saw as being central to empowering citizens. Groups in every sector of American life now complain about how difficult it is to sustain participation and even membership--churches, unions, civic associations, even block clubs only yards from where we live. Perhaps we already have reached that time which Tocqueville foresaw where, each of us, "living apart, is as a stranger to the fate of all the rest" and our children and our private friends constitute "the whole of mankind." If so, we needn't be surprised that our democratic system--which requires a somewhat broader level of involvement--is in disrepair. As Tocqueville warned, if a person "exists only in himself and for himself alone; and if his kindred still remain to him, he may be said at any rate to have lost his country" (318).

To claim a country was, for Tocqueville, "self-interest: rightly understood." Yet it meant far more than pledging allegiance to a flag. It required that we give at least some time to one another and to the "welfare of the state." It demanded that we participate in our own communities and take part in political associations seeking justice from the larger society. Above all, it meant recognizing that being a citizen was essential if we hoped to thrive as human beings. We may recite little pieces of Tocqueville today, but we need to grasp this larger point that he was trying to make as well. We ignore it at our peril.

ENDNOTES

1.   Alexis de Tocqueville, *Democracy in America*, ed. Philips Bradley (New York: Vintage, 1990), 1:305.

2.   Alexander Hamilton, James Madison, John Jay, *The Federalist Papers*, ed. Clinton Rossiter (New York: New American Library, 1961), 10:77-83.

II. Educating for a Civil Society

Chapter 7

Educating for a Humane Society: The Reclamation of Civic Virtue

Denis P. Doyle

> Culture is activity of thought, and receptiveness to beauty and humane feeling. Scraps of information have nothing to do with it. A merely well-informed man is the most useless bore on God's earth. What we should aim at producing is men who possess both culture and expert knowledge in some special direction. Their expert knowledge will give them the ground to start from, and their culture will lead them as deep as philosophy and as high as art.

> Alfred North Whitehead
> *The Aims of Education*

INTRODUCTION

When I was invited to write this essay, I took the occasion to return to my own work to find a quote that would illustrate the theme of educating for a humane society, and, as Pat Moynihan says, "backwards reels the mind . . ." More than a decade ago I wrote an article for *The College Board Review*, titled "Education and Values: A Consideration." If anything it is more apt today:

The views in this chapter do not necessarily reflect the views of the trustees, officers, or staff of Hudson Institute.

Since ancient times, philosophers and scholars have known that values and education are indissolubly bound together. Their connection was so obvious and important that it was virtually impossible to imagine value-free education. Even if education did not transmit values explicitly and self-consciously, it did so implicitly and by example. Can anyone remember a distinguished teacher or philosopher, ancient or modern, who was morally neutral?

As a people we have come to understand that no nation that ignores values in education can hope to endure. No democracy that neglects values and education can expect to remain free. The reasons, though they should be obvious, bear repeating.

The American experiment in self-government is now two centuries old. Indeed, we are not only the oldest democracy in the world; we have an unbroken tradition of self-government marked by a long history of enlarging the franchise. When our experiment began, only white men of property could vote; today all citizens over 18 may do so. They may do so because we are convinced that all adults can responsibly exercise the franchise. They may do so if they are educated.

Philosophically, the reason for including values in education is clear enough: a democracy committed to the twin principles of equality and liberty must have an educated citizenry if it is to function effectively. By "educated" I mean not just a knowledge of basic skills, but people who are liberally educated. In this connection it is worth remembering the purpose of a liberal education: it is to suit men and women to lead lives of ordered liberty. It is the embodiment of the Jeffersonian vision of a free and equal people.

CIVIC VIRTUE

Such observations, of course, would hardly surprise the Founders. To them civic virtue was the *sina qua non* of a democratic republic, and it was in some large measure imparted by the formal institutions of society, among them schools. Indeed, without such norms, civilization itself is unimaginable. Born naked, ignorant, and full of appetites, each child must learn the facts and values of the culture anew. It is no surprise that formal schooling plays a major role in that process. Schooling and civic virtue cannot be separated.

In place of the hereditary aristocracy of the Old World, the New World, according to Thomas Jefferson, would witness the emergence of a natural aristocracy of talent. In a great democracy, as all men are equal before God and the law, so too are all men free to develop their talents to the fullest. This elegant and radical idea survives to this day and for its full development, the people of a democracy must be educated.

As Lord Brougham said, "Education makes a people easy to lead, but difficult to drive; easy to govern, but impossible to enslave."

The ancient Greeks, from whom we inherit our intellectual and educational traditions, knew that there was one purpose for education and one only: to fit man to live in the polis. And the key to life in the polis is values, "civic virtue;" without it the polis, the state itself, would founder. They had the insight to know how one acquires civic virtue. Their threefold lesson is as true today as it was then. It is study, example, and practice.

STUDY

First, values are acquired by study, knowledge acquired didactically. Teachers teach and students learn. Study requires submission to the discipline of learning. Second, values are acquired by example. Virtuous men and women by example communicate values to the young and to their fellows. Third, and perhaps most important, values are acquired by practice. Virtue is acquired by behaving virtuously.

Long before the "excellence movement" there were two broad schools of thought in such matters. One is the vision of school as agent of the state, familiar enough to anyone who cares to peer beyond the totalitarian state. John Stuart Mill, who was spared the excesses of modern totalitarian and authoritarian regimes, thought that no other objective could characterize government schooling. Government education, whether the dominant power be a priesthood, monarchy, or majority of the exiting generation is

> a mere contrivance for moulding people to be exactly like one another: and as the mould in which it cast them is that which pleases the predominant power in the government . . . it establishes a despotism over the mind . . .

By way of contrast there is the perspective of a supporter of government as the instrument of civic virtue, Simon Bolivar. Addressing the Congress of Angostura, he solemnly observed:

> Let us give to our republic a fourth power with authority over the youth, the hearts of men . . . Let us establish this Areopagus to watch over the education of the children . . . to purify whatever may be corrupt in the republic . . .

There is, however, a less extreme way to think about education and civic virtue in a democracy. How should a free people inculcate those values and attitudes essential to public welfare, domestic tranquility, and the pursuit of happiness? How can order and freedom be reconciled? The task, while not easy, is not impossible. And the American experience of the past century and a half with public education--or the education of the public--is instructive.

What are the values of civic virtue? First, explicit knowledge, mastered to the point of habit, about the rights and responsibilities of citizenship, and the opportunities and obligations imposed by a constitutional republic. It is knowing, as sociologist Morris Janowitz observed, that the corollary of the right to trial by jury is the obligation to serve on a jury when called. It is knowing that one man's freedom ends where another's begins. It is knowing that rights are earned and must be protected if they are to survive. It is knowing that Supreme Court Justice Oliver Wendell Holmes was right when he observed that "taxes are what we pay for civilized society."

What is it our public schools should do to teach values? What knowledge and habits must children acquire to make them virtuous citizens? Let me look first at example, then study, then practice.

The most striking example of citizenship in all of history was offered by Socrates. He accepted the hemlock cup, not because he believed himself guilty of corrupting the youth of Athens, but to demonstrate the supremacy of law. His wisdom and his courage are captured by John Ruskin in words which contain the essence of my point:

> Education does not mean teaching people what they do not know . . . It is a painful, continual, and difficult work to be done by kindness, by watching, by warning, by precept, and by praise, but above all-by example.

As a practical matter, this means that our schools must be staffed by moral men and women who care about their calling and their craft. By the pure force of personality they must communicate their sense of commitment to their students. There is no mystery as to who these people are. They are the teachers we each remember, the teachers who made a difference in our own lives. The problem is not identifying them after the fact, but before the fact. They are the teachers who are connected to their disciplinary traditions, who are broadly and deeply educated, and who believe in the life of the mind.

These are not empty homilies. There is an internal dynamic to study and scholarship, and there are canons of the profession that themselves embody the values of a democratic society. They include honesty, fidelity, accuracy, fairness, tolerance for diversity, flexibility, and a willingness to change when new evidence is presented. Indeed, what we expect of our better teachers, is precisely the set of traits that we associate with civic virtue.

THE INVISIBLE CURRICULUM

Another name I use to describe this cluster of attributes and the outcomes they help foster is "the invisible curriculum." It is the message sent by teachers to students about what is right and what is wrong, what is acceptable and what is not. A school, for example, that sets low standards sends a powerful message: nothing much matters, get by. That is a dangerous message to give a young person because it programs him for failure. The invisible curriculum undergirds and reinforces the student's visible curriculum.

It has become fashionable in certain circles to think that education is a process, a set of skills divorced from their substantive context. That is not true. Education is contextual. It is a substantive experience which requires, among other things, learning about the great documents of citizenship. At a minimum these include an acquaintance with Aristotle's *Politics and Ethics*, Plato's *Republic*, The Magna Carta, *The Prince* by Machiavelli, *An Essay Concerning Human Understanding* by John Locke, The Declaration of Independence, the 10th *Federalist Paper*, the United States Constitution, John Stuart Mill's *On Liberty*, The Gettysburg Address, Lincoln's Second Inaugural Address and Martin Luther King's Letter from Birmingham Jail. Education is an empty concept if it is stripped of the values these documents embody. As King reminds us, "Freedom is never voluntarily given by the oppressor; it must be demanded by the oppressed."

This is first and foremost a normative statement, a statement of values. To be fully educated the student must master a body of knowledge, fact, myth, history, anecdote, not as an exercise in memory, but as an exercise in understanding and critical thought. History and context are important to education both for themselves and as the instrumentality by which people learn to think and to reason. It is simple but true: people learn to think by thinking and thinking hard. That is the essence of the Socratic dialogue, the most enduring and important teaching technique ever devised.

Think of the centerpiece of the Fifth Amendment as simply a phrase to be recapitulated without an understanding of its underlying meaning: "nor shall be compelled in any criminal case to be a witness against himself." Without understanding its purpose and its historical context it is truly nonsense. Why should a suspected criminal not have to testify against himself? Protecting all of us from testifying against ourselves emerged from a long and bitter history of the rack and thumb screw--if a man may be compelled to testify against himself who is to say no to the torturer? Certainly not the victim. Freedom from self incrimination is no more and no less than freedom from the Inquisitor and the tools of his trade. It is a strange thing in a century so convulsed by violence of every kind that this simple truth is frequently overlooked when people "take the fifth." It may be the single most important protection a free people enjoy.

As George Santayana observed, "something not chosen must chose." In exploring the idea of educating to reclaim civic virtue we must remember that values are a part of our world that is not scientifically derived. They include such human but unscientific attributes as love, loyalty, courage, devotion, piety, and compassion. These attributes give dimension, scope, and meaning to being human. It is precisely with these attributes that great literature concerns itself.

HUCK FINN

Let me draw upon a particularly telling and appropriate example, Mark Twain's *Huckleberry Finn*, published more than a century ago. It is arguably the greatest American novel, a book of such importance that no American who has not read it can be considered educated. What makes this book important? Its scope and sweep, certainly, but above all, its values. In shape it is a book for the masses. Like the Bible or *The Iliad* it tells a universal story, accessible to all. Just as it contains much with which to agree, it contains much that shocks, provokes, and even offends. As a consequence, reading the book and discussing it in a classroom requires sensitivity and discretion. It is not a book to be taken lightly.

It is interesting that the book is attacked today just as it was when first released. The far right believes Huck is venal at best, and hostile to religion at worst. They say his language is abominable, his behavior unacceptable. In sum, he is a poor example. The left is even more outspoken in its hostility to Huck. They level against him the worst of modern epithets: racist.

I will stipulate to this: Twain's purpose was to subvert the state, undermine the morals of the young, and challenge the smugness and complacency of the American *haute bourgeoise*. To this accusation I plead Twain guilty. And this is precisely the power of the book: to confront the conventional wisdom. Twain railed against the organized religion of the day and its sanctimonious piety and hypocrisy. Indeed, he found organized society, particularly the state, the cause rather than the cure for social ills. Huck and Jim, children of nature, could escape the corrupting forces of contemporary life only by physical escape.

So far as we can tell, Twain really believed that society was a sentence and the only hope was escape. The development of this idea in *Huckleberry Finn* is the best known of Twain's repeated efforts to deal with it. If this interpretation of Twain is correct, as I believe it to be, he is far more dangerous than either the left or right wings know. He is an enemy of the state.

Whether or not he should be read by callow youths, then, becomes a question with meaning. The direction assumed by other great works across the ages is the same. While the first purpose is to entertain, the more important purpose is to instruct. Such literature is almost never the servant of the state nor the advocate of the *status quo*.

Jean DuBuffet, champion of "*l'art brut*," raw or unschooled art, in a splendid twist on Plato asserted that art was subversive, that the state should attempt to suppress it, and that the artist worked best and most effectively when he was disdained by the prevailing culture. That is, in fact, a rather exaggerated version of my hypothesis here. Suffice it to say that the artist should question, at a minimum, the conventional wisdom and make the *bourgeoisie* uncomfortable.

Without dwelling on Twain, it is useful to consider great literature in general to see if the example is idiosyncratic. Are there common threads? The direction assumed by great literature across the ages is the same. While its first purpose is to entertain, its more important purpose is to instruct. It provides examples of courage, strength, and love. It shows the effects of hubris, greed, and the will to power. It reveals transcendent accomplishment and abject failure. Such literature is almost never the servant of the state or the advocate of the *status quo*. Great literature challenges assumptions, it breaks with the conventional wisdom.

Not all great books are offensive, or irreverent, or hostile to the state, but they challenge the conventional wisdom, they provoke the reader, they insist upon engagement with the subject. This is even true of science, particularly in its early stages when it is concerned with breakthroughs in basic knowledge. Galileo, Kepler, and Darwin are only the best known examples.

The controversial nature of a work, then, is a product of its power and authenticity, and it is for this reason that the inexperienced reader will frequently find the great book difficult--it is often very tough sledding. It is tough sledding because it raises fundamental questions about right and wrong. For the inquiring mind, it induces an interior Socratic dialogue.

VALUE FREE EDUCATION: AN OXYMORON

At issue in the teaching of values is an error of judgment that continues to plague our schools. An assumption was made, in all good faith, that our schools could be value-free, neutral, and objective; this would defuse the potentially explosive question of which values to teach and how to teach them. This vision of American education is an old one.

In the 19th century, what was described as value-free education was really non-sectarian Protestantism. It was not quite ecumenism, but a robust Unitarianism. Indeed, it is no accident that the early public school reformers were visionary and romantic Unitarians, builders who would use the public schools to uplift and transform each generation. As Horace Mann, with a striking sense of modernity, said in his *Annual Report to the Board of Education* in 1848:

If all the children in the community from the age of four to that of seventeen could be brought within the reformatory and elevating influence of good schools, the dark host of private vices and public crimes . . . might . . . be banished from the world.

When it came to values education, Mann, as well as his supporters and colleagues, had little problem identifying what schools should do. They knew that most teachers were poorly trained and they were the inheritors of a classical tradition that brooked little interference. In essence, the curriculum chose itself. So it was in the late 19th century that the *McGuffey Reader* enjoyed unparalleled success. It was full of pious homilies and entreaties to civic and religious virtues, the values widely shared by the community that patronized the public schools. In the 19th century, the patrons were almost exclusively white Protestants.

The emergence of a highly diverse, democratic, and pluralistic modern society means that we can no longer rely on either the classical curriculum or the Protestant consensus of the 19th century.

THE DISCIPLINARY TRADITION

In an attenuated way this disciplinary tradition does exist in the best public and private college preparatory schools. In these institutions, for example, teachers are free to choose Dryden or Donne, Spencer or Marlowe, Shakespeare or Cervantes, Twain or Hawthorne--but the freedom to choose is nearly ephemeral, because the educated person, the student, must eventually read all of them.

What has happened in American education, of course, is the virtual abandonment of the disciplinary tradition. Instead of vertical integration, elementary and secondary schools are organized horizontally.

They are not only characterized by self-contained classrooms, they are self-contained organizations with few links to the outside world. Great bands of children are grouped by age and they are given "problem areas" to study. Communications skills replace English, social studies replaces history and geography; is it any surprise that bachelor living and power volleyball enter the curriculum?

Is it any wonder that there are periodic attempts to purge Huck Finn from the classroom? With no intellectual and disciplinary anchor, the school is subject to the fads and vicissitudes of the moment. When the watchwords of the school become "value neutrality," "relevance," and "relativity," anything goes.

Nothing is imposed on anyone, except the notion that there are two sides to every question. The philosophy of the ancient Greeks and the great revealed religions, both based on moral absolutes, no longer provide answers. Not even the existential answer that teachers know more than students can be offered with conviction. It is for these reasons that the disciplinary tradition is essential.

PRACTICE MAKES PERFECT

Let me turn briefly to my final point: practice. "Happiness," Aristotle tells us, "is activity of the soul in accord with perfect virtue." We achieve this state by practice. Ironically, it is not so much in the exercise of our rights that we learn this, but in meeting our obligations. It is through submission to a higher principle that we learn to appreciate the importance of our hard-won rights.

At the level of friend and family, practice means satisfying the reciprocal demands that loyalty and filial responsibility place upon us. At the level of the community, it means meeting minimum standards of civility and good conduct.

More than just obeying the law, it means accommodation to unspoken standards of behavior. At the level of the state, it means honoring the full and explicit demands of citizenship from honesty in paying taxes, to citizen participation, to the ultimate sacrifice for a higher good in time of mortal danger.

At the level of the school, practice means doing what is expected and doing it well. But it could and should mean much more. It could and should mean service, both to the school and to the community. Although an old idea in private education, service is just now being taken seriously in the public sector.

The North Carolina School of Science and Mathematics (NCSSM), one of the nation's few public boarding schools, enrolls some of the best and brightest youngsters in North Carolina. There is a special graduation requirement that says no student may graduate without performing three hours a week of school service and four hours a week of community service.

Students from NCSSM spend time in nursing homes, orphanages, day care centers, and hospitals. And they do so week in and week out.

Every high school student in America should be expected to perform community service as a condition of graduation. No one is so poor or so elevated as to not profit from it, for that is surely its purpose. The help these young people provide, while important, is the least of what they do.

What is really important is that they are learning through practice the habits of service. That is the very foundation of civic virtue and the personal satisfaction it can provide.

What this means, of course, is that we cannot avoid the question of curriculum. What we teach we value and what we value we teach. The curriculum, both visible and invisible, is value laden. What is it we need to know as Americans, both to have a shared sense of community and a shared destiny?

COMMUNITY

At the same time, we need the support, solace, and integrity of the smaller, organic communities of which we are naturally a part. No one can be a member of a "family" of 240 million people. We can be citizens, and owe obligations and expect rights to flow from this larger body politic, but the kinds of association that most of us find deeply satisfying flow from smaller units of organizations. Any curriculum--particularly a "core" curriculum--must reconcile the demands of a continental democracy and the need to belong to a more intimate community. It must reflect the values of the whole and the part, respecting both while supporting the individual.

The need is acute because in the final analysis "excellence" in any endeavor is a solitary pursuit, requiring self-discipline and commitment. Excellence also assumes many forms--music, art, the quantitative disciplines, languages and the Humanities. And over the life of a student the pursuit of excellence calls for progressively greater specialization and more complete immersion in the peculiarities of a given discipline.

This is not to say that a "core" curriculum cannot coexist with specialization: it can. It is just more difficult to pull it off successfully. And this raises the most important question of all. If curriculum is central, and values are central to the curriculum, who will chose and of what will the curriculum consist? If it is chosen by the wise and judicious, the penetrating and the discerning, the discriminating and the disciplined--in short, by you and me--the curriculum will be a wonder to behold.

But if it is chosen by the ideologues of the left or right, the Babbits and Buffoons of American intellectual life, it will be a disaster. The fear of the latter is a real one as anyone who has read Francis FitzGerald's study of American history texts must admit. Anti-intellectualism in America is an old, powerful, and even honored tradition, and it is not at all clear that the excellence movement will, even over the long haul, change that.

Lurking beneath the surface of any discussion about the quality of American education is the nagging suspicion that we already have the schools that we both want and deserve. We do have citizen control; we do have a voice in what our schools do and how they do it, however attenuated it may be. Perhaps, after all is said and done, Americans prefer football to the life of the mind. That, after all, is what values are all about.

CONCLUSION

The life of the school, then, is defined by what is taught, and the life of the student is defined by what is learned.

What has this to do with educating for a humane society? A good deal, I think, because we are what we value, and schools cannot escape this simple truth. And at the heart of the excellence movement--if indeed it has a heart--lies the conviction that it makes a difference what children are taught and what they learn.

This quintessential and timeless expression of values and education is carved in stone on the B'nai B'rith headquarters in Washington, D.C.: "The world stands on three foundations: study, work and benevolence." And so it does.

This chapter is reprinted, with minor changes, from *Educational Innovation: An Agenda to Frame the Future*, ed. Charles E. Greenawalt, II (Lanham, Md.: University Press of America, Inc., and The Commonwealth Foundation for Public Policy Alternatives, 1994), 81-92, by permission of the author and the publishers.

Chapter 8

The Role of Heroes and Heroines in the American Story

Dennis Denenberg

THE DILEMMA

Ask almost any six or seven-year-old child to describe a stegosaurus, and you will most likely hear a complete and accurate description, including the correct spelling of the creature's name. By the way, you'll also have to listen to details about tyrannosaurus rex, because kids love that ferocious beast.

Ask that same child who "Old Joe Camel" is, and after some giggles, you will hear a fairly precise accounting of not only his appearance, but also the product he represents. In fact, according to research published in the December 1991, *Journal of the American Medical Association* and reported in major news magazines,[1] kids can identify that commercial symbol as readily as they recognize Mickey Mouse! Remember, cigarette commercials are even banned from television. Interesting too is another portion of that study about teenage smokers, a third of whom select that brand compared with less than ten percent of the over 21-year-old smokers making the same choice.

Now ask that child a third question: Who is Thomas Jefferson? You will probably receive a blank stare and an "I don't know" response. You might hear an amusing guess, such as "I think he's the man who brings our mail," or maybe a defensive reply, "We didn't learn about him." But the chance that you'll hear any accurate information about the author of our Declaration of Independence is quite remote.

Why? Because neither in our schools nor in our homes do children learn about the great men and women who have made positive contributions to our nation and our world. We teach dinosaurs "ad nauseam" in the elementary grades because they arouse kids' imaginations. Meanwhile, the all-pervasive advertising industry uses cartoons to capture kids' hearts and minds. But we ignore the many wonderful real people--HEROES--from whom children could learn so much.

HEROES

A hero is an individual who can serve as an example. He or she has the ability to persevere, to overcome the hurdles which impede others' lives. While this intangible quality of greatness appears almost magical, it is indeed most human. And it is precisely because of that humanness that some individuals attain heroic statue. They are of us, but are clearly different.

We look to heroes and heroines for inspiration. Through their achievements we see humankind more positively. They make us feel good. They make us feel proud. For some of us they become definite role models, and our lives follow a different direction because of their influence. For others, while the effect may be less dramatic, it is of no less import, for these heroes make us think in new ways. Their successes and failures lead us to ponder our own actions and inactions. By learning about their lives, our lives become enriched.

Molly Pitcher saw what had to be done and did it. Women had a defined role in the war; they were a vital support to the fighting colonials. But when her husband was wounded, and the cannon needed to be fired, she knew what she had to do. Molly Pitcher was, and is, a heroine, and her story deserves to be told and retold. Neither a great statesman or soldier, she was an ordinary person who did an extraordinary deed.

Michelangelo spent a lifetime at his craft, leaving the world a legacy of magnificent paintings and sculptures. His hard work was a daily reaffirmation in his belief of a human's creative potential. Through toil, he produced artistic monuments which have continued to inspire generations.

This world has had (and still has) many Molly Pitchers and Michelangeloes, people who set examples which inspire others. Some had only a fleeting moment of glory in a rather normal life, but oh, what a moment. Others led a life of longer-lasting glory and had a more sustained impact on humankind. All were individuals who through their achievements made positive contributions.

Where are the heroines and heroes for children today? They are everywhere! They are the figures from our past, some in the historical limelight, others still in the shadows. They are the men and women of the present, struggling to overcome personal and societal problems to build a better world.

Indeed they are everywhere, but most children know so very few of them. Quite simply, in our schools and in our homes we have removed these great people from our focus. They have become "persona non grata" instead of persons of importance. Where at one time nearly every American classroom had portraits of Washington and Lincoln gazing down upon the children, now Mickey Mouse and Snoopy hold court. The greats are still around; they have merely been removed from everyone's view.

YESTERDAY

"Once upon a time . . ." kids had heroes, and lots of them. Some of these great individuals were real (Lincoln, et al.); others were legendary (such as Paul Bunyan and Casey Jones); still others like Hercules were of a different realm altogether. Most of them were male and white, as if heroics somehow knew gender and racial lines of distinction. Frequently kids pretended to be these heroes, or at they very least their followers. Since not every boy could be King Arthur, the others could be knights of the Round Table. Yes, it was clearly better to be the King, but even as a knight, one got to slay a dragon now and then. All--kings and knights-- were capable of great deeds!

These heroes seemed to be everywhere. They were part of the curriculum, so textbooks and other reading materials (even the classic comic books) provided details of their adventures. The movies portrayed them in action, adding an exciting visual dimension not found in the books or classroom. Heroes truly came alive for kids, who not only learned about them but, often, learned values from them.

Whether or not "the Father of Our Country" ever did chop down a cherry tree is not a question of significant historical importance. What is telling is that for generations the story helped children understand the meaning of honesty. Even heroes had faults, but they were moral enough to admit their errors.

The inclusion of heroes in schools served dual purposes. In addition to learning about specific great individuals, students also were exposed to the ethical nature of those persons. The presence of heroes provided a focus for children's dreams and wishes, and those heroes were cloaked in mantles of virtuous behavior.

In some instances, those deeds were even accomplished by children. Who has not marveled at the brilliant accomplishments of that most famous of child prodigies, Wolfgang Amadeus Mozart? George Westinghouse began his successful career as an inventor and entrepreneur at the age of 12. For the next 56 years until his death at age 68, he continued building a legacy based on hard work, creativity, and a desire to improve people's lives. Indeed, heroes for children were real children of achievement.

TODAY

As the advertising industry grew, however, heroes became displaced persons and virtually disappeared from children's views. Through the wonders of the mass media, a whole new array of characters became a daily part of American culture. Cartoon creatures and company advertising mascots existed for many decades, but not until the advent of megacommunications did they intrude into everyone's lives in a seemingly unending manner. Billboards, print ads, television and radio programs, commercials, videotapes, and many other avenues provide ads "ad infinitum." Even while relaxing on the beach, one's attention is pulled skyward to read the fly-by advertisements. Mickey Mouse and his companions, Charlie Brown and his associates (especially his dog), and countless other purveyors of the popular culture are everywhere today.

The issue is not so much that they have joined the ranks of known figures, it is rather that they have totally replaced real heroes for children. Today the role models are often whatever the latest commercial fad creatures happen to be. Once the new character catches the public's attention, the merchandising machine marches on. The tee shirts, buttons, books, backpacks, greeting cards, games and toys, trading cards, movies, and of course, television series, all follow in rapid succession. The presence of the latest sensation dominates the child's world. Consciousness leads to conversation demanding the newest marketable item bearing the creature's image. And everywhere--in the child's mind, in the home, and in the classroom--the character assumes a new status of heroic proportions. It's out with Ben Franklin; here comes the Mouse!

En masse the animated beings invade--everywhere into the classroom and the school. Out go the pictures of Washington and Lincoln (except in February for a two-week period) to make room for cutouts of Donald and Goofy. This transformation occurs not because teachers think the latter are more significant than the two presidents; rather, it is most frequently done under the guise of "good teaching." Many elementary teachers genuinely believe the furry fad figures motivate and inspire kids. Because the child already recognizes Mickey from his numerous media appearances, those special ears make the child feel comfortable. Instantly, a friendly, known climate for learning is established, as familiar faces and figures abound to evoke feelings of security in the child. So teachers use the Mouse and his many compatriots on bulletin boards and every conceivable type of instructional resource. In the name of motivation, cartoon characters take over many classrooms.

Instead of seeing displays of real people or even time-tested legendary heroes, kids primarily see and experience the latest kid-culture fad hero. In the 1980s one could have guessed the correct year simply by entering a typical elementary school, visiting the classrooms, and identifying the creatures that dominated the display areas. Had the students been present, many of their personal belongings--tee shirts, notebooks, backpacks, pencils, and the occasional lunchbox--would most certainly have matched the bulletin boards. So, not only was the Mouse already there to welcome the kids to school, he often came along with them. There simply was no escaping the influence and impact of commercialism.

Do you remember the movie about Roger Rabbit? In it, there was an entire city populated by cartoon characters--they co-existed with humans, and each was able to enter and leave the other's realm whenever and wherever they chose. Farfetched, wasn't it?

But it really is not that far off the mark, is it? Children today are so surrounded by cartoon fad figures that indeed they enter and leave cartoonland every day. It is possible they awake to see Garfield emblazoned on their pillowcases, drink their morning juice from a Little Mermaid glass, grab their Snoopy lunch pail, and leave for school, wearing, of course, their Batman shirt. Once in their fourth grade classroom, they will be surrounded by these same images, staring at them from bulletin boards, ceiling mobiles, and fellow classmates' clothing. Assorted worksheets and stickers will carry the familiar fad faces too. Following school, they'll return home, where most likely bedroom posters will carry the same theme. With any luck (their opinion), tonight's rented video might be the latest Turtle adventure! It is their world, and welcome to it!

STRIVING FOR BALANCE

Should the fad figures be expelled from school and the home? No, such a drastic step is neither realistic nor desirable. Undoubtedly, the furry creatures do at times motivate students to perform well. For instance, Barney's footprint stamped on a child's perfect (or near perfect) math study sheet may be the reward sought eagerly by the youngster. But the comic characters must be moved to the backseat, and the real heroes and heroines should move to the front and start driving. Let Jonas Salk, the discoverer of the polio vaccine, be given attention and space in the classroom instead of being relegated to a token five minute portion in a health lesson. He, not some purple dinosaur, should be displayed.

Envision this issue of cartoon versus real figures as a continuum. In most classrooms, all of the displays and instructional techniques fall at the cartoon end; the emphasis is clearly skewed in favor of fads. What is needed at the very least is a balance; what is desirable, however, is a skewing toward the great people's end of the continuum.

The balance between commercially-derived figures and real people of significance is easy to achieve in some cases. For example, when Mickey Mouse is used in the classroom, give credit to the genius who created him. Walt Disney's picture should be alongside his famous drawing. His life story can be just as inspirational, or even more so, than any of the exploits in his cartoons. Mr. Disney's triumphs and failures, and most of all his perseverance, are worthy of attention and emulation.

The over-presence of fantasy characters in our schools and homes contributes to a confusion for our children and adolescents about the value of real-life human accomplishments. It is not surprising that when in 1991, a Harrisburg, Pennsylvania-area school district asked its fifth to twelfth graders to name people they most admired, the teenagers chose rock stars, athletes, and television personalities, people who often seem to be larger than life. Other than Nelson Mandela, no famous people from any other field of endeavor were mentioned. No great artists, inventors, humanitarians, political leaders, composers, scientists, doctors--none were mentioned by the 1,150 students.

It is readily apparent that as elementary-aged children grow up, their attention is turned from fad creatures to fad people. Bedroom posters of the latest animation figure gradually become life-size posters of sports, music, or movie stars. These human idols are in many instances even less desirable than the cartoon icons were.

There are real people to whom kids can turn for role models. Hard work is what makes productive people succeed. Let children learn about the creative spark humans possess, so they begin to understand that it is individuals who make a difference. If Mickey is used as the motivator, surely Mr. Disney is the real hero who ought to be given recognition too. Balancing the message requires at least equal time, space, and effort between the cartoon and the cartoonist. It is the human, not the animation, which ought to be the focus in classrooms and in homes.

A NEW APPROACH

Important individuals will be quite different from those prominently referred to before the 1960s. The heroic people we recognize today as great are of every race and ethnic origin and of either gender. No longer are heroes only white and male. The women and men who shaped this nation and the world, but who were not given a fair shake because of earlier historical shortsightedness, should now be given their day in the sun--and in the schools. Their presence is needed in classrooms to teach and to inspire. They, not the mice, cats, and dogs, should be the role models for tomorrow's leaders. Remember the child with the near-perfect math paper? Build a situation so that the student wants a Sally Ride sticker, or the letters *SR* stamped on the paper, instead of a dinosaur print. Good mathematicians can become good scientists and even astronauts; they cannot become extinct animals! Sally Ride, not Barney, can show children what hard work and dedication can achieve for real people, so it is most fitting to reward achievement in her name. She is only one of the many new heroes and heroines waiting in the wings.

Enlivening classrooms and curriculum materials with great people does not mean overwhelming children with them. Very little, if anything, is achieved by the good intentioned teacher who displays pictures of all the presidents. The outstanding men and women who never reached that high office or who earned distinction in other fields are overlooked. "Less is more" is clearly a guideline to follow in moving toward the continuum's hero/heroine end. Key individuals representing all types of heroic deeds should be employed judiciously throughout the year. By focusing on a limited number and by planning carefully their appearance and reappearances, a teacher can guarantee that these individuals will have an impact.

Think of the impression on young minds if teachers and principals begin using real heroes regularly in the school's curriculum. Currently, it takes a special day (usually a day off from school) to honor the few key people still receiving recognition. Martin Luther King, Jr.,'s photos appear in mid-January; at the end of the month they are removed and replaced by the old dynamic duo of Washington and Lincoln just in time for Presidents' Day. Sometimes, a teacher will make a sincere attempt during "Women in History" week to spotlight famous females. But these efforts are too transitory and too limited to achieve any lasting effect--especially when they are compared to the continuing and permanent presence of fad figures. The effort to inspire and motivate through great people must be ongoing and lasting if indeed it is going to influence children's thinking.

NATIONAL SUPPORT

Encouraging signs of the reemergence of heroes and heroines are already appearing, as some historians present strong arguments favoring the inclusion of more history in the school curriculum. For example, the Bradley Commission on History in Schools has asserted:

. . . Well-taught, history and biography are naturally engaging to students by speaking to their individuality, to their possibilities for choice, and to their desire to control their lives . . .[2]

Young children are fascinated by heroes, amazing deeds, fantastic tales, and stories of extraordinary feats and locales. History offers a wide range of materials to delight and engage the young learner.[3]

The *History-Social Science Framework for California Public Schools, Kindergarten Through Grade Twelve* strongly endorses the inclusion of heroes and heroines in children's studies:

To understand the common memories that create a sense of community and continuity among people, children should learn about the classic legends, folktales, tall tales, and hero stories of their community and nation . . . Children should listen to biographies of the nation's heroes and of those who took the risk of new and controversial ideas and opened new opportunities for many. Such stories convey to the children valuable insights in the history of their nation and its people; . . .[4]

Aimed at reshaping social studies education in our largest state, that important curriculum document sprang from ideas espoused by such individuals as E.D. Hirsch, Jr., and Diane Ravitch. Their thinking and writings have created a needed dialogue over the issue of more meaningful content in elementary schools.

In his 1987 best-seller, *Cultural Literacy: What Every American Needs to Know*, Hirsch develops his major premise that all citizens should share a common core of cultural information to enable communication and progress to occur.[5] To be "culturally literate" means to be familiar with a body of knowledge seen as important to the development of America and for its continuation. Hirsch argues that the disadvantaged children are particularly hurt by lacking fundamental background knowledge. "The American vagueness about what a child needs to learn in a grade seems more than any other circumstance to cause the learning gap [between privileged and disadvantaged children] to widen."[6] Today, the newly established Core Knowledge Foundation promotes the establishment of a "core knowledge" curriculum in elementary schools. A defined sequence for grades one through six has been developed, and a series of resource guidebooks (*What Your First [Second, Third, etc.] Grader Needs to Know*, Doubleday Publishers) has been written. "Model" core knowledge schools have been started in several states, with Florida and Texas in the forefront. While critics have sometimes labeled the effort as a form of "Trivial Pursuit," Hirsch clearly does not advocate memorizing endless lists of facts. "Teachers in Core Knowledge schools bring the knowledge to life in active creative ways."[7]

Hirsch's work and emphasis on engaging the young learner with meaningful content is closely related to Diane Ravitch's philosophy. In extensive writings, she has severely criticized the emptiness of the elementary school curriculum, especially in the so-called expanding environment framework of kindergarten through grade three social studies teaching.

> This curriculum of "me, my family, my school, my community" now dominates the early grade in American public education . . . It contains no mythology, legends, biographies, hero tales or great events in the life of this nation or any other. It is *tot sociology*. [emphasis added][8]

Ravitch, along with Charlotte Crabtree, were the principal writers of the California Framework, which clearly promotes the inclusion of heroes into the curriculum at all grade levels.

One textbook company, Houghton-Mifflin, has taken the ideas found in the California Framework and based a new elementary social studies textbook series on them.[9] This comprehensive work incorporates great men and women into every grade level, beginning with kindergarten.

A more revolutionary approach aimed solely at the upper elementary grades of fourth through sixth is *A History of Us*, a ten volume set by Joy Hakin.[10] It restores the story to *history* without sacrificing the need for well researched facts. Real people are brought to life as America's story is told, and heroes again reappear in social studies instruction.

In addition, to help teachers and parents in promoting real heroes, more children's books are being published about the lives of famous people. *Hooray for Heroes! Books and Activities Kids Will Want to Share with Parents and Teachers* provides over 100 clever, hands-on activities and comprehensive age-appropriate lists of biographies for children.[11] Thousands of titles are organized so kids and adults can easily find books about inventors, humanitarians, artists and so on, and then can use the activities to become actively involved with their heroes and heroines. Likewise, *Toward A Human Curriculum: A Guide to Returning Great People to Classrooms and Homes* is a brief practical guide to help make heroes come alive.[12]

CAN IT BE DONE?

Can children--young children, "older" children, teenagers--learn all this "stuff," this "core knowledge," all these heroes and heroines? The answer is an unqualified *YES*--if we who teach them in schools and in homes spend as much time making learning about heroes as interesting and exciting as we make learning about dinosaurs.

Commitment is needed first if changes are to be made, and that commitment is quite simply the recognition that most children are far more capable of learning enriching content than what we give them credit for. Someone puzzled by that statement need only count the number of questions kids ask in one day! They are eager to learn, and every good teacher and parent knows it. If students are actively and creatively engaged in their learning, any content can be taught. Brachiosaurus, and its companions can give way to Albert Schweitzer, Harriet Tubman, Beethoven, and on and on.

And, more importantly, Thomas Edison, Elizabeth Blackwell, Peary and Henson, and so many others can take the places of Mickey, Snoopy, Barney, et al. The *real* Leonardo, not his Turtle namesake, should be our focus.

Why focus on great women and men as part of our necessary knowledge base? Kids need role models, that's why. The presence of people of achievement is needed once again in today's helter-skelter world, and especially in the lives of children and young people. Parents and teachers working together through creative teaching can make a difference by exposing children to these role models. The strategy to move away from cartoon fads and toward real heroes is obviously not a quick fix for society's ills, nor is it one the results from which can be easily measured. But it is a common sense, "feels good" notion that can help change the focus in schools and homes.

Heroines and heroes and children belong together.

ENDNOTES

This chapter is reprinted, with changes, from *Educational Innovation: An Agenda to Frame the Future*, ed. Charles E. Greenawalt, II (Lanham, MD: University Press of America, Inc., and The Commonwealth Foundation for Public Policy Alternatives, 1994), 129-140, by permission of the author and the publishers.

1.   Geoffrey Cowley. "I'd Toddle a Mile for a Camel." *Newsweek*, 23 December 1991, 70. Similar articles appeared in *Time Magazine*, 23 December 1991; *Business Week*, 23 December 1991; and *Science News*, 14 December 1991.

2.   Bradley Commission on History in Schools, *Building a History Curriculum: Guidelines for Teaching History in Schools* (Indianapolis, IN: Educational Excellence Network, 1988), 5.

3.   Ibid., 16.

4.   History-Social Science Curriculum Framework Criteria Committee, *History-Social Science Framework for California Public Schools, Kindergarten Through Grade Twelve* (Sacramento, CA: State Department of Education, 1988), 43.

5.   E.D. Hirsch, Jr. *Cultural Literacy: What Every American Needs to Know* (Boston: Houghton-Mifflin, 1987).

6.   E.D. Hirsch, Jr., "Fairness and Core Knowledge," *Common Knowledge: A Core Knowledge Newsletter* 4, no.2, (Fall 1991): 6.

7.   E.D. Hirsch, Jr., "Esprit de Core," *Common Knowledge: A Core Knowledge Newsletter* 5, no.1, (Winter 1992): 2.

8.   Diane Ravitch, "Tot Sociology, or What Happened to History in Grade Schools," *The American Scholar*, Summer 1987, 343-354.

9.   Houghton-Mifflin, Social Studies (Boston: Houghton-Mifflin, 1991).

10.   Joy Hakin, *A History of Us* (New York: Oxford University Press, 1993).

11.   Dennis Denenberg and Lorraine Roscoe, *Hooray for Heroes! Books and Activities Kids Will Want to Share with Parents and Teacher* (Metchen, NJ: Scarecrow Press, 1994).

12.   Dennis Denenberg, *Toward a Human Curriculum: A Guide to Returning Great People to Classrooms and Homes* (Unionville, NY: Trillium Press, 1991).

Chapter 9

Building Community
Through Education

Eric R. Ebeling

INTRODUCTION

The pervasive sense today that social life in the United States is
degenerating is not new; many Americans had a similar feeling during the
Jacksonian period more than a century and a half ago.[1] What is new,
however, is the amount of exposure to and information about the crisis.
Modern news coverage provides the public with a continuous and graphic
view of the ravages of crime, poverty, and other ills across the entire
continent. In addition, modern social research supplies the data to actually
substantiate the country's decline when people in the past could only
surmise it.

This broad range of awareness, however, does not necessarily translate
into a correspondingly broad range of action. Although these social
problems are national in occurrence, their solutions must be local in
character. A consensus is emerging that federal and state programs *can
not* match city and town initiatives which mobilize people who are
personally concerned about the areas in which they lead their lives.
America must be turned around at the grassroots, and it is the premise of
this essay that building community is the way to effect that reform.

What role, if any, can education have in building and strengthening
community? To answer that question one must begin perforce with a
definition of community. One excellent definition, advanced by a social

theorist in the 19th century, remains viable in comprehending the notion of community and discerning its decline in the United States. Furthermore, this definition offers a theoretical framework for analyzing the impact of education on community, an impact that generally is negative but could be positive if current practices were changed. After examining some of the present realities and future possibilities of education in this regard, this essay concludes with a look at three educational movements that are building community today in America and their implication for policy makers.

A DEFINITION OF COMMUNITY

In the vernacular "community" typically refers to a group of people who share the same locality or interests. Occasionally, the term is used interchangeably with "society," but to those attentive to nuances of meaning, the two words are not completely synonymous. The differences between them emerge when they are contrasted: "community" is more intimate, concentrated, and bounded while "society" is more impersonal, diffuse, and extensive.

These connotations are not accidental, for they reflect an important analytical distinction advanced by social theorists of the past. Beginning with Plato, a number of thinkers have addressed this distinction, but the German scholar Ferdinand Tönnies deserves credit for explicating it in the most comprehensive manner. In 1887, he published a work entitled *Gemeinschaft und Gesellschaft* in which he explored the concepts of community and society in a way that has affected sociological inquiry ever since.

Although there are no equivalent words for Gemeinschaft and Gesellschaft in the English language which capture all their implications, *Gemeinschaft* is usually translated as "community" and *Gesellschaft* as "society." As ideal types or mental constructs, neither of these exists in the real world by itself. Instead, they together provide a useful polarization for comparing different settings of social life.

Gemeinschaft signifies "intimate, private, and exclusive living together."[2] It is characterized by understanding, agreement, cooperation, and solidarity. In elaborating the concept, Tönnies identified three manifestations of it distinguished by the type of bond involved. He called them the Gemeinschaft of blood, of place, and of mind.

The Gemeinschaft of blood refers to kinship, especially the family, where people are literally related to each other. Tönnies located this form of community in the home which brings its members together in household activities as a consequence of their biological proximity. The Gemeinschaft of place refers to neighborhood where people are related to each other through shared local concerns. Tönnies located this form of community in the village which brings its members together in civic activities as a consequence of their physical proximity.

Finally, the Gemeinschaft of mind refers to friendship where people are related to each other through common interests or beliefs. Tönnies located this form of community in the town or church which brings its members together in cultural or religious activities as a consequence of their intellectual or spiritual proximity.

In contrast to Gemeinschaft, Gesellschaft represents the "mere coexistence of people independent of each other" (34). It is characterized by distrust, opposition, competition, and detachment. Unlike Gemeinschaft which "is the lasting and genuine form of living together," Gesellschaft "is transitory and superficial" (35).

What governs human interaction in Gesellschaft is the contract, an agreement which people enter into only to effect a transaction. Once that transaction has concluded, their association ends. As a consequence of this mercenary aspect, Gesellschaft is marked by pretense and manipulation:

> Its supreme rule is politeness. It consists of an exchange of words and courtesies in which everyone seems to be present for the good of everyone else and everyone seems to consider everyone else as his equal, whereas in reality everyone is thinking of himself and trying to bring to the fore his importance and advantages in competition with the others. For everything pleasant which someone does for someone else, he expects, even demands, at least an equivalent (78).

Tönnies came to these constructs through his belief that all human interaction is an expression of human will and priorities regarding ends and means. He connected Gemeinschaft with what he called "natural will" in which people affiliated with each other to have a relationship they valued as an end in and of itself. In contrast, he linked Gesellschaft with what he called "rational will" in which people associated with each other to achieve a common goal using their association as a means to that end, even if they personally were indifferent or even hostile to each other on other levels. In Tönnies's words, their interaction was "the resultant of two divergent wills, intersecting in one point" (71).

In identifying Gesellschaft with rational will, Tönnies was not implying that Gemeinschaft is completely irrational. In fact, he indicated that Gemeinschaft groups also exhibit rational aspects, and he ranked family, neighborhood, and friendship accordingly in order of increasing rationality. For Tönnies, friendship was the highest form of community because it was based on relationships free of compulsion.

As a summary of his theory in the words of Rudolf Heberle, Tönnies showed that both Aristotle and Hobbes were correct in their respective views on social life:

> Man was indeed by his very nature a social being who would unfold his essence only by living in communities of kinship, space (neighborhood), and spirit, but who was also capable of forming and, at certain stages in history, compelled to form new kinds of associations by agreements--associations which could be understood as instruments for the attainment of certain ends-- whereas those "older" communities were taken as ends in themselves and therefore could not be understood by a utilitarian approach (xi-xii).

THE DECLINE OF COMMUNITY

Tönnies arrived at his analysis from the vantage point of 19th century Germany. There he observed firsthand the effects of the rise of urbanization, industrial capitalism, and the nation state in post-Reformation Europe. He admitted that Gesellschaft initially seemed "innocent"--the harbinger of "progress" and symbol of "fairness, reason and enlightenment." Its emergence, however, had negative as well as positive ramifications:

> But a rational scientific and independent law was made possible only through the emancipation of the individuals from all the ties which bound them to the family, the land, and the city and which held them to superstition, faith, traditions, habit, and duty. Such liberation meant the fall of the communal household in village and town, of the agricultural community, and of the art of the town as a fellowship, religious, patriotic craft. It meant the victory of egoism, impudence, falsehood, and cunning, the ascendancy of greed for money, ambition and lust for pleasure. But it brought also the victory of the contemplative, clear and sober consciousness in which scholars and cultured men now dare to approach things human and divine (202).

From his observations Tönnies concluded that rational will and Gesellschaft over time replaced natural will and Gemeinschaft. In discerning this development, he also anticipated the problems of modern society: "The less human beings who remain or come into contact with each other are bound together in relation to the same Gemeinschaft, the more they stand opposite each other as free agents of their wills and abilities" (46). Without the ties of community to connect them, people would become antagonistic toward each other in the struggle to achieve their own individual ends.

Today, more than a century after Tönnies presented his theory to the world, social life in the United States provides compelling evidence of his remarkable foresight. The notion of community which he articulated seems so lacking, especially in large urban areas where families, neighborhoods, and even friendships in the sense that Tönnies characterized them are in decline. Crime, illegitimacy, and other problems manifest the deteriorating quality of social life as people without communal attachments become callous and abusive in seeking their own personal agendas. Human interaction in many sectors seems governed by a calculus of individual benefit and exploitation instead of mutual benefit and reciprocity. The losers in the interchange lash out in resentment, and the vicious cycle continues.

Certainly there are many things that have contributed to the current crisis, among them the developments of modernization that Tönnies and other scholars have identified. While the impact of some factors is obvious, the effect of others is less evident. Education, for example, may not appear to be a contributing force in the weakening of community. As the following section will show, however, education actually exerts a deleterious influence on community in the United States today.

EDUCATION AGAINST COMMUNITY

In laying out his theory, Tönnies provides a framework for assessing the impact of education on community. The ensuing discussion will illustrate how some current educational practices are often antagonistic to the communities of family, neighborhood, and friendship that Tönnies identified in his analysis. It will also touch on how education works against his notion of relationships as ends in and of themselves.

Education Against Family

Education in the United States today works against families in a number of ways. Compulsory attendance laws, enacted to ensure that children receive a formal education, also serve to take boys and girls out of the home for the school day. In addition, extracurricular activities extend the separation of young people from their parents. The result is that fathers and mothers have little time to spend with their children.

While these educational policies may be well-intentioned, they act to supplant parents in their natural and traditional child-rearing roles. As a consequence, adults often neglect their responsibility to teach their children because the schools provide them with the excuse to do so. The almost unquestioned supposition today is that only schools educate; parents merely house, clothe, feed, and care for their offspring (although schools are beginning to assume some of these duties as well). While educators may argue that parental indifference and neglect have prompted the intervention of the school, the causal link may actually go the other way.

Ironically, while teachers effectively work parents out of the educational picture by monopolizing the role of instructor, they simultaneously try to work them back into it, prodded by research which shows that academic achievement increases with parental involvement. Consequently, educators clamor for the participation of fathers and mothers in the learning process. The only participation acceptable, however, is on the school's terms; parents are expected simply to support the curriculum and assist with homework. Adults outside the educational establishment typically have no voice in determining more weighty matters such as the content and method of their children's education. Where parents supposedly have a role in making school decisions, they usually are involved only in a token way.

The implication of these policies is that parents, in the eyes of professional educators, are not qualified to teach their children. In some instances they are even viewed as obstacles in the educational process, as backward or biased parties who hamper their children's development. In addition, the entire familial dimension of educational experience--the values, traditions, and background which form a potentially relevant and meaningful part of each child's world--is likewise ignored.

Education Against Neighborhood

Just as some educational practices currently works against the family, they also work against the neighborhood. Perhaps the most obvious manifestation of this is the school facility itself. Even where campuses are physically located in the community they serve, they are set off from the community in other ways. School buildings are not open to everyone; instead, only designated personnel can enter them. Similarly, academic resources and facilities are reserved for students and staff. Although these polices may provide children with certain benefits, they also tend to distance the rest of the community and restrict the interaction of young people with it.

In many settings the campus is physically removed from the local community as well. As a result of the consolidation of districts and the use of busing to achieve racial integration, many schools take youngsters out of their neighborhoods and place them with youngsters from other areas who do not share the same local backgrounds or concerns. Frequently, the teachers and administrators who work in the school also come from other locations and therefore have little connection to or interest in the communities of the children.

Not only are students and staff imported into schools, but so is the curriculum which is often dictated by officials in distant state offices. In a sense, standardized and mandated curricula imply a rejection of community life because they suggest that local considerations do not matter. Instead, the priorities of the state predominate. Consequently, the curriculum is often irrelevant to community life. As another result, community members feel they have no part in what goes on in schools. The school in their midst is not their school, and the only connection they may have with it is as boosters of its athletic teams.

This delineation of boundaries between the school and the community is a manifestation of how schools have arrogated educational authority to themselves. As education has become more and more the field of "experts" with special credentials which qualify them to instruct the young, it has become less and less the field of parents and other community members who traditionally exerted an educational influence in the lives of the rising generation. There is almost an implicit assumption that uncertified individuals do not know how to teach children. In addition, the local dimension of educational experience--the history, composition, and problems of the neighborhood--is neglected as educators focus on remote state, national, and world agendas in the curriculum.

Education Against Friendship

Even if students in educational settings all come from the same local area, a number of current school practices weaken community in other ways. For example, age-grading assigns children to artificial groups, restricting their associations to peers who represent a very narrow segment of society. This policy precludes children from forming friendships with other people who might share their interests or background. It has also abetted the rise of both a youth culture which is often antagonistic to other groups and a juvenile market which is exploitative of young people. In a more abstract way schools compartmentalize knowledge as well as children. Separate classes for each subject dispense information isolated from any broader context. As a result, education degenerates into a trivial exercise almost devoid of interdisciplinary discourse. Students fail to see the connections between fields of knowledge and leave school ill-prepared to make those necessary connections in an integrated world.

On another level, education in many schools fails to address any transcendent dimension of human experience such as religious belief. These areas of inquiry are off limits because they are deemed controversial and divisive. Consequently, opportunities for meaningful interaction between students and teachers are lost.

Education Against Relationships

Not only the content but also the method of schooling works against community. Instead of encouraging cooperation, testing, grading, and ranking practices based on comparisons foster competition among students who strive to surpass each other in their academic work. Schooling becomes a zero-sum game in which each child's goal is to look better than his classmates. The overemphasis on educational achievement as measured by standardized tests encourages students to view other people as potential instruments in helping them to achieve high scores.

In their defense, educators sometimes draw analogies between academic attainment in schools and vocational success and personal aggrandizement outside the institution which are widely esteemed as the most desirable goals in American society. However, the pursuit of any of these objectives reduces social relationships to utilitarian associations. "What can you do for me" becomes the measure of all human interaction.

Sex education in schools encapsulates the four ways described above in which education works against community. Traditionally a responsibility of parents and logically a concern of the family, sex education is now a learning objective of the academic establishment. While the problems of sexual abuse and illegitimacy are frequently local issues, teachers rarely consider the neighborhood settings which give rise to them. The material is often taught in a clinical fashion as a unit in a health class, and consequently transcending notions of love and religion have no place in the discussion. Finally, the emphasis on methods and precautions gives young people an instrumental view of sex. As a result, it often becomes a tool in exploiting others for selfish ends.

EDUCATION FOR COMMUNITY

In acknowledging the emergence of Gesellschaft over time, Tönnies did not suggest that Gemeinschaft was not totally eclipsed in the process. Instead, he maintained that "the force of Gemeinschaft persists, although with diminishing strength, even in the period of Gesellschaft, and remains the reality of social life" (232). His work implies that pockets of community not only can exist within the larger society but also can be fostered there. Although education can be hostile to community, it can be supportive as well. Again, Tönnies's analysis provides a framework for exploring some examples of the potentially positive impact education can have on families, neighborhoods, and friendships as well as on relationships as ends in and of themselves.

Education for Family

The family has always been and continues to be the most basic educational unit. Whether they realize it or not, parents have a primary and inescapable role in their children's education. Obviously, adults directly influence what their sons and daughters learn when they take time to deliberately teach them--for example, when they discipline them or help them with their homework. Less obviously, fathers and mothers also indirectly influence what their children learn to the extent they determine what experiences they will have. In particular, adults take part in the education of their offspring by exercising (or not exercising) control over how they spend their time and what they are exposed to through the television shows they watch, the music they listen to, the literature they read, the activities they participate in, and the people they associate with. Simply by living with their parents, boys and girls have learning experiences that would be different if they lived somewhere else with someone else.

Consequently, the educational influence of parents is unavoidable. Even the most negligent father or mother at least indirectly determines some of what his or her children will learn. Educators, therefore, must acknowledge and deal with this reality by encouraging parents to fulfill their educational role in a responsible and beneficial manner and by coordinating the instructional agendas of parents and other agencies so that children learn what they should in the most efficient way.

In this discussion, the issue of who should control the education of the young is paramount. Given the direct and indirect influence that fathers and mothers exert on what their children learn, logically parental interests must predominate. In other words, if parents have the right to raise their own children, then they also have the right to control their education. The legitimacy of private schooling as an alternative to public education in this country is predicated on this assumption.

With parents in control, school curricula and programs should be designed to accommodate their concerns, and government intervention should be limited to allow families the greatest possible freedom in educating their children. The school must be an extension of the home, not a replacement of it. Only when educators recognize the vital part that fathers and mothers play and both allow and require them to play that part will parents respond accordingly.

Tönnies himself addressed the educational role of parents as an extension of their roles in bringing children into the world. He implied that their responsibilities as teachers were among their most important and satisfying obligations:

Thus, the idea of authority is, within the Gemeinschaft, most adequately represented by fatherhood, or paternity. However, authority, in this sense, does not imply possession and use in the interest of the master; it means education and instruction as the fulfillment of procreation, i.e., sharing the fullness of one's own life and experiences with the children, who will gradually grow to reciprocate these gifts and thus to establish a truly mutual relationship (39).

If parents esteemed and shouldered their educational role accordingly, many children would not be the orphans they effectively are today.

Education for Neighborhood

Parents are not the only individuals with an interest in the education of the young. Every individual and organization with an investment in a locality should also have an interest in its children who affect the well-being of the community today and its vitality tomorrow. Consequently, the education of children should also be the concern of their neighbors.

Education is justifiably a local matter because the very existence of communities is testimony to their viability. In a sense, communal life is validated in part by its continuation, and the desire of older members to pass on that life to younger ones is therefore legitimate. This is not to say that all communities are perfect; many in fact are quite parochial. But as a point of departure, local community life deserves a hearing in education, and teachers should work to build bridges between it and the larger world.

Education can also help build communities because raising children is a concern which cuts across all the lines that divide Americans into conflicting groups. Poverty may be the peculiar problem of the lower class and prejudice the peculiar problem of minorities, but raising youngsters is everyone's challenge. Children are born into families from all parts of the economic, racial, ethnic, and religious spectrum, and their parents all face similar difficulties in guiding them through their formative years.

This discussion has many implications. For example, if there is a cost to educate the young, then that cost should be borne by the community in which they live. Certainly parents should shoulder the expense to the extent they are able; after all, they are responsible for bringing their children into the world and adding them to the community. But if some parents do not have the resources to pay for the education of their offspring, then other parties in the community with a stake in its future should supplement their efforts. The current system of state and federal financing of education tends to erode communal control by shifting the locus of power to distant officials who almost always impose mandates in exchange for funding.

Community members should be involved not only publicly and collectively in education but privately and individually as well. Education must become a lifelong activity for everyone, not just a temporary experience for the young. The belief that education is synonymous with schooling and the consequent notion that the former ends with the latter must be dispelled. In effect, the school walls must be extended to envelop the entire community, making everyone both a learner and a teacher.

Concurrently, those involved most directly with the formal educational process (students, teachers, and educational leaders) must also reach out into the community. Local experiences, issues, and conflicts should be topics of intense personal interest to everyone in school. As an outgrowth of this focus, students should participate in community life through clubs, service projects, reform initiatives, and other programs designed to integrate them into their local world.

Education for Friendship

As children mature, their interests may expand beyond the neighborhoods in which they live. Those who direct their educational path must recognize this development and encourage it by linking them with others who share their concerns. The friendships that result can provide lifelong growth and fulfillment for the young.

Another way to connect children to the larger world is reflected in the fact that "community" and "communicate" are related words. In building community through education, students must not only be taught the mechanics of speaking, reading, and writing but also be provided with something to communicate about: the shared culture that serves as the basis for human discourse. In essence, education is the project that attempts to transmit everything worthy in the cultural capital accumulated from the past to the young who, in turn, will enlarge that legacy as well.

Finally, the inescapable moral component of education provides another vital link in communities of friendship. Helping children acquire a moral sense means helping them to recognize their relationships to others and to develop appreciation for and consideration of their fellow human beings. Morality is not an individual matter; rather, it is a prerequisite for positive social interaction.

Education for Relationships

Educating for membership in the community means educating the whole individual, not just one academic component of his or her makeup. Relationships in community are holistic; they involve the total person. As education enriches human lives, it makes those lives worth sharing. People who really enjoy each other's company cannot entertain thoughts of exploiting their friends for personal gain.

Ultimately, education is all about relationships, for teaching and learning are not solo activities. Certainly, the people who comprise the social world of the child bestow meaning on every experience he or she has. Yet there is nothing in education that surpasses the generative quality of relationships in which both parties grow in symbiotic interaction. In these partnerships, spending time together becomes the best way to learn and the end in itself.

EDUCATIONAL MOVEMENTS WHICH
BUILD COMMUNITY

Tönnies's analysis provides a valuable conceptual framework for assessing the impact of education on community. Educational practices have attenuated families, neighborhoods, friendships, and relationships, but different approaches, if implemented, could strengthen these forms of community. In short, the way to build community through education consists of a two-pronged approach: involve communities in education and involve education in communities. This strategy applies to each of the three forms of community Tönnies identified, and it also leads to an elevation of human relationships as ends in and of themselves.

Although much of current educational practice exerts a negative impact on community, there exist some educational movements today in the United States that are building community in the way described above. These include home education, private schooling, and telecommunication networks.

A growing number of parents are choosing to teach their children at home in lieu of sending them to school. Whether they are motivated by religious, academic, or safety reasons, these parents are discovering many advantages in their approach. Not surprisingly, their families are stronger as a result.

In some locations, specialized private schools are opening that focus on particular populations. Many of these institutions are religiously based while others are tailored to racial or ethnic groups. In their ongoing efforts to integrate schools, some educators seem bewildered by the rise of these schools, especially African-American academies which serve black students exclusively by capitalizing on their distinctive experience and culture. This phenomenon will probably become more widespread, reflecting as it does a desire for the communities of place and mind.

Finally, the growing web of affiliations made possible through telecommunication technology links like-minded people all over the nation and world. The Internet and other electronic networks provide ways for those who share similar ideas or beliefs to communicate and build communities. In conjunction with conferences that bring these people together in face-to-face gatherings, these interactions portend a future of more liberating relationships which are chosen instead of imposed.

The implication of these developments is significant. Citizens of the United States enjoy a number of basic rights, among them the right to have children, to live where they choose, and to associate with whom they will. Each of these rights is connected to a form of community which Tönnies described. Given this fact, policy makers must either deprive citizens of these rights or else acknowledge and capitalize on them through educational efforts directed at building community.

In the effort to build community, education can also be used to enlarge it, to extrapolate from the personal and meaningful relationships of local environments to the shared concerns of the broader world. Indeed,

Tönnies himself mentioned that "one could speak of a Gemeinschaft comprising the whole of mankind" (34). In one sense, this means ceasing from viewing other people and peoples so instrumentally. In another, it means emphasizing the elements that are common instead of the aspects that are different in social interactions. As Tönnies described people in the two constructs he employed, "in the Gemeinschaft they remain essentially united in spite of all separating factors, whereas in the Gesellschaft they are essentially separated in spite of all uniting factors" (65). If the citizens of the United States are to remain united in all their diversity, then the communities they inhabit must be built and strengthened. Education can and must be part of that construction project.

ENDNOTES

1.   See David Rothman, *The Discovery of the Asylum: Social Order and Disorder in the New Republic* (Boston: Little, Brown and Company, 1990).

2.   Ferdinand Tönnies, *Community & Society (Gemeinschaft und Gesellschaft)*, trans. and ed. Charles Loomis (East Lansing, MI: The Michigan State University Press, 1957), 33.

Chapter 10

Can Schools and Colleges Help Restore Citizenship?

John W. Cooper

INTRODUCTION

It has become commonplace to decry the fact that many of today's high school and college graduates are woefully ignorant of geography, history, and the principles of government in a free society. Indeed, nearly all Americans have lost touch with the intellectual roots of our civil society.

Civic illiteracy, cultural rootlessness, and alienation from "the system" are a seriously troubling problem for American society and other democratic pluralist societies. One rightly wonders how a democracy can survive if its schools and colleges--and the extended educational apparatus of families, churches, and the media--eschew their moral mission to inculcate civil values.

Be certain, however, that this is not a question of indoctrination or brainwashing. Schools should never be the instruments of state control any more than they should be mere adjuncts to an economy in need of skilled labor.

Education for a civil society, including the restoration of citizenship and the preparation for an American civil society in the 21st century, requires several ingredients. First, we need to *take a fresh look at the curriculum* in our schools and colleges to honestly assess whether students have a realistic chance of developing civil literacy. Second, we must *examine the value system* that appropriately governs an educational institution in a pluralistic society. Third, we need a strategy to *prevent the politicization of education* by the proponents of "political correctness" on the Left or Right. Fourth, and finally, we must *reconceptualize schools and colleges as civic institutions properly understood.*

What follows are some modest proposals intended to further these four goals in our schools and colleges.

EXPLORING CIVIC VALUES IN THE CURRICULUM

A fresh look at the curriculum of our schools and colleges is required for many reasons. Some people are concerned about the impact of technology on American education. Others worry about the need to reject the "factory model" of schooling. The concern here is to explore how some specific curricular innovations could better build the American civil society of the next century.

Education for a civil society can be done in countless ways and at many educational levels: at the elementary level, through the study of national holidays and heroes, and through visits to monuments and polling places; at the secondary level through the reading of history, the study of governmental structures, and the careful analysis of current events; at the collegiate and graduate school levels through the study of political philosophy and public policy and through internships and fellowships in law offices, think tanks, and government agencies.

While a thorough proposal for curricular modifications at all levels of schooling is beyond the scope of this essay, suggested here is a scenario for the general direction of changes. Imagine, if you will, a high school or college seminar that aimed to "teach the basics" of how to build and maintain a civil society.

This hypothetical course would attempt to teach about civil society by concentrating on one brief but profound text, the Declaration of Independence.

This course is called "Values and Democracy." It is a seminar for 12 to 20 students. The course is genuinely interdisciplinary. As such it presupposes that students have some exposure to American history and government and perhaps some familiarity with philosophy and religious ethics. At the college level, the course can be listed in the catalogue as an interdisciplinary seminar or as an offering in any of several departments, including philosophy, history, political science, religion, and American studies. Students are divided into groups of four or five for projects and class presentations. Individual assignments include objective testing and substantial written work that is evaluated by the instructor at the first-draft and the final-draft stages. The primary texts are: The Declaration of Independence, the Constitution, selections from *The Federalist Papers,* a substantive intellectual history of the Revolutionary period such as Forrest McDonald's *Novus Ordo Seclorum,* basic works of early modern political theory such as Richard Hooker's *The Laws of Ecclesiastical Polity* (1593), Francisco Suarez's *On Laws and God the Lawgiver* (1612), John Locke's *Second Treatise of Government* (1690), and selections from contemporary works of political philosophy such as Jacques Maritain's *Man and the State,* John Rawl's *A Theory of Justice,* and Robert Nozick's *Anarchy, State and Utopia.*

The opening class session focuses immediately on the central text, two sentences from the second paragraph of the Declaration:

> We hold these truths to be self-evident, that all men are created equal, that they are endowed by their Creator with certain unalienable rights, that among these are Life, Liberty and the pursuit of Happiness. That to secure these rights, Governments are instituted among Men, deriving their just powers from the consent of the governed.

The instructor might ask students to imagine that the Declaration is an anonymous document--forgetting for the moment their knowledge of the Anglo-American conflict during the Colonial Era, forgetting the Revolutionary War, the Constitution and two hundred years of relatively stable American self-government. In the *abstract,* what does the text say? The text places a set of general propositions before the reader's eyes for inspection. "With which of these propositions do *you* agree?" the instructor might ask.

The opening session will probably reveal a wide range of opinion and may become a no-holds-barred exchange. Ideally, students will begin to debate each other on the meaning and coherence of the text's propositions. Students should note well their initial reactions to the Declaration--perhaps in a succinct two-page essay--so that they can compare it with their thoughts at the end of the course.

The next two or three sessions might be devoted to filling in the historical background. What were the colonists' specific complaints about the British monarchy's policies in the 1760s and 1770s? Most of them are listed in the Declaration itself. What kind of people were the colonists and what kind of life had they fashioned for themselves? Contrast the revolutionaries with the loyalists. Ask students to play the opposing parts in a mock debate. Is there a cogent argument for the loyalist position? After the colonists had made the Declaration, was it inevitable that they would have to fight a war for the independence? Were the high ideals of the Declaration upheld in the conduct of the war? In the Articles of Confederation? In the Constitution?

After a brief historical analysis, the course then turns once again to the text. A detailed analysis of each proposition, with reference to a broad range of secondary materials, should constitute the bulk of the course. In succession, students and the instructor might discuss the following sets of questions.

We hold these truths. What is truth? Is there a difference between fact and truth? The "facts only" world view might lead to a too-easy pragmatism or a materialist philosophy of life. But a truth-fact distinction, or a value-fact distinction, raises the deeper questions of epistemology. How do we know truth? On what authority? Observation of nature? Reason? Revelation?

We hold these truths to be self-evident. What is a "self-evident truth"? What is the nature of the "evidence"? Or is there no evidence, just a call to blind faith? Do the text's later references to the "Creator" and "Nature's God" suggest a transcendent grounding of truth? Given the Judeo-Christian-Deist background of the Colonial-era intellectuals, is it accurate to invoke a classic model that locates each term in a "two-storied universe." Does the revelation-reason model of truth provide sufficient freedom for the intellect? Is reason corrupted by sin and/or ignorance and thus in need of revelatory correction? Does the agnostic "operate" only in the lower half of the model? And can the believer "meet him there" in full agreement on the rules and ends of a pluralistic society?

That all men are created equal. "That all men are created" suggests a number of questions. Are humans, indeed, *created* beings? Is there a creator? If so, what purpose lies behind the creation? Is God-the-creator the ultimate source of truth and values, whether revealed or rationally deduced? Although, in fact, the Founders had a variety of opinions about God and the Divine Nature, it is nevertheless possible to delineate a common-ground view of the deity in the Declaration. Students might be asked to critically compare the Deist and Judeo-Christian conceptions of God. "Created equal" suggests the key concept that humans have rights, including equal treatment before the law. Are all persons equal "in God's sight"? Is equality before the law essential to justice?

That they are endowed by their Creator with certain unalienable rights.

That rights are "unalienable," or more properly inalienable, is the pivot between the idea of man's relationship to God (primary) and the idea of man's relationship to others in society and state (secondary). In other words, limited government means that certain aspects of human life and action are, and should be, beyond the reach of state power. On what basis can we say that people are rights-endowed? Why should governments be limited in their power? The Founders believed that natural rights and limited government were God-revealed or at least "written into" nature itself. Student discussion might focus on the proposition that persons have rights *over against* government. This is a radical proposition, uncommon in world history and rarely accepted by actual governments.

That among these rights are [equality,] life, liberty, and the pursuit of happiness. The Founders listed only a few specific rights by name. In the previous sentence, they mentioned equality and here they summarized the full range of rights as "life, liberty, and the pursuit of happiness." Students might start by making a longer list of human rights. Freedom of speech, the right to fair trial, freedom from cruel and unusual punishment, and the like come immediately to mind. In recent times greater emphasis has been placed on "positive" rights: rather than restraining governmental power these establish a claim of the individual against the state (e.g., the right to a job, to health care). But what was the focus of the Founders' concern? *Equality* meant that all franchised citizens were equal before the law. No judge or jury could mete out arbitrary or prejudiced punishments. That is the gist of that curious phrase, "a government of laws, not of men." Equality did not mean that all men were identical, not in talents, not in energy, not in temperament. To the Founders it was perfectly logical that some men would attain greater power, fame, or wealth. The Declaration does not envision "equality of result" but rather "equality of opportunity." Today that distinction is questioned by some and defended by others.

The "right to life" can be seen as a fundamental human right. The state cannot take a life without due cause (e.g., in a war of self-defense, as punishment for murder). Indeed the sacredness of life leads many even to question the legitimacy of defensive war or capital punishment. Students might discuss how our views of human nature or the soul affect our opinions about life-and-death public policy issues. The contemporary use of the phrase "right to life" by the opponents of abortion indicates that an issue like abortion cuts to the bone, it forces a society to ask itself the most fundamental questions about justice.

A "right to life" and a "right to liberty" suggests a further restriction on state power. Not only is the state forbidden to take life or to imprison without due cause, but there is an ideal of individual freedom implicit here that requires the state to respect the conscience as well as the person of each citizen. Thus there is an oblique connection to the first amendment language concerning the "free exercise of religion." Rights, liberty, freedom, and their cognate linguistic forms suggest a depth of respect for the individual that goes even deeper than protection of life and liberty. Indeed freedom of conscience, even more than the right to life itself, is *the* primary human right. Students might discuss some of the worst instances of the abuse of human rights by governments, including both abuses against persons' bodies and against their consciences. How should individuals react if given the choice between death and the renunciation of their most deeply held beliefs?

The "pursuit of happiness" had a special meaning for the Founders. In fact, as is well known, there was a debate over whether to substitute here the word "property." The right to possess one's property--to create and then to own a tangible or intangible good--was considered fundamental by the authors of the Declaration. One's property should not be taken by the state without due process. Taxation is a form of due process. But, at a certain point, excessive taxation becomes confiscation. And the colonists had a legitimate complaint about both excessive taxation and lack of due process ("taxation without representation"). All that said, however, property is not an end in itself. It is a tool that we use to live, to relieve life's burdens, to pass along as inheritance, to give away in charity. Thus the Founders concluded that it is not property per se that we have a right to, but the use of property to pursue happiness. Property is not only money and tangible goods but also the time and labor of the so-called "non-propertied" classes.

Property can be misspent, misused. It can even become an instrument for abusing the rights of others. That is why government regulation and enforcement of commercial relationships and contracts are essential in a democratic society. Furthermore, "property" suggests a whole set of realities necessary to a fair and free economy: reliance on markets and fair competition, the use of financial incentives as a motivator, the need for a private social welfare system that sustains the economically disabled. Students might discuss the implicit economic theory behind the Declaration. Why are economic rights and political rights so closely intertwined? Why do problems arise when the former are subordinated to the latter? In the contemporary world, why are the democratic countries more likely to have relatively humane market economies, and vice versa? *That to secure these rights, governments are instituted among men, deriving their just powers from the consent of the governed.* Implicit in what has already been said is the idea that the state should serve man, not man the state. Governments should not be instituted to perpetuate and increase their own power. They should be formed to "secure" something that already exists: namely, rights. Why do our rights need protecting? Because they are threatened by others--by other people and sometimes by governments themselves. Students might reflect on the uses of power. What instances of the unjust use of power come to mind? What are some instances of the just use of power? How is the claim to a just use of power grounded? The Founders believed the ultimate basis of just power was the consent of the governed. The colonists were well aware of the concept of popular consent in the writings of John Locke and Thomas Hobbes: the idea of an original state of nature followed by a social contract based on either implied or explicit consent. Students might be asked to debate the idea of a social contract. Is "the consent of the governed" a weak concept? What if people give consent to a tyrant like Hitler? Is that consent misguided and therefore not true consent? Once in power, if a ruler becomes a tyrant, how is consent withdrawn? Here students might discuss the right of revolution, and the parallel rights of recall and impeachment, as these concepts developed over time. How did "the divine right of kings" clash with the right of revolution?

These and many more questions will arise in any thorough discussion of the Declaration of Independence. Toward the end of the course, the instructor might ask students to reflect on what the Declaration means today. Do most Americans understand it? Would most Americans agree with its propositions? Should we teach the Declaration to America's children? Should we tell children that Jefferson, Madison, Hamilton and others were heroes--and that King George was the villain--in a great drama about how society should be governed? How do we teach values in a pluralistic society in a way that is intellectually honest and not ideological?

As a final exercise, students might be asked to compare their initial reactions and opinions about the Declaration--from their first essay assignment--to their current views. The instructor can imagine several creative ways to allow students to say how their minds have changed. If the course has been a success, it will be evident in the liveliness of the final discussion.

Do courses like the one described above already exist? They probably do, in some more or less similar form. Would such courses begin to address the problem of civic illiteracy in our society and would they become a building block for civil society in the 21st century? Yes. This brief exploration of a hypothetical course is suggestive of the ways that further curricular reform could help restore civil society. Careful attention to the special needs of students of all ages--primary, secondary, and post-secondary--would yield encouraging results.

But beyond course content and the curriculum, there are several other issues that affect schools and colleges which must be dealt with.

THE VALUE SYSTEM OF SCHOOLS AND COLLEGES

Another perspective on the efforts of schools and colleges to prepare students as citizens in a civil society focuses on the value systems of our educational institutions. Should schools and colleges teach morality and ethical decision-making to students? Do they really have a choice? After all, teachers play a major role in forming not only the intellect, but also the character, of their students. Teachers teach morality, whether they intend to or not. Thus, teaching morality is another key component in helping schools and colleges restore civil society.

After decades of attempting to create a value-neutral educational system, educators are today realizing that schools and colleges not only can, but must, teach morality.

A recent Gallup poll found that 84 percent of public-school parents want moral values taught in schools and 68 percent want educators to develop strict standards of "right and wrong."

Another survey, conducted by Louis Harris and Associates for the Girl Scouts, found that 47 percent of students would cheat on an exam, 66 percent would lie to achieve a business objective, and 36 percent would lie to protect a friend who had vandalized school property. Clearly the need of a carefully designed program of moral education has never been greater.

One example of careful thinking about which values should be emphasized comes from the Board of Regents of Florida's State University System. In 1987, they adopted a bold statement on the values that Florida's universities are committed to uphold. The statement built upon the pioneering 1983 report of the Maryland Values Education Commission.

The statement implicitly rejects the value-neutral philosophy that has for too long dominated the educational establishment. It sets forth principles that are specific enough to be meaningful and broad enough to be acceptable in a pluralistic culture.

What are these values that educators ought to promote?

1. Personal integrity that is rooted in respect for truth and love of learning.
2. A sense of duty to self, family, and the larger community.
3. Self-esteem rooted in the quest for the achievement of one's potential.
4. Respect for the rights of all persons regardless of their race, religion, nationality, sex and age, physical condition, or mental state.
5. The courage to express one's convictions, and recognition of the rights of others to hold and express differing views.
6. The capacity to make discriminating judgments among competing opinions.
7. A sense of, and commitment to, justice, rectitude, and fair play.
8. Understanding, sympathy, concern, and compassion for others.
9. A sense of discipline and pride in one's work; respect for the achievements of others.
10. Respect for one's property and the property of others, including public property.
11. An understanding of, and appreciation for, other cultures and traditions.
12. A willingness to perform the obligations of citizenship, including the obligation to cast an informed ballot, jury service, participation in government, and respect for the rule of law.
13. Civility, including congenial relations between men and women.
14. A commitment to academic freedom as a safeguard essential to the purposes of the school or college and to the welfare of those who work it.
15. The courage to oppose the use of substances which impair one's judgment or one's health.

This is an agenda that teachers, parents, and students at every educational level should adopt. It challenges us to think about how these values could be taught creatively. What readings, discussions, and assignments would be appropriate for elementary children? For high-school students? For college students?

Educators and the "consumers" of education would, indeed, benefit from clear thinking about values, ethics, and morality. As New Hampshire high school teacher Margaret Carlson puts it, "There are some values--like courage and honesty, responsibility and self-control--that really aren't debatable. Getting away from them has impoverished our people."

Hence, it is clear that in addition to a curriculum that teaches about civil society, we need schools and colleges that are themselves models of civil society--with value systems that are solid and courageous. Our educational institutions should teach about values, but they should also adopt, promote, and defend a set of traditional American values such as that outlined above.

To be self-consciously committed to teaching values in our schools and colleges admittedly runs the risk of slipping into a self-justifying political correctness. Can we teach values without politicizing the campus?

THE DANGERS OF THE POLITICIZATION OF EDUCATION

One of the most bizarre ironies of life on America's college campuses today is the contrast between the predominant liberalism of most faculty members and the moderate conservatism of most students. A 1989 Carnegie Foundation study found that philosophically liberal professors outnumbered conservative faculty members by 2-to-1. In the humanities, the ratio was almost 4-to-1.

Students, by contrast, register to vote as Republicans and Democrats in roughly equal numbers. In other words, college students more nearly reflect the political orientation of the general population. In fact, by some measures, students are slightly more conservative than their elders.

So, what's happening on campus these days? The answer may surprise you: a radical politicization of the curriculum, an attack on standards, truth, and merit, an effort to transform totally the institutions of higher education in the name of "multiculturalism" and "diversity."

How can we guard against the politicization of academic life today? The problem is acute on our college campuses but it is also real in our schools, and even reaches into the lower grades.

By looking at the problem of political correctness on college campuses, perhaps we can gain insights that apply throughout the educational arena and that will guide us in making our schools and colleges genuinely civic institutions.

In a groundbreaking book, *Illiberal Education,* Dinesh D'Souza has catalogued the disturbing trends now sweeping American campuses. D'Souza, an iconoclastic young researcher of East Indian descent, found that today's leading universities often teach that "standards and values are arbitrary, and the ideal of an educated person is largely a figment of bourgeois white male ideology," that "individual rights . . . should be subordinated to the claims of group interest," and that "the multiracial society cannot be based on fair rules that apply to every person, but must rather be constructed through a forced rationing of power among separatist racial groups."

The multiculturalist revolution manifests itself through a rigid system of reverse discrimination that gives special privileges to members of selected ethnic groups, women, and homosexuals--a system that distorts the process by which students are admitted to schools and colleges, and faculty members are hired, retained, and tenured. The revolution often enforces a dogmatic philosophy that denigrates the "great books" of Western civilization and excludes them from the curriculum in favor of victims' literature from the Third World. Ironically, today's multiculturalist curriculum reformers are as hostile toward non-Western classics such as Confucius and the Koran as they are toward Plato and the Bible.

This multiculturalist revolution seeks to impose a set of beliefs and attitudes known as political correctness and is willing to subordinate freedom of speech in order to achieve it. In recent years at the University of Connecticut, for example, the President's Policy on Harassment provided for penalties ranging from reprimand to expulsion for "the use of derogatory names," "inconsiderate jokes," "misdirected laughter," and "conspicuous exclusion from conversation."

One of the most socially corrosive practices on many college campuses today is the extensive use of racial quotas in admissions policies. At the University of California at Berkeley in 1986, the mean Scholastic Aptitude Test (SAT) scores for entering freshmen were 952 for African-Americans, 1,014 for Hispanic-Americans, 1,082 for native Americans, 1,232 for whites, 1,254 for Asian-Americans. Since Berkeley attempts to admit students in racial proportions equal to the composition of the population at large, "affirmative action" applicants are up to 20 times more likely to be admitted than Asian-American students with the same qualifications.

But, what about the "beneficiary" of affirmative action? Is not the individual black or Hispanic-American student *fortunate* to be admitted to Berkeley under the racial quota system? No, he or she is immediately placed at a disadvantage compared to non-quota students because the academic competition is simply too much for an underprepared student to handle.

The problem of "academic mismatch" is dramatized in the graduation figures: 65 to 75 percent of white and Asian students graduate from Berkeley within five years, as do 55 percent of regular-admission Hispanic students, 22 percent of affirmative-action Hispanic students, 42 percent of regular-admission black students, and 18 percent of affirmative-action black students. In other words, four-fifths of the black and Hispanic individuals who enter Berkeley as "special admits" drop out.

The tragedy of the individual black and Hispanic students who drop out of Berkeley is that their academic futures are sacrificed in the name of social engineering. These are not, for the most part, weak students. They are young people who, if they enrolled in another college that was only marginally less competitive, would likely have successful collegiate careers. Under the quota system, they are as victimized as the non-quota students who are denied admission simply because they do not meet the ethnic criteria.

Where does the politics of racial preferences ultimately lead? In 1990, the California legislature actually considered bills introduced by Tom Hayden and Willie Brown that could have required all state colleges to admit, grade, promote, and graduate students at the same rate for all racial groups.

In all of this--reverse discrimination, the rejection of the values of Western civilization, the thought-control methods of the "political correctness" gang--there are profound threats to our schools and colleges. As D'Souza notes, "Universities are a microcosm of society. But they are more than a reflection or mirror, they are a leading indicator."

If the colleges are, indeed, a "leading indicator," then all Americans have reason to worry when these institutions succumb to philosophically misguided principles. In a civil society, schools and colleges must stand for a sound curriculum, a merit-based policy in student admissions and faculty hiring, and a campus atmosphere of open inquiry and freedom of speech.

If America can avoid the temptation to politicize the campus, then our educational institutions will have a better chance to fulfill their potential as truly civic institutions.

AMERICAN SCHOOLS AND COLLEGES AS CIVIC INSTITUTIONS

We have seen how America's schools and colleges might help restore civil society in the 21st century by reforming their curriculum, examining their value systems, and eschewing the siren song of political correctness. With those modest proposals in mind, let us turn finally to the issue of the self-conception of our schools and colleges. *Should* our educational institutions think of themselves as civic institutions? If so, what are the philosophical commitments that would help schools and colleges stay attuned to their mission?

In a recent essay, historian Manfred Stanley placed a challenge before the American university by suggesting that it has become, like it or not, "a civic institution with quasi-sacred functions." But, do universities want this role? American schools and colleges are "civic" because, whether publicly-supported or independent, they occupy a central role in the public square, in the "social construction" and "social maintenance" processes. Schools and colleges are "quasi-sacred" because they aspire to a holistic vision of truth and the good, in the classical sense of the philosophers, with or without a theological-transcendent referent.

Furthermore, our schools and colleges are profoundly ambivalent about their civic and quasi-sacred character. After all, the present situation arose as much from social circumstances as from a conscious attempt by administrators and faculty to make these institutions a matrix of public value-formation. Observers of America's schools and colleges will immediately see several obstacles that would mitigate against their success as keepers of the civic health of America. But properly understood, these obstacles can become opportunities for American schools and colleges.

The first obstacle is excessive social differentiation. Excessive social differentiation occurs when schools and colleges become psychologically divorced from the rest of society. Excessive social differentiation, or institutional compartmentalization, occurs when specialized institutions generate their own meaning systems and, thus, their own competing public philosophies. Several types of institutions have, on occasion, stumbled over this obstacle: the professions, corporations, the polity, religious communities, the media, labor unions, and voluntary associations. Indeed, when the various institutions in a pluralistic society have radically different visions of reality, dislocation and even revolution can result. The most recent such period in American history was the 1960s, but there have been other similar periods, such as the Revolutionary era and the Civil War.

Insofar as our schools and colleges become excessively socially differentiated from the rest of society, they will fail to fulfill their duty as civic institutions. But, social differentiation can also become an opportunity for the university and for society when it is made the focus of a pedagogical strategy that examines all societal phenomena as interdependently determined. In other words, differentiation need not and should not become excessive or lead to compartmentalization. We ought to teach young people that, just as there are three branches of government--executive, legislative, and judicial--there are three sectors of society--the political, the economic, and the moral-cultural. (Schools and colleges belong primarily to the moral-cultural order.) Like government, these sectors do and should operate in a check-and-balance relationship to each other. The genius of our system is *freedom*: in politics freedom means democracy, in economics it means market choice, in culture it means pluralism, tolerance without relativism.

Professionalism is a second obstacle for schools and colleges that seek to be civic institutions. A false view of professionalism breeds contempt for ordinary citizens and a jargon that insulates the professional from his or her "customer/clients." The wrong kind of professionalism can become a vehicle for institutional compartmentalization and a form of self-justifying *gnosis* that is immune to all external criticism. But, professionalism can become an opportunity rather than an obstacle when faculty and curricula emphasize the historical roots of the idea of a profession. The medieval monastics were the first "professionals" because they professed a belief, they served a cause (the Christian evangelization of society), and they saw themselves as promoting the common good. The Reformation emphasized *vocation*, a parallel concept. But as "professional" came to mean "expert," the idea was subtly modified to connote a function independent of, and sometimes even preying upon, society. Schools and colleges must recover the authentic notion of professionalism as vocation in the service of the common good.

Third, the idea of the school or college as a civic institution is sometimes hampered by confused notions of citizenship. Does a belief in citizen self-government conflict with good public policy? Does wise public policy depend exclusively on experts, professional pundits, and politicians? Are citizens the passive objects of imputed rights devoid of any positive obligation to community-building? A better view of citizenship would underscore the fact that, when it comes to the most important decisions in our lives, the "values" decisions, *everyone* is an expert. Amateur citizenship is the only genuine citizenship. So citizenship ought to be informed and self-critical, in short, a refined art.

Furthermore, there is no harm in proclaiming one's values as a citizen and engaging in *civic* and *civil* systems. Genuine toleration in a genuinely pluralistic society means, as Richard John Neuhaus said, talking about "differences that make a difference." When this perennial task of civic dialogue becomes real--in institutions, in communities, in the lives of persons--a genuine civic faith can emerge. That is to say, true civic discourse can generate a common set of commitments: to truth, to democratic procedures, to solidarity, and to communal loyalty. Such a "civil religion"--to invoke a term that should only be used metaphorically--will be, first and last, a self-critical and constantly reforming public philosophy.

When schools and colleges teach such a public philosophy, encourage a concrete and nuanced concept of citizenship, educate young people to take on the true disciplines of the professions, and counteract the compartmentalization of social reality, they can and should be "civic institutions with quasi-sacred functions."

SCHOOLS AND COLLEGES CAN FULFILL THEIR OBLIGATION

There is, finally, a role for schools and colleges that want to help restore civil society. They can teach civility and civics. They can adhere faithfully to profound values systems. They can resist politicization, social compartmentalization, and over-professionalization. They can engage their students in a perennial dialogue on the nature of citizenship. And, if they do these things, they can take satisfaction in their role as genuine civic institutions.

Schools and colleges do have an obligation to help restore genuine citizenship in the 21st century. The ultimate rationale for this reform effort is that it is of substantial value to students. In short, our students deserve it.

III. Politics, Law, and America's Public Discourse

Chapter 11

Beyond Governmentalism: The Diminishing Possibilities of Public Policy

Don E. Eberly

INTRODUCTION

America is in the midst of a great ferment in how it thinks about and treats social problems. Many are giving up on conventional approaches to human problem solving. America's deepest social troubles have cultural and behavioral roots, which means that finding solutions will involve more than developing a new set of legislative initiatives. Almost no one is prepared to defend our existing welfare system. Those recommending bureaucratic solutions of any kind possess little credibility. The social sciences are out of gas. The heartening news, however, is that, if history is any guide, these developments mean that real change may finally be in the air.

While society and public policy interact and influence one another, politics is increasingly the dependent, not the independent variable. Politics will always have major consequences and will remain an important platform for debating ideas and values, but politics more reflects than it shapes the culture. Politics for decades has run on the basis of raising ever higher expectations about the possibilities for broad-based societal reforms. The tendency is strong for every new victorious administration to lay out for consideration *the* great new policy agenda and sweeping reforms that will take America to new heights.

There are no revolutionary new paradigms for promoting renewal through politics, which is perhaps itself a revolutionary idea. Management guru Peter Drucker predicted that one of the most consequential developments in the 20th century would be the death of the notion of salvation by state, which has perhaps been this century's most dominant idea. What individual Americans do to advance national renewal will be far more important than what is done for them under any capitol dome. The scale of social change now needed will likely come independent of and prior to political change.

Americans have been subjected to a never ending debate over Democratic "governmentalism" on the one hand, and Republican "incentivism" on the other, neither of which has significantly affected reality in American neighborhoods lately, and which has instead kept the focus of attention on what someone in some distant place should or should not do on everyone else's behalf. H. L. Mencken said that this seems to be the entire aim of practical politics.

The surest way to put modern minds at ease in the centers of American political and cultural power when vexing social problems of the day come up is to change the subject to programs or economics. The language of government and economics is pleasingly impersonal--it is about the things which are quantifiable and subject to expert study and calculation, and it makes every human ailment appear to be one House or Senate resolution away from solving. This is often true whether one is a government-minded Democrat or business-minded Republican.

This fixation with governmentalism offers a vivid reflection of the great conceit of our time: that the deeper problems of mankind can be solved entirely through rational, technical, material means. This conceit has been advanced by most of the social sciences, particularly the policy and management sciences. It is the assumption of much of society's policy elites that the trees move the wind. And so we have amassed this huge and hugely prosperous class of experts who try very hard to assure us that there is some technical-material solution just around the turn.

One should not confuse a discussion of public policy's limitations, however, with more traditional arguments for limited government. A host of government functions remain vital and are not about to disappear, whether social programs ranging from Head Start to the GI Bill or the critical public protection functions ranging from the Forest Service to the Coast Guard. The issue being raised here is the limitations of public policy agendas--anyone's, liberal or conservative--to seriously reverse the kinds of societal problems being addressed in this book. The tendency in America is to translate every public problem into the language of legislative initiatives and bureaucratic programs, which diverts attention and energy away from more vital initiative-raking at the individual, family, and neighborhood level.

Disorder resulting from this hubris is now enveloping the nation and the Western world. At home, many are coming to realize that alternating periods of Democratic and Republican control have not offered, and perhaps cannot offer, what most Americans prize the most: a humane and civilized society.

Neither the private sector or public sector alone can provide solutions for the deepest problems confronting the country. For those suggesting that private sector growth is sufficient, it was during the 1980s, the decade of surging economic growth, foreign policy successes, patriotism and traditional values boosterism, that the cultural indicators either remained stagnant or went steeply southward, as if to suggest that the culture is on a separate track, and that policy tools and platforms are no match as a determinant of national destiny. On the public sector side, the 1990s is being spent containing, not expanding the state, as evidenced by attempts to streamline existing bureaucracy through reinventing government schemes, stemming the growth of entitlements, trimming the deficit, and attempting to end welfare as we know it. These attempts at reform seem to suggest that the public sector will no longer be seen as the engine of social change.

AMERICA'S CULTURAL DILEMMA

Cultural disorder produces problems that are largely beyond the capacity of government to solve. Administrations come and go, promising much but accomplishing little more than minor tinkering with bureaucracy, programs, and tax and criminal codes. The government and the economy are both too large, and the country's problems too complex, for public policy tools to make a significant difference. As pointed out in the introduction, the debate in America for the balance of this century will focus on what may be the greatest modern paradox: how can a society that has produced more wealth than any in history, and been so generous in its distribution, also increasingly lead the world in many categories of social pathology?

Some have contended that human civilization has arrived at some final destination point, some Hegelian synthesis, in mankind's long ideological struggle. Yet, liberal democracies may be in for their own surprises.

Neither democracy nor our market system are strong enough, by themselves, to withstand the influence of cultural-moral forces. T. S. Eliot said "the term democracy does not contain enough positive content to stand alone against the forces that you dislike--it can easily be transformed by them." Russell Kirk has said precisely the same about capitalism. Material foundations cannot "preserve, unaided, order and justice and freedom" and that those who believe that production and consumption are the ends of human existence become materially as well as spiritually impoverished."

Aging capitalist nations must come to grips with what sociologist Daniel Bell called the cultural contradictions of capitalism, the tendency of capitalism's success in producing prosperity to weaken the very virtues of self-discipline, hard work and industry that produced the wealth in the first place. Commerce without a moral compass can easily degenerate into a scramble for luxury that completely confuses means and ends. Alexis de Tocqueville was deeply concerned about a pernicious materialism that would substitute wealth for work, replacing a culture of virtue with a consumer culture that simply values consumption, amusement, and impulse gratification.

Columnist George Will describes the contradiction of those who would see "no connection between the cultural phenomena they deplore and the capitalist culture they promise to intensify." A culture of extreme individualism that reinforces the unfettered self, cut off from community or transcendent purposes, is a culture that almost certainly will push rights-based politics and demands for more entitlements to ever greater extremes. (Tocqueville called it "democratic despotism.")

What Americans seem to have forgotten is that politics and economics are only two legs on a three-legged stool of Democratic capitalism. The third stool--the cultural-moral realm--already affects America's health at home and may constrict her strategic power abroad. Economic and political freedoms are simply empty vessels into which the contents of culture are poured.

Contemporary economics tends to view man as little more than a relentless market maximizer: a unit of production and consumption. By contrast, the founder of modern economics, Adam Smith, a moral philosopher, believed the success of market capitalism was inseparably linked to the possession of elementary virtues like honesty and trustworthiness. Any system based upon a respect for property and on minimal government, to survive, depends upon the preservation of values, not just the calculation of self interest. If market participants have not been moralized by the institutions of family and religion, they will only invite more external regulation. In other words, to paraphrase Edmund Burke, man is prepared for his freedom in exact proportion to his willingness to regulate himself and his own passions, and the less there is within the more there will be without.

Zbigniew Brzezinski, in *Out of Control*, argues that "the global relevance of the West's political message could be vitiated by the growing tendency in the advanced world to infuse the inner content of liberal democracy with a life-style that I define as permissive cornucopia," which is the "defining trend in the current American culture." Brzezinski concludes ominously that "unless there is some deliberate effort to establish the centrality of some moral criteria for the exercise of self-control over gratification as an end in itself, the phase of American preponderance may not last long, despite the absence of any self-evident replacement."

Brzezinski has said that history has not ended, but has become compressed, it is accelerating in "velocity" and is "highly uncertain in its trajectory." America, he says, will have to deal increasingly with painful internal contradictions between subjective expectations and objective socioeconomic realities.

All of this is to say that the course of America, domestically and abroad, will be determined less by traditional economic indicators and more by social reality: the social capital that is comprised of human character, competence, and values. What Brzezinski recognizes is that society has always been linked to spiritual and moral foundations. Only recently have we dared think otherwise. From the period of the nation's Founding, through bouts of crisis as well as bursts of social progress, America saw itself as undergirded, empowered and ennobled by a guiding hand that has been spiritual, not simply technical or rational.

THE POLICY CONSEQUENCES OF SOCIAL DECAY

Politics is more shaped by, than it shapes, social realities. Thus, we should look to changes in individual and social behavior, as well as changes in policy to create the impetus for national renewal. The current issues of health care, crime, and poverty provide examples. On health care, for instance, former Health and Human Services Secretary Louis Sullivan said that if we could eliminate sexual disease, AIDS, premature births, crack babies, alcohol-related injuries and deaths, and drug-related violence, health care costs would be brought down dramatically.

The most intractable and costly social problem in America may be crime. Per capita spending on prisons has increased 400 percent over the past 20 years. In the 1980s alone, America spent 30 billion dollars doubling its prison capacity. Over one million Americans go to sleep behind bars--more than any nation, with only South Africa and the former Soviet Union coming close. Like so many policy debates, the debate about crime is governed more by partisan needs than any real grounding in reality. Political promises to reduce crime center mostly on the need to "lock 'em up," which wrongly assumes that Americans are willing to pay any price for any amount of prison space, even though corrections spending is already the fastest growing category of state government budgets, with no end in sight.

Governors, mayors, and police department chiefs who are supposed to be the recipients of all this money are privately indicating that no amount of increased money or personnel will be sufficient to stem the tide of crime. Dismissing crime as a function of too few convictions and incarcerations on the one hand, or too few programs to combat joblessness, poverty and illiteracy on the other, (deterrence versus prevention) is to miss the point. Neither squares with the evidence of history.

America's leading crime expert James Q. Wilson has written extensively on the root causes of crime. Wilson searched for correlations between outbursts of criminal violence and economic deprivation. Paradoxically it was during the times of economic dislocation--for example the industrial revolution, rapid urbanization at the turn of the century, and the depression--that crime significantly decreased. Wilson found that crime is, in large measure, not a function of money, but rather of changing morality. Crime will not be significantly reduced until the institutions that impart character, particularly the family, are rebuilt.

As the makeup of the prison population demonstrates, crime is frequently a direct outcome of the weakening of the family and other social institutions. Family scholar Barbara Dafoe Whitehead has said that the relationship between crime and one-parent families is so strong that "controlling for family configuration erases the relationship between race and crime, and low income and crime." Seventy percent of the occupants of juvenile detention centers are from fatherless families. The failure in family life could not have a greater impact on children, one in four of whom live in poverty. A recent Unicef report names America as a leader in child poverty and youth homicide. The U.S. poverty rate is twice that of any other industrial nation; the homicide rate five times that of its nearest competitor Canada.

No one chooses poverty, but the gap between rich and poor would be substantially narrowed, and American society would be significantly more just and fair, if behavioral reforms could be promoted. According to the National Commission on Children, chaired by Senator Jay Rockefeller, while 43 percent of mother-only families live below the poverty level, only seven percent of two parent families are poor. Poverty, particularly its length and duration, is very heavily influenced by a person's decisions in the area of education, family, and work ethic. This is not to dismiss the very real hardship associated with the loss of manufacturing jobs to the suburbs, the South, and places like Singapore. Since the 1960s, low-skilled urban residents dependent upon factory jobs have been dramatically worse off by the transition from a manufacturing economy to service and technology. But these realities have not prevented newly arriving immigrants from prospering under the same harsh economic circumstances. In fact, differences between one group and another, even taking remaining racism and economic deprivation into account, are differences rooted in large part in behavior.

Once again, the debate about poverty in America is almost completely focused on the failed incentives of the welfare state. Liberals blame the slashing of programs in the 1980s and the lack of good jobs and good wages, health care and other programs. Conservatives such as Charles Murray, explain dependency as the legacy of an ill conceived welfare state and distorted incentives. These polar positions have something in common, according to Boston University economist Glenn Loury. They both implicitly assume that "economic factors lie behind the behavioral problems. . . . Both points of view suggest that behavioral problems in the ghetto can be cured without, by changing government policy, by getting the incentives right. Both smack of mechanistic determinism, wherein the mysteries of human motivation are susceptible to calculated intervention."

Myron Magnet, who has written about the cultural roots of poverty, has criticized the assumptions of social policy in recent years, charging that it views the individual as independent of a social milieu. Individuals are seen as rationally calculating, "able to weigh costs and benefits with admirable nicety," and are assumed to be "the spontaneous creation of nature rather than the triumphant product of a long, laborious cultural development."[1] These competing causal theories are completely powerless to explain why people groups of all kinds, today, everywhere and always throughout history, succeeded in the face of the most inhospitable circumstances. Whatever the odds, people have always risen above obstacles on the basis of some deeper reservoir of spiritual strength.

BEYOND THE TECHNICAL, RATIONAL, MATERIAL

In more ways than we may be aware, social policy today is the product of the 20th century's dominant ideologies--Marxism and Freudianism, for example--which viewed the individual as a hapless victim of social or psychological forces. Each ideology has contributed to the pervasive idea today that individuals are helpless to overcome their condition unless or until some structural reform has been arranged in the broader social system. Many in politics believe that history is shaped predominantly by what people in government do or do not do, which is one reason why they are often indifferent to spiritual and cultural renewal. It is the one thing that would be entirely spontaneous, and thus beyond the power of social planners to arrange or take credit for.

Deterministic theories destroy the vision and hope of a people and reinforce the message that individuals are passive clients in a society run by enlightened professional bureaucrats and social workers. Problems are permanent, in part, because an entire class of problem-solvers are dependent upon them for jobs. A staggering number of middle class social workers, administrators, therapists, analysts, and government workers make their living off of caring for people whose problems are never solved, nor really are they expected to be.

As First Lady Hillary Rodham Clinton has said "we are all recognizing that the kinds of rationalistic, scientific, technical, organizational responses to human needs in the past several centuries are not sufficient to respond to people's deeper yearnings, their spiritual desires and the way they treat one another."

Much has been made of the anti-religious bias in our society. Most recently, Yale University professor Stephen Carter's book, *The Culture of Disbelief*, has argued that religiously-based arguments have been rendered wholly illegitimate. Forcing Americans for whom faith is central to hide from it, and pretend that it is peripheral, is entirely at odds with the American tradition. But one wonders whether this is the cause or the effect of our deep public faith in technical-material solutions. The process of subjecting all human experience to the tools of scientific analysis and management is spiritually impoverishing. It produces a desacralized world of cold intellectualism.

Spiritual renewal has been a particularly powerful force in rescuing the urban poor. Marvin Olasky, in his study of American charity, found urban conditions in the late 19th century just as despairing as today's. Thousands of orphans roamed the streets. Infant mortality rates were ten times present levels. New York Police Commissioner Thomas Byrnes estimated that 40,000 prostitutes worked the city. Opium slaves lined the streets.

These urban plagues were confronted head on at the turn of the 20th century, not by an army of government specialists, but by the charitable action of religious groups and individuals. Thousands of families were raised out of poverty. Sixty thousand orphans were rescued and given homes. Churches provided services ranging from meals to job training. Urban decay is not new, and neither is the great dislocation resulting today from our transition from one economic era to another. We have been through large scale shifts before in our economy and society, and these shifts have always produced winners and losers. The economic incentives have never been good enough; there has never been enough capital; there have rarely been enough jobs; and it has never been easy for all but a few to gain and keep financial independence.

Admittedly, the isolation of our current poor resulting from middle class flight poses a greater challenge for our cities today than in previous periods. Still, one of the great enduring characteristics of a country with deep religious traditions is that spiritual change causes men and women to reach out to the less fortunate.

The story today is how people are turning away from the cold paradigms that absorb the minds of academics and policy wonks and are building communities of mutual aid and interdependence based largely on spiritual strength. They are not waiting for new policies to arrive, and their initiatives are working because they are treating the whole man with holistic care.

Most American problems today are defined in terms of the failure of the affected group to gain enough political power. But those who operate on this theory should be challenged to ask themselves: what amount of power would be capable of changing the poverty of mind and soul? Too many Americans still subscribe to the myth that America's rebirth will occur when the right combination of people and policies are adjoined under the capitol dome. It is more likely the case that renewing power will flow in the opposite direction.

A new framework for problem solving must be created that depoliticizes problems, at least those that are beyond the power of politicians to solve. America needs a new civil public discourse, a willingness to escape the sterile debates of Left/Right, where possible, a new moral ecology, and the restoration of the habits of a humane civilized society.

The greatest needs in America are for hope and healing. No policy agenda, by itself, will significantly change aimless and estranged individuals. No policy agenda, by itself, will cause us to apply true compassion, seek true justice, or offer true repentance and healing of our racial wounds, because these are the miracles that no government can perform. They are gifts of mercy that come to those whose hearts have been changed.

None of this is to suggest that government agencies or well designed public policy programs will not continue to perform a vital role. But the endless cycles of debate about criminal and tax code reforms, reinventing government, and reforming bureaucracy have not and will not restore America and civic society.

CONCLUSION

While politics continues to be absolved in its own reality, Americans are coming to grips with a new and different kind of reality: the realization that the quality of life for a great many is declining, and that this has a lot less to do with the economy or national politics than the press and many politicians would have us believe.

Perhaps we are nearing the end of a long cycle. Eric Voegelin was confident in predicting in the 1950s that there are no more great thinkers of the types that altered history, such as Marx and Hegel. He said "we have had them all." Perhaps Voegelin's prediction is about to come to pass. We are living in the midst of a period of change more dramatic than has perhaps come along in several centuries.

Ages come and ages go, and with an age's passing, its political alignments, its assumptions, its methods, and its dominant values yield to something new. What lies immediately ahead for America's citizens, institutions, and patterns of life is less clear than what is passing: the politics, ideologies, and major intellectual currents of much of the 20th century.

It is as if the great cosmic hand of history has reached down and turned the page. According to futurist William Van Dusen Wishard

All the major currents of 20th century intellectual thought are dried up. Marxism has collapsed. Socialism is vanishing. Totalitarianism is discredited. Even the French are losing faith in rationalism. Liberalism inspires few hearts and little action. Modernism has deconstructed. While science continues unabated, few believe that the objectivity of science provides ultimate meaning in life.[2]

All of this according to Wishard, "leaves us groping for authority and legitimacy in the body politic and for some transcendent belief in society at large." What is becoming painfully clear is that the deeper roots of personal and cultural order are those that the 20th century's scientific materialism has been inadequate in treating: issues of alienation and the search for meaning.

ENDNOTES

1. Myron Magnet, *The Dream and the Nightmare: The Sixties Legacy to the Underclass* (New York: William Morrow and Co., 1993), 29.

2. William Van Dusen Wishard, "The Cultural Context of a Sustainable Future," (Speech before the World Business Academy, Dallas, Texas, 25 March 1993).

Chapter 12

Political Parties and the Replacement of Civic Responsibility

Colleen Sheehan

INTRODUCTION

Do political parties have anything to do with good, democratic government? Or are they simply the arenas in which power politics and crafty maneuvering constitute the horizon? Contemporary Americans tend toward the latter view, contending that politics is a dirty business and that most party leaders (whom they usually refer to as "bosses") are scoundrels. Given that there is no shortage of evidence for this view, the American people's distrust and pessimism about politics today is neither surprising nor unwarranted. Although the decadence that characterizes the contemporary political scene has bred cynicism among the citizenry, it has not produced apathy. A study by the Kettering Institute has found that the American people are not apathetic. They care very much about the current condition of their political life, but feel they are powerless to do anything about the problems confronting them. It would seem that the *modus operandi* of party politics is too entrenched and the government it creates too big and stolid. What can ordinary citizens do, really, in the face of this massive, unwieldy Leviathan? After all, it takes so much of our free time and energy just to steer our own little life rafts through the political and bureaucratic debris that ever threatens to capsize us and our families. Such is the voyage of life and its seeming limitations on the cluttered political sea of the 1990s.

The American people are not wrong in their assessment. As a nation, as a people, we have, in fact, been drifting--at first slowly, then more swiftly, and now almost uncontrollably--swept by forces seemingly larger than our powers and paddles can handle. There is still, however, the possibility that we can steer clear of the danger, *if* we are able and willing to see our predicament clearly and face it with courage, and before we are completely engulfed by it. But the republic of America cannot endure, no more than could the republic of Rome, if its attempts to close the flood gate come only after the torrent has rushed through and rent its destructive force.

What has caused our dangerous predicament? How can we avert it?

THE QUELLING OF CIVIC RESPONSIBILITY

The danger to us is caused, at least in part, by overgrown government. Especially since the 1960s, the growth of government and its increasing dominion over our lives is the history of a government that presumes to master us rather than exists to serve us. And we ought not be misled to think that the overgrowth of the national government has resulted in the reduction of power at the state and local levels, for they too have significantly increased their domains.

The danger of governments puffed and swollen by enormous power is not the sole cause of our present, menacing predicament. Overgrown, unlimited government has been encouraged and propelled along its destructive path by the current political parties of our land. Indeed, the distention of government could not have happened, and could not continue, if it were not for the present, reprobate state of party politics. Together, miscreant government and roguish party politics have caused significant damage to American political life. Hand in hand they have in recent years accomplished what no good American ever wished for and what many once thought impossible: the quelling of the spirit of a free people. It is the suppression not just of democratic participation that we are at present witnessing, but the suppression of American citizenship.

Why blame our predicament as much, or perhaps even more, on party politics as on big government? After all, don't we all know that party politics is by its nature rather crass and unprincipled, certainly more part of the problem than part of the solution? Don't we expect political parties to be maneuvering machines of dirty tactics and dastardly ploys, while we at least hope that government will be something of the opposite?

Americans do tend to think this way, but we must ask whether this really makes sense. The broader landscape of democratic life extends far beyond governmental policy formulation and implementation. It begins and ends in the day to day civic ethos, or way of life, of the citizens. We see who we are in how we associate with one another; this, and not government, is the most fundamental expression of our view of justice. Government is simply the surface manifestation of what is happening underneath and all around it.

THE LOSS OF VOLUNTARY ASSOCIATIONS

All across the land we still witness something of what Alexis de Tocqueville once observed, the multitude of private and voluntary civic organizations providing the cornerstones of American democracy. There are families, churches, schools, neighborhood leagues, community recreation clubs, veterans' organizations; youth groups, charitable organizations, and political clubs.

While there is yet a myriad of such associations in America, it would be misleading to imply that they are as vigorous or flourishing as they were in Tocqueville's time, a century and a half ago. Will they continue to form and increase at the same rate as previously, or provide the rootedness, participation, and sense of responsibility to God, community, and family that they once did? In recent years government has undertaken nothing less than to substitute itself for the private and free, voluntary associations that have traditionally and successfully provided the training sites for personal and civic responsibility in the American polity.

In a large and populous democratic republic there is always the risk that government will increase its powers and get away from the people because it is difficult to collect the will of so many people spread over so large a territory. Thus, in order to prevent the extension of governmental power beyond its proper limits, leaving the people in possession of their own provinces and partnerships, it is crucial that there be an effective vehicle to collect the public will and carry the public voice to the political forefront. This is the job of the political party in a large, populous territory, a job invented in America by James Madison, who gave the concept of party a wholly new meaning. The political party in America was invented to perform the function of *the* architectonic civic organization; it was to be the most encompassing and decisive expression of our common republican opinion and civic character.

THE FAILURE OF POLITICAL PARTIES

The idea of the political party as the vehicle for the creation of a common republican opinion and character is virtually nonexistent today. Political parties are simply not fulfilling their civic function in the American republic. Contemporary political parties have failed us for either one of two reasons.

There is the one party that rejects the crucial importance of private and civic associations. Instead, it looks to the legal institution of government to solve all of society's ills. This means that citizenship is minimized to an occasional vote and that the ordinary person and his or her association with others really does not matter. He or she has little if anything to do with shaping the common life of his land; he has only to plead with the government to help him through the maze of regulations. For this party, the government of America is no longer a manifestation of the association of the American people, except perhaps by default, having largely succeeded in sapping their vitality. The people are thus severed from their government, and they feel, not surprisingly, remote and politically feeble.

The other party does not think we should look to government as a panacea for all our social woes. Many of its members have taken to mere naysaying, without much real success. But one does not merely say no to bigger and more powerful government, one says no to it for a reason. Only *limited* government provides the conditions necessary to protect and promote the cause of a free citizenry. Furthermore, the cause of a free citizenry is always in need of articulation, defense, and advancement. What is the purpose of our freedom? That this question is left unasked and unanswered by contemporary American political parties means that there is nothing that animates the greatest American civic organizations, that in fact, they do not understand that they have any civic responsibility at all.

Political parties that are devoid of purpose, or whose only purpose is the increase of governmental power and proprietorship, fail to protect and promote the freedom that is the condition of their own existence. These developments have meant the abdication of the original purpose of the party, and in turn have allowed and encouraged government to chart a course largely independent of the people themselves. The unfortunate, but logical, result is the inefficacy of public expression and the feeling among the people of a pervasive powerlessness and despair.

THE NEED TO REEXAMINE OUR CIVIC ETHOS

We are all aware of the tattered fabric of contemporary American life: violence continues to increase, drug problems soar, and our schools are abysmally failing our young; the collapse of families continues at an alarming pace, the demands to satisfy any and every possible desire are more and more shrill, and teenage suicide is now a fact of life. These are the cries of a people in crisis. They are the cries of the American people, more pummeled and worn than at any other time in our nation's history.

There is nothing more needful for us today than to reexamine the civic ethos of the American people. If there be any possibility of success, it will take all of our candor and courage and spiritedness, and none of the helplessness that has become so fashionable. Who are we and what have we been becoming? How do we conduct our public lives? What characterizes us when we associate publicly and politically? How does the nature of our political partnership reveal itself in the vignettes of American political life? For it is within this broader political frame that the soul of our democracy dwells.

As a professor of politics, I have time and again asked myself if politics has anything to do with the things we care most about. And time and again I had answered yes. Sure, I'd say, politics is about petty ambitions and power and false glory, but these things are not the whole of it. Politics is also about trying to understand and establish the conditions that allow us to give meaning to our short lives, to treat others with decency and justice, and to offer genuine hope to young people whose souls long for something more than the empty rhetoric of "change."

I had said these things with urgency, but I now understand that my urgency was not then born of full understanding and conviction. It may have been the result of relentless hope in the face of the tragic alternatives. For, outside of a small community of close friends, I had never before seen the kind of politics I talked about--that is, until two years ago.

In June of 1992, I happened to be in California. On election night I visited the many campaign suites at the hotel headquarters, finding much that was familiar and, to tell the truth, bearing little hope for our country's future. With curiosity I watched the perfectly groomed young men in their Brooks Brothers suits, each with the perfunctory walkie-talkie attached to the end of his arm as if it were part of his natural body, go up and down the elevators. Dozens and dozens of them, up and down and up and down, in dizzying monotony. What could be their purpose? What was the cause of their youthful self-importance? And then there were the middle-aged women sporting shiny dresses, heavy, expensive perfumes, and Newport tans. And of course there were the many politicians, followed by trails of supporters, who relentlessly competed for the attention of the media--which had come to follow the politicians but could not attend to them all at once.

Then I set off for a gathering of friends and workers of a Senate candidate. I was hesitant because I knew things did not look promising for this particular campaign. I was afraid the room might be almost empty and any lingering people despondent. As I approached the party, the band was playing some country and western tune which I knew was famous, but could not identify. The room was full, and folks had on their Sunday best. I describe the dress this way because one could tell that a number of the people there were definitely not part of the upper and higher-upper American middle class. Some of them did not get "decked out" too often. When they did, they went all out, as best they could, sort of like Prom Night in a small town.

There was a whole array of people who defy categorization. They were homemakers, army generals, preachers, college students, business men and women, doctors, unemployed individuals, and school teachers, in skin tones of black, white, brown, yellow, and red. There was one fellow with long hair in a ponytail, wearing canvas sneakers and a charming smile.

All of these folks spoke easily to one another. Despite the fact that "victory" would not be forthcoming in this election, festivity embraced the assemblage. And among them there was none of the unbearable self-importance of being that seems to accompany the politico set. These folks were simply not interested in the same things as the others at the hotel that night. There was something else occupying their attention. Sure, they wanted to talk about the election results as they came in. But their eyes gleamed when they spoke about what really brought them there that evening.

Self-government, they called it. The story was told in a hundred different voices in as many different ways, like a mountain echoing out the expressions of its hiking travelers and their various experiences. But they all understood each other, and in their shared understanding they had become a community of citizens. They spoke the common language of republicanism. Most of them spoke rather quietly, but with unmistakable depth and urgency in their voices. Their political lives had been transformed, and they wanted to say so. It was for them as if there had occurred a political revelation, and America was no longer the home of despair but had become in their eyes the citizens' promised land.

Their's was no ordinary political journey. They were traveling to a place that for a long time had been hidden in shadows. They were rediscovering the lost soul of American politics. They wanted the senseless killing that has become so much a part of the American landscape to stop. They wanted to retain a fair wage for their days' labors. They wanted to send their children to schools of their own choosing, and they longed for a decent education and life for all of America's youth. Most of all, these folks wanted the government to cease treating them like dependents, mendicants, and servile incompetents. In a word, they wanted to govern themselves.

These people did not just say the word "change," they meant it--and not the kind of change that merely brings new programs of governmental interference by new governmental masters. They meant the change--the transformation--of the *people* of this land into genuine *citizens*.

The skeptic might well claim that their vision is uncommon and unrealistic. Perhaps. Perhaps not. I am reminded of a book by John Barth, entitled *The Last Voyage of Somebody the Sailor.* The book is about the life of a common sailor on an extraordinary journey. Somebody embarked on his voyage because he considered himself a sailor, but it was the voyage that *made* him a sailor. The dangers and obstacles along the way were exceedingly real, but so was Somebody's willingness to face them. It was not an heroic or singular valor on Somebody's part; it was only the common courage of a good sailor on, perhaps, his last voyage.

Like so many Somebodies, the people of this Senate campaign claimed no extraordinary virtue. Their journey to the land of self-government was made because they considered themselves citizens. But it was in traveling there that they truly *became* republican citizens. You might ask them to describe their voyage. In response, they may recite to you their remarkable tales of political adventure; but then, quietly and urgently, they will tell you to make the voyage and see for yourself.

THE FOUNDING OF THE FIRST PARTY

Is the desire for responsible self-government unique to our era? Is our dilemma unprecedented? James Madison wrestled with these issues and longed to construct a constitutional republic that could last through the ages. Could it last a century? Could it last two? And beyond? Might it avoid the fate of the Roman Republic and the seemingly endless cycle of the rise and fall of regimes? Madison asked.

Americans usually remember Madison as the Father of the American

Constitution. They are not generally aware that he was also the founder of the first American political party. Or, indeed, that the origins of this first party were intricately connected with Madison's vision of what is required to make a republic that could last. Ultimately, he believed, paper constitutions and even practical institutional arrangements, though necessary, are not enough. Thomas Jefferson agreed, calling for the constitution to be written in the minds and hearts of the citizens. In other words, what truly constitutes or makes a free public lives in the souls and characters of the people themselves, or it lives nowhere. Believing that republican government depends, finally, on the making of "the republican cause," Madison, with Jefferson by his side, worked to forge a permanent place for citizenship and self-government in American political life. This vision of the cause of a free and responsible people led them to found the Republican party of the 1790s.

Shortly after the establishment of the new government under the United States Constitution, Alexander Hamilton was busy at work preparing documents supporting governmental involvement in financial and manufacturing enterprises. Madison, Jefferson, Henry Lee, and others disagreed with the growth of governmental power recommended by Hamilton. They feared that government officials were not only expanding the means that could be used to achieve the enumerated objects of the federal Constitution, but also that they were illegitimately enlarging the governmental objects themselves. The latter was the more serious threat, they said, for it would result in unlimited government and mean the death knell of free government. Whether or not Hamilton's measures were as dangerous as Madison and others contested, certainly their grave concern about opening the door to a government unlimited in its scope and powers, and the threat that such a government poses to the people's freedom, has proven all too portentous.

The predominant historical interpretation is that Hamilton's opponents sounded the alarm in defense of strict constitutional construction and states' rights. While this is not incorrect, it is only a partial description of the matter. It is true that Madison believed that the national government was unconstitutionally usurping state authority, but this was not his principal reason for opposing Hamiltonian policies. His primary reason concerned the relationship of the United States government to the people. The government, he said, was not operating in due dependence on the authority of the people, and this amounts to the subversion of the fundamental tenets of free, republican government. Despite the seemingly kind, patronizing tones of those who think they know and can decide the people's interests and good, better than the people themselves, it is just the old despotic game of making authority the sun and liberty but its satellite. When the few rule the many, teaching them simply to obey and submit-- that they will do for the people because they cannot do for themselves-- this is not free government.

Hamilton was rather surprised at Madison's censure and opposition in the early 1790s. After all, he and Madison had collaborated a few years earlier in writing *The Federalist Papers*; they had even spoken in one voice, signing all the essays "Publius." What had become of their united project? What was all the fuss about? Hamilton suggested the scoundrel Jefferson was at the bottom of this rift.

Madison tried to explain, at first refusing to make his rebuke of Hamilton's programs into full-fledged opposition to the administration of government. The logical continuum to the theory of republican government presented in *The Federalist*, he said, requires a fuller attention to the role of public opinion in free societies. It is not sufficient for a free people simply to elect others to do the job of governing for them; they must, in the most fundamental sense, govern themselves. Representative government is part of the solution to how they might do this well, for the republican representative or statesman is responsible for educating the public on important measures. But this is only part of the solution. The other and equally important component of republicanism is that the enlarged and educated opinion of the republic is the vital and determinative force in popular government.

Madison argued that in a republic the government must be intimately connected with, indeed dependent on, the opinion of the people. If the public voice is silenced or made ineffectual, then government is left to a *"self directed course."* And a powerful, self-directed government independent of the people, he asserted, is anti-republican. In a country as large as America was then and as extensive in territory as it would become, the threat that government may become unlimited and tyrannical is especially great. This is because it is difficult to combine and call into effect public opinion in such a vast, populous territory. Nonetheless, Madison maintained, this is a difficulty we must live with and find ways to counteract, because a small territory cannot provide the requisite strength against foreign powers and it cannot sufficiently deter unjust interest groups and factions from taking over domestically. A large territory can do these things, but then to keep the polity free there must be other provisions made so that the people through their representatives will rule, and not an independent band of governmental masters. While the government is designed to control the *passions* of the public, the *reason* of the public must control the government and provide the decisive, ruling voice of the polity.

To achieve a genuine republican citizenry, Madison concluded, requires the existence of an effective vehicle to refine, unite, and carry the public voice to the political fore. Thus, in 1792, he founded the original Republican party, whose purpose was to form and effectuate the "republican cause." The adherents of this first American political party saw themselves as breaking with the old notion of party prevalent in England. They were not advocating the organization of powerful and partial interests corruptly tied to government officials. Rather, they understood their purpose as advancing the common cause of the whole, and in this sense the traditional definition of "party"--the definition that seems to have reasserted itself today--is a misnomer. The Republicans of the 1790s claimed rightful allegiance to the good of the whole because the underlying cause of their unity was the republican principle of the equality of all human beings. The sharing in a common human nature meant to them not only that government must derive its powers from the consent of the people, but also that governmental operations derive their legitimate authority from, and only from, the ongoing authority of public opinion. The purpose of America's first political party was the establishment of the free civic association *par excellence*--the voluntary association of republican citizens upon whose majority opinion and sense the government itself must depend.

THE GREAT EXPERIMENT IN SELF-GOVERNMENT

Whether or not the association of a free people could check and control the tendency of government toward unlimited powers was to receive its test in America. The even greater test, however, was whether the people themselves were able and willing to remain consistent to the principles of their republican constitution. America was to be the soil, the Founders proclaimed, upon which would be tried the great experiment in self-government.

Was success possible? That depends, Madison said, on your view of human nature. He argued in *Federalist 55* that "there is a degree of depravity in mankind which requires a certain degree of circumspection and distrust." But he also believed that "there are other qualities in human nature which justify a certain portion of esteem and confidence." If there are not these qualities among human beings, then "nothing less than the chains of despotism can restrain them from destroying and devouring one another." Republican government does not suppose that people are angels, nor that checks on the baser human passions of avarice, selfishness, and the like are unnecessary. But it does presuppose that there can be *sufficient* virtue among ordinary citizens for the ennobling exercise of self-government. In the America Madison envisioned in *Federalist 57*, he saw not only citizens capable of restraint and decency, but also a people actuated by the vigilant spirit which "nourishes freedom, and in return is nourished by it."

The question for the Founders was never whether we could banish clever maneuvering and dirty tactics from politics. Nor did they believe that the solution to all human woes is just around the corner. The baser human passions as well as the limitations that necessarily accompany human life have and ever will remain with us, they believed. It is only folly to pretend otherwise. Despite the realism that characterized the Founders' judgments, they deliberately engaged their generation of Americans, and future generations to come, in the trial of self-government. Fully cognizant of the lesser angels of our human nature, they thought it possible for ordinary people to embark on the extraordinary voyage of republicanism.

It is worth contemplating how the many Americans who refused to feel helpless or feeble, even in the face of attempting an experiment as yet untried, might assess our situation today. Must all regimes, finally, go the way of Rome? Does every people, sooner or later, take together what will be their last voyage? Or is the capacity of a people to govern themselves in freedom always within the reach of ordinary people possessing a common degree of willingness and courage?

Perhaps the citizens who came before us would smile at our last inquiry and tell us that we must see for ourselves, adding quietly, that Somebody once thought so.

An early version of this chapter was delivered as a lecture at the Heritage Foundation in Washington, D.C. in January 1994.

Chapter 13

Citizenship: Transcending Left and Right

A. Lawrence Chickering

INTRODUCTION

Toward the end of his book *Good-Bye, Darkness*, William Manchester relates the nightmare of the U.S. Marines' fight for Okinawa, the last battle of World War II before the planned invasion of Japan. His friends are dying all around him--there is blood and carnage everywhere. He looks at the hideous reality, and something inside him snaps: the bond between him and the Marine Corps. He will fight on and continue to do the job, but his passion and idealism are gone.

Moments later he is wounded--only superficially, but enough to remove him from the field and send him to a hospital. It is a "million-dollar wound, the dream of every infantryman." But later, as he lies in the safety of his hospital bed, eating hot food on clean plates and listening to rebroadcasts of radio programs from the States, he learns that his unit has been ordered to attempt an amphibious assault behind Japanese lines. So he jumps hospital, goes AWOL, and rejoins his unit.

For many years he could not account for his behavior. "It was an act of love," he later wrote. "Those men on the line were my family, my home. They were closer to me than I can say, closer than any friends had been or ever would be. They had never let me down, and I couldn't do it to them." These words are almost incomprehensible today, especially for the generation of Americans who did not know World War II, for those whose only real war was Vietnam.

Manchester's world was devoted to the traditional virtues: duty, honor, sacrifice. In that world, good and evil were clear, patriotism was nothing to be ashamed of, roles were well defined. The traditional authority of family and church was strong, and the word responsibility defined and symbolized a way of life for most people. People focused their lives on getting a "good job" in order to "make good." That world started to unravel around 1960, and it has continued to do so for three decades.

This unraveling has had a number of important consequences. One of the most striking is that it has undermined and greatly damaged the coherence of American political life, destroying in the process much of the confidence that people feel in our politics. The result is a crisis in our political culture that is occurring, ironically, just at the moment when the American system of democratic capitalism has completed an ideological victory over its primary adversary, Marxist-Leninism. People across the political spectrum agree that at its moment of triumph, American liberal democracy suffers problems of its own so serious that no one feels like celebrating.

Although conservatives and liberals point to very different examples of America's troubles, the sense is felt across the political spectrum that something is deeply wrong. For liberals the sickness is revealed in growing problems of the homeless and the underclass, in Wall Street cheating, and in the violation of trust between the executive and legislative branches over Irangate. Conservatives see decay in rising rates of crime and illegitimacy, and in declining standards of educational achievement. While conservatives and liberals view our trouble differently, both sides see a fundamental crisis of values--a personal and social crisis of understanding about how we can affirm our highest purposes, and even whether we have any purposes.

Our crisis of values is caused by our deep-seated, philosophical uncertainty about what values are true--by our uncertainty about whether any values can be known to be true. According to Alasdair MacIntyre, in his book *After Virtue*, our moral consensus has collapsed, and we lack the terms of argument to persuade each other about the great political and moral issues we face. So we say nothing. Having lost our consensus about what is true, we have no way to speak or appeal to our responsibilities or obligations to each other. Instead, our political vocabulary concerns itself with rights, sneaking appeals to social responsibility through a polemical back door. Our courts are thus jammed with people claiming their rights and other people's responsibilities.

Opponents today rarely acknowledge commonalities of interest. They rarely acknowledge weaknesses in their own arguments. Our preoccupation with exposing falsehood as the means of defining truth has relieved us from the burden of having to examine ourselves and affirm our beliefs in a positive way. The lack of real dialogue is intensified because the principal words and concepts we use do not mean anything concrete. Even words like "conservative" and "liberal" have come to mean so many conflicting things that coherent talk about politics has become all but impossible.

How can the word "conservative" mean anything coherent when it supposedly describes Milton Friedman and the Moral Majority? How can one make sense of a word that describes Friedman's libertarian commitment to the modernist values of individualism, freedom, reason, and progress, and the Moral Majority's diagnosis of the modern torment as being caused by the assault of those same (liberal/libertarian) values on traditional virtues? "Liberal" is no more meaningful; it can signify almost anything today. Liberal includes the commitment of the American Civil Liberties Union to individualism, freedom, and rights as well as the antigovernment spirit of anarchists. The longer one ponders the words "conservative" and "liberal," the more one suspects that each means nothing more than "not-the-other."

The failure to mount a serious discussion of our crisis of values has less to do with actual differences between political groupings than with how we approach major issues. Our political vocabulary no longer speaks to the major issues we face. This presents an intellectual challenge that must be solved if any of the major ideological positions are to regain coherence and value. The challenge is how to reconcile and integrate our traditional commitments to individual freedom and rights with a sense of values beyond the self and a commitment to the larger good. The nature of the dilemma explains a lot about the incoherence of our political debate, as each ideological grouping struggles to integrate a freedom side and an order side--the one side focusing only on the rights of the individual and the other focusing on the obligations to the community.

No matter how we emphasize the differences between most political opponents, the commonality of their quest to integrate freedom and order is far more important. As modern people, whether on the Left or the Right, we cannot live without freedom *and* order. Reconciling these ideals is crucial to solving the crisis of values that will otherwise overwhelm our civilization and all we hold dear.

If the search to integrate freedom and order is the dominant impulse within the major political groupings in the American political system, the solution to all major policy issues also now depends on it. Whether the issue is poverty, race, the environment, women's rights--you name it--the solution depends on finding a response to the larger challenge of integrating freedom and order.

THE AMERICAN HISTORICAL EXPERIENCE

Alexander Hamilton made clear the nature of the challenge faced by the American Founding Fathers when he emphasized it in the opening paragraph of essay 1 of *The Federalist.*

> [T]he people of this country must decide the important question, whether societies of men are really capable or not of establishing good government from reflection and choice, or whether they are forever destined to depend for their political constitutions on accident and force.

A few lines later he focused on the crux of the issue: "Happy will it be if our choice should be directed by a judicious estimate of our true interests, unperplexed and unbiased by considerations not connected with the public good." The challenge for societies is freely to choose the obligations ("our true interests") that are necessary for good government. The challenge is the same for individuals.

Half a century later, Alexis de Tocqueville saw a partial solution to Hamilton's quandary in the voluntary association he found everywhere in this country. But he remained deeply concerned. "The prestige of royal power has vanished," he wrote in his classic *Democracy in America,* "but has not been replaced by the majesty of the law; nowadays the people dispute authority but fear it, and more is dragged from them by fear than was formerly granted through respect and love." Therefore, he called for a "new political science to establish new sources of authority and values, and encourage individual responsibility.

Tocqueville's distress at what he saw in America 150 years ago precisely anticipated our current dilemma. He expressed his concern in terms that anticipated the despair many on both the Left and Right feel over the present-day crisis of values:

> Have all ages been like ours? And have men always dwelt in a world in which nothing is connected? Where virtue is without genius, and genius without honor? Where love of order is confused with a tyrant's tastes, and the sacred cult of freedom is taken as scorn of law? Where conscience sheds

but doubtful light on human actions? Where nothing any longer seems either forbidden or permitted, honest or dishonorable, true or false?[1]

Our commitment to integrate individualism and free choice with a moral and social vision of the good life is central to our politics, as Tocqueville suggested, because each value is incomplete without the others. They are complementary values, because freedom without obligation or virtue is nihilism, and obligation or virtue without freedom is authoritarianism. An integration of these values leads to the ultimate ideal of conservatives and liberals alike: that individuals, left free, will choose the good.

FREEDOM, ORDER, AND CONTEMPORARY POLITICS

Defining the political Left and Right became a problem in the late 19th century when liberalism began to take on a new and contradictory meaning. The original liberalism, dating from the early 19th century referred to the Lockean belief in protecting individual liberty against the state. It was thus associated with laissez-faire economics. Later, however, English liberal theorists such as Matthew Arnold and T. H. Green developed a broader theory of liberty, encouraging state intervention to relieve poverty and promote social welfare. In the United States, which never had a conservative tradition in the European sense, "conservative" came to connote a combination of the original tradition of European liberalism and a commitment to traditional moral and social authority-- family, church, and local community. "Liberal," in America, came to stand for the later European *etatiste* tradition, and for a commitment to freedom from the traditional social and moral order.

As a result, the American concepts of conservatism and liberalism each acquired qualities of freedom and order, leaving contemporary politics with *four* rather than two contending political ideas. The Left and Right each divided into two sets of ideas--one embracing freedom, individualism, and rights; and the other supporting virtue, order, community, and equality. Conservatism is therefore divided into libertarian (freedom conservative) and traditionalist (order conservative) parts; and liberalism includes freedom liberals (anarchists, the counterculture, civil libertarians) and order liberals (socialists, welfare state liberals).

The conflict between these two sets of ideas within the Left and Right-- one set (order, community, virtue) coming to us from the ancients, the other (freedom, individualism, rights) appearing only in modern times--has come to infect all of the major terms in our political vocabulary. This conflict is also evident in disputed definitions of "capitalism," "socialism," and other basic stables of our political discourse.

The need to reconcile and integrate these ideas is not only important theoretically; it is also crucial to accomplishing the most practical challenges of governing. For liberals, the key question of governance may be: How can order (or social democratic) Left hope to use the government's powers to achieve social justice when the freedom Left (for example the ACLU), in its commitment to freedom and individual rights, unrelentingly undermines citizens' trust and confidence in government? And in their turn, how can Republicans and conservatives expand personal freedom--which they argue is under great threat from welfare state liberalism--when the order Right pushes for using government coercion to enforce traditional standards of personal morality?

The dilemma of freedom and order appeared in the American experience because of our historical commitment to freedom from the old European order. Two centuries of increasing individual freedom have delivered to us the crisis of values (that is, of order) that we now face. Our challenge is now to rediscover an order to which we can freely commit ourselves--a self-governing order.

Until the integration between freedom and order is accomplished, politics will remain in crisis--a form of war (to paraphrase Clausewitz) carried on by other means. Until the integration is accomplished, conservatives will continue to see the freedom Left represented by the ACLU and the counterculture as carriers (respectively) of moral relativism and nihilism, and the order Left (heirs of the socialist tradition) as authoritarians. And liberals will continue to see the freedom Right (libertarians) as exponents of greed, and the order Right (traditionalists) as authoritarians.

The reality is that each view is correct but incomplete; all these factions await the integration that still eludes us.

The problem is in the loss of agreement about personal obligations, all concepts of which remain based on tradition. In Hamilton's time, and in Manchester's, there was widespread consensus about order and obligation. When there is agreement about personal responsibilities--about what the people's "true interests" are--the problem of integrating freedom and obligation is relatively small. But when obligations are unclear, as they have become, the decline of tradition, integrating freedom and order becomes extremely difficult.

One thing is clear. Integration of freedom and order--or individualism and community--depends on belief in the self- governing capacities of all human beings. It depends on the belief that the principle venue of moral improvement is local--individuals and their local communities, participating in and working through various levels of government. This is true no matter what role is ultimately conceived for the central state. Unless the underlying values of a society are healthy (with freedom and order integrated) those who administer government policies will pursue their own, rather than public, ends. Moreover, if people do not live by their responsibilities to treat each other with dignity and respect, government policies will be forced to operate in a hostile environment that will relentlessly undermine any good they may do.

The need for healthy values highlights a major difficulty we must overcome. That difficulty resides in the fact that our entire debate on issues of freedom and order centers on politics--especially the politics of central governments. Thus it speaks only to centralized entities, almost never to private or decentralized action and values. There will be no hope of accomplishing the synthesis of freedom and order we seek unless we stop vesting all hope in centralized public action. There will be no hope until we move beyond traditional politics and broaden our concern about values to include the realm of the private and the local.

MOVING BEYOND POLITICS

Integrating freedom and order is possible only if we move beyond our preoccupation with negative freedom (freedom from tradition) and search actively for new sources of authority and values--values that respond to our need for choice and for conscious engagement in moral life. Such new views would be personal because they would be individually affirmed; but in giving purpose, meaning, and connection beyond ourselves, they would also define the individual's obligation to his society. Integrating freedom and order would thus allow us to have the Left's commitment to social justice and the libertarians' to individual freedom.

To address the problem of integration seriously, however, the discussion must move beyond traditional politics and consider deeper issues. Specifically, it must consider the question of how and in what personal and political circumstances people would freely choose to be obligated. Under what conditions would they choose order and responsibility? And what would be the nature of the order they would choose? These questions apply not only to individuals relating privately to one another, but also to them as citizens, participating through institutions of public life of the large community and state.

Since freedom and consciousness pose problems for individuals, we cannot avoid considering certain social and psychological issues that focus on individuals. These include understanding, first, *why* people increasingly demand freedom and reject traditional morals, and second, understanding *how* individuals, consciously working in and through freedom, might establish the sense of purpose and connection beyond themselves. These issues are important in considering the search for obligation and responsibility in both public and private life.

Society's need to move away from traditional politics to a politics informed and animated by psychology (perhaps of a new kind) reflects the crucial role that conscious individuals will need to play in this process. The new politics must encourage self-knowledge and allow people to find purpose and meaning by making commitments and reaching beyond themselves. The crucial political point, however, is that much of this process must take place outside and beyond the realm of central governments. It must be focused on the search for new, self-governing institutions at the local level that engage individual citizens to work for common purposes.

All of the major ideological positions in our political debate have parts of what is needed to move beyond governments to create systems of citizen governance. The challenge we face is to reach across traditional ideological lines to develop new institutions.

THE DILEMMA OF NEOCONSERVATIVES

The neoconservatives' concern about tradition and order is important. The great threat to free institutions lies in the possibility that the search for new forms of authority and values will fail, and that people will end up demanding that order be imposed on them, as many of the most educated did during the 1960s. They did this when they embraced the full program of the order Left, which, through statements like the Kerner Commission's report on urban race riots, called in essence for a social revolution led by the federal government. Radical demands for an imposition of order, though in a more military form, are now the principal threat to the newly independent republics of the former Soviet Union. People will not tolerate chaos and anarchy indefinitely; at some point they will demand that authority, even the military, step in and restore order.

While traditional conservatives (including neoconservatives) are effective in warning about the dangers we face if we do not rediscover strong sources of order and values, they have no remedy for the problem except to return to traditional authority. They are limited to renewed appeals to faith and virtue, the same approach adopted by less sophisticated people. Such an appeal may work for ordinary working people, but they are not the problem. Traditional authority does nothing to convince intellectuals and highly educated people, including intellectual conservatives. In fact, society has changed so much in the past 25 years that one cannot even be so sure about "ordinary people." There is considerable evidence that tradition and habit have an ever weaker hold on them as well.

THE DILEMMA OF THE LIBERTARIANS

Libertarians are the political group most explicit in embracing individualism and free choice. Their entire social and political program is based on a desire to maximize free choice. They too, however, avoid the real issue of individualism.

If traditional conservatives cannot propound a vision of order that includes freedom, libertarians are preoccupied only with freedom; they have no serious vision of order. They focus solely on the external conditions of freedom, for they take freedom to be man's natural condition and assume that everyone else feels the same unqualified desire for it. From this they conclude that people who lack their enthusiasm must lack "the facts." And so they spend their energies writing "objective" arguments for unrestrained freedom, which they imagine will put their opponents right.

Although traditional conservatives have been correct that the decline of social authority--family, church, and local community--would undermine the social and psychological foundations of liberal democracy, they stumbled in their diagnosis of the problem and therefore failed to prescribe a workable solution. The reason for this is that they did not take individualism seriously. Libertarians, on the other hand, failed to see the need for order to complement their emphasis on individualism. They focused exclusively on the external conditions for freedom and democracy, confining their concern for politics. For them, it was enough that government interfere less in the private lives of citizens. Unfortunately, focusing on the external architecture of freedom avoids the really difficult questions that we must face to resolve the problem of freedom and order.

Their failure to deal with moral and social values encourages the conclusion that libertarians, whose favorite institution is capitalism, are inherently materialistic. The misapprehension is not made only of libertarians; it applies also (for the most part) to free-market economists who appeal constantly to self-interest. "If there is one thing you can trust people to do," the libertarian economist Armen Alchian once remarked to me, "it is to put their interest ahead of yours." The cynicism is amusing, but it serves the ideals of capitalism and freedom badly.

LIBERALS OPT FOR ORDER

If the Right suffers severe problems, the Left is in full-blown crisis. The Left's dilemma, like the Right's, lies in the apparent contradiction between its freedom and order tendencies. One tendency--the order Left--looks to politics, especially centralized politics, to realize its visions of community and equality. The order Left dominates the Democratic party in the United States because its principal constituent interest groups are of the order Left. These include labor unions, environmentalist organizations, the women's movement--all of them committed to using the federal government to realize political, economic, and social objectives.

The other tendency--the freedom Left--emphasizes individual rights against the traditional political and moral order and, especially in the counterculture, celebrates extreme, individualistic behavior. This position is most evident in civil liberties organizations such as the ACLU, in *avante-garde* art circles, and among the clientele of counterculture institutions such as coffeehouses. It is also prominent in entertainment, such as movies showing government officials pursuing sinister ends with savage indifference to citizens' rights. Oliver Stone is the most prominent filmmaker of this school, as he demonstrated most recently in *JFK*, his movie about President Kennedy's assassination.

The order Left emphasizes obligations and responsibilities; the freedom Left focuses on freedom from responsibilities--at least in the traditional form. One group looks toward politics, and especially centralized government; the other looks away from politics to other arenas of life, while actively encouraging citizens at every turn to distrust their government. Most people on the order Left, finally, are committed to using reason, science, and the forces of material "progress" as a means of helping and defending ordinary working people. The freedom Left rejects traditional bourgeois values, is highly suspicious of science, actively opposes progress, and often celebrates intuition and feeling over reason.

The conflict between these positions explains why coherent Left-liberal government has become impossible. Until a way is found to integrate the freedom and order tendencies in a single version, the order Left will continue trying to use central government power to impose its programs on people--which is all it knows how to do. If it succeeds, it will provoke an inevitable reaction not only from the Right, but from the freedom Left, which seeks to be free from imposed order.

It is interesting to consider how the freedom and order Left relate to their counterpart positions on the Right. One can see in their evolution a struggle to integrate freedom and order, as the Left and Right, in different periods, emphasized first one ideal, and then the other, trying to find the right balance between the two. That they have not succeeded in finding a balance is because they cannot: the issue is not balance, but integration.

The dilemma of the Left in the United States is the dilemma of the order Left. In a country that is inherently liberal (in the classical sense), the order Left can thrive only given an economic catastrophe such as the Great Depression. Without an open social upheaval, it has a great problem selling its centralized policies to a populace that has always distrusted powerful central governments. The order Left's dilemma comes from its reflexive desire to throw money at problems. This instinct is in complete contrast to liberal society's focus on self-governing individuals and communities.

ORDER WITHOUT COLLECTIVISM

In trying to understand the modern crisis of values, both the order Left and the order Right--the social democratic Left and the traditional Right, which are both often suspicious of capitalism--puzzle about what has "gone wrong" in human society. Although they begin with very different judgments about the nature of man, they come to surprisingly similar conclusions about his problem.

To simplify greatly, the Left, after Rousseau, believes man is born free and good, but is corrupted by institutions--meaning traditional institutions. Conservatives, on the other hand, take original sin as their starting point: they believe that man is born flawed and needs institutions and tradition to contain his appetites. Despite this difference in judging what has gone wrong, the order wings of both Left and Right come to interestingly similar conclusions: both blame misdirected freedom and individualism for encouraging preoccupation with self and disregard for higher values. And both, therefore, opt for collectivism as the solution--collective solutions imposed on individuals. The order Left does this in its reliance on the central state, and the order Right does it by urging a return to traditional institutions, especially traditional religion.

It is important to be clear that only the order Left and order Right are preoccupied by the crisis of values. The freedom wings worry about it, but indirectly and in a different way. Both freedom Left and freedom Right see collectivism as a problem, not the solution.

A closer look at these issues will reveal that today's crisis of values has nothing whatever to do with "capitalist" or "socialist" institutions. It is a by-product of individualism, and rises to the extent that a people is modern and not traditional. Moreover, this crisis is most sharply felt among intellectuals and artists, not among those who continue in large measure to live by tradition and habit.

Solving this and other problems that result from modern individualism requires understanding their source. Most important, we must stop blaming fictitious enemies; we must stop blaming "systems." The real source of these problems is in us, as we search for a way to integrate the modern emphasis on individual self-expression with a vision of values, community, and purpose that transcends the individual self--a way to integrate freedom and order.

Capitalism and socialism have a role to play in the search for a solution. They represent not conflicting, but complementary, ideas. The real conflicts are, in fact, *within* in each idea--between the freedom element and the order element in each--which push against each other as they struggle for reconciliation, even as the same conflicts do so within the Left and the Right.

RETHINKING LEFT/RIGHT POLITICS

The political winds are filled with criticism, both from the Left and the Right; yet both sides issue only high-minded calls to do more of what has been shown to fail. Lacking a principle of order and obligation that is consistent with our commitment to individual freedom, both conservatives and liberals call for reform in familiar ways: conservatives argue for less government; liberals call for more. President Reagan, for example, led an extraordinary counterattack against the growth of the federal government but provided little leadership in developing the local public and private self-governing institutions that would resuscitate our deteriorating political and social life. Reagan's was a negative vision in important respects; President Bush substantially continued Reagan's program with even less positive vision.

Order liberals retreat to ideas they call "progressive," but that are, in fact, only repackaged versions of outmoded involuntary concepts of order. Although Bill Clinton showed signs at the 1992 Democratic convention of wanting to move in new directions, in the campaign he returned to the safety of centralized politics. He, like other democratic leaders, had to mollify powerful political constituencies that have no interest in or understanding of citizens' desire for more control over their own lives. Feminism, environmentalism, and other similar movements offer new versions of socialism's characteristic tendency to coerce behavior through the power of government.

We must undertake a fundamental rethinking of our politics. Such a rethinking is crucial now, as geopolitical changes suggest a radical reduction of the state's original central function: national defense. Although liberals in the United States hope that reduced military spending will make possible a "peace dividend" that will allow increased government funding of social programs, the opposite may well happen. The decline in the government's geopolitical function may well accelerate voters' declining confidence and interest in the federal government. This may leave little public appetite for any ambitious expansion of what many voters see as federal programs.

Order liberalism finds itself in crisis for the same reasons, in general, that order conservatism does: because each, unable to incorporate the human impulse to seek freedom, ultimately retreats and embraces a coercive order to further its ends. Each sees opposition to its policies not as a demand for freedom but as an ominous rejection of its values. Each concludes, therefore, that society must "go back." Order conservatives say that society must go back to the traditions of the past; order liberals say the state must break up and destroy the oppressive effects of tradition, restoring society to its original humanness. Both visions treat citizens as children, treat their demands for the freedom to make their own commitments to responsibility as hugely mistaken.

The social problems that are the concern of the order Left are troublesome and real, and they deserve serious attention. But solutions will require far more dedication than can be provided by government spending alone. Social critics on the Left often excoriate Americans for believing they can buy anything with money. But the same misconception also applies to social problems: we cannot buy solutions to these, either. Thinking we can trivializes the problems; a much deeper approach is required.

Liberals have never viewed aggrandizement of the state as an end; they have seen it as a means to liberate the individual, releasing him from the false consciousness rooted in tradition. But after two centuries of experimentation with state intervention to solve social problems, it is clear that, although tradition continues to decline, the state shows no signs of withering away in response. The state has become an increasingly decadent political form, whose only end is its own perpetuation. Belief in the redemptive state rests on confidence that those who run it--both elected politicians and bureaucrats--are somewhat immune from the false consciousness that afflicts less enlightened members of society. This is, of course, a mistake. Although great statesmen do appear from time to time, their appearance is unpredictable.

THE REDISCOVERY OF SELF-GOVERNANCE

Any serious plan for renewal must include institutions that empower citizens to participate in and govern all public institutions that are essentially local in nature. An important element of such institutions is that participation must be voluntary. People must be able to leave, to opt out, to seek alternatives, if they feel institutions are not meeting their needs--whether in housing, education, or other areas of their lives. When laws and constitutional rules encourage and expand individual choices and opportunities for participation in governance, citizens at all levels of society are freed to contribute in a multitude of ways to economic and social progress. When they narrow or even deny choices, the effect can be to exclude a large fraction of a country's citizens from participating in its formal (as opposed to informal or underground) economic and social activities.

Self-governance depends on the idea that people should govern their own lives--that their doing so is good in itself, independent of questions of efficiency. It views inputs (human effort) as having a nonmaterial, even spiritual, worth. This allows self-governance to value both inputs and outputs independently; it allows one to see the contributions of, say, a bank president and a gardener as equal in some fundamental sense.

The self-governing model appreciates value at two levels. One is tangible, objective, economic; the other is intangible, subjective, and human. The two-dimensional value system underlies the self-governing approach to the world, which borrows the best of both capitalism and socialism and combines them in an integrated vision. It celebrates both the capitalist commitment to individual freedom and the socialist commitment to cooperation and community.

The problem of moving to a new kind of politics, grounded in the self-governance of individuals and communities, has two dimensions. One is objective and tangible and has an institutional solution: it is concerned with achieving an end. The other dimension is subjective: it is focused primarily on the means to that end--on a change in the *spirit* of individuals and the community that comprises them. The ultimate challenge to the creation of a really new conception of politics is whether people can embrace, for themselves and for others, the idea of participation, both subjective and objective, that is the heart of self-governance.

ENDNOTES

This chapter is a compilation of excerpts from *Beyond Left and Right: Breaking the Political Stalemate* (San Francisco: ICS Press, 1993), by permission of the author and the publisher.

1.   Alexis de Tocqueville, *Democracy in America* [1835], ed. J.P. Mayer and Max Lerner (New York: Harper and Row, 1966), 1:11.

Chapter 14

Federalism, Citizenship, and Community

Eugene W. Hickok, Jr.

INTRODUCTION

There is something wrong with politics in America today. The average citizen, so the polls inform us, lacks confidence in both the individuals in and the institutions of our national government. He feels a distance--a sense of separation--from the government, and a sense that the government cannot deal effectively with difficult issues. Americans, who have always been skeptical of government, have become cynical of it as well.

Needless to say, there is plenty of fuel available to feed that cynicism. In many ways, American politics came of age a generation ago with Watergate. Since then, one crime or controversy after another has visited the nation's capital. Every administration has had to cope with political brushfires fed by scandal, gossip, malfeasance, corruption, or incompetence. The Congress has produced its share of horribles as well. While there have always been those in the House and the Senate whose conduct has created controversy and harmed the reputation of the Congress, more recently it is the integrity of that institution itself which has come into question. Contributing to all of this, of course, is the anxiety created by the fact that the world in which the United States exists and to which it must respond is very different from the world of just a few years ago, and it continues to change rapidly.

The popular sense of governmental breakdown is heightened, no doubt, by the nature of the issues Americans continue to care about and have to grapple with. Violent crime continues to plague society. Some cities have become war zones; some schools seem to be more like armed camps. Even small towns and rural America have had to come to grips with the fact that violent crime knows no boundaries. In the eyes of many, America is an unsafe place. Education, once this nation's greatest achievement, has become its worst embarrassment. The reform of the welfare system has been on the national agenda virtually since that system was established. More recently, reform of health care has emerged with similar prominence and surely progress in that area will parallel the fits and starts that have marked welfare reform. The changing nature of the family in America, the startling statistics about unwed mothers and teen pregnancies, the breakdown of traditional values; these represent the most important issues confronting society, both as a challenge to our way of thinking about things and as a symptom of just how bad things have become.

It can be argued, of course, that much of what the nation confronts is inevitably associated with life in a modern, highly developed society. And there is more than a kernel of truth to this. But the fact remains that the vital signs of the body politic are weak, and in a democracy that can be dangerous, if not deadly.

THE DECLINE IN THE QUALITY OF DEMOCRACY

The thesis presented here is that what we as a nation are experiencing is a decline in the quality of our democracy. On a superficial, but telling level, the decline in voter turnout and the lack of popular confidence in government are obvious evidence of this decline. But they are symptoms of a larger illness. At its very core, democracy means self-government, and it is at its very core that democracy in America is decaying. Simply put, the anxieties and lack of efficacy people feel toward their government can be traced to a transformation in the understanding citizens have of their relationship to the government.

In the abstract, citizenship can best be understood as the working out of the relationship between an individual and his state. There exists in every regime laws and statutes which establish how citizenship is defined by that regime. But within these sometimes broad parameters, the essence of what citizenship means to an individual is determined by how the individual relates to the government and vice versa. In a liberal democracy such as the United States, the individual is free, by and large, to fashion for himself or herself his or her own brand of citizenship. Because all individuals are believed to possess natural rights, no special obligations are placed upon them and relatively few special rights or privileges are awarded to them. Citizenship in the United States, in other words, may mean a great deal or very little indeed; it is pretty much up to the individual. The paradox of this, however, is that healthy democracies rely upon citizens for both support and direction.

In the United States, a nation of citizens who make responsible choices and elect individuals to make responsible choices has been transformed into a nation of consumers of government who purchase government with their tax dollars and expect the government to deliver the goods and/or services they have purchased. Citizenship has become consumership. Individual citizens who once were agents for change in society and in government have become passive subjects of an immense nation-state. Today, it is commonplace for people to look to the government for relief from the most ordinary sorts of concerns, support for the most basic kinds of endeavors, and vindication for the most elementary of damages. People have become clients of the state as opposed to the masters of it. They have become dependent upon government rather than government being dependent upon them.

This decline in the quality of democracy--self-government--can be traced to many things. But interestingly, it is a decline that those who created the American republic anticipated and sought to avoid. Moreover, it is a decline that can be reversed if Americans are prudent enough to reconsider some of the arguments mounted during the formative years of the Republic and to seek ways of applying those arguments to contemporary politics.

THE INNOVATION OF FEDERALISM

It is an overstatement to say the U.S. Constitution is nothing but a bundle of compromises. Those who gathered in Philadelphia in 1787 were not only practical men of politics, they were also students of public affairs and history and political theory. The Constitution they created reflected this, as much as the need to forge a compromise that might work. One of the principal features of that compromise was one of the novel inventions of the Constitutional Convention: federalism.

The debate over the definition of the relationship between the states and the new central government not only captured the attention of the delegates to the Philadelphia Convention, it also was the overriding debate

among those who would decide the fate of the Philadelphia constitution--
the delegates to the various state ratification conventions. While it is
unnecessary to dwell on all the issues in those debates, it is instructive to
consider how the arguments mounted during the ratification period
sprouted from two very different approaches to government in general and
embraced differing understandings of citizenship, community, and
individual rights. We shall see that the issues that led to disagreement and
debate in 1787 are not unrelated to the sorts of concerns Americans
confront today as they struggle to redefine their democracy and sense of
self-government.

Concerns of the Anti-Federalists

The concerns of the opponents of the new constitution, the Anti-
Federalists, should be examined first. The term Anti-Federalist is used
here in reference to that unorganized, loose coalition of men throughout
the 13 states who wrote in opposition to the ratification of the Constitution
and argued against it during the state ratification convention. Because
they lost the ratification debate, their arguments are too often ignored. But
the Anti-Federalists' position reflected a firm grounding in republican
political theory and practical political experience. Moreover, most
Americans at the time would have been comfortable with their arguments.
    Citizenship was a critical concern to the Anti-Federalists. Simply put,
good government required an informed, engaged, vigorous citizenry. The
only way to accomplish this was through structuring the relationship
between an individual and his government so that citizenship was nurtured.
People must be close to government, reasoned the Anti-Federalists, if they
are to be able to watch it, participate in it, and control it. A distant
government loses touch with those whom it is supposed to serve. A
distant government can develop a will of its own. Most importantly, a
distant government undermines the political efficacy every citizen in a
democratic republic must sense in order for that republic to prosper
politically.
    In order to nurture citizenship, the government must be subject to
popular access and accountability. For the Anti-Federalists, this meant
keeping government simple. Citizens need to be able to understand public
debate in order to remain interested in it and to contribute to it.
Citizenship, after all, was all about self-government; people actively
participating in the public affairs of their communities and states. When
this happens, the tendency all people have to pursue their own individual

self-interests can be blunted by a concern for a wider general civic responsibility.

This concern with managing the tension that can exist between individual self-interest and the community or public interest was at the very root of the Anti-Federalists' understanding of republican political theory and their embrace of citizenship. Popular government, in order to succeed, required public-spirited citizens. A sense of what was once called civic or republican virtue needed to be cultivated and nurtured within the society. This civic virtue would be promoted by the interaction of citizens with one another as they sought to pursue their common interests. Civic virtue was what citizenship was built on. Citizens interacting with one another in the discussion and pursuit of public issues within a community in which each citizen recognizes his well-being is related to the well-being of his fellow citizens. The new Constitution-- with its relatively sophisticated institutional arrangement of checks and balances among separated powers, its distance from the people, and its national executive and legislature--was at odds with almost everything the Anti-Federalists had read and been taught because it ignored the importance of the relationship between citizens and their government. How could citizenship be nurtured by a government that was so far removed from the people and how could community be nurtured in a nation as large as that created by a union of the several states?

The Anti-Federalists looked to other institutions in society to cultivate civic virtue and good citizenship as well. Religion was important; it fostered those habits of thought and action that temper selfishness, materialism, and greed. Civic organizations, including newspapers and social/fraternal clubs, helped to bring people together to discover and explore common values, heritages, and concerns; contributing to that sense of community that citizenship is nourished by and nurtures. Education was critical. Education, for those privileged and able, was crucial to molding citizens.[1] Many schools and colleges were founded on the principle that students in a republic should be taught that they are public persons: individuals who had public responsibilities as well as private opportunities. The economic culture of the people mattered as well. Civic virtue, it was thought, was more easily promoted in an agricultural society where the virtues of hard work, self-discipline, and teamwork were prized. It was important to stay in touch with the land.

For the Anti-Federalists, the states and local political subdivisions were the political entities where citizenship, republican government, and self-government could flourish. A distant, consolidated government was inimicable to all of what they cherished.

Concerns of the Federalists

Their opponents, those who advocated a stronger central government under a new constitution, had been taught these same ideas. But the practical problems of the times had convinced them that some modifications in republican theory were needed. They too cherished citizenship, but they saw its limitations. They had come to harbor doubts about the cultivation of civic virtue among individuals. They tended to see people for what they are--capable of doing good and bad things--and felt the ability to mold individuals into good citizens was more theory than reality; and there was evidence everywhere to support that position. For the Federalists, good government did not depend on good citizenship; it depended on a proper regard for the design and structure of the institutions of government. The proximity of the government to the governed mattered less as long as the government had only certain, defined powers and the people maintained ultimate authority over it. Even a distant government could be a responsible government accountable to the people, if it was structured properly.

The product of their musings was a constitution calling for a national government of limited, enumerated powers, operating within a system of separation of powers and checks and balances that would help to keep the government in its place. The Constitution created an extended, commercial republic which recognized first and foremost the natural self-interest of man and asserted the natural rights of man over and above the formal obligations of citizens.[2] Such a republic was at odds with a concern for civic virtue, not only because of its size but also because an emphasis on commerce encourages individuals to pursue their personal interests. Civic virtue might flourish in a homogeneous society where individuals know and care about each other, but in a large republic, the concerns of citizens gradually will be diverted from the community interest toward an overriding regard for self-interest.

The Federalists understood all this and understood the anxieties of the opposition. And while they did produce a new government derived from what they referred to as a "new science of politics," they did not casually dismiss the importance of citizenship, community, and civic virtue to the success of popular government. The Constitution they supported called for a central government of limited enumerated powers that would be responsible only for national/international affairs. It was government that was to be preoccupied with matters relating to interstate and foreign commerce, national defense, and international affairs. Most of the day-to-day concerns of politics would remain in the hands of the citizens at the state and local level.[3] It was there where citizenship might be nourished. Experience had taught the Federalists that more was needed from government than the states and localities alone could provide. Even an alliance of states under the Articles of Confederation was inadequate. Good government required more. But the Federalists also understood the importance of state and local government to the political vitality of the nation and the future of self-government.

Common Ground: Citizenship, Community, Civic Virtue

For both the Federalists and the Anti-Federalists, then, citizenship, community, and civic virtue were important. Both recognized the necessity of an informed, public spirited citizenry to the success of republic government. James Madison, often revered as "the Father of the Constitution," went so far as to argue that "to suppose any form of government will secure liberty or happiness without virtue in the people is a chimerical idea."[4] John Adams, writing to Mercy Warren in 1788, argued that if pure virtue

> . . . the only foundation of a free government cannot be inspired in our people, in a greater measure than they have it now, they may change their rulers, and their forms of government, but they will not obtain a lasting liberty.[5]

For the Anti-Federalists, popular government was impossible without good citizens and a strong sense of community. For the Federalists, it was possible to have it all--a large commercial republic, good citizens, and flourishing communities--as long as most of what happens in public life occurs where the people are and they maintain control over it. Federalism, then, was critical to nurturing citizenship and community, as well as limiting the power of the new central government.

The Question of Rights

A common political theory and heritage among the generation of public men who framed the debate over the Constitution shaped their understanding of the role government plays in securing basic political rights as well. Both the Federalists and the Anti-Federalists embraced a theory of natural rights and understood the importance of government to the security of those rights. They differed on the necessity for a national Bill of Rights, but there was no disagreement on the primacy of rights. All possess certain natural rights that governments are created to secure. It is a theory of natural rights for all individuals.

For the Anti-Federalists, the best way to secure rights was through bills of rights in state constitutions and an informed and active citizenry protecting their rights. Citizens, they reasoned, are in the best position to safeguard rights because they control the government. It is a theory of rights which recognizes a citizen's responsibility to protect rights, as well as a governmental responsibility to secure rights. Wary of the creation of a new, national government under a new constitution, the Anti-Federalists argued that a national bill of rights was needed to protect the citizens' rights against that government and to protect the authority of the states against that government. At each of the ratification conventions, amendments to the proposed constitution were supported. The First Congress, meeting in 1789, delivered what the opponents to the Constitution had sought, the Bill of Rights.

The Federalists, who also embraced natural rights theory, did not see the necessity of a national bill of rights. Consistent with their opponents, the Federalists felt rights were best protected at the state level. Their response to those who felt a national bill of rights was needed against the new national government was that the new government was a limited one--limited by a written Constitution creating a government of enumerated powers. It made little sense to say the national government could not abridge freedom of speech; the Constitution had not delegated any such power to the government in the first place. In other words, the Federalists argued that the best way to secure individual rights was to carefully proscribe the powers of government so that rights would not be endangered and to structure the political system so that the primary security for rights remained at the state and local level. A healthy federal system was the key to the maintenance of rights.

Federalism--born of compromise at the Constitutional Convention--was understood by both those who supported the new government and those who opposed it to be the critical principle under the Constitution. It was critical for a host of reasons, among them the maintenance of the states as sovereign entities and a means of keeping the new government in its place. But at its very heart, federalism was understood to be a means of maintaining the political vitality of the people and the communities in which they resided as well as securing individual liberty. It could provide a way to offset the obvious disadvantages accompanying the new, distant national government. Federalism was understood as a means for nurturing the relationship between the individual and the government, to the benefit and security of both.

Balanced Tension Through Federalism

Defining and managing the relationship between the states and the national government emerged quickly as a political issue. Much of the early history of the Republic reflects the political give and take between advocates of state sovereignty and proponents of a stronger nationalism. The magnitude of that debate took on epic proportions, due to slavery, plunging the union into civil war. But for much of the time before the middle of the 19th century, the federal nature of the Republic was taking shape and as it did it reflected some of the advantages those who had helped to create the system had hoped it would.

In the 1830s, Alexis de Tocqueville traveled through America attempting to capture for his countrymen the essence of the unique character of the Republic. In *Democracy in America*, he provides a glimpse of how federalism was working at that time. According to Tocqueville, America benefitted from the advantages of both large and small size. Being an immense country, it had the resources, natural wealth, and great variety of regions, cultures, and climates that could produce unprecedented economic growth. Moreover, large size carried the additional advantage of national defense; America was protected by two oceans and its size meant it was virtually impossible to conquer. But what captured Tocqueville's attention was the fact that within this huge nation were countless communities within the various states--communities in which citizens participated with one another in self-government. They were communities, he noted, that were nourished by civic associations, religious organizations, business groups, local newspapers, and political parties. They were communities which erected public schools and taught the importance of political and civic responsibility in those schools.

According to Tocqueville, America seemed successful at balancing individual self-interest with citizenship and community spirit because the government was a federal one. It was the vitality of local government that especially impressed the young Frenchman. It was through local government that individuals were drawn into public affairs and a sense of community was instilled that seemed to moderate the natural tendency to pursue one's self-interest. Local institutions placed liberty

. . . within the people's reach. Local liberties which induce a great number of citizens to value the affection of kindred and neighbors, bring men constantly into contact, despite the instincts which separate them, and force them to help one another.[6]

The federal system and vital local government, according to Tocqueville, promoted a type of patriotism or civic virtue that "in the end becomes, in a sense, mingled with personal interest." The citizen, he observed, comes to view his nation's prosperity "first as a thing useful to him and then as something he created."[7] It is a civic virtue born of enlightened self-interest and, in Tocqueville's eyes, it was the great virtue of American government.

Tocqueville seemed to identify two factors which were critical to the maintenance of this public spirit in America: active local government in a federal system and a belief on the part of the people that they are free to be the masters of their own fate. An individual's belief in himself seemed to matter as much as his commitment to community. And in a particularly moving passage, Tocqueville warned that it would be difficult for America to maintain the balance it had achieved through federalism. Citing a unique sort of despotism that tends to undermine democracies, he warned of the dangers that accompany the centralization of government. Seeking to "trace the novel features under which despotism may appear," Tocqueville wrote that, "the first thing that strikes the observation is an innumerable multitude of men, all equal and alike, incessantly endeavoring to procure the petty and paltry pleasures with which they glut their lives." A nation of strangers--individuals so self-interested and self-involved as to be indifferent to the fate of others or of the state. It is a nation in which the individual "exists but in himself and for himself alone; and if his kindred still remain to him, he may be said at any rate to have lost his country." A nation in which individuals are governed by the state as opposed to the state governed by them.

Above the race of men stands an immense and tutelary power, which takes upon itself to secure their gratifications, and to watch over their fate. The power is absolute, minute, regular, provident, and mild. It would be like the authority of a parent, if, like that authority, its object was to prepare men for manhood; but it seeks, on the contrary, to keep them in perpetual childhood: it is well content that the people should rejoice, provided they think of nothing but rejoicing. For their happiness such a government willingly labors, but it chooses to be the sole agent and the only arbiter of that happiness; it provides for their security, foresees and supplies their necessities, facilitates their pleasures, manages their principal concerns, directs their industry, regulates the descent of property, and subdivides their inheritances: what remains, but to spare them all the care of thinking and all the trouble of living?[8]

Such a government, argued Tocqueville, "renders the exercise of the free agency of man less useful and less frequent" and "gradually robs a man of all the uses of himself."[9] It is a government that promotes individual self-interest because it caters to it; a government that weakens the spirit of individuals, leading eventually to a decline of citizenship and community because the people no longer care. It is a transformation in the minds of men that is brought about by the nature of the government. The despotism Tocqueville warns of is a tyranny of men's minds, as citizens no longer practice citizenship while they reside in communities in which there are no neighbors.

FEDERALISM'S DECLINE

The federalism created during the formative years of the Republic and praised in *Democracy in America* has succumbed to the sort of centralization that so concerned Tocqueville. Indeed, much of the history of America is a history of the decline of the Framers' federalism. The Civil War undermined the political and constitutional legitimacy of state sovereignty as the linchpin of federalism. While states would reassert their political independence after that war, in the end, state sovereignty offers little challenge to national authority. As Lincoln pointed out, before the Civil War we referred to ourselves as a union of sovereign states: the war was fought to forge a nation.

The Great Depression challenged the very survival of the states, as well as the nation, and the New Deal solution to that Depression created the national welfare state that transformed American government. With the New Deal, a limited enumerated government was replaced by an active government of immense power. The full flowering of the welfare state during the last half of this century has produced a national government with almost plenary power over the states and reduced states to the role of administrative subunits for Washington. The emergence of a national and then international economy provided sound economic as well as political arguments for discarding the restraints inherent in a federal system. Federalism, as the Framers envisioned it, has been turned on its head.

Contemporary discussion of American federalism bears little

resemblance to the deliberations that led to the birth of federalism 200 years ago. There is talk of "New Federalism" with each new administration. But most of what passes for a concern with federalism is really a desire to improve the management of intergovernmental relations-- that enormous system of programs, grants, and regulations that flow from Washington to state and local governments. The more recent talk of "reinventing government" or "downsizing government" represents the most recent management approach to dealing more effectively with the way government works. Federalism, as the Framers understood it--as a concern with quality of the relationship of citizens to one another and to the government--is no longer an issue in America. And that is part of the problem.

Contemporary American politics suffers from a decline in the vitality of citizenship and community as animating principles of our democracy. Ironically, as we as a nation have become more democratic than ever, our ability to talk with one another and to work together to resolve the issues confronting society has diminished. Even more ironically, as we enjoy the benefits of technology that allow every American to participate directly in public affairs and to watch as events unfold before us on television, we have become a society that has chosen to observe public affairs rather than to participate in them. And most interestingly, as we have become a better informed and more knowledgeable society, our doubt, distrust, and cynicism toward government has grown.

One telling legacy of the contemporary decline in the character of our citizenship is the emphasis most Americans place on rights. While basic rights have always been a fundamental concern of Americans, until relatively recently, a concern with individual rights was balanced with a recognition of individual responsibilities. This was a modern twist on the idea of citizenship, civic virtue, and community that concerned the Founding generation. More recently, however, America has become a society almost obsessed with rights. Political discourse today is so much "rights talk" as individuals and groups assert their rights against government and against one another.[10] Moreover, a concern with individual rights has been displaced with a concern for group rights, asserted by groups that argue the need to correct for alleged past wrongs.

This shift to group as opposed to individual rights is of fundamental importance. At the most basic level, it is at odds with the theory of rights embraced by the Declaration of Independence and the Constitution. That is a theory of individual natural rights possessed by all people equally. It is a theory that asserts what all people have in common. The assertion of group rights involves claims being made by one group against another, which invariably involves inequalities and making distinctions among people. It is an approach to rights which forces people to dwell on what they do not have in common, undermining any deeper sense of community that might come to shape the contours of our politics.

The emphasis on group rights also leads to a blurring of the distinction between rights and interests and rights and entitlements. For example, it is commonplace in the United States today to hear of a right to a job, to an education, to welfare benefits, to health care, etc. A previous generation of Americans would not have framed those issues in the context of rights but in the context of political interests. It is in the public interest to promote employment, education, help for the needy, etc. Hence the government, at the direction of the citizens, develops programs to respond to these concerns. Gradually, however, as generations come to expect these programs, they come to depend upon them--as though they have a right to them--thereby shifting the terms of political discourse and changing the focus of debate: Rights become something one seeks from and receives from government as opposed to something an individual possesses by nature.

It is the popular understanding of basic rights, along with the general disaffection with public life that many Americans feel that attests to the decline in American citizenship and community spirit. And no tinkering with the management of Washington will revitalize citizenship and community in America. Self-government, by definition, begins with the individual. And it is at that level that any attempt to reinvigorate citizenship must commence.

TODAY'S RENEWED HUNGER FOR CITIZENSHIP AND COMMUNITY

While there is something wrong with politics in America today, there is evidence that change may be occurring. Recent surveys suggest Americans are beginning to turn away from the conventional avenues of politics and government and are seeking other ways of dealing with those important issues which effect their lives and which government seems to be particularly ineffective at resolving. It is not that citizens have lost all confidence in government. Rather, it is a growing sense, according to a recent study by the Kettering Foundation, that politics and government as usual are somewhat irrelevant to getting the job done locally. Surveys suggest that as this attitude matures and spreads, there will be growing momentum for "grass-roots" movements by citizens eager to organize outside of government to deal with issues through non-governmental channels. This resurgence of what might be labeled grass-roots democracy is the product of the sort of disaffection discussed previously and may represent the best remedy for the political illness currently afflicting this country.

At its very root, grass-roots democracy is fed by the hunger for citizenship and community that animated political life when this Republic was born. It is a desire to take charge of those aspects of public life that most directly effect citizens in the conduct of their daily lives. It is nourished by the gradual recognition that self-government is not the product of a series of policy choices posed by politicians and bureaucrats and then administered by them, but the product of ongoing discussion, deliberation, and decision-making by those individuals who will have to live with the consequences of their decisions. It represents the restoration of citizenship as central to the health and prosperity of the American democratic republic, and there is mounting evidence that it may become the single most important source for the reform of American politics in the coming years.

Citizens who care about the quality of education offered in their public schools have gradually come to understand that it is shortsighted and inefficient to wait for the government--in the statehouse or the White House--to enact fundamental reforms that will work. It will require taking over local school boards and taking charge of education where education takes place. It will require challenging the educational establishment from within that establishment, pushing for more flexibility to enable localities to enact policies that de-bureaucratize public education, and developing sources for revenue that build on the strength of a community rather than weakening it further. And in those areas where local control of education has already succumbed to the heavy hand of state and federal regulation and where local school boards are little more than symbolic relics of a bygone era, citizens will have to form parent and taxpayer groups that will redefine education in their communities.

Citizens who are concerned about violence and crime in their community are gradually coming to realize that there are limits to the degree to which policy emanating from Washington can deal effectively with crime on Main Street. They are beginning to see through the rhetoric of such ideas as "three strikes and you're out" and are seeking to take charge of their streets and neighborhoods. In communities throughout the nation, citizens are forming neighborhood patrols and watches, police assistance networks, and safe streets groups. In some towns the constable--the uniformed foot patrolman who provides a police presence and helps to deter criminal activity by his mere presence--is making a return. Local newspapers have become instrumental in the grass roots "war on crime" and in some cases have become partners with citizens and local law enforcement authorities in the effort to report and punish criminal conduct. It is an approach to local law enforcement that recognizes that a successful strategy to reduce crime will require the judicious combination of sufficient funding with local control to deal with the unique problems that confront every community.

Perhaps the most influential citizens groups are the ones seeking fundamental reform in tax policies and in government itself. It is no accident that term limitations on state elected officials are being considered across the nation. In some states there have been mini-revolutions in taxing and spending policy. But the real success of these groups is not the reforms they have been able to promote but the questions they are causing citizens everywhere to ask: What should government do and what level of government should do it? These are the sorts of fundamental questions that force individuals to reflect upon the quality of their politics and the nature of their citizenship.

FEDERALISM'S RESTORATION THROUGH LOCAL GOVERNANCE

The restoration of citizenship and community in America will depend in no small measure upon a restoration of federalism as a fundamental aspect of our politics as well. For all the reasons discussed at the beginning of this chapter, self-government cannot thrive in a large centralized state. Such a state inevitably does too many things and does very few of them well. Moreover, such a state inevitably loses touch with those deeper and lasting popular sentiments and sympathies that must always direct the action of a republic. It is a state that measures the public interest in terms of public opinion polls, confusing popular government with popularity of government, thereby responding to the fluctuating trends of opinion rather than the long term interest of the nation. What is needed to counter this tendency is a return to the sort of federalism envisioned by those who created the Constitution; a revitalization of the political efficacy of state and local government. It is time to recognize that not every issue demands national scrutiny and a national prescription; not every national problem is best solved through a single national policy. Indeed, it is time to recognize (as the Framers did so long ago) that most of the domestic problems that confront modern society are regional or local in scope and the purpose of government should be to make it easier for citizens in those regions and localities to deal with those problems.

There is evidence everywhere of the subtle but important restoration of citizenship and community that is transpiring in America. It is a transformation bred of frustration with the political status quo and fed by the sense of decline in democracy outlined previously. But it is a transformation that will in all likelihood fail to achieve all that it might unless it is accompanied by fundamental reform of our institutions of government as well. What is needed in order to truly restore citizenship and community in America is broad and radical reform of government at all levels in this country. Reform that seeks to tap the very foundation of government and seeks to return government to its roots and founding principles. No institution should be immune from scrutiny. It should be reform that is guided by the proposition that what matters is not how much power and influence the government has but how much power and influence the citizens have and how government can help citizens exercise that power and influence.

In all likelihood, reform of this sort will require the expenditure of energy, discipline, and courage by those in government who might very well end up as losers, in a parochial sense, should real reform be implemented. It will require politicians practicing a sort of statesmanship and deliberation that have become all too rare in government today. In the end, paradoxically, the restoration of our democracy--the restoration of self-government--must begin with a renewal of citizenship and community so that both citizenship and community can once again be the cornerstone of our politics. For the true measure of our democracy will always be the ability of its citizens to generate the political will to take control of their destinies and to define the future course of their government.

ENDNOTES

1.   Benjamin Rush wrote, (*Selected Writings* [Dagobert Runes, NY: Philosophical Library, 1947], 88), "Next to the duty which young men owe to their creator, I wish to see a regard to their country inculcated upon them."

2.   Alexander Hamilton, James Madison, John Jay, *The Federalist Papers*, ed. Clinton Rossiter (New York: New Americn Library, 1961), nos. 10 and 51.

3.   See *The Federalist Papers*, no. 45.

4.   Douglas Adair, "Clio Bemessed," in *Fame and the Founding Fathers*, ed. Trevor Cobourn (New York: W. W. Norton, 1948), 103.

5.   See Gordon Wood, *The Creation of the American Republic, 1776-1787* (Chapel Hill, NC: University of North Carolina Press, 1968), 571.

6.   Alexis de Tocqueville, *Democracy in America*, ed. J. P. Mayer (New York: Alfred Knopf, 1968), 511.

7.   Ibid., 233.

8.   Ibid., 692.

9.   Ibid.

10.   See Mary Ann Glendon, *Rights Talk* (New York: The Free Press, 1991).

IV. American Civil Institutions

Chapter 15

Man, Woman, and the Family: Difference and Dependency in the American Conversation

Barbara Dafoe Whitehead and David G. Blankenhorn

The world is divided into two very distinct classes of people: men and women. Neither can exist without the other and, practically speaking, significant accomplishment by either alone is impossible. Is it not good sense, therefore, for us to be concerned about how they live together and whether this common life promotes the accomplishment and happiness of each?

Paul Sayre, 1939

SEXUAL IDENTITY IN THE PUBLIC SQUARE

What is the meaning and role of gender in America's current policy debate and public discourse? Few topics are more important, for what is ultimately at stake is nothing less than how we raise our children and what kind of people we wish to be.

Yet it is also a dangerous, almost forbidden topic. Indeed, to say anything interesting about this subject is probably to give offense to much of our nation's policy and opinion elite. For ironically, in a society that ·purports great interest in all things sexual, our elite discussion of gender policies is almost quaintly repressed and sublimated, governed primarily by taboo, euphemism, and silence, and undergirded by a cast-iron orthodoxy that insists on the fundamental social irrelevance of sexual differences between women and men.

In comparison, our private, grass roots discourse is much more pluralistic and, on the whole, much more open and direct about gender differences. In fact, we surmise that elite conversations on this topic in Washington, D.C. and Los Angeles would be much improved if they sounded more like kitchen table conversations in Paducah and Omaha.

We focus here primarily on the policy debates and public discourse surrounding marriage and parenthood. Certainly other issues, such as adolescent sexuality or care for the aged, are also relevant. But viewed from the vantage point of public policy, we submit that the two most important things to know about man and woman are that they get married and have children.

We agree with the opening quotation of Paul Sayre, founding president of the National Council on Family Relations. While we do not uncritically accept the separate-spheres gender philosophy of our parents' and grandparents' generations, we do believe that, on the whole, our own generation's prevailing gender philosophy--typified by its adamant denial of difference and dependency--has harmed, rather than helped, the search for a "common life" for man and woman that promotes "the accomplishment and happiness of each."

Specifically, we believe that current public discourse on gender policies is dominated by twin ideals of androgyny and expressive individualism. The result is a public philosophy that undermines families, neglects children, and makes individual adult happiness more difficult to achieve. The solution is a public philosophy that seeks to improve the social ecology of family life. These are large claims. Let us explain.

HUSBANDS AND WIVES

Our culture's transvaluation of the marital bond over the past three decades constitutes the most socially consequential change in family life in this century. Indeed, Lawrence Stone, in *Road to Divorce*, describes the recent transformation in the West from "largely non-separating and non-divorcing" societies to "separating and divorcing" ones as "perhaps the most profound and far-reaching social change to have occurred in the last five hundred years."[1]

In the United States in 1960, there were 35 divorced persons for every 1,000 married persons. Today there are 142--a 406 percent increase in 30 years.[2] During that same period, the proportion of children living with only one parent jumped from nine percent to 25 percent.[3] Between 1960 and 1985, the percentage of all childbirths occurring outside of marriage increased from five to 22 percent;[4] the percentage of teenage mothers who were unmarried increased from 15 to 58 percent;[5] and the overall proportion of American adult life spent in residence with both a spouse and at least one child dropped from 62 percent, the highest in our nation's history, to 43 percent, the lowest in our history.[6]

These numbers reflect the twin processes of deinstitutionalization and dejuridification. The former denotes the erosion of marriage as a social institution embodying widely shared moral values. The latter refers to the shrinking of the legal regulation of marriage, which assists deinstitutionalization by legally transforming marriage from a binding social commitment to an essentially private, freely terminable lifestyle option.[7] In essence, divorce has become a "right"--less a judicial issue than an administrative procedure.

For some time now, the social consequences of this rapid transformation have prompted popular anxiety and alarm. More recently, even elite discourse, including influential scholarship, has recognized the profound social costs, especially as regards the well-being of children, of the divorce revolution and the redefinition of marriage.[8]

What caused this momentous change? More specifically, what is the relationship of contemporary sexual identity--the meaning and role of gender in our culture--to this transvaluation of marriage in our time?

Let us begin by looking at language. Consider the single most important new word to emerge in our public discourse during this phenomenon: "no-fault." Almost all of our grandparents, as well as most of our parents, would be amazed and distressed by any claim that the act of marital dissolution is largely unconnected to issues of fault and morality. Yet in 1969, California became the first state--indeed, the first jurisdiction in the Western world--to eliminate all fault-based grounds for divorce. Over the next 15 years, this new type of divorce law--and this new word--spread rapidly across the country. By 1987, 40 states plus the Distict of Columbia had revised their divorce laws in ways that, according to Mary Ann Glendon, tilted "decidedly toward easy nonfault divorce."[9]

During this time in the United States, Glendon continues:

[T]he "no-fault" idea blended readily with the psychological jargon that already had such a strong influence on how Americans think about their personal relationships . . . [and] fit neatly into an increasingly popular mode of discourse in which values are treated as matters of taste, feelings of guilt are regarded as unhealthy, and an individual's primary responsibility is assumed to be to himself.[10]

The ideology and practice of no-fault thus transforms marriage both personally and socially. Personally, the no-fault idea tells us that, when a marriage ends, no one is to blame. People change; people grow apart; people must above all pursue their own happiness. These are facts, not to be censured or repressed, but rather to be accepted and even celebrated, since even failed relationships can foster personal growth and self-realization.

Socially, the terminology of no-fault tells us that marital formation and dissolution is a private matter, designed essentially for the fulfillment of the individual spouses. Other prospective stakeholders in the relationship--such as children or even the society as a whole--are understood to be at best minority shareholders whose claims should be effectively without standing and therefore unenforceable.

This idea stands in sharp contrast to the common wisdom of our parents' generation, perhaps best summarized in a famous essay by Roscoe Pound, who insisted that family law "must distinguish the individual interests in domestic relations from the social interest in the family and marriage as social institutions." This social interest is twofold: "the maintenance of the family as a social institution" and "the protection of dependent persons, in securing to all individuals a moral and social life and in the rearing and training of sound and well-bred citizens for the future."[11]

Finally, the ascendancy of the no-fault idea reflects, in microcosm, a much broader set of newly regnant elite cultural values that substantially redefine our society's understanding of love, mating, and adulthood. As Ann Swidler points out, these new values celebrate above all "a new concern with the survival, wholeness and autonomy of the self that makes self-sacrifice seem weakness, and self-realization seem a moral duty."[12]

In the largest sense, Swidler argues, our new cultural story of love and marriage "validates adulthood as a period of continuing crisis, challenge, and change"[13] in which "adulthood provides no resting place from demands on the self."[14] Because it rejects the idea of "the self" as "a stable achievement,"[15] the new story fails to "make the achievement of adult commitment, fidelity, intimacy and care themselves seem heroic, meaningful achievements."[16] Traditional marital norms, therefore, are transmogrified:

> The obligation to sacrifice oneself for another is replaced by the duty to respect the other person's separateness, to recognize the other's need for growth and change, and to give to the other in return for what one receives . . . We no longer believe that an adult's life can be meaningfully defined by the sacrifice he or she makes for spouse or children.[17]

Swidler also explores the ways in which gender differences shape the new values that redefine our society's "love myth." In the United States, she argues:

> [T]he love myth is, at least symbolically, differently shaped for men and women. In women's literature the happy ending is still marriage, and love still allows people to find themselves as they find each other. High culture, on the whole, is dominated by men and by the male version of the myth, in which the man escapes both women and society in his lonely quest for selfhood.[18]

Our currently ascendent story of love and mating, therefore, reflects a sharp cultural tilt, involving women as well as men, toward these traditionally "male" (and adolescent) aspects of the love myth--the emphasis on individualism and isolated self-mastery, as embodied in cowboy or detective myths, in which dependencies and permanent commitments are seen as obstacles rather than pathways to fulfillment.

These values carry wide-ranging consequences. In our society, divorce is approaching a rough parity with marriage as an expectation, ritual, and experience of adult life. In a remarkable demonstration of what Norval Glenn terms the "decline in the ideal of marital permanence", the proportion of Americans who believe that couples who do not get along should not stay together for the sake of the children has increased, in just three decades, from a decided minority to an overwhelming majority.[19] A divorced man talks to his former stepson, who is now living with his mother and a second stepfather:

> I assured him that marriage did work, and that just because his parents' marriage hadn't, it was no reason to give up on the institution. He looked at me patiently and said: "Dad, none of my friends parents are still together. Everyone gets divorced sooner or later. Don't worry, I'm all right. I can take care of myself. Love 'em and leave 'em. Right?"[20]

The ubiquity of marital dissolution, though most apparent among elites, has penetrated every aspect of our culture. A national magazine, *Divorce*, was launched in 1987.[21] The *Style* page of the *New York Times* chronicles divorce parties along with debutante parties. Greeting card companies now include divorce cards ("Think of your marriage as a record album. It was full of music, both happy and sad. But what's important now is YOU: the newly released hot new single!") in their inventories of "occasion" cards. A liquor ad in one magazine features two women in conversation and simply reads: "He's crazy about my kid. And he drinks Johnnie Walker."[22]   Numerous religious denominations--including Lutherans, United Methodists, Episcopalians, Unitarians, and the United Church of Christ--have incorporated divorce prayers and accompanying rituals into their liturgies.[23] A new line of children's books includes titles such as *The Divorce Workbook: A Guide for Kids and Families*.[24]

What is to be done? The challenge, clearly, is not primarily economic or political. It is cultural. The problem is especially rooted within elite culture. As Christopher Jencks has pointed out in his analysis of family dissolution among the poor:

> Single parenthood began its rapid spread during the 1960s, when elite attitudes toward sex, marriage, divorce, and parenthood were undergoing a dramatic change . . . we moved from thinking that society ought to discourage extramarital sex, and especially out-of-wedlock births, to thinking that such efforts were an unwarranted infringement on personal liberty.[25]

The central challenge, therefore, is to directly confront the newly ascendent cultural values that are eroding the institutions of marriage and family.   In this regard, the most effective tool is also the most controversial: the reestablishment of the social stigma that has traditionally accompanied voluntary family dissolution. Today the word "stigma" is generally used pejoratively, as are such related words as "guilt," "shame," or "blame." But if our principal negative imperative is to banish the language and idea of "no-fault" from our family issues lexicon, surely our key positive imperative is to reclaim our appreciation and use of stigma.

As a rule, stigmatizing any behavior will reduce the frequency of that same behavior. For confirmation of this rule, ask anyone who would, other things being equal, prefer to smoke in crowded restaurants, litter a beach, or use racially derogatory language on television. Conversely, the fact that de-stigmatizing a behavior will increase that behavior is an anthropological commonplace. Without this type of values shift, little effective change will occur, irrespective of what policymakers do.

At the same time, politics also affects culture. Laws and public policies do more than distribute resources and establish rules and incentives. They, too, convey normative messages. They help shape our public conversation--our cultural stories--about who we are and who we want to be. Accordingly, the politics of family life remains important, especially as regards marriage. As Bruce Hafen has observed, "regulation of marital status has always been a fundamental element in helping human society induce the behavior needed for social as well as individual survival."[26]

Reform of our marriage laws, therefore, can contribute, at least indirectly, to a broader cultural renewal of the marital relationship. The first priority is surely to reverse the legal trend toward easy, no-fault, little-responsibility divorce--especially when the separation is contested by one spouse, and most especially when minor children are involved.

In this regard, it is important to understand that much of the no-fault idea is rooted in the assumptions of androgyny and individualism. No-fault divorce laws tend to assume, for example, that the division of marital property is the principal means for settling the financial aspects of divorce. After the divorce, it is assumed, each spouse can and should be largely self-sufficient. If we look at the real-life facts of gender roles and dependent relationships, however, the flaws in these assumptions become clear:

1. Roughly three-fifths of all divorces involve minor dependent children who, overwhelmingly, end up in the custody of their mothers.[27]
2. Most ex-wives, due in part to pre-divorce work and childrearing arrangements, have much less earnings capacity after divorce than do their ex-husbands.

The result of ignoring these gender and dependency realities is that, after divorce, the living standards of women and children tend to drop, often dramatically, while the living standards of men tend to rise.[28] Moreover, child support payments by non-custodial parents, almost always fathers, tend to be quite low--in part because judicial discretion allows judges, operating on the self-sufficiency assumption, to award low payments and in part because the absence of meaningful post-divorce supervision means that only a minority of mothers receive full payment of support that has been awarded.[29]

These facts help explain why women, rather than men, have emerged as the most persistent and eloquent critics of our current divorce laws. As Mary Ann Glendon has put it, "American divorce law in practice seems to be saying to parents, especially to mothers, that it is not safe to devote oneself primarily or exclusively to raising children."[30]

MOTHERS AND FATHERS

The androgynous imperative within elite discourse is most clearly evident, and especially harmful, when it seeks to suppress or deny the differences between mothers and fathers. This imperative impoverishes our understanding of ourselves in several ways. Most fundamentally, it contests thousands of years of precisely those aspects of our bio-evolutionary history that have favored, above all, the survival of the human infant. By shifting the focus of family life away from the nurture of children and toward adult satisfaction, the new imperative assaults those cultural norms of parental sacrifice and denial that are essential to successful childrearing. Ultimately, therefore, the androgynous imperative challenges the central prerequisite of social life: fostering the competence and character of the next generation.

Again, consider the key words "mother" and "father." What are their meanings in today's elite discourse? Historically, of course, the definitions of these words go far beyond "female parent" and "male parent." The Oxford English Dictionary devotes six pages to the word "mother" and its cognates and four pages to "father" and its cognates. Few, if any, words in our language are more richly invested with personal, social, cultural, moral, and religious meaning.

Similarly, no other words are more essential to our understanding of gender differences. Certainly anthropologists, sociobiologists, endocrinologists, ethnologists, and obstetricians would all resist, on professional grounds, the obfuscation of these words. (So, for that matter, would most babies.) Yet elite discourse in our public square increasingly, and adamantly, insists that we speak, not of mothers and fathers, but of the androgynous and even non-familial "parent" or "co-parent."

Typical is a 1978 parents' manual written by the Boston Women's Health Collective. In a section entitled "We Are Now Co-Parents," they say:

> In anticipating parenthood, whether natural or adoptive, we both eagerly awaited our child's arrival and worried about ways our life together would change. We are no longer simply "lovers," "friends," "partners," but co-parents in another kind of venture altogether.[31]

This deracination of our vocabulary of sexual differences has its ironic side. In a culture drenched in the imagery and language of adolescent sexuality--a culture that tolerates, and at times promotes, the onset of sexual activity at ever younger ages--we detect a curious primness about mature sexual differences. When it comes to mothers and fathers, elite culture shies away from fecund women and virile men and seems much more comfortable with interchangeable androgynes.

Irony aside, however, the substitution of "parent" for "mother" and "father" serves explicit political and cultural objectives. First, it aims at establishing what Alice Rossi terms an egalitarian ethos in child nurture:

> The egalitarian ethos urges several programmatic changes in family organization: a reduction of maternal investment in children to permit greater psychic investment in work outside the family, an increased investment by men in their fathering roles, and the supplementation of parental care by institutional care.[32]

Second, the gender-neutral "parent" also seeks to establish moral equivalency among family types. To achieve this goal, the word "parent" is deployed in order to avoid making any explicit distinctions that might convey implicit value judgments. Thus married mothers and fathers, single mothers and fathers, lesbian and gay custodians of children--all become equalized as the same thing: "parents." By liberating us from the concreteness of traditional familial statuses and sexual identities, the new "parent" encourages us to embrace as equivalents all possible childrearing forms and to remove any distinctions of gender and family form from our understanding of parenthood.

Moreover, "parent" can be isolated not only from gender and family status, but also from kinship itself. A 1991 conference publication from the Child Welfare League proposes a "many parents" model of childrearing that approvingly establishes equivalency among the "many parents"--"biological parents, kinship care parents, family foster parents, group care or house parents, and adoptive parents"--of our children.[33]

Consider another word that is essential to a vocabulary of difference: pregnancy. Pregnancy is the physiological condition of carrying a child. It is a state unique to female mammals and a primary expression of biological difference between the sexes. Moreover, the word "pregnancy," like the words "mother" and "father," is historically redolent with positive cultural meaning: it is a "blessed event," the state of "expecting" and of "being with child." These definitions helped convey the story of pregnancy in our culture--a story that aimed at sacralizing a physiological event and valorizing the pregnant woman.

"And why shouldn't most women love being pregnant?" asks *The Expectant Father*, published in 1964. It continues:

Despite the temporary distortion of their figures, they usually bloom physically and emotionally in every way. They are in good spirits most of the time. Their complexions become transparent and rosy; their eyes shine brightly, they carry themselves as well as a protruding abdomen allows, with a majesty they never had before and will seldom have again.[34]

Today, we increasingly tell ourselves a quite different story. Consider a typical version of the new story, written in 1977 in *A Guide to Pregnancy and Parenthood for Women on Their Own*: ". . . pregnancy is a momentous event in any woman's life, married or single, and it helps to understand your initial feelings, which may include any of the following, or even several mixed up at the same time." The list of feelings includes pleasure, doubts and fears, embarrassment, apathy, activity, running away, and suicide.[35]

Perhaps these two examples represent the extremes. But the extremes reveal much about our cultural narrative. Today, pregnancy is increasingly portrayed in our discourse as problematic and difficult--a source of anxiety, fear, and unwelcome dependency. A number of specific trends undergird this story, including the changing age of primiparous women; the pressures on, and desires of, mothers to participate in the paid labor force; the growing number of single mothers; and our general cultural devaluation of children and parenthood.[36] The overall result is a new cultural definition: pregnancy as a disability.

Certainly both popular wisdom and medical opinion dispute this understanding of pregnancy as a disability. Yet neither of these sources of authority guided the legislative establishment of pregnancy leave in the United States. Passed as an amendment to the Civil Rights Act of 1964, the Pregnancy Discrimination Act was part of a larger effort to secure equal rights for women in the workforce and to provide statutory protections for all workers without regard to gender.

Cast as an issue of civil rights and argued in the familiar American idiom of individualism and formal equality, pregnancy can no longer be viewed as a healthy condition unique to women. Instead, it must be construed as a temporary disability, like a broken leg, no different from any other temporary disability that might handicap any other worker.

This redefinition of pregnancy--from blessed event to disability--reflects a broader change: the cultural shift from a family-based ethic to an employment-based ethic. Historically, pregnancy has been exclusively a family event, *extra-commercium*. It is now increasingly a workplace event, mediated by the money world.

Consider the meaning of this shift. The family perspective understands pregnancy and childbirth as the central event of family life, to be welcomed with ceremony, thankfulness, and celebration. The labor force perspective understands pregnancy as a workplace disruption that weakens employees' attachments to their jobs, increases absenteeism, and reduces productivity.

The old story of pregnancy and childbirth accentuated the differences between men and women--physical, emotional, and social--and reinforced the cultural ideal of separate and complementary spheres. A classic rendering of that story is found in *Anna Karenina*. As Tolstoy describes it, the scene is one of radical separation, with a clear division of physical and emotional labor. Levin waits in an anteroom as his beloved Kitty goes into labor with their first child. Kitty submits to the physical pains of childbirth while Levin experiences emotional anguish as devastating as her physical pain:

> Leaning his head against the doorpost in the next room, he stood there listening to someone shriek and moan in a way he had never heard before, and he knew these sounds were coming from what had once been Kitty. He no longer had any desire for a child. Now he hated that child. He did not even want her to live any more; all he wanted was an end to this horrible suffering.[37]

Levin's emotional vulnerability, his fear and ignorance, contrast sharply with Kitty's emotional strength, physical courage, and womanly knowledge. These are the familiar elements of the old story. With a winking apology to Tolstoy, one might even compare Levin to Ricky Ricardo in the famous January 1953 television episode of *I Love Lucy*--an episode that captured the largest audience share in American television history. Rotund and serene in her impending maternity, Lucy arrives at the hospital carrying her own suitcase, while Ricky is pushed alongside in a wheelchair, emotionally unhinged and temporarily disabled. He is loving but weak. She is strong.

The old story, moreover, extends these differences into the post-partum period. Popular advice literature warns a husband that his wife will experience new emotions; she may, in fact, lavish more affection on the new baby than on him. Family life will change, the old story warns. A new baby exacts new and different sacrifices from mother and father-- sacrifices that result, however, in life's highest rewards. As Dr. Spock puts it in his classic *Baby and Child Care*:

> Taking care of their children, seeing them grow and develop into fine people,

gives most parents--despite the hard work--their greatest satisfaction in life. This is creation. This is our visible immortality. Pride in other worldly accomplishments is usually weak in comparison.[38]

The new story explains these same physical, psychological, and social components of pregnancy and childbirth, but through a radically different narrative. Underlying the new story is the cultural ideal of androgyny. It minimizes, rather than celebrates, the differences between mothers and fathers. It focuses not on family and biological identity, but on individual rights and options. In short, it recasts the experience of pregnancy and childbirth into the familiar terms of the marketplace and of what Robert Bellah terms the therapeutic model.[39]   Accordingly, pregnancy and childbirth become yet one more path to greater individual freedom and self-expression.

In the old story, pregnancy separates women from men. In the new story, pregnancy brings the sexes together. Men, in fact, join women in the state of pregnancy, so that couples versed in the latest linguistic fashions tell their friends that "we are pregnant." Men should join women in the delivery room, since mothers and fathers should share as equally as possible the pain and pleasure of childbirth.

At the same time, the woman in the new story must be free to pursue her autonomy and her rights which are firmly anchored in a very particular conception of female freedom and independence. In *Your Baby, Your Way*, Sheila Kitzinger urges the expectant mother to draw up a birth plan designed to achieve an autonomous birth. This task aims, not simply at achieving an obstetrically trouble-free birth, but at liberating the pregnant woman from medical, social, and legal constraints. Childbirth is a political act:

> Through striving to achieve autonomy in childbirth--the biological act that epitomizes a woman's role as mother, nurturer, homemaker--conformists become nonconformists, assimilators become dissidents, charming, polite, compliant women become political activists.[40]

Yet paradoxically, the emphasis on rights and options only makes pregnancy more problematic. According to Kitzinger:

> [A] woman's experience of pregnancy and birth is likely to be fraught with a sense of inadequacy and powerlessness. At the point when she is bringing new life into the world and a tremendous power is released in her body, she feels most helpless. She is trapped in a situation outside her control.[41]

We are now looking at exact opposites. In the old story, pregnancy empowers. In the new story, it disempowers.

The current demand for autonomy in pregnancy, intended to overcome female powerlessness, is clearly evident in the affirmation of single motherhood through artificial means--one of many "options" promoted in contemporary guidebooks. In *Having A Baby Without a Man*, 38-year-old Elaine tells her story:

> I started looking around me and felt that family life could be different from what I had grown up with. I read in the newspaper that one out of five children were being raised by single mothers and realized that I could and should be able to do it on my own too . . . When I realized that I could be assured of having the father be anonymous yet also mentally and physically healthy, my mind became made up. Here was the optimal way to be a mother in my situation.[42]

Where do these new definitions come from? What underlying trends have produced this new story of mothers and fathers? We recognize, of course, the important demographic, technological, and economic trends of the late 20th century: the internationalization of the economy; the stagnation of real wages; new contraceptive technologies; rising levels of higher education; the societal ripple effects created by the huge baby boom generation as it moves through the life cycle; the impact of the broadcast media; and many others. But as we seek to identify the shaping influences of the new story of mothers and fathers, we do not, in the final analysis, look to economics, demographics, politics, or technology.

Again, we look to culture. We do not, therefore, interpret cultural values as a "superstructure" that can be understood as a reflection of a materialistic "base." Accordingly, we do not interpret changes in our cultural story of parenthood--or for that matter, family change in general-- as essentially adaptive and situationally induced, caused primarily by institutions and material conditions outside the family itself. We believe that the heart of the matter--not merely a reflection, but rather the basic source of the new story--is a shift in cultural values.[43] Specifically, we look to the growing influence of the twin cultural values of androgyny and expressive individualism. Consider three principle tensions in our public discourse which reflect the shift toward these values.

Man and Woman Versus the Universal Male

One strain of feminist thought has been particularly influential in the drift toward androgyny. Most powerfully articulated by Simone de Beauvoir, this view sees freedom and independence as the natural state of only one sex: the male sex. As Michael Walzer points out in his essay on de Beauvoir:

[T]here is only one universal life, and it is men--beings of transcendence and ambition--who have lived it. The fact is that culture, civilization, and universal values have all been created by men, because men represent universality.[44]

Many contemporary feminist philosophers share this belief. In their utopia, as Christina Sommers has pointed out:

[G]ender in the choice of lover or spouse would be of no more significance than eye color. There the family would consist of adults but not necessarily of different sexes and not necessarily in pairs. There we find equality ensured by a kind of affirmative action which compensates for disability. If women are somewhat weaker than men, or if they are subject to lunar disabilities, then this must be compensated for.[45]

Consequently, although the ideal is androgyny, the new public story also embraces the idea of the universal male. As Alice Rossi puts it with admirable precision:

[T]he authors and dramatists of both the mating and parenting scripts in the new perspectives on the family are just as heavily male as the older schools of thought about the modern family, if not in the generic sense, then in the sense that parenting is viewed from a distance, as an appendage to, or consequence of mating rather than the focus of family systems and individual lives.[46]

Parental altruism versus expressive individualism

In *Reclaimed Powers*, a cross-cultural study of gender patterns in aging, David Gutmann describes a pivotal event in human development: the "parental emergency." Young parents respond to the emergency in two ways. First, they assume the gender-specific roles learned during early socialization--roles they may have modified, experimented with, or even ignored before they became parents. Second, they abandon narcissistic strivings toward omnipotentiality. They voluntarily limit their potential freedoms in order to secure the physical and psychological well-being of the dependent child.[47] As Gutmann puts it,

> There is general agreement that parents will, as part of their general servitude, accept deep restrictions on their own needs and deep revisions of their own psychological make-up in order to meet their children's essential needs.[48]

In short, parenthood demands that children come first. Its essential requirement is sacrifice and denial. Its result is "the routine, unexamined heroism of parenting . . ."[49] In Gutmann's cross-cultural studies, parental altruism approaches the status of a universal norm, since it is essential to the survival of the species.

Yet to what degree is this norm reflected in our public discourse and policy debate about gender roles and childrearing? The answer is unsettling. Clearly, the dominant discourse seeks to extend, rather than suppress, the narcissistic tendencies of young adulthood. For parents, no less than non-parents, the self--not the other or the neighbor or the child or the family--constitutes the governing moral idea of contemporary culture.

Even a casual reading of advice literature for new parents reveals this tendency. Compared to the old story, far greater emphasis is attached to recognizing and affirming adult "needs" as against baby's demands. In the old story, the arrival of a new baby ushered in a period of mutual sacrifice. In the new story, a baby tests the parents' own sense of independence with its assertion of neediness. Parents must "balance" the baby's needs against other social and personal "needs." The very title of one parenting manual, *Ourselves and Our Children*, succinctly states the new set of priorities: parents come first.

> We want to develop a strong bond with our child and at the same time maintain our partnership, our adult friendships, as well as our involvements with the outside world. What we discover even before we have a baby is that our lives are thrown off balance once we become parents and we need time to establish a new equilibrium . . .[50]

In the new story, the fascination is not with the developing child; it is with the constantly evolving adult.

Family Culture Versus Jobs Culture

In his essay *The Invasion of the Money World*, Robert Bellah argues that the values and language of the marketplace are invading the family realm and, more broadly, the realms of church, neighborhood, and community. Activities once assigned to families--child care, meals, even outdoor play--are increasingly monetized: converted to services that are bought and sold in the marketplace. As part (but only part) of this trend, mothers, who have traditionally dominated the realms of family and community life, now pursue, or at least are strongly expected to pursue, regular paid employment outside the home.[51]

As a result, the separate sphere of family and community life is both shrinking and losing its distinctive character. Increasingly, this sphere simply fails to constitute an independent moral realm containing relationships and values different from those of the commercial realm. This trend helps explain why women are no longer considered--nor, at least in the dominant discourse, would they want to be considered--more virtuous or innocent than men. More importantly, this trend tells us why home and family are no longer expected to serve as the essential base of women's power and self-esteem.

Precision in criticism requires precision in praise. Certain revisions in traditional gender roles, we believe, have been beneficial for both men and women. Women today have far greater opportunities for a public life, with its considerable recognition and rewards, than did the previous generation. This is good. Moreover, as the life span increases and as the proportion of life devoted to childrearing concomitantly decreases, women clearly have more time, over the course of the life cycle, to devote to work in the marketplace. We see benefits for men as well. Men no longer must bear sole responsibility for breadwinning. With a mutual, if not equivalent, commitment to both the worlds of paid work and of family, husbands and wives who stay together may achieve a greater harmony of interests and perhaps even greater emotional closeness.

At the same time, separate spheres of philosophy--properly, we believe-- located life's most enduring virtues and satisfactions not in the marketplace or even in the public square, but in the home. Indeed, 19th-century feminism hoped to reform the world according to the model of home and family. Domesticating the marketplace, not commercializing the domestic realm, was the central focus of much early feminist thought.[52]

Thus, the current identification of home and family as the source not of woman's strength, but of her weakness, stands as a sharp departure from earlier feminist traditions. And when contemporary feminists attack traditional family life as oppressive, they frequently fail to recognize that men, as well as women, have historically embraced the sacrifices and restrictions of family life as their best chance for happiness and individual fulfillment. In an important respect, the gender script of our parents' generation was intended to be less blatantly sexist than aggressively familistic.

As much as our culture in the 1950s worshipped Mom in the kitchen, it celebrated Dad in the den. Father's Day became an important national holiday during this period, as Hallmark cards iconized the "at-home" dad, with his pipe and newspaper. Television viewers seldom saw the father of *Father Knows Best* at work. We never knew what Ozzie Nelson or Ward Cleaver did for a living. For these television dads, the pathway to the good life ran, not through the office, but straight to the backyard with the kids. As one contemporary magazine article entitled "Are You a Dud as a Dad?" put it:

> Here is one area of your life which doesn't depend on "breaks" or ability or education or money. A man can be a success as a father, a real "dad," if he cares enough to try . . .

As Elaine Tyler May notes in her analysis of this article, "nowhere was it easier for a man to be his own boss than in fatherhood."[53]

In contrast, the contemporary vision of individual happiness and social progress, as reflected in elite discourse, is increasingly less identified with building a family. The new vision focuses on achievement in the marketplace. It is rooted, above all, in the assumption of a fully mobilized workforce.

In this story, both women and men find fulfillment and contribute to the good of society through their participation in the workforce and in their behavior as paid workers and consumers. Of course, the economy of the 1950s mobilized consumers as well, but the primary unit of consumption was the family, not the individual. Today it is affluent individuals, including children--with appetites for imported cars and designer toys-- who are most eagerly courted by advertisers. Mom, Dad, and kids, though still desirable, are considered slightly down-scale, with tastes running more to Kmart than to Cuisinart.

Our public policy debate on child care is clearly dominated by this economic perspective. To a remarkable degree, the debate centers less on what is best for the parent-child relationship than it does on what is best for the labor force. To the degree, for example, that the mother-child relationship conflicts with the mother-job relationship, the mother-job relationship is almost always treated as primary.

This overwhelmingly economic focus in our child care debate reflects, in large part, the remarkable success of the "work-family" movement of the 1980s--a broad coalition of corporate consultants, policy think tanks, business leaders, legislative lobbyists, and others, who seek, in the words of one prominent organization, "new approaches for balancing the changing needs of America's families with the continuing need for workplace productivity."[54] A national work-family conference in 1988, entitled "Child Care: The Bottom Line," elaborates this perspective:

> Never before in the history of the United States has the issue of child care been so inextricably linked with the state of the nation's economy. Not only does the availability of affordable, high-quality child care affect the well-being of the majority of American families, it affects the bottom line of every business in the nation and ... inevitably ... affects the United States' ability to compete successfully in a global economy.[55]

As one national leader of the work-family movement put it, "Child care is really an economic development issue" that is "as essential for getting people to work as public transportation."[56] This approach became truly bipartisan during the 1980s, defining the discourse of Republicans as well as Democrats. The most influential child care report of the Reagan Administration, for example, organized by the Department of Labor, was entitled "Child Care: A Workforce Issue."[57]

Such an approach sends a clear message to both policymakers and families. The message to policymakers is that child care is a matter of economic policy, designed almost exclusively for mothers who work fulltime in the paid labor force. Thus, for U.S. Representative Patricia Schroeder, probably the nation's most influential advocate of the work-family agenda, to argue that child care policies should recognize the role of non-employed parents is "like saying the highway program must recognize people who don't drive."[58]

For policymakers, the flaw in this approach is not merely philosophical--it leads to specific and dubious policy consequences. Most of the child care debate in the 1980s, for example, assumed that the goal is to allow more parents, especially mothers, to achieve a new "balance" that, in practice, would mean less time with children and more time at work.

Yet considerable evidence suggests that many mothers want precisely the opposite: to spend less time in the workplace in order to spend more time with family.[59] The chief policy recommendation of the economistic assumption is more day care centers. In contrast, the chief recommendation of the familistic assumption is more part-time work and other options to reduce, rather than increase, hours of paid employment.

For families--or again more specifically, for mothers--the message of today's child care debate is not to feel "guilty" or overly constrained by the responsibilities of childbearing and childrearing. The new imperative is not to permit the demands of children to stand in the way of work responsibilities.

In sum, we identify three major tendencies in our current public discourse and policy debates on parenthood: the universalization of the "competitive male model,"[60] the denial of parental altruism, and the invasion of the family culture by the jobs culture. These tendencies contribute to a regnant cultural ethos, especially strong among elites, based on the twin ideals of androgyny and expressive individualism. We believe that this ethos is harmful to the quality of our public discourse and to the well-being of families, particularly children. Let us state more explicitly our basic reasons for this assertion.

First, today's individualistic and androgynous "parenting script" is antithetical to childrearing on both biological and cultural grounds. In essence, the egalitarian perspective seeks to deny biological difference, claiming that motherhood and fatherhood are determined by externally imposed and outmoded socialization processes. Therefore, public discourse as well as public policy should seek to reform the socialization process in ways that make men and women equally competent in the care and nurture of the newborn.

We offer only one cheer for this idea. Babies can certainly benefit from a father's attention. (So can fatigued mothers). We believe that "real men" can change diapers. Yet as Alice Rossi convincingly argues, bio-evolutionary theory, as well as endocrinological evidence, clearly suggests:

[T]here may be a biologically based potential for heightened maternal investment in the child, at least through the first months of life, that exceeds the potential for investment by men in fatherhood . . . Mating and parenting are activities linked more closely for females than males.[61]

From a cultural perspective, David Gutmann similarly demonstrates that, across time and cultures, mothering and fathering appear as sharply differentiated (and complementary) activities. Fathers protect the vulnerable infant from physical harm by defending the perimeters of the domestic realm. Mothers provide emotional nurture to the child and sustain the domestic realm as the center of nurture. This role differentiation does not derive primarily from either social convention or individual choice, as current elite discourse would have it. Instead, it is the result of a bio-evolutionary process that selects for capacities that will favor the survival of the vulnerable human infant and ultimately the species itself.[62]

Historical and sociological evidence leads to similar conclusions. As David Popenoe puts it:

> Universally, women have cared for very young children, and men have typically played the child-care roles of provider, protector and back-up assistant . . . [Men] have different sexual drives, different propensities toward children, different perspectives on relationships, and perhaps different conceptions of morality. They also have different reasons for marrying."[63]

Second, as Christina Sommers suggests, elite discourse on family life is frequently at odds with the experiences, norms, and moral values of ordinary men and women.

> [P]olitically and morally, lack of respect for common sense fosters illiberalism and elitism. Here we have a radical temper that often advocates actions and policies wildly at odds with common opinion--from infanticide to male lactation, from no-fault divorce on demand for children to the "roommate test" for marital relationships.[64]

In the realm of everyday life and practical morality, most Americans, if asked, say that they seek happiness through family life, not through their careers.[67] Most women want to be mothers and prefer staying home while their children are very young. Most women want and expect financial and emotional support from husbands and fathers. Many, we suspect most, divorced mothers view divorce as harmful to children. Yet our dominant elite discourse about love, marriage, and parenthood would have it quite the other way on each of these issues.

Finally, the ideals of androgyny and expressive individualism fail to deliver on their basic promise: they do not make for greater individual happiness. Individual happiness and family obligation are not, as the elite story would have it, antithetical. Survey research shows quite compellingly that happiness with marriage and family life remains by far the strongest predictor of personal happiness and overall life satisfaction.[66]

GENDER IDENTITY IN PUBLIC POLICIES

We conclude an essentially cultural analysis of marriage and parenthood with a political question: Should public policies strive explicitly to counteract the prevailing tilt toward androgyny and expressive individualism? To what degree can, and ought, politics seek to influence culture in the area of gender differences and dependencies?

Certainly a case can be made for public policies that affirm gender differences. For example, the family policies of the U.S. armed services are rigorously gender-blind. They accord no special status to nursing mothers, single mothers, or married parents simultaneously called into active service. In this instance, gender-blindness leads to the traumatic separation of mothers and children during wartime. It also risks turning children into orphans. These military policies typify a work-family perspective that puts work over family. Although such policies are hospitable to the employment needs of working parents, they are almost self-evidently hostile to the needs of children.

Similarly, consider policies that protect a woman's right to a job that is potentially harmful to her reproductive system. Such policies certainly contribute to greater opportunities and equality for women in the labor force. But they do not, to speak with moderation, promote the well-being of the developing child.

Finally, our society's new divorce laws, firmly rooted in the assumptions of androgyny and individualism, simply fail to acknowledge, to a remarkable degree, the roles of most mothers within most marriages. Our no-fault divorce laws, in fact, constitute a clear embodiment of the universal male model--a model which rewards autonomous achievement in the marketplace while largely ignoring our social and individual interests in the family and in caring for dependent children. In this case, current policy goes beyond simply the formulation of gender-neutral legal categories. These new laws are indifferent, even hostile, to important social interests.

Yet despite these caveats, as a general rule, public policies should seek to be gender-neutral--they should generally refrain from directly defining gender identities or assigning gender roles within the family, or in the workplace, or in public life.

In the area of divorce, for example, our laws must offer more protection for women and children. Yet this imperative does not require the law to establish gender-specific legal categories. It requires only that the law acknowledge the divisions of labor within marriage and the social importance of childrearing. In the area of custody, for example, we do not have to say: "Custody shall go to the mother." We only have to say: "Custody shall go to the person who is already providing the most day to day care for this child." Sometimes, that person will be the father. Most times, not.

In the workplace, as well, policies should steer this middle ground. They should be family-friendly. They should not simply embody the norms of the competitive male model. But neither should they seek explicitly to define the gender identities and roles of workers. Thus we favor generous "parental" leave, not "maternity" leave, even as we know that most workers who use it will be mothers. The same principle should govern wage and hour policies, employee benefits, and others workplace policies. Such policies would, in practice, affirm and promote formal equality of opportunity for women in the workplace and in public life, while at the same time respecting the importance of family commitment and obligation.

This conclusion rests on the principle of "subsidarity," drawn largely from Catholic social thought. In this instance, the idea of subsidarity suggests that cultural problems require primarily cultural, not political, solutions. Controversies over gender differences are, as a rule, simply too complex--and too important--to be settled through legislation or political campaigns. Instead, we must turn to the institutions of civil society--the family itself, the church, the local community--to direct us in the important task of naming gender differences, affirming familial dependencies, and reasserting the permanent and binding character of relationships within the family.

Budding signs--some reasons for hope--are emerging that the United States in the 1990s will substantially revise its currently dominant elite stories of man and woman. Our culture is now acknowledging the limits and costs of expressive individualism as a reigning norm. We sense, even within elite discourse, the beginning of a renewed appreciation of differences and mutual dependencies between men and women. We anticipate, in short, a new cultural tilt toward improving the ecology of family life in the 1990s.

For example, David Gutmann's recent scholarship on the evolution of gender roles during the life cycle finds a popular echo today--both in the declining popularity of the "superwoman" model and, concomitantly, in the growing popularity among women of "sequencing" job and family responsibilities.

For Gutmann, the end of the "parental emergency" permits both men and women to resume, albeit in different ways, their quest for omnipotentiality. Indeed, according to Gutman, something of a sex-role convergence occurs within many couples. Wives, no longer responsible for the daily care of children, become more independent, self-centered, and publicly ambitious. Men, as they age, become more dependent, other-centered, affiliative, and private. Gutmann writes,

[S]enior men and women can reclaim, for themselves, those aspects of self that were once disowned inwardly, though lived out externally, vicariously, through the spouse.[67]

Sylvia Ann Hewlett aptly summarizes this theory when she declares:

When I was younger I wanted to insist on a 50/50 division of love and work every single day. But now I see my 50/50 shot occurring over the course of a lifetime.[68]

Looking at contemporary U.S. culture, David Popenoe finds a new realism about family matters:

The gender-role debate is turning more in the direction of frankly discussing gender differences. In view of the new work roles of women, many men are becoming more actively involved in childrearing. A growing number of women have begun to rethink their lives and their careers along lines different from men, with a new interest in sequencing work and family pursuits that enables them to spend more time with very young children.[69]

Several recent surveys support Popenoe's observation. According to separate surveys conducted in Washington, D.C. and Los Angeles, a majority of working mothers would prefer, if finances permitted, to stay home with young children.[70] In 1985, the Virginia Slims Opinion Poll survey reported that 21 percent of women surveyed believed that "nothing gets slighted when mothers work." In the 1990 survey, that figure had declined to 14 percent.[71]

The 1990 Yankelovich Monitor, the annual survey of social values and consumer attitudes, finds a similar tilt toward family and children. In 1987, 21 percent of women said "putting more energy into homemaking" was a good reason to stop working. In 1990, the figure rose to 28 percent. "Having a baby" also became an increasingly popular reason to give up paid employment, increasing from 18 percent in 1987 to 24 percent in 1990. Overall, the survey points to a "major shift away from work and more toward home," according to Peter Stisser, a Yankelovich vice president and *Monitor* analyst.[72]

Moreover, the currently large number of childbirths in our society--over four million in 1990, more than any year in American history--suggests that a large proportion of the baby boom generation will be experiencing the "parental emergency" at roughly the same time over the coming decade. This demographic event, with its myriad social and cultural ripple effects, may well lead to an upturn in parental altruism within the society and to a renewed commitment to family well-being.

We are essentially pessimistic about the state's ability to define and enforce gender roles and identities. At the same time, we are optimistic about our cultural capacity in the years ahead to renew the language of difference and dependency in our public discourse about man and woman, to leave behind a story that is impoverished and anemic and to refashion for our time a story of "a common life" for man and woman that "promotes the accomplishment and happiness of each."[73]

ENDNOTES

This chapter is reprinted, with changes, from *First Things* published in New York City by The Institute on Religion and Public Life (Issue 15 August/September 1991), 28-35, by permission of the authors and the Institute on Religion and Public Life.

1.   Lawrence Stone, *Road to Divorce: England, 1530-1987* (Oxford: Oxford University Press, 1990), 422.

2.   U.S. Bureau of the Census, *Current Population Survey* (March 1990), unpublished report. If the divorce rate is measured as the number of divorces per year per 1,000 people, the U.S. rate for both 1989 and 1990 is 4.7, down slightly from its peak of 5.3 in the years 1979 and 1981 -- a drop probably due largely to the aging of the large post-war baby boom cohort. (Source: National Center for Health Statistics, *Monthly Vital Statistics Report*, 39 (No. 10, February 19, 1991) and 38 (No. 13, August 30, 1990). Nevertheless, the rate has "stabilized" at unprecedentedly high levels; the United States has, with the possible exception of Sweden, the highest rate of marital break-up in the world.

3.   U. S. Bureau of the Census, "Household and Family Characteristics: March 1990 and 1989," *Current Population Reports* P-20 (No. 477, March 1990).

4.   Sar A. Levitan, Richard S. Belous, and Frank Gallo, *What's Happening to*

the American Family? (Baltimore: Johns Hopkins, 1988), 114, 120.

5.   U. S. Bureau of the Census, "Marital Status and Living Arrangements: March 1988," *Current Population Reports* P-20 (No. 433, March 1988).

6.   Susan Cotts Watkins, Jane A. Menken, and John Bongaarts, "Demographic Foundations of Family Change," *American Sociological Review* 52, no. 3 (1987): 346-58.

7.   See Mary Ann Glendon, *Abortion and Divorce in Western Law* (Cambridge, MA: Harvard University Press, 1987), 63-64.

8.   See Irwin Garfinkel and Sara S. McLanahan, *Single Mothers and the Children: A New American Dilemma* (Washington, D.C.: Urban Institute, 1986); Lenore J. Weitzman, *The Divorce Revolution: The Unexpected Social and Economic Consequences for Women and Children in America* (New York: Free Press, 1985); Judith S. Wallerstein and Sandra Blakeslee, *Second Chances: Men, Women and Children a Decade after Divorce* (New York: Ticknor and Fields, 1989).

9.   Glendon, *Abortion and Divorce in Western Law*, 76.

10.   Ibid., 107-108.

11.   Roscoe Pound, "Individual Interests in Domestic Relations," *Michigan Law Review* 14 (No. 177, 1916): 177.

12.   Ann Swidler, "Love and Adulthood in American Culture," in *Themes of Work and Love in Adulthood*, eds. Neil J. Smelzer and Erik H. Erikson (Cambridge, MA: Harvard University Press, 1980), 139.

13.   Ibid., 130.

14.   Ibid., 134.

15.   Ibid., 127.

16.   Ibid., 126.

17.   Ibid., 136, 138.

18.   Ibid., 145.

19.   Norval D. Glenn, "The Family Values of Americans," unpublished paper

for the Institute for American Values (January 1991), 13.

20.   Steven O'Brien, "One Son, Three Fathers," *New York Times Magazine* (December 28, 1986): 36.

21.   "A Magazine Called Divorce," *New York Times* (July 7, 1987).

22.   *New York Times Magazine* (June 5, 1988), 92.

23.   "Finding Solace: Prayers Accepting Divorce," *New York Times* (August 31, 1987).

24.   Sally Blakeslee Ives, David Fassler, and Michele Lash, *The Divorce Workbook: A Guide for Kids and Families* (Burlington, VT: Waterfront Books, 1985).

25.   Christopher Jencks, "Deadly Neighborhoods," *The New Republic* (June 13, 1988): 28, 30.

26.   Bruce C. Hafen, "The Constitutional Status of Marriage, Kinship, and Sexual Privacy--Balancing the Individual and Social Interests," *Michigan Law Review*, 81 (No. 3, January 1983): 470.

27.   Glendon, *Abortion and Divorce in Western Law.*, 93.

28.   Weitzman, *The Divorce Revolution*, 323, *passim.*

29.   Glendon, *Abortion and Divorce in Western Law.*, 92-93.

30.   Ibid., 111.

31.   The Boston Women's Health Book Collective, *Ourselves and Our Children: A Book By and For Parents* (New York: Random House, 1978), 49.

32.   Alice Rossi, "A Biosocial Perspective on Parenting," *Daedalus* 106 (1977), 1. See also Alice Rossi, "Gender and Parenthood," *American Sociological Review* 49 (February 1984).

33.   Child Welfare League of America, "Children in Crisis: A Response for the '90s" (Pamphlet announcing the 1991 Mid-Atlantic Regional Training Conference of the Child Welfare League of America, Washington, D.C., June 16-19, 1991).

34.   George M. Schaefer, M.D. and Milton L. Zisowitz, *The Expectant Father* (New York: Simon and Schuster, 1964), 48.

35.   Patricia Ashdown-Sharp, *A Guide to Pregnancy and Parenthood for Women on Their Own* (New York: Random House, 1975; Vintage Original, 1977), 19-21.

36.   Norval D. Glenn, *The Family Values of Americans.*, 16.

37.   Leo Tolstoy, *Anna Karenina* (New York: Bantam Books, 1960), 761.

38.   Benjamin Spock, M.D., and Michael B. Rothenberg, M.D., *Dr. Spock's Baby and Child Care* (New York: Pocket Books, 1985), 23.

39.   Robert N. Bellah, Richard Masden, William M. Sullivan, Ann Swidler, and Steven M. Tipton, *Habits of the Heart* (Berkeley, CA: University of California Press, 1985).

40.   Sheila Kitzinger, *Your Baby, Your Way: Making Pregnancy Decisions and Birth Plans* (New York: Pantheon Books, 1987), 313-14.

41.   Ibid., 6.

42.   Susan Robinson, M.D., and H. F. Pizer, PA-C, *Having a Baby Without A Man: The Woman's Guide to Alternative Insemination* (New York: Simon and Schuster, 1985), 21.

43.   Glenn, *The Family Values of Americans*, 1-2.

44.   Michael Walzer, *The Company of Critics: Social Criticism and Political Commitment in the Twentieth Century* (New York: Basic Books, 1988), 161-62.

45.   Christina Sommers, "Philosophers Against the Family," in *Person to Person*, eds. George Graham and Hugh LaFollette (Philadelphia: Temple University Press, 1989), 734.

46.   Rossi, "A Biosocial Perspective," *Op. cit.*, 16.

47.   David Gutmann, *Reclaimed Powers: Toward a New Psychology of Men and Women in Later Life* (New York: BasicBooks, 1987), 195-96.

48.   Ibid., 190.

50.   Ibid., 198.

51.   Boston Women's Health Book Collective, *Op. cit.*, 33.

52.   Robert N. Bellah, "The Invasion of the Money World," in *Rebuilding the Nest: A New Commitment to the American Family*, eds. David Blankenhorn, Steven Bayme, and Jean Bethke Elshtain (Milwaukee: Family Service America, 1990), 230-31.

52.   See, Ann Douglas, *The Feminization of American Culture* (New York: Avon, 1977; Doubleday, 1988); Catherine Beecher, *Treatise on Domestic Economy for the Use of Young Ladies at Home and at School* (1846).

53.   Elaine Tyler May, *Homeward Bound: American Families in the Cold War Era* (New York: Basic Books, 1988), 149, but also 146-49, *passim*.

54.   From a description of the Families and Work Institute, excerpted from a brochure entitled "Mainstreaming a Work-Family Agenda," published jointly by The Conference Board and the Families and Work Institute, New York (February 1991).

55.   Barbara Riesman, Amy J. Moore, and Karen Fitzgerald, *Child Care: The Bottom Line*, (New York: Child Care Action Campaign, 1988), 9.

56.   Barbara Riesman, quoted in "U.S. Plan on Child Care is Reported to be Stalled," *New York Times* (January 27, 1991).

57.   U. S. Department of Labor, *Child Care: A Workforce Issue* (Washington, D.C.: U.S. Government Printing Office, 1988).

58.   Patricia Schroeder with Andrea Camp and Robyn Lipner, *Champion of the Great American Family: A Personal and Political Book* (New York: Random House, 1989), 84.

59.   The Roper Organization, Inc., *The 1990 Virginia Slims Opinion Poll* (1990), 10, 68, 75. Cf. The Roper Organization, Inc., *The 1985 Virginia Slims Opinion Poll* (1985).

60.   Sylvia Ann Hewlett, *A Less Life: The Myth of Women's Liberation in America* (New York: William Morrow, 1986), 33.

61.   Rossi, "A Biosocial Perspective," *Op. cit.*, 24.

62.   Gutmann, *Reclaimed Powers.*, 190-191.

63.   David Popenoe, "The Declining American Family: Taking a Reasoned Moral Stand," (Paper presented at the "Consultation on Religion, Family and Culture" conference sponsored by the University of Chicago Divinity School and

The Johnson Foundation, held at the Wingspread Center of the Johnson Foundation, Racine, Wisconsin, November 9-11, 1990), 21, 24.

64. Sommers, "Philosophers Against the Family," *Op. cit.*, 747.

65. Glenn, *The Family Values of Americans*, 4-8.

66. Ibid., 8-11.

67. Gutmann, *Reclaimed Powers*, p. 203.

68. Sylvia Ann Hewlett (Comments made at the "Consultation on Religion and Family Ethics" Conference sponsored by the University of Chicago Divinity School and The Johnson Foundation, Racine , Wisconsin, November 9-11, 1990).

69. Popenoe, "The Declining American Family," *Op. cit.*, 24.

70. *The Washington Post Poll* (June 11-July 7, 1990); Mark Baldassare & Associates (Irvine, CA), *The Los Angeles Times Poll* (July 19-23, 1990).

71. The Roper Organization, Inc., *Op. cit.*

72. "Focus shifts from goods to feelings," *Dallas Times Herald* (February 25, 1991), D-1.

73. Paul Sayre quoted in Ruth H. Jewson and James Walters, *The National Council on Family Relations: A Fifty-Year History, 1938-1987* (St. Paul, MN: National Council on Family Relations, 1988), 1.

Chapter 16

The Role of Normative Values in Rescuing the Urban Ghetto

Glenn C. Loury

INTRODUCTION

I am a social scientist, but I confess to being pessimistic that social science can ultimately contribute very much to the alleviation of ghetto poverty. This is not to say that research and evaluation on problems of unemployment, teenage motherhood, drug addiction, and so fourth should be abandoned. Billions have been spent in this vein over the last 30 years, creating great demand for the services of academic economists like myself, statisticians, sociologists and so on. We have learned something, although we remain ignorant about even more.

My point is not to disparage the often ingenious efforts that analysts undertake to fathom the intricacies of human behaviors, bureaucratic machinations, and structural transformations. Rather, I intend to question whether real improvement in the conditions of the ghetto poor, real change in the lives of real people, depend much at all on answers to the kinds of questions that social scientists pose.

Why this skepticism? Because modern social science and policy analysis speak a language of cause and effect: "if we design this program then they will respond in that way." Yet it is my conviction that the core problems of ghetto poverty require for their solution a language of *values*: "we *should* do this; they *ought* to do that; decent people *must* strive to live in a certain way." In the discourse of the "policy wonk," there is no place for language like this.

We now know that much of the problem of ghetto poverty is connected with the dysfunctional patterns of behavior adopted by young people in these communities. The issues raised by behavioral dysfunction, and the questions of who bears what responsibility in the face of that dysfunction, are inherently moral and political questions for which our nation, as a political and a moral community, must produce answers. To find these answers, we must have the will to examine ourselves: how we live, what we value, what we believe. And this self-examination should not involve just the poor, but all of us.

SILENCED VOICES AND EXHORTATIONS

As a number of critics have emphasized recently, there is a relationship between the behavioral problems of the poor, and the cultural crisis affecting the middle and upper classes in America, as evidenced by rising divorce rates, the spread of venereal disease, problems of our education system, increases in teen suicide, alcohol and drug abuse, our problems in international competitiveness, our flight from responsibility into various therapies which stress our victimhood, and so forth.

At issue here is our capacity as a moral and political community to engage in an effective discourse about values and ways of living, and to convey normative judgments which arise out of that discourse. I am dubious, for example, that it will ever again be possible for the federal government of the United States through the Congress or the executive, to put the force of its considerable power behind the simple and sensible normative proposition that children ought to be born to parents after marriage, not before. In the last quarter-century it has become increasingly more difficult for a public figure to give voice to this belief, one which not so long ago would have been universally seen as appropriate.

National campaigns have, aimed at some aspects of behavior, have indeed been waged with positive results. Smoking is the obvious example, successfully inveighed against over the last generation, with both public and private efforts. Our national consciousness of environmental issues has been raised in recent decades, in part through the use of public rhetoric and exhortation which has had a powerful normative aspect to it. One only need read Al Gore's book *Earth in the Balance* to see that. But efforts as public exhortation about sexuality, marriage, and childbearing are far more contentious because, unlike in these other areas, such efforts cut against the ideological grain of the great "liberation" movements which have swept through our society in past decade.

What has all this to do with the ghetto poor? Stated directly and without benefit of euphemism, the conditions under which many people live today in poor black communities reveal as much about the disintegration of urban black society as they do about the indifference or hostility or racism of white society. Institutional barriers to black participation in American life still exist, of course, but they have come down considerably and everybody knows that. Everybody also knows that other barriers have grown up within the urban black milieu in these last decades--and not only there--which are profoundly debilitating.

Neither the social scientists nor the politicians know what to say, or what to do, about this disintegration. The analysts cannot account for it; the public spokespersons dare not speak of it. Euphemisms abound, but the clear expressions of fear, disgust, dismay, contempt--sentiments which we all know are widespread--have no place in our political discourse. Giving public voice to such judgments is something most of us prefer to avoid.

Yet the absence of such moral language, and of the power of that kind of public discourse, has consequences. Remarkably, electoral campaigns can be waged in cities riven by the social disintegration of their ghetto communities without the language of values ever being directly invoked. Incredibly, campaigns of reconstruction are mounted--in South Central Los Angeles, for example--in the absence of any effective normative discourse aimed at judging the behaviors of those whose lack of discipline and restraint have proven so costly for their community.

Instead, we hear familiar intonations of platitudes and empty phrases: "racism," "inadequate funding," "no jobs," "no hope." And, of course, if it needs to be said, I do not hold that racism has vanished, or that funding is entirely adequate. I am saying, though, that we lapse all too easily and comfortably into a public rhetoric that avoids engaging fully the moral problems that confront us. We prefer to evoke certain ready-at-hand symbols which leave important facets of those problems hidden. Even as the collapse of social life among the inner-city poor worsens, we have these pat, ritualistic public conversations full of platitudes about "caring" and "compassion," but devoid of hard-edged judgments about decency and personal morality.

MECHANISTIC DETERMINISM AND PERSONAL MORALITY

The fundamental assumption behind our public language about ghetto poverty is a materialist viewpoint: economic factors are supposed ultimately to underlie behavioral problems, even behaviors involving sexuality, marriage, childbearing, and parenting; matters which reflect people's basic understandings of what gives meaning to their lives. The view is that these behavioral problems can be cured from without, that government can change these behaviors, that if you can just get the incentives right, then everything will be fine. This reflects a philosophy of mechanistic determinism, wherein the mysteries of human motivation are supposedly susceptible to calculated intervention, if only the government were sufficiently committed to try.

This economic determinists' view of social disorder in the inner-city lends itself easily to the favored lines of political argument about social policy. Those who favor expanded government can argue that we either pay now for social "investment" programs, or pay later, for welfare and prisons. Those who want the federal budget to shrink can cite the worsening conditions of the ghetto, in the face of social spending growth over the last generation, as evidence that the Great Society failed. Those who seek a middle way can split the difference by talking about how the receipt of benefits must be accompanied by an acceptance of responsibility on the part of the poor, though the government must provide services which help the poor to accept their responsibilities, and so on. We are all familiar with this language.

These debates are sterile and superficial. They fail to engage questions of personal morality. They fail to talk about character and values. They do not invoke any moral leadership in the public sphere. The view seems to be that in a pluralistic society such discussions from public officials are inappropriate. Nor do we teach in our schools--the schools serving this very population--the comparative virtues of alternative ways of living. We give only muted public voice to the judgments that it is wrong to be sexually promiscuous, to be indolent and without discipline, to be disrespectful of legitimate authority, or to be unreliable or untruthful or unfaithful. We no longer teach values, but offer "clarification" of the values that children are supposed to have somehow inculcated in them without any instruction. We elevate process ("How does one discover his or her own values?") over substance ("What is it that a decent person should embrace?").

The advocacy of a particular conception of virtuous living has virtually vanished from American public discourse. And it is unthinkable that it would be evoked in the context of a discussion of race. Marriage as an institution is virtually dead in inner-city communities of our country. The vast majority of poor black children are now raised by a mother alone. But who will say that black men and women *should* get together and stay together more than they now do, for the sake of their children? Who will say that young people of any race *should* abstain from sexual intimacy until their relationships have been consecrated by marriage? These are, in this present age, not matters for public discourse.

Most Americans believe that one and a half million abortions a year are far too many, and that this constitutes a profound moral problem for our society. Yet, the public discourse on this issue is dominated by the question of a woman's right to choose, not the moral content of her choice. Nearly all of us would prefer, on moral as well as pragmatic grounds, that our 15-year-olds not be sexually active. But to publicly take this rhetorical stance in response to an epidemic of sexually transmitted disease among young people is to invite ridicule from the highest government officials. Government, it would appear, should confine itself to dealing with the consequences of these moral lapses, rather than taking the issue of morality directly.

Now, I am not one for tilting at windmills. The emergence of morally authoritative public leadership seems highly unlikely at this late date. Evidently we are going to have to look to nongovernmental agencies of moral and cultural development in particular communities to take on some of the burden of promoting positive behavioral change. In every community there are agencies of moral and cultural development which seek to shape the ways in which individuals conceive of their duties to themselves, of their obligations to each other, and of their responsibilities before God. The family and the church are primary among these.

These are the natural sources of legitimate moral teaching--indeed, the only sources. If these institutions are not restored, the behavioral problems of the ghetto will not be overcome. Such a restoration obviously cannot be the object of programmatic intervention by public agencies. Rather, it must be led from within the communities in question, by the moral and spiritual leaders of those communities. The "bully pulpit" of public leadership, however, can be used to encourage rather than disparage these private efforts at the inculcation of specific moral codes.

SPIRITUAL PROBLEMS AND COMMITMENTS

Now, the mention of God may seem quaint, or vaguely inappropriate here, but it is clear that the behavioral problems of the ghetto (and, again, not only there) are spiritual in part. A man's spiritual commitments influence his understanding of his parental responsibilities. No economist has yet to devise an incentive scheme for eliciting parental involvement in a child's development as effective as the motivations of conscience deriving from the parents' understanding that they are God's stewards in the lives of their children.

Although public policy should not reflect particular religious doctrines under our form of government, this is no reason to keep an understanding of the importance of spirituality out of public discussions of poverty and many other social problems. Everything worth talking about in public need not issue in a government program or a federal statute! We should recognize the importance of the efforts, ongoing in many communities but still woefully inadequate to the challenge, to reconstruct systems of beliefs and values from which individuals derive meaning, and around which people can organize their lives.

This line of reasoning has an implication for how we black Americans should approach the problem of ghetto poverty--a problem which threatens, in a way that southern segregationists never could, to derail our march forward into an estate of full and complete equality in American social life. A great, existential challenge faces black America today--the challenge of taking responsibility for our future by exerting the moral leadership that is needed within our communities. We must choose whether to commit ourselves to making the sacrifices of time and resources so as to build the social institutions which do not now exist, but which are ultimately the only means by which the problem of social disintegration in the inner-city can be solved. I am not saying that government has no place. I am not suggesting that we do away with Head Start, or that we withdraw funds from public schools.

Rather, I am arguing that the normative dimension to the problem of behavioral dysfunction is not amenable to government remedy, because government has neither the will or the instruments to address it. It is a problem that communities need to address for themselves. For that to happen, the intellectual, religious and political leadership of this community must embrace their responsibilities. No matter how contentious the policy debate between Democrats and Republicans about the size of the next federal budget, the challenge remains for leaders of the black community to build the communal institutions which can instill in our youngsters a normative framework sufficient to allow them to partake of the great opportunity which this society offers.

Indeed, it is to make a mockery of the idea of freedom to hold that, as free men and women, blacks ought nevertheless to leave the determination of the normative framework of our communal life to the vicissitudes of government policy. A truly free people have to accept responsibility for the behavior of their children. And when that behavior has gone badly astray, they must work to correct it. This is not simply a pragmatic observation intended to promote greater economic advancement among blacks. This concern goes straight to the heart of the issues of dignity and equal standing and respect for blacks in our society.

THE PRICE OF OUR SOULS

The ideological presuppositions of current black American political advocacy simply ignore the truth of what I am saying here. Some leaders, in civil rights organizations and the halls of Congress, remain wedded to a conception of the black condition, and a method of appealing to the rest of the polity, which undermines the dignity of our people. They seek, it would seem, to make blacks into the conscience of America, even at the price of our souls. Remarkably, they think that the mere announcement of the small number of blacks who attain a certain achievement constitutes an indictment of society, and not of us. The rhetoric is: "It costs more to keep a young black man in jail for a year than it does to send him to Yale for a year"--as if the difference between his being in jail or at Yale is a matter of the size of somebody's budget, rather than the behavior of the young man himself.

If we want to see this young man at Yale and not in jail, we should not talk to President Clinton; rather, we should talk with his parents, his neighbors, his pastor, and his teachers. These are the people who are, or at least who should be, intimately involved in his life. These are the people who are connected to him by bonds of blood. But racial advocacy in our time directs itself to the political world outside of the community, rather than to the moral world inside of it. Instead of working to construct the social infrastructure that would make Yale a possibility for the young man, advocates cite his condition as basis for a claim against the rest of society. It is as if we count the bodies and then pile them up on the doorstep of politicians so as to present a bill for a certain sum. This is a wholesale abdication of moral responsibility of astounding proportion.

Consider the blood that has been shed, the sacrifices that have been made, the determination, the organizational skill, the commitment and dedication that has been shown by blacks of previous generations, who struggled with much less opportunity against much greater odds in order that our generation might live as free and prosperous American citizens. This great legacy of struggle against the "enemy without" deserves to be respected by our having the courage to take-up the current struggle against the "enemy within."

I hold that we blacks ought not to allow ourselves to become ever-ready "doomsayers," always alert to exploit our own suffering by offering it up to more or less sympathetic whites as justification for incremental monetary transfers. I hold that such a posture gives evidence of a fundamental lack of confidence in our own abilities as to make it in this country, as so many millions of immigrants have done and continue to do. And, even if we succeed with the advocacy, in the end it is impossible that genuine equality of status in society could lie at the end of that road.

It is, however, possible to understand how things have come to this pass. The fact there has been in the United States such a tenuous commitment to social provision to the poor, independent of race, is one reason why we have ended up in this ideological trap. Leaders and intellectuals among the African-American population think they have to cling to victim status as a way of making claims to the rest of the society, because it provides their only secure basis upon which to press for attention from the rest of the polity.

The desperate plight of the poorest makes it unthinkable that whites could ever be "let off the hook." Americans bear a responsibility, as a national community, to help poor people in the ghetto, and elsewhere. When we do not live up to that responsibility as a national community-- and we often have not--we make it nearly impossible for the kind of thinking about personal responsibility which I advocate here to flourish among black intellectuals and political leaders.

POLITICAL RISK AND MORAL NECESSITY

Nevertheless it remains true that, whatever the outcome of the policy debate, we blacks must let go of the past and take responsibility for our future. What may seem to be an unacceptable political risk has also by now become an absolute moral necessity. The circumstance is a genuine dilemma. The temptation can be overwhelming to adopt the posture of the aggrieved claimant, the historical victim, the one whose violation accounts for his every disability, who, in his helplessness, is, indeed, nothing more than the creation of his oppressor.

Yet such a posture inhibits the attainment of genuine freedom and true equality, for its militates against an emphasis on personal responsibility and morality within the group. It is difficult to overemphasize the self-defeating dynamic which can be at work here. The dictates of political advocacy encourage an ideology in which personal inadequacies among blacks are inevitably attributed to "the system." The emphasis on self-improvement is denounced as irrelevant, self-serving, and dishonest. Individual black men and women simply cannot fail on their own, they must be seen as never having had a chance. They cannot be living immorally--in a way inconsistent with communal values which black leaders stand ready to affirm--they must, instead, be seen as victims.

But the crime, violence, drug use, promiscuous sexuality, unwed child-bearing, parental neglect, abuse and irresponsibility, and a general failure to seize opportunity--these are all maladies affecting inner-city black communities for which we blacks, as a community, must accept responsibility. We have to acknowledge the personal moral failings which lead to these problems. We must not simply blame these conditions on society or racism or capitalism or whatever.

If we do not grasp the horns of this dilemma, if we continue to respond to the plight of the ghetto poor in terms of our historical victimization, then we shall pay a terrible price. No one but us can provide the moral and spiritual leadership which is essential to reverse the social disintegration now so well advanced. Too many black leaders and spokespersons, confronting their people's need and their own impotency, believe they must continue to portray us as the "conscience of the nation." And yet, as I have said, the price extracted for playing this role, in incompletely fulfilled lives and unrealized personal potential, amounts to a loss of our own souls.

Consummate victims, we lay ourselves at the feet of our fellows, exhibiting our own lack of achievement as evidence of our countrymen's failure, hoping to wring from the American conscience what we must assume, by the very logic of our claim, lies beyond our own capabilities. All the while, indeed, bemoaning how limited that sense of conscience seems to be. On this path lies not the freedom so long sought by our ancestors, but instead, a new and dismaying and permanent second class status in this society.

Chapter 17

Building the Well-Ordered Society: Subsidiarity and Mediating Structures

T. William Boxx

INTRODUCTION

The term "order" in social order indicates the absence of chaos and the presence of principles of cohesion. It refers to the condition of all the parts of society working harmoniously for the good of the whole in service to the members of society. Society itself may be broadly understood as being comprised of three interrelated macro systems of organization--political, economic, and cultural--within each of which various institutions facilitate the satisfaction of the diverse material and intangible needs and desires of the members. The question of social order, then, is how social relations are most satisfactorily governed among individuals and the institutions that make up society.

Social order, however, cannot be properly conceived of as only the structure of the sociological units. Most fundamentally, what gives order is the collective sense of the norms and values of the people, rooted in the interaction of beliefs and the practices of everyday life. The principles by which people live in society, whether articulated or not, have the quality of being absolutes in the sense that they are assumed to be universal--everyone more or less lives by them and they are accepted as both true and useful. Otherwise to the extent that social principles are widely violated, disorder prevails. Thus, social order is, metaphorically, the spirit that animates the societal body or the public philosophy that arises from tried and true social relationships. When the validity of values and norms weaken, and when the presumptive truth and utility of certain fundamental social institutions are swallowed by the encroachments of others, the harmony and ordered balance of society dissipates.

SOCIAL ORDER AND CULTURE

It should be clear that much of the social order depends upon the cultural sphere. Social order and particular cultural foundations are not invented per se, though they obviously reflect human choices, but rather evolve over long periods of time in complex and innumerable interrelationships. Culture cannot be successfully constructed whole overnight or in one or two generations. Tragically, it can fall in a short space and it is then no simple matter to rebuild. As T. S. Eliot put it, when culture goes "you must start painfully again, and you cannot put on a new culture ready made. You must wait for the grass to grow to feed the sheep to give wool out of which your new coat will be made."[1] As the old order declines, there follows a deepening twilight of uncertainty and diffusion, the signs of which a growing many now detect. Our practical task then, must be one of renewal and rejuvenation, not *creatio ex nihilo,* to push back the approaching long dark night, if we can.

The social order falls when the culture has become discredited and the people no longer have confidence in the formerly presumed norms out of which decisions were made and public life progressed. Many sense such decline, and the nightly pictures of social dissolution and human wastage incrementally reinforce the prophecies of inevitability. We fear that a destiny of ruin awaits us, as surely as the biblical writing on the wall: "you are weighed in the balance and found wanting." As fell Babylon to the Persians, we wonder about our fall, not to an external force but rather to the self-destructive tendencies of postmodernism. Thus, like Scrooge's desperately hoping inquiry to the spirit of the future, we also are led to ask: "Are these the shadows of the things that will be, or are they shadows of the things that may be only?"[2]

The heart of culture is morality, so that at bottom, ours is a moral crisis. Will Herberg observed over 25 years ago that it is not just that moral standards are too often violated; thus has it always been. It is the far more distressing fact that "the very notion of morality or moral code seems to be itself losing its meaning for increasing numbers of men and women in our society."[3] Herberg saw the pervasiveness of relativism as leading towards a "non-moral, normless culture," where the idea of truth is denied and therewith any sense of natural or divine law.

The validity of morality itself rests upon it being conceptualized as transcendent of mere human invention, either by virtue of the natural order or by divine design or both. The moral order is discovered (and to the theologically committed, also revealed) and while changing circumstances engender new insights and interpretations, such do not alter the conviction that the essence of the moral life is rooted in nature and its Creator. It is hard to fathom how morality conceived of as mere preferences of lifestyle and variable personal values, constrained basically only by isolated individual choices, could sustain a civil and humane order. Yet that is the prevailing elite paradigm. Fortunately, the mass of people, although less confidently perhaps, have not as yet lost hold of their common sense notion that moral habits and the qualities of good character are defined and compelled by less arbitrary authority. Almost everyone in American society believes in God, and the renewal of social order fails if it does not take our civil heritage of belief into account.

Moral norms fundamentally restrain negative, selfish tendencies as well as promote a vision of the good and meaningful life. It is obvious that those who have little or no moral discipline, that is, who are not restrained in private life, will not be restrained in public life. Moral relativism simply does not work and cannot inspire a vital culture or effective social order. In challenging moments, weakly formed moral sentiments will too easily give way to expediency and selfishness or to passion and appetite. Michael Novak put it thus: "For how can a people profess to be capable of self-government--of government of, by and for the people--if they cannot govern their own passions? How can a people govern a whole society who cannot, each of them, govern themselves?"[4] It is senseless to speak of political freedom without moral standards. In a democratic polity such moral laxity translates into accelerating demands for government provision and diminishing expectations of personal responsibility.

We are made to be moral-cultural beings, both by biological necessity and, if you will, by our transcendent nature. Particular human behavior is largely learned--it is not instinctive. Through natural processes our precursors emerged as creatures of culture whose very survival was dependent upon learned behavioral patterns of culture. Those who exhibited moral-like qualities, perhaps grounded in affection for the young and familial attachment, leading to mutual cooperation and social affiliation, were more successful.[5] We have the capacity and necessity for culture, including moral judgment. Although the mechanisms for moral-cultural judgment are ingrained, however, the surety of their expression is not. It is important to emphasize that the moral capacity is one of predispositions only with no guarantee of their on-going effective manifestation. Successful and stable patterns of culture are required for their proper nurturance and encouragement. Social policy that works against this nature, however well-intended, is bound to be dysfunctional in the end.

The human person is part of nature and its natural processes but also transcendent of nature. We are self-aware with a unique consciousness and rational capacity that sets us apart from the rest of creation. Particular biological developments are the necessary conditions for the existence of our transcendent qualities but ultimately, I would affirm, we owe their emergence to the transcendent Creator and cannot be satisfactorily explained otherwise. As rational beings, we discover the moral order in creation and as creatures of the Creator we are called to likewise be responsibly creative within that natural order. Thus, morality and creativity are in our nature as potentialities and our cultural arrangements and social institutions must reflect and facilitate the manifestation of that nature.

Because we are transcendent creatures and biocultural beings, personal moral responsibility and a concomitant societal moral consensus are requisite conditions of our existence. Our human nature is such that cultural arrangements cannot be subject to limitless reconstructions which might, for example, present a false dichotomy between the individual and society or which would tend to blur the distinctions or which would diminish the validity of moral life. Individualism in its extreme form, on the one hand, and socialism, on the other, are errors of some magnitude because they have a distorted view of human nature--a nature which entails both personal moral responsibility and social cooperation.

RESPONSIBLE FREEDOM

Moral responsibility presumes the freedom to make moral judgments so that freedom is a necessary condition of moral life. We must be free to choose, but because human life in its fullest is not possible absent social cooperation, which requires the presumption of established norms, individual choice cannot in all cases be the ultimate standard for social resolution or organization. Society must be ordered so as to encourage the exercise of responsible freedom, for both personal and social well-being.

It is necessary to leave much to individual preferences and life decisions for the sake of freedom, but the institutions of society must have the vigor and presumption of rightness to confidently uphold certain standards of behavior and social order. In other words, there must be a strong sense of what is normal and good, in spite of deviations which might be freely chosen by some individuals. Radical individual freedom cannot be established as the super-value that automatically overwhelms the normative institutions of society whenever conflicting claims are pressed, which has too often been the legal and policy tendency in the moral-cultural field of our time. The economic sphere, however, is another story where freedom has tended to be overrun by the lopsided demands of the state.

The question then is, how do we best promote responsible freedom through culture and the social order? Social order must be rooted in human nature if it is to be successful. That is, if it is to call forth the best potentialities in the people and assure the propagation of civil society. The good society presumes that some measure of what was classically known as virtue must exist in the people. The ancient Greeks recognized four cardinal virtues--prudence, fortitude, temperance, and justice, to which Christian theology would add faith, hope, and love. Plato understood that the human person was by nature oriented to the Good, but virtuous character must be vigorously inculcated in the young until they come to love the Good on their own. And Aristotle recognized that one acquires virtuous habits by the practice of virtue. You learn moral habits by doing, which requires the prevalence of examples to follow and social reinforcement. If the precepts of the virtuous or moral life are not widely held and affirmed by key institutions, society collapses. And then what is freedom when everyday life is a struggle and basic security becomes precarious? The late Dr. Russell Kirk insightfully expressed the contingencies of freedom: "Out of faith arises order; and once order prevails, freedom becomes possible. When the faith that nurtured the order fades away, the order disintegrates; and freedom no more can survive the disappearance of order than the branch of a tree can outlast the fall of the trunk."[6] As we lose our moral foundations, we will hardly be able to hold onto civic freedom in any meaningful sense.

THE AMERICAN ORDER

The founders of the American regime, themselves students of the classics, presumed a republican citizenry that possessed the characteristics of virtue. As James Madison rhetorically inquired: "Is there no virtue among us? If there be not, we are in a wretched situation. . . . To suppose that any form of government will secure liberty or happiness without any virtue in the people is a chimerical idea."[7]   He knew that the political order must comport with human nature and called government "the greatest of all reflections on human nature."[8]

The American republic was founded upon the presupposition that there were such things as "truths" about the human endowment and a rightness of order derived from "nature and nature's God." Political organization and public life in general cannot be established upon relativistic assertions about human nature, and it is foolishness beyond *hubris* to think any civilization can be sustained by such.

The new American political order was not cut complete from new cloth. Americans were accustomed to political freedom and largely unimpeded commerce, flowing principally from the ideas and social arrangements of the British civilization to which they belonged.   That is what made the hardening restrictions and disdainful behavior of King George's government so intolerable.   They certainly in a compelling sense established a "new order for the ages," a new political order, but it was founded upon the widely held "rights of Englishmen" and the philosophy and beliefs of the European culture to which they were heir.   It was not a radical revolution along the lines of the near contemporary French revolution of 1789 or the Russian communist revolution of 1917.   They did not create from nothing but rather built upon the deeply rooted values of the people and the best of their culture.   Thus their social history was the social history of Europe, and therefore of Rome, of Athens, and of Jerusalem.

The American social order was constituted of Judeo-Christian religious traditions as well as the philosophical insights of Enlightenment thinking. That is how the Founders could presume a certain degree of virtue in the people and how they could speak of "self evident truths." And that is how they could propose a system of government that was, as John Adams said, "made only for moral and religious people."[9]   In this sentiment the Founders shared the thought of their British contemporary Edmund Burke: "We know and what is better, we feel inwardly, that religion is the basis of civil society, and the source of all good and of all comfort."[10]   A well ordered American society requires the renewal of political culture, such as envisioned by the Founders and statesmen like Burke, with its moral and philosophical presuppositions. And, I might add, citizen-statesmen who can put the common good above narrow and special interest and self-interest.

Yet in the last several decades especially, decades of accelerating social dysfunction, our political order--through the courts and legislated policy--has pushed the religious foundations of morality out of the public square and fostered an environment of hostility towards traditional values. During the very time when the anomic influences of postmodernism most needed countering by confident public moral reaffirmation, the leadership of key societal institutions gave over to the false dualistic rationalism of secular extremism.   What is wanted is a renewed understanding of the indispensable connection of morality to social order and to freedom.

SUBSIDIARITY AND MEDIATING STRUCTURES

The "well ordered society" means that the key spheres and institutions of society work harmoniously and effectively in consort with the highest qualities of human nature, including the promotion of responsible freedom. It follows that no one part can be allowed to encroach upon and diminish the other parts and that the principles and norms behind public life be transmitted and upheld in vigorous fashion.   This, the concept of subsidiarity, proposes and a vital system of mediating structures presumes.

The term subsidiarity was originally formulated in Roman Catholic social teaching. It comes from the Latin and connotes a helping function as the purpose of higher political and social organizations or communities in relation to lower ones. Mediating structures refer to those institutions or communities within society that mediate, or stand between, the individual and the state such as families, neighborhoods, local communities, churches, and voluntary associations.   As a system of thought, these concepts put the emphasis on the institutions and communities closest to the individual.   For instance, the vitality of the family as the closest mediating institution to the individual should not be weakened by, say, federal government policy but rather, the federal government as a higher community should serve to help maintain the vitality of the family.

Subsidiarity first came into prominent public discourse in 1931 by Pope Pius XI's encyclical *Quadragesimo Anno,* which was written as a commemoration of the 40th anniversary (hence the Latin title) of Pope Leo XIII's landmark social encyclical *Rerum Novarum* (New Things). The theme of Pius's encyclical was, appropriately, "On Reconstructing the Social Order," a phrase contained in the fuller title.

Pius XI led the Roman Catholic Church from 1922 to his death in 1939. During his pontificate, he faced the social and political disruptions which followed in the aftermath of the first World War: the Great Depression, the rise of fascism and Nazism, the expanding influence of communism, and the looming threat of the second World War. Human society itself seemed threatened in this time with dehumanizing regimes in the ascendancy and economic systems in turmoil or out of balance. He saw that the world needed true peace and a return to moral law with the principles of justice and charity at the heart of right social order.[11]

Pius objected both to what he called liberalism, which might be more appropriately called a type of libertarianism today, and socialism--that is, radical individualism and collectivism. Liberalism was seen as an error because it failed to take into account the *social* character of private property and denied public authority any control over economic life. Great concentrations of wealth were the result to the detriment of the mass of working people. Furthermore, it was thought, those few in control of the wealth tended to inordinately influence the state, thus becoming an economic imperialism and denying the state its proper function.

Collectivism, either in the form of socialism or communism, on the other hand, was in error by its denial (in contrast to liberalism) of the *individual* character of the right of property. The themes of class warfare and abolition of private property were recognized as damaging to human society whether variously tempered or not. Socialism's emphasis on production and the material was such that the higher goods of the human person, including freedom, were relegated to secondary importance. It implied a level of unacceptable coercion and made no place for true social authority, which rests on the Creator and not on temporal and material advantages. Thus Pius emphatically affirmed that true socialism is incompatible with Christianity. He also warned against those who downplayed the dangers of the brutal and inhumane communist regimes then in power. His warnings, were vindicated in the fall of the Soviet communist empire beginning in 1989.

Quadragesimo Anno has three major parts. The first division (paragraphs 16-40) comments on the contributions of Leo XIII's *Rerum Novarum,* which focused on the conditions of workers. The second division (paragraphs 41-98) elaborates on certain aspects of Leo's encyclical and applies its teaching to modern conditions. The final part (paragraphs 96 - 110) deals with the changes in economic life since Leo, the development of socialism, and the causes of socioeconomic evils and the necessity of moral reform.

It is in the second part that the concept of subsidiarity is offered, which builds upon Leo's political economy as interpreted by Pius in the preceding part. Pius calls for the reform of institutions and morals with the state as the most prominent of the institutions to be considered. He qualifies the importance of the state by denying to it the ability to create "universal well-being" by its activities. He perceives that the "rich social life which was once highly developed through associations of various kinds" has become nearly extinct with only individuals and the state remaining. This situation he wishes to correct with a right understanding of how the state ought to function within society.

With the moribundity of this former "structure of social governance" the state has assumed the burdens formerly borne by associations, such that it has become overwhelmed by "almost infinite tasks and duties," causing great harm to the state itself. In other words, there is a limit to what the state should be expected to do. Even recognizing the changing conditions of history, Pius nevertheless affirms what he calls "that most weighty principle, which cannot be set aside or changed," and which must remain a "fixed and unshaken" social philosophy. This social philosophy, placing the state in the context of the overall society, he describes as follows:

> Just as it is gravely wrong to take from individuals what they can accomplish by their own initiative and industry and give it to the community, so also it is an injustice and at the same time a grave evil and disturbance of right order to assign to a greater and higher association what lesser and subordinate organizations can do. For every social activity ought of its very nature to furnish help to the members of the body social, and never destroy and absorb them.(79)

Thus, the state should not absorb the roles of the various other institutions and associations in society in the same way that individuals should not be relieved of their responsibilities. The state, according to Pius, should "let subordinate groups handle matters and concerns of lesser importance" leaving to it the things only it can do, which functions are characterized by "directing, watching, urging, restraining, as occasion requires and necessity demands." Those in authority should assure that "a graduated order is kept among the various associations" of society. This above described social philosophy and order he terms the principle of "subsidiarity function," that is, an order of helping relationships that respects the proper function of each social unit (80).

Quite clearly, the state is conceived of as an important part of society but only a part and not, in effect, synonymous with society. Most particularly, Pius presumes that the state is not superior to the natural rights of individuals (elsewhere discussed in the context of the right of private property) because the human person is "older than the state" and families are "prior both in thought and in fact to uniting into a polity"(49). The fundamental function of the state is to preserve the common good. To be sure, Pius can be interpreted as allowing quite vigorous action upon the part of the state in carrying out this duty, nevertheless, his rule is for the state to help maintain the vitality of all the parts of society and not to absorb them nor abolish the inherent freedom of the human person. The inference is that society is built upon human nature; that is, the human person as one who is simultaneously a free, morally responsible, and social creature.

Pope Pius's current successor, John Paul II, reaffirmed the importance of subsidiarity as the organizing principle for social teaching in his 1991 encyclical *Centesimus Annus,* written for the one 100th anniversary of *Rerum Novarum.* Building upon Pius, John Paul interprets the implications of subsidiarity as requiring that: "A community of a higher order should not interfere in the internal life of a lower order, depriving the latter of its functions, but rather should support it in case of need and help to coordinate its activity with the activities of the rest of society, always with a view to the common good" (*Centesimus Annus* 48). The viability of mediating institutions must be affirmed and supported by the state which is subsidiary, that is, a help to society. This is so because the social nature of the human person is such that it is "realized in various intermediary groups, beginning with the family and including economic, social, political, and cultural groups that stem from human nature itself and have their own autonomy, always with a view to the common good"(13).

For these reasons, John Paul is particularly critical of the contemporary welfare state or what he calls the social assistance state. He employs the concept of subsidiarity to define the state's proper role so as to avoid "enlarging excessively the sphere of state intervention." Such a misunderstanding of the state creates the "malfunctions and defects" of "bureaucratic ways of thinking" leading to an "inordinate increase of public agencies" and enormous increases in spending as well as misspent human energies. He affirms that needs are best understood and satisfied by those closest to them, which obviously assumes a prominent role for mediating institutions in providing support (48).

Like Pius implied, John Paul recognizes the family (founded upon marriage) as the primary mediating institution of society, which he calls "the first and fundamental structure for human ecology." In the family, the human person receives his or her "first formative ideas about truth and goodness and learns what it means to love and to be loved, and thus what it actually means to be a person." He reveres the family "as the sanctuary of life"(39). The state cannot truly provide or replace these functions without totalitarian pretensions although it can support or hinder the social environment necessary for family vitality.

In the context of limited state intervention, one of the most widely discussed concepts in *Centesimus Annus*, and something of a watershed in contemporary Catholic social teaching, is John Paul's strong affirmation of the free economy. Whereas Leo's and Pius's criticisms of both liberalism (imprecisely assumed to apply to American capitalism) and socialism led many Catholic thinkers to explore for a "third way" in political economy, John Paul seeks to put that quest to rest. He supports capitalism understood as "an economic system which recognizes the fundamental and positive role of business, the market, private property, and the resulting responsibility for the means of production as well as free human creativity in the economic sector"(42). Perhaps because the term capitalism has somewhat of a pejorative connotation in some circles where human failings and precapitalistic political economics have been mistakenly judged as indicating the inherent fallacy of the capitalistic system, he prefers the terms "business economy, market economy or simply free economy." In any event, the free economy is rooted in human freedom which is a requirement of human dignity.

The state has strong and decisive limitations in terms of interventions but John Paul is not proposing a strictly libertarian political economy. His teaching on capitalism entails a free economic sector which is "circumscribed within a strong juridical framework which places it at the service of human freedom in its totality and which sees it as a particular aspect of that freedom, the core of which is ethical and religious"(42). The economic system must function within a moral-cultural context and the rule of law. The state serves society by watching over the common good and intervening in limited ways when necessary (especially on behalf of the weakest) and in a manner that is supportive of intermediary groups and individual responsibility.

One sees in Catholic social teaching a recognition that society must be organized on the basis of human nature, a nature that is inherently free and social. It is also a nature that tends toward the good but is capable of evil. Therefore, right social order must especially respect the family as the primary social unit wherein the moral life and highest values of humanity are irreplaceably first nurtured. Likewise the fuller social nature of the human person presumes a network of various other affiliations, which the state is bound to respect, along with human freedom, in its service to civil society. The concept of subsidiarity is conceived of as harmoniously balancing the individual and social aspects of the human person and orienting human activity toward the common good.

MEDIATING STRUCTURES AND PUBLIC POLICY

The indispensability of healthy mediating structures for a well balanced society has steadily gained broad recognition over the last couple of decades among social scientists and policy experts. A pivotal point for greater attention to the subject was a 1977 monograph by Peter Berger and Richard John Neuhaus sponsored by the American Enterprise Institute and partially funded by the National Endowment for the Humanities.[12]

In *To Empower People: The Role of Mediating Structures in Public Policy*, Berger and Neuhaus examined the welfare state in light of two apparently contradictory tendencies in American public opinion. One tendency is the desire for a high level of provided services and the other is distrust of big government. Given the assumption of the predominant existence of the welfare state for modern society, their approach was to propose "alternative mechanisms" in providing welfare state services so as to address both tendencies. Their concern was not, however, merely for efficiency of delivery but more significantly for a recognition in public policy of the necessary "meaning and identity" bestowing functions of mediating structures. The premise of this social vision is that mediating structures can more humanly serve the purposes of the welfare state and bridge the meaning gap between the isolated individual and the "megastructures" (most notably, the state) of modern society.[13]

Berger and Neuhaus chose to focus on four mediating structures, which most people could relate to and which were relevant to problems of the welfare state. Those mediating structures--the neighborhood, family, church, and the voluntary associations--are the kind of key institutions that relate the political order to the "values and realities of individual life" and thus, provide its moral foundation.[14]

The crippling risk of cynicism when political life becomes detached from the foundational values of individual and community life was recognized by Berger and Neuhaus. Although promising political and social movements have transpired since the time of their writing, the credibility of the political order, to say the least, remains a serious problem. A majority of the population believes that most federal representatives are corrupt and sizable portions of the electorate do not see much point in voting. It is exceedingly unhealthy in a democratic republic for politics to be held in such disrepute as it is today. While one could examine a number of causal possibilities, the continuing breach between the life and work of ordinary citizens and that of the political leadership is no small consideration. The term limits movement is one understandable reaction to this detachment between ordinary life and its values and a political system perceived as unresponsive and irresponsible.

A significant step towards amelioration of denigrated political life is a renewed emphasis upon, as Berger and Neuhaus phrased it, "the value-generating and value-maintaining agencies in society."[15] To help implement this effect, *To Empower People* presents three propositions for government that would enhance the legitimacy of domestic public policy and therefore, of the political order:

1. Mediating structures are essential for a vital democratic society.
2. Public policy should protect and foster mediating structures.
3. Wherever possible, public policy should utilize mediating structures for the realization of social purposes.[16]

Government concern for mediating structures does not necessarily presuppose a particular set of policies (though such needs to be offered) but it does entail taking into account the effect of proposed and existing public policies upon, especially, the family and local community affiliations, wherein real people really live. It also means that mediating institutions and non-governmental associations should be (with all responsible considerations) favored mechanisms for public policy implementation over bureaucratic systems. Along the lines of cost-benefit analysis, there should be a mediating structures analysis and impact statement with social welfare programs.

To effectively involve religious institutions, the current political system will need to modify the prevailing radical church-state separation ideology and return to something more resembling the founding intent of the First Amendment, which was simply not to establish a state church (as in England) and no state persecution of religious diversity, rather than the wholesale exclusion of religion from the public square. To suppose that, as Richard John Neuhaus has disparagingly put it, "wherever the writ and coin of government run, religion must retreat," is to abuse one of civil society's most valuable institutions and to disturb the balance of social order in favor of the voracious state.[17] True civic pluralism and freedom requires no less. Religion's unnatural exclusion (for example, in education) and limitation through counter-productive or denuding regulatory conditions perpetuates the perverse identification of all things public with governmental exclusivity.

Renewed emphasis on the significance of mediating institutions (whether the exact terminology is used or not) has arisen through various sociopolitical themes in recent years. Much of their animating force stems from the social deconstruction undeniably progressing, as starkly enumerated by William Bennett in *The Index of Leading Cultural Indicators*. The data reveals that over the last 30 years there has been more than a 500 percent increase in violent crime, an over 400 percent increase in illegitimate births, a tripling of the percentage of children living in single parent households, a tripling in the teenage suicide rate, a doubling in the divorce rate, and a 75 point drop in SAT scores. All of this has been accompanied by tremendous increases in government spending including inflation-adjusted increases on welfare of 630 percent and on education of over 200 percent.[18]

Such sociopolitical orientations as the communitarian perspective, empowerment strategies, family values initiatives, volunteerism, character and virtue education, cultural renewal projects--all of these intellectual and civic endeavors seek, in one way or another, to restore a lost balance between the individual and social nature of the human person for the sake of civil society. Two such sociopolitical approaches will be briefly sketched to exemplify these common chords of concern for institutional well-being: communitarianism and the empowerment movement.

A salient feature of the communitarian perspective is that it recognizes that the "preservation of liberty depends upon the active maintenance of the institutions of civil society."[19] Such institutions as family, education, and local communities are the spheres in which shared values and responsible citizenship is fostered. The family as the primary socializing institution, requires special attention. Generally, the communitarian perspective recognizes that the best interests of children are served by stable two parent families and that social policy should encourage this mother-father child-raising pattern as normative. Schools also should support the role of the family in the moral education of children, teaching basic values that Americans share (for example, honesty, thrift, respect, responsibility, democracy) and creating an environment where good character and civil behavior is normative. The raising and educating of children is of first level importance for, among others, the reason David Popenoe identifies: "Successful civilizations heretofore have been based on a family foundation, one that assured that children were taught the values, attitudes, and habits of the culture and became, as adults, reasonably well integrated into society."[20]

The balancing of rights and responsibilities is also an important aspect of communitarian thinking. It aims for, as Amitai Etzioni has said, "a judicious mix of self-interest, self-expression, and commitment to the commons--of rights and responsibilities, of I and we."[21] By its nature, communitarian thought obviously perceives that the current imbalance is weighed in favor of the rights side and that community commitments need to be added to the equation without significantly tilting to either side.

The principles of sociopolitical organization that follow from a communitarian perspective echo the basic tenets of subsidiarity. In general, social responsibilities should not be assumed by higher level or larger institutions than necessary. This applies to social groups as well as governments so that many typical welfare state functions are best handled by those closest to the need, to the extent possible. A preference for viable local communities means that higher levels of government should only be involved when "other social subsystems fail, rather than seek to replace them." There may be roles for government and private partnerships but government must not, in effect, replace local communities.[22]

As would be suspected, there are many and varied facets within communitarian thought, and views about social policy and political economy are diverse, which cannot here be reviewed. What is important is that common threads and connections across sociopolitical orientations can be identified, towards the revivication of social order.

The empowerment movement is another important development for sociopolitical reform that seeks to reorder domestic policy in favor of individual, familial, and communal responsibility. Its approach is to empower individuals and communities through grass roots organization and public policy reform. Empowerment strategies are oriented to helping individuals and local communities take charge of their lives and to put an end to dysfunctional social conditions. Empowerment is a practical and real life application of the movement to restore civil society.

Policy initiatives focus on housing, welfare, education, economic development, and crime and other social problems. An empowerment approach to public housing is to turn management over to tenants and to promote private ownership. Housing controlled by tenants themselves or where owned by individuals, is more efficaciously maintained and social pathologies (for example, crime, drugs, prostitution) are less present in the environment. When people are systematically empowered to accept responsibility through self-management and ownership, they tend to accept it and have more incentives to do so.

People need to be allowed the dignity of responsibility, the freedom to make individual choices, and the opportunity to change their lives for the better. That should be the overarching paradigm of all welfare state policies. In welfare assistance programs, this approach favors initiatives that promote two parent families, savings and ownership, and work opportunities. In other words, it works to bring the poor and marginalized into mainstream society rather than perpetuating dependence. The perverse incentives of the current system are a scandal to the good intentions of most Americans and ruinous to the citizens and communities they are designed to help.

Empowerment means better and greater choices in life and that is nowhere more applicable than the education of one's children. Education is the key to the future as most parents realize. Parents should have the opportunity to send their children to the schools that best meet their goals and needs. In many places, especially in economically depressed urban areas, predominantly minority communities, it is parochial and independent schools that clearly provide a superior learning and social environment. The monopolistic and centralized approach to education has most dramatically failed people who are poor and they, above all, know it. A voucher system empowers parents and their children and would help spur the educational revival the country as a whole increasingly needs to compete in the world and to provide an expanding quality of life.

We have to overcome the notion that public education necessarily means government-run education. The principle of subsidiarity, recognition of mediating structures, and communitarian principles, as well as the failing achievement of many government schools, all logically compel a revamping of the way education has come to be primarily delivered. One of the crucial misjudgments in the history of education was the trend of centralization and consolidation of schools away from their natural communities as well as increasing political control. Education is fundamentally parental and communal in nature and the dominant political system has largely absorbed and displaced these qualities, sometimes in service to special interests, rather than helping to support them.

Other empowerment approaches focus on economic development and job opportunities through such programs as enterprise zones, investment assistance, technical assistance, and so forth. Efforts to restore community security through crime watch and other neighborhood programs are also important. Fundamentally, the empowerment approach seeks to eliminate barriers to individual and community betterment and to inspire citizens and policymakers to this orientation.

Across the spectrum of responsible and pioneering sociopolitical thought, the common principles of social governance that emerge involve a recognition of four things:

1. The practical and moral indispensability of reinvigorated mediating institutions, especially the family, for a free and civil society.
2. The vital necessity of moral renewal and social reinforcement of responsible behavior.
3. The understanding of government as a help to and not a master of individuals and mediating institutions--government as a *servant* of civil society.
4. The fundamental duality of freedom and responsibility and the individual and social nature of the human person, which is at the heart of each of the above.

CONCLUSION

Building the well ordered society, or restoring the social order, entails reinvigorating the mediating institutions of society that transmit and reinforce personal and social responsibility and moral constraint--and it entails restoring the public (including the state) recognition of normative values that bind citizens and their institutional affiliations into a truly civil society. In a country where the state has incrementally absorbed many social functions and where the political system has become so debased as to have largely lost its moral and philosophical moorings, the renewal of political culture needs necessarily to be among the high priorities in rebuilding the well ordered society.

American society is in trouble and almost everyone knows it. We are in trouble because too many of us and our intellectual, social, and political leaders have forgotten or denied that society is not endlessly malleable just as individuals are not. We must return to the understanding that there is a created human nature out of which flows a moral order and "self evident truths." A democratic republic is an experiment in ordered liberty and cannot be grounded on less than the presumption of enduring principles and the rightly formed character of its citizens.

The shaken Scrooge had asked if the dark shadows of the future which were shown to him might yet be changed. And from the innate well springs of the hope of a converted man he answers his own question: " ...if the courses be departed from, the ends will change. Say it is thus with what you show me!"[23] Say it is thus.

ENDNOTES

1.   T.S. Eliot, *Christianity and Culture: The Idea of a Christian Society and Notes Towards the Definition of Culture* (New York & London: Harcourt Brace Jovanovich, 1948), 157.

2.   Charles Dickens, "A Christmas Carol," in *Christmas Books and Stories*, Volume 1 (London: The Hawarden Press, 1899), 160.

3.   Will Herberg, "What is the Moral Crisis of our Time," *The Intercollegiate Review* (Fall 1986): 7.

4.   Michael Novak, "Virtue and the City," (Public Arguments) in *Crisis: A Journal of Lay Catholic Opinion* (May 1994): 9.

5.   See James Q. Wilson, "What is Moral, and How Do We know It?" *Commentary* 95, no. 6 (June 1993): 37; and his *The Moral Sense* (New York: The Free Press, 1993) for a fuller study.

6.   Russell Kirk, *The Wise Men Know Wicked Things are Written on the Sky* (Washington, D.C.: Regnery Gateway, Inc., 1987), 110.

7.   James Madison, quoted in the introduction to *The Federalist Papers by Alexander Hamilton, James Madison and John Jay*, ed. Gary Wills (Toronto: Bantam Books, 1982), xxi.

8.   James Madison, *Federalist 51, Op.cit.*, 261.

9.   John Adams quoted in John Eidsmoe, "The Religious Roots of the Constitution," *The New Federalist Papers*, eds. J. Jackson Barlow, Dennis J. Mahoney and John G. West, Jr. (Lanham, New York & London: University Press of America, 1988), 274.

10.   Edmund Burke, *The Speeches of the Right Hon. Edmund Burke, with Memoir and Historical Introduction by James Burke, Esq., A.B.* (Dublin: James Duffy & Co., Ltd., 1858), 445.

11.   Terrance P. McLaughlin, "Introduction," in *The Church and the Reconstruction of the Modern World: The Social Encyclicals of Pope Pius XI* (Garden City, NY: Image Books, Doubleday & Co., 1957), 1-23.

12.   Peter L. Berger and Richard John Neuhaus, *To Empower People: The Role of Mediating Structures in Public Policy* (Washington, D.C.: American Enterprise

Institute, 1977).

13. Berger and Neuhaus, *To Empower People*, 3.

14. Ibid.

15. Berger and Neuhaus, *To Empower People*, 6.

16. Ibid.

17. Richard John Neuhaus, *Doing Well and Doing Good: The Challenge to the Christian Capitalist* (New York: Doubleday, 1992), 273.

18. William J. Bennett, *The Index of Leading Cultural Indicators: Facts and Figures on the State of American Society* (New York: A Touchstone Book, Simon & Schuster, 1994), 8.

19. *The Responsive Communitarian Platform: Rights and Responsibilities* (Washington, D.C.: The Communitarian Network, undated), 1.

20. David Popenoe, "The Family Condition of America: Cultural Change and Public Policy," in *Values and Public Policy* eds. Henry J. Aaron, Thomas E. Mann, and Timothy Taylor (Washington, D.C.: The Brookings Institution, 1993), 82.

21. Amitai Etzioni, *The Spirit of Community: The Reinvention of American Society* (New York: A Touchstone Book, Simon & Schuster, 1993), 26.

22. *The Responsive Communitarian Platform*, 6.

23. Dickens, "A Christmas Carol," *Op. cit.*, 160.

Chapter 18

Religion in the Civil Public Square

Os Guinness

INTRODUCTION

George Washington's home, Mount Vernon, is among America's most visited sites. But one of the most fascinating things at Mount Vernon is one of the least noticed--the key to the Bastille, the forbidding Paris fortress whose fall on July 14, 1789, became the symbol of the French Revolution. The key hangs in the hall at Mount Vernon, oversized for its classically proportioned surroundings and often overlooked. But it once spoke eloquently for the highest hopes in both nations. Six weeks after the ratification of the U.S. Constitution in September 1787, Jefferson rejoiced at the meeting of the Estates General and the prospect of applying revolutionary American principles to France. In that same spirit, the Marquis de Lafayette took the key of the Bastille in 1789 and sent it to his good friend Washington as a symbol of their common vision of the future.

Jefferson's and Lafayette's hopes were to be dashed. Sobered by the reign of terror and the revolutionary ugliness from Robespierre and Danton to Napoleon, both Americans and French supporters of the United States revised their views. Gouverneur Morris, for example, the U.S. Ambassador to France, wrote home in disgust: "They want an American Constitution with the exception of a king instead of a President, without reflecting that they have no American citizens to uphold that constitution."[1]

Two hundred years later, that discussion sounded astonishingly fresh as the stirring events of 1989 unfolded. Old hopes and fears that the framers' generation would have understood were alive again. Issues that echo those discussed by Washington and Jefferson were in the air--how realistic is it to view democracy as a model set of political arrangements to be exported? What is the role of technology as a force for freedom and democratic change? For democracy to prosper, does a nation have to have certain ideals and assumptions, or is it enough to copy institutions and political arrangements, such as free, recurrent elections, separation of the executive and judiciary branches, and respect for civil liberties?

Opinions differ sharply over the answers to these questions. But what seems odd in a century clouded by state repression and sectarian violence is that no part of the American experiment stands out more clearly yet is less appreciated or copied as a key to modern troubles than the Religious Liberty clauses of the First Amendment. For in the tensions and challenges now surrounding the clauses are some of the deepest and most significant issues of our time. Above all, there is the simple but vital question: How do we, in an age of expanding worldwide pluralism, live with our deepest--that is, our religiously and ideologically intense-- differences? In short, what is the relationship of religious liberty and American democracy today?

This chapter examines perhaps the most critical task of rebuilding a civil society--reforging the public philosophy. The overall purpose is reconstitution--the genuine reappropriation of the constitutional heritage through citizens engaging in a new debate reordered in accord with constitutional first principles and considerations of the common good.

The present situation confronts Americans directly with a three-fold choice first stated by supporters of democracy in Greece and restated by John Courtney Murray in the early 1960s. The choice is as follows: As the crisis of the public philosophy deepens and controversies over religion and public life continue to arise, will Americans respond as "tribespeople," in the sense of those who seek security in a form of tribal solidarity and are intolerant of everything alien to themselves (a problem that grows from a distortion of communitarianism and an exaggerated view of group sensitivities, whether religious, racial, sexual, or ethnic)? Or will they respond as "idiots," in the original Greek sense of the totally private person who does not subscribe to the public philosophy and is oblivious to the importance of "civility" (a problem that grows from a distortion of libertarianism and an exaggerated view of individual and personal rights)? Or will they respond as "citizens," in the sense of those who stand for their own interests but who also recognize their membership in a "commonwealth" and who appreciate the knowledge and skills that underlie the public life of a civilized community?[2]

Agreement over the place of religious liberty in a civil society is only one component of the wider public philosophy, but a vital one because of the personal importance of faiths to individuals and to communities of faith in America, and the public importance of both to American national life, a common vision of religious liberty in public life is critical to both citizens and the nation. It affects personal and communal liberty, civic vitality, and social harmony directly. Far from lessening the need for a public philosophy today, expanding pluralism increases it.

AMERICA'S FIRST LIBERTY

The first step in reforging the public philosophy is to show why the notion of religious liberty remains important to the public philosophy today. For, to underscore the point once more, to many Americans, especially the thought leaders, the question of religion in public life has become unimportant. It is viewed as a nonissue or a nuisance factor--something that should be purely a private issue, which inevitably becomes messy and controversial when it does not stay so, and which should therefore revert to being private as quickly as possible.

A more helpful way of seeing things is to see that the swirling controversies that surround religion and public life create a sort of sound barrier effect. At one level, the issue appears all passions, problems, and prejudices. But break through to a higher level and it touches on several of the deepest questions of human life in the modern world. Once these are appreciated, it clearly becomes in the highest interest of the common good to resolve the problems rather than ban the topic out of personal disdain or fear.

There are at least five reasons why religious liberty remains a vital part of America's public philosophy. First, religious liberty, or freedom of conscience, is a precious, fundamental, and inalienable human right--the freedom to reach, hold, freely exercise, or change one's beliefs, subject solely to the dictates of conscience and independent of all outside, especially governmental, control. Prior to and existing quite apart from the Bill of Rights that protects it, religious liberty is not a luxury, a second-class right, a constitutional redundancy, or a sub-category of free speech. Since it does not finally depend on the discoveries of science, the favors of the state and its officials, or the vagaries of tyrants or majorities, it is a right that may not be submitted to any vote nor encroached upon by the expansion of the bureaucratic state. Since it is a free-standing right, it is integrally linked to other basic rights, such as freedom of speech, but it does not need them to supplement its legitimacy.

Unless America's public philosophy respects and protects this right for all Americans, the American promise of individual freedom and justice is breached.

Second, the Religious Liberty clauses of the First Amendment are the democratic world's most distinctive answer to one of the entire world's most pressing questions: How do we live with our deepest--that is, our religiously intense--differences?

Some regions of the world (for example, in western Europe) exhibit a strong political civility that is directly linked to their weak religious commitments; and others (for example, in the Middle East) exhibit a strong religious commitment directly linked to their weak political civility. Owing to the manner of the First Amendment's ordering of religious liberty and public life, American democracy has afforded the fullest opportunity for strong religious commitment and strong political civility to complement, rather than threaten, each other.

Unless America's public philosophy respects and protects this distinctive American achievement, the American promise of democratic liberty and justice will be betrayed.

Third, the Religious Liberty clauses lie close to the genius of the American experiment. Far more than a luxury, let alone a redundancy, the First Amendment is essential and indispensable to the character of the American republic. Not simply a guarantee of individual and communal liberty, the First Amendment's ordering of the relationship of religion and public life is the boldest and most successful part of the entire American experiment. Daring in its time, distinctive throughout the world both then and now, it has proved decisive in shaping key aspects of the American story. It is not too much even to say that as the Religious Liberty clauses go, so goes America.

Unless America's public philosophy respects and protects this remarkable American ordering, the civic vitality of the American republic will be sapped.

Fourth, the Religious Liberty clauses are the single, strongest non-theological reason why free speech and the free exercise of religion have been closely related and why religion in general has persisted more strongly in the United States than in any other comparable modern country. In most modern countries, there appears to be an almost ironclad equation: the more modernized the country, the more secularized the people. America, however, is a striking exception to the trend, being at once the most modernized country and having the most religious of modern peoples.

The reason lies in the effect of the American style of disestablishment. By separating church and state, but not religion and government or public life, disestablishment does two things. It undercuts the forces of cultural antipathy built up against religious communities by church-state establishments--historically speaking, established churches have contributed strongly to their own rejection and to secularization in general. At the same time, disestablishment throws each faith onto reliance on its own claimed resources. The overall effect is to release a free and unfettered competition of people and beliefs similar to the free-market competition of capitalism.

Unless America's public philosophy respects and protects this enterprising relationship, both American religious liberty and public discourse will be handicapped.

Fifth, the interpretation and application of the First Amendment today touches on some of the deepest and most revolutionary developments in contemporary thought. A generation ago it was common to draw a deep dichotomy between science and religion, reason and revelation, objectivity and commitment, and so on. Today such dichotomies are impossible. All thinking is acknowledged to be presuppositional. Value-neutrality in social affairs is impossible. To demand "neutral discourse" in public life, as some still do, should now be recognized as a way of coercing people to speak publicly in someone else's language and thus never to be true to their own.

Unless America's public philosophy respects and protects this new (or restored) understanding, the republican requirement of free democratic debate and responsible participation in democratic life will be thwarted.

One conclusion is inescapable: The place of religious liberty in American public life is not merely a religious issue, but a national issue. It is not only a private issue, but a public one. Far from being simply partisan or sectarian, religious liberty is in the interest of Americans of all faiths or none, and its reaffirmation should be a singular and treasured part of the American public philosophy.

CHANGES, CHALLENGES, AND CONTROVERSIES

The second step in reforging the public philosophy is to analyze the factors behind the recurring conflicts over religion and public life, and assess the challenge they pose for American religious liberty and the public philosophy today. The conflicts themselves need no elaboration, though it is helpful to draw a distinction between cases where religion itself is directly the issue and cases where its influence is indirect. Abortion is the principal example of the latter and examples of the former are common—school prayer and New Age meditation, creation science, secular humanism, textbook tailoring, prayer before high school sporting events, Muslim prayer mats in government offices, Gideon's Bibles in hotel rooms, the Ten Commandments on school walls, blasphemy in films and novels, the Pledge of Allegiance, Mormon polygamy, "Christian Nation" resolutions, day care centers, and so on.

Some of these conflicts are critical, others less so. But they are all flashpoints along the contested boundaries between religion and public life. For a full generation now, this issue has been highly contentious, with an endless series of disputes and the whole subject surrounded by needless ignorance and fruitless controversy, including at the highest levels. Too often, debates have been sharply polarized, controversies dominated by extremes, resolutions sought automatically through litigation, either of the Religious Liberty clauses set against the other one, and any common view of a better way lost in the din of irreconcilable differences and insistent demands.

The temptation is to take a quick glance at the contestants, apportion the blame, enlist on one side or another, and treat the whole problem as largely political and capable of having a political solution. From that perspective, the problem is one that has been created by a series of overlapping conflicts: an ideological clash (the fundamentalists versus the secularists) that overlaps with a constitutional clash (the accommodationist "low wallers" versus the strict separationist "high wallers") that overlaps with a historical clash (the biblical and republican tradition versus the Enlightenment and liberal tradition) that overlaps with a clash of social visions (the communitarian "rootsers" versus the libertarian "rightsers") that overlaps with opposing views of morality in public life (the maximalists versus the minimalists) that overlaps with a psychological clash (the "bitter-enders," who insist on commitment regardless of civility, versus the "betrayers," who insist on civility regardless of commitment), which has produced, in turn, two extremist tendencies (the "removers," who would like to eradicate all religion from public life, versus the "reimposers," who would like to impose their version of a past or future state of affairs on everyone else)--all this, of course, potently reinforced by technological factors, such as direct mail and its shameless appeals to fear and anger.

Such analyses may be accurate as far as they go. But they stop before they take into account some of the deepest factors. All of the above conflicts amount to a series of responses--which raises the question of what are the deeper forces to which they are responding. I would argue that behind the recent conflicts lie several developments that stem from the explosive acceleration of modernization in the last generation. Two factors are especially important to this argument: the reversal of roles in the relationship of church and state and the current expansion of pluralism.

"Church and State" has become a thought-numbing category that misleads as much as it illuminates. As Judge John Noonan has pointed out, the phrase is triply misleading because it suggests that in America there is a single church, a single state, and a simple, clear distinction between the two. But this confusion is only the beginning of the complexities. Harold J. Berman, the doyen of American scholars on law and religion, builds on that and shows that the framers' more common terms were religion and government, not church and state. But not only have religion and government each changed over the course of 200 years under the impact of modernity, the relationship between them has also changed to the point of being a complete "exchange of roles."[3]

Berman analyzed the involvement of religion and government over 200 years in three areas, family life, education, and welfare. He summarized the two main consequences of the role reversal:

> In the 1780s religion played a primary role in social life . . . and government played a relatively minor, though necessary, supportive role, whereas in the 1980s religion plays a relatively minor, though necessary, supportive role and government plays a primary role. On the other hand, the role played by government in the social life of America in the 1780s (and for almost a century and a half thereafter) was openly and strongly influenced and directed by religion, whereas in the 1980s that is much less true and in many respects not true at all, while the role played by religion in the social life of America in the 1980s is openly and strongly influenced and directed by government.[4]

Berman builds his case with care, but states his conclusion with force. "Whereas two centuries ago, in matters of social life which have a significant moral dimension, government was the handmaid of religion, today religion--in its social responsibilities, as contrasted with personal faith and collective worship--is the handmaid of government."[5]

The second, and equally important, factor is the recent expansion of pluralism. This is a worldwide phenomenon that links current American tensions to similar trends around the globe. How do we live with each other's deepest differences? That simple question has been transformed by modernity into one of the world's most pressing dilemmas. On a small planet in a pluralistic age the all too common response has been bigotry, fanaticism, terrorism, and state repression.

Multiculturalism and expanding pluralism is no stranger to the American experience. It has always been a major theme in the American story, with tolerance generally expanding behind pluralism. But the last generation has witnessed yet another thrust forward in religious pluralism in two significant ways. First, American pluralism now goes beyond the predominance of Protestant-Catholic-Jewish and includes sizable numbers of almost all the world's great religions--Buddhist and Muslim, in particular--though an astonishing 86.5 percent of Americans identify themselves as Christians. Second, it now goes beyond religion altogether to include a growing number of Americans with no religious preference. In 1962, as in 1952, secularists--or the so-called "religious nones"--were two percent of Americans. Today they are between ten and 12 percent, and strikingly higher on the West coast than anywhere else.[6]

This latest expansion of pluralism is one of the social facts of our time, though consciousness of it has been reinforced and somewhat distorted through a combination of modern technologies and postmodern theories. The effect has been to complete the profound sea change initiated by the "new immigration" of the beginning of the century. The United States has shifted from a largely Protestant pluralism to a genuine multifaith pluralism that includes people of all faiths and those who claim no religious preference. The effect can be observed at two different levels in American society. In the first place, the effect of exploding diversity can be seen in the demographic make-up of contemporary American society. The state of California, for example, has America's most diverse as well as its largest population. It now accepts almost one-third of the world's immigration and represents at the close of the century what New York did at the start--the point of entry for millions of new Americans.[7]

California's schools have a "minority majority" in all public school enrollments. This will be true of the population of California as a whole soon after the year 2000. (The same situation already exists in all of the nation's 25 largest city school systems, and half of the states have public school populations that are more than 25 percent minorities.[8]) The result is a remarkable mix of the diverse cultures of Africa, Asia, Europe, and Latin America.

The effect of the exploding diversity can also be seen in what is a form of cultural breakdown--collapse of the previously accepted understandings of the relationship of religion and public life and the triggering of the culture wars. As a result, a series of bitter, fruitless contentions over religion and politics has erupted, extremes have surfaced, the resort to the law court has become almost reflexive, many who decry the problems are equally opposed to solutions to them, and in the ensuing din of charge and countercharge any sense of common vision for the common good has been drowned.

As always with the trends of modernity, the consequences of increased pluralism are neither unique to America nor uniform throughout the world. Nor are the consequences of pluralization simple. On the one hand, increased pluralism deepens old tensions. Under the challenge of "all those others," many are seemingly pressured to believe more weakly in their own faith, to the point of compromise--the more choice and change, the less commitment and continuity. In reaction, however, others tend to believe more strongly, to the point of contempt for the faith of others. On the other hand, increased pluralism helps develop new trends. Today's dominant tensions are not so much between distinct religions and denominations. As often as not, they are between the more orthodox and the more contemporary within the same denomination.

In sum, like it or not, modern pluralism stands squarely as both the child of, and the challenger to, religious liberty--whether because of its presence (given the democratic conditions arising out of the Reformation and the Wars of Religion), its permanence (given the likely continuation of these conditions in the foreseeable future), or its premise (that a single, uniform doctrine of belief can only achieve dominance in a pluralistic society by two means: through persuasion, which is currently unlikely because unfashionable, or through coercion by the oppressive use of state power, which at anytime is unjust and unfree). If religious liberty makes pluralism more likely, pluralism makes religious liberty more necessary.

CHARTER FOR THE THIRD CENTURY

The third step in reforging the public philosophy is to introduce the concept of covenantalism, or chartered pluralism, as the basis of the public philosophy. This means to examine its contribution to the civil society and to show its advantages over the two existing visions of religion and public life that are now deadlocked--namely, communitarianism, the social vision that degenerates into "tribalism," and libertarianism, the vision that degenerates into political "idiocy." Anyone who appreciates the factors behind the present conflicts is confronted with tough questions. Above all, can there be a healing of the schism of the spirit, a resolution to the culture wars, and an adjustment to the new pluralism without endangering the logic of religious liberty in public life? Can there be an agreed center of national unity that complements, rather than contradicts, American diversity? Is there a way in which diverse faiths can fulfill their respective responsibility to the requirements of order, freedom, and justice without favoring one of the three at the expense of the other two?

At first sight, the search for a just and commonly acceptable solution to these challenges seems as futile as squaring the circle or searching for esperanto. The question of the public role of religion in an increasingly pluralistic society appears to be a minefield of controversies, with the resulting ignorance, confusion, and reluctance an understandable outcome. Yet if it is correct to trace the problem to forces, such as pluralism, as much as to ideologies, individuals, and groups, then we have more victims than villains over this issue, and the wisest approach is to search together for a solution, not for a scapegoat.

In fact, the present stage of the conflict offers a strategic opportunity in the 1990s. Extreme positions and unwelcome consequences are readily identifiable on many sides, and a new desire for consensus is evident. But where and on what grounds could consensus emerge? As so often, the most constructive way forward is to go back--or, more accurately, to reforge the public philosophy through the renewal of a concept that is at the heart of American democracy and the American constitutional tradition--covenantalism.

Historical Covenants

The recovery of the idea of covenant as a key to American democracy and the American constitutional tradition is one of the freshest and most important findings of recent scholarship.[9] Far from being completely new and startlingly original, the Constitution of 1787 is now seen to be the climax of a long tradition of covenants, compacts, and charters that goes back to the earliest colonial experience. Far from being the legacy of John Locke in the 17th century or Whig and Enlightenment thinkers in the 18th century, the American constitutional tradition was in place and operating strongly by the 1640s when John Locke was not yet a teenager and Charles-Louis Montesquieu, Jean-Jacques Rousseau, and William Blackstone had not been born.

Seen in this new light, the American Constitution and the constitutional tradition grew directly from the seedbed of Puritan ideals and institutions that were rooted in the notion of covenant. Dissenting English colonists relied on Swiss, Dutch, and German theologians who themselves relied on the biblical principles of a Jewish covenantal republic to create a distinctively American style of government. The term "federalism" did not come into use until later, but Puritan notions, such as "federal liberty," were the twin-concepts to "federal theology" and all went back to the core of covenant (*foedus* in Latin and *B'rit* in Hebrew). The foundational covenant was the one between God and human beings, but there were multiple extensions to different levels of community--the covenant of marriage, the local church, the town, the colony, and eventually the nation.

The Mayflower Compact on November 11, 1620, was the first explicitly political use of the religious covenant form and a historic milestone on the road to the more secular and national covenant of the "miracle in Philadelphia" in 1787. But in all the dozens of cases that made up the early American system of institutions and set of ideals, one feature was unmistakable: The covenant/compact/charter represents a distinctive combination of unity and diversity, commonality and independence, obligation and voluntary consent.

This idea of covenantal, or federal, liberty holds the promise of a resolution of our present problems through the concept of chartered pluralism. At the base of the notion is a defining feature of modern experience: The present state of intellectual divisions in modern pluralistic societies does not permit agreement at the level of the *origin* of beliefs (where justifications for behavior are theoretical, ultimate, and irreconcilable). But a significant, though limited, agreement is still possible at the level of the *outworking* of beliefs (where the expression of beliefs in behavior is more practical, less ultimate, and often overlapping with the practical beliefs and behavior of other people).

The Three Rs: Rights, Responsibilities, Respect

Covenantalism, or chartered pluralism, is therefore a vision of religious liberty in public life that, across the deep religious differences of a pluralistic society, guarantees and sustains religious liberty for all by forging a substantive agreement, or freely chosen compact, over three things that are the "Three Rs" of religious liberty: rights, responsibilities, and respect. The compact affirms: first, in terms of rights, that religious liberty, or freedom of conscience, is a fundamental and inalienable right for peoples of all faiths and none; second, in terms of responsibilities, that religious liberty is a universal right joined to a universal duty to respect that right for others; and third, in terms of respect, that the first principles of religious liberty, combined with the lessons of 200 years of constitutional experience, require and shape certain practical guidelines by which a robust yet civil discourse may be sustained in a free society that would remain free.

The social vision of covenantalism is a modern form of "federal liberty" that combines the best, and avoids the worst, of the libertarian and communitarian visions. Put differently, the notion of chartered pluralism is an example of what John Rawls calls the "overlapping consensus" that is needed in a liberal democracy. The core of its principled pact over the Three Rs is a variation of what Jacques Maritain described as "a sort of unwritten common law, at the point of practical convergence of extremely different theoretical ideologies and spiritual traditions." Maritain used himself to provide the example of the difference between the theoretical and the practical levels.

> I am fully convinced that my way of justifying the belief in the rights of man and the ideal of liberty, equality, fraternity, is the only one which is solidly based on truth. That does not prevent me from agreeing on these practical tenets with those who are convinced that their way of justifying them, entirely different from mine, or even opposed to mine in its theoretical dynamism, is likewise the only one that is based on truth. Assuming they both believe in the democratic charter, a Christian and a rationalist will nevertheless give justifications that are incompatible with each other, to which their souls, their minds and their blood are committed, and about these justifications they will fight. And God keep me from saying that it is not important to know which of the two is right! That is essentially important. They remain, however, in agreement on the practical affirmation of that charter, and they can formulate common principles of action.[10]

The covenantal element in chartered pluralism is obvious. The social vision is solidly founded on such a principled pact that it can be seen to give due weight to the first of its two terms. It is therefore properly a form of *chartered* pluralism, or pluralism within the framework of a principled charter that spells out the rights, responsibilities, and respect required by religious liberty. So long as the pact over the Three Rs of religious liberty remains strong, the vision avoids the respective weaknesses of relativism, interest-group liberalism, or any of the minimalist approaches to unity that rely solely on "process" and "proceduralism." (For example, claims that seek to go beyond proceduralism but only a little, such as: "We are held together by the coherence of our moral disagreement and argument within an ongoing cultural conversation."[11])

But at the same time the area of public agreement is strictly limited in both substance and in scope. The pact does not pretend to include agreement over religious beliefs, political policies, constitutional interpretations, or even the philosophical justifications of the three parts of the compact. Chartered pluralism is an agreement within disagreements over deep differences that make a difference. It therefore gives due weight to the second of its two terms, and remains a form of chartered *pluralism*. By doing so, it avoids the equal but opposite maximalist approaches to unity, such as the dangers of majoritarianism, civil religion, or any form of overreaching consensus that is blind or insensitive to tiny minorities and unpopular communities. Thus social unity is maintained, but religious liberty and diversity are respected in that religious unity is either made dependent upon persuasion or deferred as a messianic hope to be fulfilled only at the end of time.

Chartered Pluralism

Several features of this compact at the heart of chartered pluralism need to be highlighted indelibly, if the compact is to pass muster under the exacting challenges of the present situation. First, the character of the compact is not a form of civil religion or public theology. Its content does not grow from shared beliefs, religious or political, because the recent expansion of pluralism means that we are now beyond the point where that is possible.[12]

Second, the achievement of this compact does not come through the process of a general dilution of beliefs, as in the case of civil religion moving from Protestantism to "Judeo-Christian" theism. It comes through the process of a particular concentration of universal rights and mutual responsibilities, within which the deep differences of belief can be negotiated.

Third, the fact that religious consensus is now impossible does not mean that moral consensus (for example, "consensual" or "common core" values in public education) is either unimportant or unattainable. It means, however, that moral consensus must be viewed as a goal, not as a given; something to be achieved through persuasion and ongoing conversation rather than assumed on the basis of tradition. Thus chartered pluralism means that there is a way to give positive meaning to public life without coercive imposition, and at the same time to foster an emphasis on freedom and diversity that need not lead toward fragmentation.

Fourth, the fact that the different religious roots of the public philosophy are largely invisible in public does not mean that they are unimportant or that the public philosophy is secular in a secularist ideological sense. On the contrary, a cut-flower public philosophy will not work. So the health of the public philosophy depends not only on a public conversation of citizens across the divisions of creed and generation, but on the private cultivation of the first principles of the public philosophy within each home and faith community. Should the diverse roots of those first principles ever grow weak or be poisoned from some antidemocratic source, such a private crisis would have inevitable public consequences.

Fifth, chartered pluralism allows even "radically monotheist" religions, such as Judaism and the Christian faith, to balance the twin demands of theological integrity and civil unity. Such faiths can never be content with religious liberty as freedom *from;* to them it must always be freedom *for*. Chartered pluralism therefore allows them to exercise their responsibilities to their conceptions of order, freedom, and justice, yet without infringing on the rights of others or becoming socially disruptive. Whereas the "idiocy" bred by libertarianism can be notoriously casual about order, and the "tribalism" bred by communitarianism on the Right and the Left can grow blind to freedom and justice for others, the federal liberty of chartered pluralism makes room for the free exercise of transcendent faiths that can address all three concerns with their own integrity, yet without compromise to themselves or damage to civil unity. The only proviso is that such influence is generally best exercised spiritually rather than politically, indirectly rather than directly, and persuasively rather than coercively.

Deficient Alternatives

Viewed in the light of the alternatives, chartered pluralism provides a way between communitarianism and libertarianism. Communitarianism, found on both the Left and the Right, virtually equates politics with morality. When transferred to the level of a public philosophy, it tends to see everything in terms of its ideology writ large all over public life. Whereas libertarianism, also found on both the Left and the Right, virtually excludes morality from politics. When transferred to the level of a public philosophy, it tends to see everything in terms of an individualism that sucks the commonness out of public life altogether.

Curiously, both social visions betray their inadequacies as candidates for the public philosophy, partly because of the ironies they exhibit and partly because they rule themselves out on the grounds of their own principles. In the politically unlikely event that communitarianism were to prevail as the public philosophy, it would become a form of majoritarianism. In seeking to impose a style of traditional solidarity on modern pluralism, it would end in denying pluralism (a smaller and milder recapitulation of the totalitarian error). On the other hand, if the communitarian vision does not seek to prevail as the public philosophy--which the majority of communitarians probably prefer anyway--the effect of communitarianism on public life would be to reinforce relativism, not community.

Libertarianism, in contrast, sets out to widen the sphere of public freedom by relativizing all faiths. Everyone will be more free if no one's position is "imposed" on anyone else because "everything depends on where you're coming from." But the effect is to relativize all positions except relativism and so to assert a new imposition in public life--that of a dogmatized relativism and a universalized libertarianism. Thus if communitarianism ends in denying the reality of pluralism, libertarianism ends in distorting it. For currently pluralism goes more closely with particularism than with relativism. Most believers who make up today's pluralistic society want to affirm their distinctives. They believe that the beliefs that make them different are finally right and important. They are committed to them in terms of absolutes--just as for many relativists relativism itself has become the last surviving absolute. Thus libertarianism rules itself out as a candidate for the public philosophy too. Ironically again, if American public life is to retain and strengthen the sphere of liberty, it cannot be on the basis of libertarianism as the public philosophy.

Expressed differently, chartered pluralism owes much to John Courtney Murray's valuable insistence that the unity asserted in the American motto, *E pluribus unum*, is a unity with limits. And therefore that the Religious Liberty clauses are "articles of peace" rather than "articles of faith."[13] But Father Murray's distinction, which was borrowed from Samuel Johnson, must never be widened into a divorce. For one thing, the articles of peace are principled before they are procedural, and they need to stay principled if principled procedures are not to be sucked into the nihilism of empty proceduralism. The articles of peace are not sacred or ultimate themselves, but they derive from articles of faith and cannot be sustained long without them. For the same reason, genuine civility is substantive before it is formal. It is not a rhetoric of niceness, let alone a fear of nastiness. Nor is it a psychology of social adjustment. Civility is both an attitude and a discourse shaped by a principled respect for people, truth, the common good, and the American constitutional tradition.

For another thing, neither chartered pluralism nor the notion of articles of peace should be understood as leading to unanimity, but to that unity within which diversity can be transformed into richness and disagreement itself into an achievement that betokens strength. Again, the old term "federal liberty" carries rich meanings. As Murray wrote, "The one civil society contains within its new unity the communities that are divided among themselves; but it does not seek to reduce to its own unity the differences that divide them."[14]

Understood properly, these three ideas--covenantalism, chartered pluralism, and federal liberty--are critical to reforging the aspect of the public philosophy that bears on questions of religion and American public life, especially in the light of the deficiencies of the alternatives. They therefore contribute vitally to keeping democracy safe for diversity. If this vision of a promise-keeping covenant gains acceptance in the three main arenas of conflict--public policy debates, the resort to law, and public education--and if it succeeds in addressing their problems constructively, chartered pluralism could serve as a public philosophy for the public square, truly a charter for religion and public life in America's third century of constitutional government.

OUR PAGE IN THE STORY

The last step in reforging the public philosophy is to set out some of the foreseeable principles and pitfalls that should shape prudential judgments as to the best way forward through the controversies.

First, certain conditions for a constructive solution are necessary politically to achieve justice. To be realistic, the issue is never likely to become a popular cause--if only because so many American thought-leaders are largely oblivious of religion and so many American believers are largely oblivious of serious thinking. Solid concepts and good will are therefore not enough. What is required is intellectual foresight that will tackle problems today; moral courage to tackle problems not necessarily considered "problematic" on the current political agenda; magnanimity that in the present situation will act generously, regardless of its own political position, with regard to the interests of others and especially those of the weaker parties; and all these qualities gathered up in bipartisan leadership of a Lincolnesque stature that begins in the White

House and reaches out across the land.

Second, there are two unlikely outcomes. These outcomes are all but inconceivable, but are worth stating because they form the stuff of activist propaganda and counterpropaganda. On the one hand, the conflicts would degenerate into Belfast-style sectarian violence. On the other hand, they would result in an Albanian-style repression of religion, especially in the public square. The combined logic of America's historic commitment to religious liberty and the depth of religious diversity today makes these outcomes virtually impossible.

Third, two undesirable outcomes, in the sense of two broad possibilities, might occur should there be no effective resolution of the current conflicts over religion and public life. The milder, shorter-term possibility is of a massive popular revulsion against religion in public life. This could take the form of "A-plague-on-both-your-houses" reaction to religious contention and therefore lead, ironically, to a sort of naked public square created, not by secularists or separationists, but by a wrongheaded overreaction to an equally wrongheaded religious overreaction.

Fourth, there are two unfortunate outcomes, in the sense of two broad possibilities that might occur even if chartered pluralism succeeds or if current conflicts simply fade away without apparent damage to national life. The first possibility is that, in the generally civil conditions of pluralism, the way is opened for some faith or worldview to play the game only to win the game and end the game for others (existing candidates from the secular left and the religious right are equally dangerous here). The second possibility is that, in the same civil conditions of pluralism, civility will itself become so corrupted that, in turn, pluralism is debased into a relativistic indifference to truth and principle. The result would be a slump into apathy, the logic of laissez-faire freedom gone to seed. The outcome would be that corruption of the republic from within of which the framers warned.

For some Americans, mention of these dangers only confirms the risks of chartered pluralism they feared all along. But mention of the framers is a reminder that the risks are not new. They were built into the experiment from the very start and, even before that, they were present in all the variations of covenant. From Sinai onward, covenants require free and continuing consent because the spirit of the compact is as important as its letter. Such risks are the reason why the American experiment is open-ended, and why the task of defending religious liberty is never finished.

Yet the risk is only half the story. The very open-endedness that is the source of risk is also the source of potential renewal. That is why each citizen and each generation matter. Each adds a new chapter to the story. As so often, Tocqueville saw this point and applied it to the two great revolutions of his time. "In a rebellion, as in a novel," he wrote, "the most difficult part to invent is the end."[15]

ENDNOTES

Reprinted, with changes, from "Tribespeople, Idiots or Citizens?" (Chapter 13) in *The American Hour: A Time of Reckoning and the Once and Future Role of Faith* by Os Guiness. Copyright 1993 by Os Guiness. Modified by the author and reprinted with permission of the publisher, The Free Press, Macmillan Publishing.

1.   Gouverneur Morris to William Carmichael 2, 10 July 1789, *The Life and Writings of Gouverneur Morris*, ed. J. Sparks (1832), 75.

2.   John Courtney Murray, "The Return to Tribalism," *The Catholic Mind*, 60 (January 1962), 6.

3.   Ibid., 48.

4.   Ibid., 42.

5.   Ibid., 43.

6.   The Williamsburg Charter Foundation, *The Williamsburg Charter Survey on Religion and Public Life* (Washington, D.C.: The Williamsburg Charter Foundation, 1988). See also *The New York Times*, 10 April 1991, A1, A18.

7.   Harold L. Hodgkinson, *California: The State and its Educational System* (Washington, D.C.: The Institute for Educational Leadership, 1986) No pp.

8.   Harold L. Hodgkinson, *All One System: Demographics of Education, Kindergarten through Graduate School* (Washington, D.C.: The Institute for Educational Leadership, 1985) No pp.

9.   See Donald S. Lutz, "Religious Dimension in the Development of American Constitutionalism," *Emory Law Journal* 39 (Winter 1990): 21; Elazar, "Covenant as the basis of Jewish Political Tradition," *Jewish Journal of Sociology* 2, no. 5 (1978): 5-37.

10.   Jacques Maritain, "The Possibilities for Co-operation in a Divided World,"

(Inaugural Address to the Second International Conference of UNESCO, 6 November 1947).

11.   Steven Tipton, "Religion in an Ambiguous Polity," *Emory Law Journal* 39 (Winter 1990): 196.

12.   See John Rawls, "The Idea of an Overlapping Consensus," *Oxford Journal of Legal Studies* 7, no. 1 (1987) No pp.

13.   John Courtney Murray, *We Hold These Truths*, 49.

14.   Ibid., 45.

15.   Alexis de Tocqueville, Recollections, ed. J. P. Mayer (New York: 1959), pt. I, chap. 5.

V. Perspectives on Civil Society

Chapter 19

Traditionalist: Strengthening the Bonds of Civil Society

Allan C. Carlson

THE TRADITIONALIST PREMISE

Traditionalist society rests on submission to the Divine spirit and will. Its members find these manifest, to some evident degree, in human nature and the order of Creation. All social constructs strive for harmony with this Divine intent.

THE PREMIER SOCIETAL BOND: MARRIAGE

Civil society builds on marriage, the first and most natural social bond. Marriage holds these distinctions, for it is self-renewing, rooted in the mutual attraction of man to woman, and of woman to man, both of whom feel their incompleteness when existing alone. They come together, of necessity, so that the human species might endure. Most cultures place marriage at or near the center of religious ritual, but the marital institution can be found even among pagan or animist savages, testifying to its universality.

The author gratefully acknowledges various sources of inspiration for this article, including Aristotle, St. Augustine, G.P. Murdock, Frederic LePlay, Carle Zimmerman, Robert Nisbet, Liberty Hyde Bailey, Thomas Fleming, David Ricardo, G.K. Chesterton, Ralph Borsodi, Sigrid Undset, Joseph Schumpeter, Russell Kirk, Wendell Berry, and Peter Berger.

In this sense, marriage is the only true anarchist institution. It pre-exists every other human bond, be it clan, village, city, state, or nation, and it has the endless capacity for renewal, even in periods of general social decline and moral degradation. Each new marriage is an affirmation of life, love (real or potential), and continuity against the darkness which threatens to overwhelm the human spirit. Every new marriage is an act of rebellion against grasping political and ideological powers that would reduce human activity to that of automatons. And each marriage contains within it the power of biological reproduction, a throw of the genetic dice that brings to life new beings, unique and unpredictable in their manifest details.

At the same time, marriage forms the foundation on which humans build other social bonds. Marriage is, at one level, a covenant between two individuals, a man and a woman who agree to give each other mutual care, respect, and protection, and who open their future to the life issuing from their sexual union. Marriage fulfills this role, and functions properly, only when the bond is indissoluble. Without that mutual promise, the efforts toward forming one flesh of man and woman can never succeed. The marital partners, out of fear for the future, will withhold some part of their investment of time and energy into the marriage. The promise of indissolubility alone encourages the man and woman to negotiate through the great differences between them in mind and body, and to bring some resolution to their common life. Incompleteness in the promise, of any sort, operates as would a crack in the foundation of a great edifice, spreading ever further.

Each marriage is also a covenant between the couple and their kin. In marriage, two families merge, in a manner that perpetuates and invigorates both. Even in the denatured societies of the modern West, family members will travel great distances to attend the wedding of a cousin, nephew, or niece, still recognizing through residual instinct the importance of both the promise and the event to their own identity and continuity.

More broadly, marriage is the innate solution to human society's universal dependency problem. Every community must resolve the same issue: who will care for the very young, the very old, the weak, and the infirm? How shall the rewards given to productive adults be shared with those who are not or cannot be productive? In the natural human order, these tasks fall on kin networks, where spouses care for each other "in sickness or in health," where parents nurture, train, and protect their offspring, until they are able to create marriages of their own, where the aged enjoy care, purpose, and respect around the hearth of their grown children, and where kin insure that no family member falls through the family's safety net. Acceptance of these duties passes from generation to generation, as each child views the treatment bestowed by his parents on his grandparents, great aunts and uncles, and so on. These observations teach children, as well, the duty and enlightened self-interest to be found in their own begetting of children, so that the chain of obligation within a family might not be broken.

Marriage is also a covenant between the couple and the broader community. Procreation within marriage offers the best promise of new community members who will be supported and trained by parents *without* being a charge on others and who will grow into responsible adults able to contribute to the community's well-being. Predictably, children reared within marriage will be healthier, brighter, harder working, and more honest, dutiful, and cooperative than those raised in other ways. They will be more likely to acquire useful skills and knowledge and less likely to slide into violent, abusive, or self-destructive behaviors. As such, each marriage represents the renewal of a community, through the promise of responsible new members to come, which is why every healthy human society invests so much ceremony and rhetoric in the event, and why a boundless array of informal pressures strive to hold the marriage together. These are symbols to the husband and wife of the solemn importance that this event holds to neighbors beyond their intimate relationship and biological families. Humans instinctively understand that the strength of their community is dependent on the strength of their marriages. If the marital institution weakens--or worse, if it is politicized--then the social pathologies of suicide, crime, abuse, poor health, and crippling dependency surely follow. If continued over several generations, these pathologies born from the decay of wedlock will consume the community itself.

THE SECOND NATURAL BOND: THE HOUSEHOLD

Marriage, in turn, creates a new household, the multitude of which gathered together form the second institutional tier in natural social life, and the one on which all political life is built. The household will normally encompass the wedded man and woman, their children, and aged or unmarried kin, joined in some cultures by apprentices and servants. Successful households are the natural reservoir of liberty. They aim at autonomy or independence, enabling their members to resist oppression, survive economic, social, and political turbulence, and renew the world after troubles have passed. Complete households must have the power to shelter, feed, and clothe their members in the absence of both state and corporate largesse. Such independence from outside agency is the true mark of liberty, making possible in turn the self-government of communities. Households functionally dependent on wages, benefits, or goods-in-kind paid by an economic corporation or a state have surrendered their natural liberty, and have accepted a kind of dependency indistinguishable, at its roots, from servanthood. Independence requires that responsible adults in a household be able to walk away from outside income, if necessary, and still be able to insure the survival of themselves and other household members.

THE STABILIZING EFFECTS OF LAND

The basic human need for functional independence in food, clothing, and shelter dictates the eternal importance both of a household's bond to the land and of husbandry skills. Autonomy requires, at the least, the capacity to produce a regular supply of edible goods, and the ability to preserve a substantial share of this bounty for consumption during the adverse seasons. The keeping of grazing and meat-producing animals adds further to the independence of households and their ability to survive wars, famines, stock market crashes, depression, inflation, and bad government, the recurring challenges to human survival. In arable climates, intensive cultivation of as little as an acre of land can provide the necessary bounty that delivers such autonomy; five to 20 acres of soil and timber offer an independence more sure and complete.

Accordingly, traditionalist society views land, particularly arable land, as different-in-kind from other commodities. The most critical of social, political, and economic tasks becomes the appropriate partition, distribution, and use of the land, where ownership is spread as widely as possible, and where freedom of use is conditioned by a responsible stewardship toward future generations. Both of these principles dictate the need for active measures to prevent the industrialization of agriculture. This event would reduce the number of persons in contact with the soil, forestall a political structure of ordered liberty, and insure the ruin of the land.

Attachment to growing things and to the soil also brings the human spirit into synchronization with the rhythm of the seasons and the beauty and violence of the natural world. It means contact with the wind, rain, and the living fertility of the soil. Familiarity with domesticated animals, a defining feature of *civilized* human life from the beginning, also delivers a natural wisdom unobtainable in any other way.

THE POWER OF HOUSEHOLD PRODUCTION

Together with land, the autonomous household also needs control over the means of production. The industrial revolution of the 18th and 19th centuries, dependent on balky power sources such as flowing water and the reciprocal steam engine, gave a monopoly on power to centralized factories, and stimulated the "great divorce" of work from home, which shattered the old and settled world. The 20th century, however, has delivered successive waves of new technologies which return "power," in both senses of that word, to the household economy. Innovations of this sort include electric motors, the internal combustion engine, and the photovoltaic cell. Each of these allows the household to apply power, in efficient manner, to productive work in the homestead. Household computers, fax machines, modems, and duplicators are other useful tools once confined to central work units. In short, the gains formally enjoyed by central factories and offices can now be reproduced in households. Where the competitive advantage in the 19th century clearly lay with the industrial factory, the advantage today in many areas of production may actually lay within the homestead (remaining apparent disadvantages often derive from marketing and distributive manipulations that distort real price, or from the corruption of free markets by a corporate-influenced state).

THE IMPORTANCE OF SELF-SUFFICIENCY

Rejecting an extreme division-of-labor, traditional society also focuses on generalized skill, and the well-rounded human life. It celebrates and rewards craftsmanship, the creative application of one human intellect to the fashioning of useful devices. It encourages self-sufficiency.

Accordingly, every household needs to be equipped with *ownership* of basic tools: the implements needed to grow food; the utensils to process and store produce; the hand and power tools necessary to build and repair shelter and to make clothing; and the transportation vehicles, communication devices, and information storage and processing units necessary to engage in the world of commerce. Whenever possible, householders should employ devices which they can comprehend, assemble, and repair themselves. Again whenever possible, the sources of power should be renewable and independent of outside suppliers, giving further security to the household, particularly in times of emergency and crisis.

Each household also requires an authority structure, where all family members defer to the wisdom of elders, where children defer to the guidance of parents, and where wives defer to the public authority of husbands. In the healthy civic order, all other loyalties to state, nation, ideology, or corporation are subordinated to or mediated through this household structure.

A central function of the household is the education of children, for which parents, supplemented by extended kin, are responsible. The household bears the obligation and natural power to transmit to children the spiritual doctrines and beliefs of the family, the customs and folkways by which the household lives, the practical skills necessary for the later creation and sustenance of new households, and the knowledge required for successful engagement in the world of commerce. While outside agencies, such as apprenticeships and parent-controlled schools, may be usefully employed for part of these tasks, those households fail which abdicate the bulk of them to others. The education of children, properly engaged, must be home-centered, where parents impart *their* visions, values, virtues, and skills to the new generation.

Relative to the world, each household exists as a small socialist collective, organized on the principle: from each according to his or her ability to each according to his or her need. The members of a household share with each other on the basis of love and altruism, without any accounting of individual gain or loss. Under some circumstances, this same principle of justice may extend to other kin, or even to small communities, where the generosity and altruism can be tempered by a practical knowledge of individual character and the discipline which a tight-knit community can bring to bear on its members. This socialist organization on a small scale may exact a price through some loss of efficiency, but it more than recovers this cost through the emotional rewards that household and community life bring.

THE THIRD SOCIETAL BOND: THE COMMUNITY

Indeed, the village, town, tribe, or neighborhood, forms the next layer of order. A broad society of households allows for the diversification and specialization of skills, within a context of general competence and an expectation of fair exchange. Such collectives operate best when bonded by other affections: a common religious faith; a shared ethnicity; a binding sense of history; the intermingling of a relatively small number of kin groups. Within such communities, the individual internalizes restraints on behavior and ambition, recognizing the threat posed by any form of abrupt innovation. In this level of civic order, children receive a kind of communal rearing, where the sharp edges or peculiarities found in each household can be tempered. Such close community also offers the only *effective* protection of individuals from pathologies *within* households, allowing social intervention to occur without threatening the normative pattern of family living. The town, tribe, or neighborhood imparts to the young the duties which constitute membership in a community, and models of behavior and rectitude beyond those found in one's immediate household. Public actions are guided most commonly by custom and convention, with formal law generally aimed at the regulation of the stranger. When deviance from community norms occurs, informal and non-aggressive measures such as shunning are normally effective in restoring order and bringing the wayward back into harmony with the community.

Leadership at this level of society emerges spontaneously, as persons living in close proximity to each other easily come to recognize the character strengths and weaknesses of their neighbors, and accept the guidance and wisdom of persons who ably practice both self- and household-governance. They give deference, as well, to the experience of age, a kind of public memory that carries a record of past successes and errors. This natural leadership may be formalized through councils of elders or trustees, or it may be left informal. In either case, the leaders accept the great responsibility of protecting their neighbors from internal or external threats that would subvert the bonds of community. Organized community militias, composed of men who study "the arts of war," provide defense against open aggression or gross challenges to public safety. The more complex dangers lie in alien ideologies and technologies that would strike at the heart of healthy community life. Community leaders properly judge such ideologies and technologies, and seek to prohibit or restrict those which would damage the basis of social life, even at the cost of "enlightenment" and "efficiency."

Commerce occurs between households, through markets. Communities rely on sentiments of common humanity to soften the rough edges of competition, to insure principles of fair exchange, and to preserve the household basis of the economy. Communities strive to forestall a complete industrialization of human economic and social life. The labor of family members, including that of children, normally occurs within the family enterprise. When employment outside the household develops, customary arrangements control the corrosive effects of competitive wages by limiting such industrial labor to only one household member and by expecting a family-sustaining wage in return.

Social life at this level also depends on the attachment of individuals to the landscape in which they grow, live and act, and to the flora and fauna of their native place. Actions such as walking, fishing, hunting, and gardening secure this bond, creating affection for the physical and biological environment which has, in a way, also given life to the individual. This grounding in a small niche of the natural world is vital to the full development of the human personality, and necessary to the attachments which define and hold households and communities together. Deep affection for a place is normally the product of growing up there, whether it be the flat grasslands of an Illinois prairie or the soaring mountains and canyons of Utah. Persons without this sense of native place, such as the children of missionaries in an earlier age or the offspring of international technocrats today, are left psychologically crippled. They often become perpetual nomads, given to grand visions and ideological constructs designed to fill the emptiness in their hearts. As such, they become a danger to their more settled fellows.

THE FOURTH SOCIETAL BOND: THE STATE

The next tier of society is the state. It exists to protect villages, households, and their members from external threat, and to mediate disputes between households and communities that cannot be resolved at a lower level. Having no fixed metaphysic, the structure of the state can vary from place to place, and circumstance to circumstance. The sole guiding principle is the limitation of its power. Natural authority resides in households and communities, where it is conditioned by innate human affections. These entities cede to the state only the minimum power necessary to keep foreign armies and other alien pressures at bay. Constitutional arrangements need insure, as far as possible, that most authority remain in local and household hands, that power granted to the state remain strictly circumscribed, and that leaders of the state be persons of character and self-restraint. Citizenship in the state is granted only to those who fulfill certain duties: participation in the common defense through membership in the militia; maintenance of personal independence through a homestead embracing arable land; ownership of the basic means of production; marriage and the acceptance of responsibility for the next generation; and acceptance by one's neighbors as part of their community. Traditionalist states have existed as monarchies, oligarchies, and republics. Monarchical organization has the important symbolic claim of providing leadership of a society of households *by* a household. Oligarchies and republics have the ability to draw from a wider pool of talent and virtue. All three forms of traditionalist governance rely on a natural aristocracy of property owners committed to constitutional duty.

The great danger posed by the state is its propensity, rooted in institutional interest, to become an end in itself, exercising authority *not* ceded by the foundational social units, but rather claimed as right. Working to destroy the traditionalist order, this rogue state will assert power to "protect" individuals from the rooted authority of households and communities. It will build "state schools" to impart a state morality. It will create artificial "rights" that bludgeon traditional authority. At its most perverse, this wayward state will set wife against husband, husband against wife, children against parents, and household against household. Aggrandizing its own power, this state will weaken the institution of marriage, subsidize illegitimacy and divorce, seize the dependency functions of care for the young, the old, and the infirm, transfer the concept of "autonomy" from the household to the individual, and invert the meaning of liberty, casting it as the gift of the state. Such actions destroy natural society, and erect in its place an order where all individuals become wards of Leviathan. An order of free men becomes a "client society," where bureaucrats minister to the needs of "citizen subjects." Such arrangements invariably bring economic and social decline, since they rest on abstract or imaginary "rights" that are divorced from a sense of duty and from the authentic human affections toward kin and neighbors. Moreover, human "needs" have no natural endpoint, and the effort to meet them through social agency will ultimately consume the wealth of a people.

THE BROADEST SOCIETAL BOND: THE NATION

The last social tier is the nation. It rests on commonalities that transcend households, communities, and states, among them religious belief, language, a shared history, a common ecosystem, inherited folkways, and blood. The consciousness of nationhood may wax or wane, encouraged at times by rallying voices who remind a people of "their common destiny," discouraged at other times by voices urging "universal brotherhood" or the creation of transnational "empire," or even forgotten during periods of social and political chaos.

"Nation" and "state" are rarely found in a perfect unity. The vagaries of history, jealousy, and chance prevent such an ordering. Yet danger lies in even an incomplete merging of these two social tiers, for such a bond inevitably augments the state's claims against households and communities, by appealing to "the needs of the nation" in a quest for taxes, conscripts, and territory. A sense of nationhood, while necessary to a complete or full social life, is properly mediated through the foundational tiers of state, community, and household. Any attempt by large numbers of individuals to swear *first* loyalty to the nation, or by the nation to sweep aside the social structures lying between it and the individual, must bring in its wake another form of crisis, and probable ruin.

SOCIETY'S UNBRIDLED FACTION: THE CORPORATION

The wild card in human social relations is the corporation, understood as an artificial, voluntary union of persons toward some overriding common end. This purpose may be religious (as in a Medieval monastic corporation), economic (as in the modern multi-national corporation), or intellectual (as in academies of sciences). The common characteristic of the corporation is the manner in which it transcends the natural social constructs of household, community, state, and nation, by claiming the direct and primal loyalty of individuals. These persons give up their bonds to the tiers of a traditionalist order, accepting a single new master.

So understood, corporations appear to have existed in every historical age. Whether its task be missionary conversion to a faith or the production and sale of a commodity, the corporation is part of the human experience. It serves as an agent-of-change, disrupting inherited ways, and reordering the context in which natural society operates. Where natural society tends toward stability, each corporation represents a push for instability, for "creative destruction." Conflict between these social visions is inevitable. If the challenge by the corporation is too great, the result can be the distortion or destruction of traditional social life. At the same time, though, the corporation can indirectly help renew natural society, by stimulating a positive response to challenges. Moreover, some kinds of innovation can augment community solidarity and decentralization, seen at least potentially in this century through the development of products like the gasoline engine, the home computer, and high-yield seed. While traditional society can suppress corporate-induced change to the point of stagnation and decline, natural society can also tame, or humanize the explosive force of innovation, turning it to constructive ends. The great test facing any age is to find a workable balance between the satisfactions of continuity through community and the disruptions spawned by corporate-driven change. Serious imbalance, either way, threatens the dignity and fullness of human existence.

The nihilist foes of society understand that order and liberty rest on this pyramid of relationships: a submission to the sacred; the creation of marriages which flow into households; and the formation of households into communities, states, and nations. While ready to twist or subvert any of these tiers of society, they probably vent their greatest fury against the Divine source of life and the institution of marriage, for it is on these two pillars that all else rests. Accordingly, defense of the sacred canopy and of the marital covenant becomes the moral and political imperative for a traditionalist order. When they rule, all else tends to follow, and human existence knows a certain joy and peace.

Chapter 20

Communitarian: A New Balance between Rights and Responsbilities

Roger L. Conner

INTRODUCTION

Three key issues will be addressed in this chapter. First, in recent years the United States has experienced a massive decline in particular values that are critical to a healthy representative democracy. Second, the problem is getting worse because the decline in values is rooted in some of our greatest successes as a country--things we like about ourselves. Third, America's historic capacity for self-renewal is not exhausted; as we search for ways to reverse these trends, communitarian ideas offer a helpful framework.

A DECLINE IN DEMOCRATIC VALUES

America is in the midst of a massive collapse in responsibility for self and to others. Responsibility is a complicated word. Here, in this context, responsibility refers to feelings which impel us to voluntarily act or restrain ourselves on the basis of empathy for others, respect for community norms, and appreciation for the invisible hands of society that constantly protect and lift us. These are values associated with voluntary restraint, mutual obligation, and civic responsibility. The evidence of this decline is all around us. For example, in 1993 Daniel Yankelovich reported on an opinion survey that asked Americans in which system of morality they believed. One system says that you should play by the rules even if nobody is there to catch you if you do otherwise. The other maintains that if there is an advantage to be obtained you should violate the rules so long as you incur no penalties. He found only 41 percent of Americans believe in playing by the rules. More ominously, while Americans aged 60 and older believe in "respecting the system" by more than two to one, younger Americans aged 18 to 24 favored a "beat the system" morality by almost two to one.

In his book *The Spirit of Community*, Amitai Etzioni reports the results of a similar opinion poll. When asked to list the most important rights they enjoy in this country, most Americans put the right to trial by jury at the top of the list. When asked whether they would willingly serve on a jury if called, a majority said that they would try to get excused.

During the savings and loan crisis, a member of Congress held a community meeting in her district. While she was explaining how much the bailout was going to cost and that Congress would have to raise taxes or reduce other social programs, someone in the back of the room stood up and said, "Wait a minute, why do the taxpayers have to pay for the savings and loan bailout--why doesn't the government do it?"

There are hosts of social problems that give us battle fatigue, including crime, the loss of safety and civility in public spaces, public housing that does not work, the budget deficit, family breakups--the list seems endless. All too often we talk about these individual social problems as if they were isolated, and we fail to recognize them as manifestations of a deeper trend--the collapse of responsibility for self and to others.

One way to understand the magnitude of changes over the past 30 years is to draw a graph, in the form of a bell curve, which portrays the entire population of the United States in 1950 with regard to responsibility. Out on one end of the base line would be Mother Theresa, my next door neighbor who has been ministering to the sick and the frail in her circle of friends for a lifetime, and dedicated high school teachers in inner city schools. On the other extreme would be the serial murderers and criminals who kill other human beings for a pair of tennis shoes and experience no feelings of guilt or remorse. In the middle are people who pretty much play by the rules so long as temptation is not overwhelming.

Next, using the same base line, imagine what the graph would look like today with respect to the same values. In the intervening years that entire curve has shifted in the direction of self-absorption and away from responsibility to the community. Statisticians say that when a bell curve shifts, the percentage changes are much larger in the tails of the distribution. Thus, both the dramatic rise in grotesquely antisocial behavior and the dramatic decline in self-sacrificial heroes, which we have experienced in recent years, should be seen as warning signals that the values of our citizens across the board are shifting in the wrong direction. Some social critics see the increase in violent crime, to take one example of our most persistent social problems, as evidence of the failure of particular subgroups within our society, an indication that we need to work on *them*. To respond solely with tougher jail sentences for criminals fails to follow the first rule of effective reform: the hole and the patch should be commensurate.

This image--of an entire bell curve which has shifted away from responsibility for self and to others--is the only way to make sense out of the daily news. For example, in Albuquerque, New Mexico, a fellow got drunk. He staggered past the parking garage attendant on the way to his car, went upstairs, wandered around looking for his car, and fell out of the garage. What was his response? Of course, his response was to sue the city because the parking garage attendant had not stopped him.

In Pennsylvania, there was the dentist who lost his license after being convicted of engaging in sexual relations with his female clients while they were under sedation. He filed a claim with his insurance company saying that he was entitled to disability payments because he had been diagnosed with "frotterism." The definition of frotterism is "the irresistible impulse to touch the private parts of women." So, therefore, this dentist considered himself a victim who should be given disability payments by his insurance company just as if he had taken a bad fall or developed multiple sclerosis.

And, from New York, comes the doctor whose medical school education was paid for by the federal government in exchange for a promise to work in under-served communities for five years. This particular doctor got to West Virginia and decided that West Virginia was a drag compared to New York City. So she and her husband filed for bankruptcy, seeking to have all of their obligations discharged, including their obligation to the federal government to serve in an indigent community.

Finally, consider the group of Americans who went to college on subsidized loans and then never repaid them. Years later, when the federal government instituted a program through which colleges could use the IRS to track down people who had not paid their college loans, the former students, now successful professionals, defended themselves in court. Too much time had passed, they argued (successfully!). Blame for their default lay with the college for failing to pursue them more aggressively.

These are more than humorous and mildly irritating anecdotes. They are illustrations of a deeper trend, a society-wide shift away from the values associated with voluntary restraint, mutual obligation, and civic responsibility. If you wish to see a collapsing country, look about you.

THE FRUITS OF OUR SUCCESS

Unless we take action, this problem will only become worse, because the trends are rooted in our finest accomplishments as a country. The first cause is the sustained economic growth and stability enjoyed by this country in the post World War II period. Daniel Yankelovich suggests a phrase, "the affluence effect" to describe what happens when several generations in a row enjoy affluence and economic success without war, pestilence, or massive economic discontinuities. He argues that a slow and steady erosion in the value of self-restraint occurs. Depressions, famine, war, and disease teach entire generations that you do not just live for today, because people who live for today get hurt. According to Yankelovich in *Values and Public Policy* published in 1993 by the Brookings Institution, without direct experience of these maladies, "people . . . start to live for today and for their own self-satisfaction, on the assumption that tomorrow things will take care of themselves."

Yankelovich's analysis is similar to the conclusions drawn by historian David Musto of Yale University who studies drug epidemics. Musto explains that addictive drugs go through predictable cycles. In the early stages, few young people have direct experience with a particular drug. A large number of young people experiment with it, thinking that this drug, unlike more dangerous ones, will offer the benefits of escapism and alternative states of awareness without the risks of addiction. Experimentation leads to addiction for many, and their friends and relatives see the destructive effects at close hand. Use of that particular drug then declines until enough time passes so that the generation which lived with the drug is dead or otherwise unable to pass on the knowledge gained from their direct experience. Then use of the addictive drug surges, and society goes through another cycle.

Yankelovich's argument--long sustained economic success results in the loosening of social bonds--sounds more deterministic than it turns out to be. As with most trends, this one cannot continue indefinitely. Economic decline will follow social decline unless we do something about it. Like the frog in a beaker of water raised one degree per day, a society beset with a decline in values may not sense the danger until too late.

The opportunity for geographic mobility is another blessing that has eroded responsibility for self and to others. Not so long ago, most people expected to live their lives in the same community, so that misbehavior carried lifelong consequences. Today, we have people who have been repeatedly convicted of child molestation moving to new states to work at day care centers. The chance for a new start is a great and liberating American tradition, one that no one is willing to sacrifice. It inevitably weakens, however, society's capacity to impose penalties for violations of community norms.

Yet another mixed blessing is the capacity of our economy to produce products people enjoy and to herald them through modern communications technology. A popular bumper sticker in Washington asserts "He who dies with the most toys wins." Every advertisement on television, every mail-order catalogue, every billboard pummels us with the message that more material goods are the way to happiness and fulfillment. If you become convinced by that message, what sense does it make to work for the interest of your community or restrain yourself in any way that reduces your earning power?

The post-war expansion in individual rights is another factor leading to the decline in responsibility. When I was in law school, we were taught that the way to solve social problems was to get them *out* of politics and *into* courts. There would sit the judge in his black robe, his (they were nearly all men in the early 1970s) faithful law clerk at his side and a huge black bag nearby. The judge would reach into his bag, pull out a bolt of lightening, and fling it downward, crying, "Discrimination, stop!" And discrimination would cease. Again he would reach into his bag and, again, fling down a bolt of lightening, declaring, "Housing, be built!" And up would go housing. All we had to do to solve social problems was to create a right, allow the people to go to court, and move on to the next problem.

It took me a long time to figure out why this model of problem-solving is so attractive to lawyers. It turns out that judges are nothing but lawyers dressed up in black robes. The "rights" model shifts the forum for resolution of problems to courts and away from the nasty, dirty, world of politics where we have to convince all of these unwashed, uncaring, unintelligent people. In our preferred forum, lawyers are king. We use a specialized language, and write on specialized forms. With rare exceptions, non-lawyers cannot even speak to the judge in their own voice, without the interlocution of the lawyer's questions.

One small problem which our law professors did not anticipate was how everyone else in the country would listen to what they were saying in court. The language of rights which we developed in court seeped outside the courtroom and became a part of normal discourse. Lawyers taught Americans that our rights are, to quote Mary Ann Glendon of Harvard Law School, "individual, absolute, and disconnected from any sense of social obligation." Lawyers are often blamed for America's current fixation on rights. In truth, the language of the law only gave strength and greater momentum to a trend driven by the other forces mentioned in this article. The importance, however, of the lawyers' contribution should not be belittled. They gave the rest of society the words, phrases, and ideas to justify the thought, "I have a right to what I want." Thus, we have seen a steady escalation of every interest and every interest group seeking to elevate its interest to the status of a right.

To illustrate the process, there was a lawsuit recently filed in South Carolina to establish a constitutional right to pick your own doctor. The case arose when a Health Maintenance Organization (HMO) discovered that doctors were using a brief stint on the HMO staff to recruit patients before setting up a private practice. So the organization added a restriction to the basic contract preventing any doctor who left for private practice from taking patients that had once been assigned to them by the HMO. Years later, a doctor came, identified a list of patients who she could woo, and sued, claiming that the HMO requirement violated the patient's constitutional right of privacy.

This escalation in the scope of individual rights which courts will vindicate is another example of how our positive achievements are weakening our society. What some critics deride as "the rights lobby" was extremely important to opening up the American community to minorities, women, and other excluded groups. It was not very long ago, for example, that a Janet Reno would have been excluded from law school. She would also have been ostracized for failing to form a family, and told to go home and raise children instead of being a hard-driving prosecutor and fulltime public servant. If this were 1950, she would not have been considered for attorney general, she would have been considered a failure. Blacks were excluded entirely from our definition of members in the community as were many ethnic groups, from Jews in Minneapolis to Irish Catholics in Boston. My house in Washington, D.C., which is less than 75 years old, bears on its deed a restrictive covenant, now stricken, preventing sale to blacks or Jews.

Vilma Martinez, the lawyer who founded the Mexican American Legal

Defense and Education Fund, was told by her high school counselor not to aspire to anything beyond a secretarial job. She would waste her time applying for college, said the counsellor who was attempting to be kind. Just ten years before I entered law school, a friend of mine applied to Yale Law School. She had excellent test scores, good recommendations, and top grades at Radcliffe. Her meeting with the admissions officer was going well. At the end of the interview she asked him, "What is my chance of getting in?" He answered, "Well, our quota is three women in each entering class at the Yale Law School, but I will do everything I can to make sure you're one of the three women." We need to be reminded of how far the rights movement has brought us in a positive direction. It is one of America's great successes, one the rest of the world's people eagerly hope to follow. But as with economic security and geographic mobility, it is progress with a catch. Neighborhoods which are trying to regain control over their streets and parks from crime and disorder are constantly blocked by extreme interpretations of the constitution. Virtually every interest group in society is trying to emulate the civil rights movement, arguing with great passion that to reject their argument is to deny their rights, all of which drives society further away from a balance between rights and responsibilities.

TOWARD AN AMERICAN RENEWAL

Our predicament today is loaded with irony. As argued above, crime, the deficit, collapsing communities, and disorder have been caused by sustained economic growth, a greater emphasis on the worth of the individual, and courts which invite expanded definitions of individual rights. Yet economic security, individual autonomy, and judges prepared to defend individual rights are *good*, not *bad*. No one wants to go back to 1950.

Seen in this light, the challenge faced by thoughtful Republicans and Democrats who value freedom is very complex. In most of our political battles we fight evils--such as racism or big government. Today we are called to a very different campaign, one which involves seeking a balance between competing goods, rather than rallying the forces of good against the forces of evil. Individual autonomy is a good thing, it is being fought for by people all over the world. It is not bad. It is good. What we must do is find a balance between the pursuit of individual autonomy and individual wants, on the one hand, and the fulfillment of civic responsibilities on the other. It is a little bit like riding a bicycle. If you are riding a bicycle and feel yourself leaning in one direction and you overcorrect the other way, you still fall down. You only keep going forward if you keep your balance.

Three principal themes have emerged from the communitarian movement on how to lean in the direction of responsibility without overreacting. The first theme is that we urgently need to start a "multi-log" about responsibility. The word multi-log was coined by Amitai Etzioni, the founder of the communitarian movement. A multi-log is like a dialog, except that millions of people are involved in the conversation all at once. We need a multi-log about the place of responsibility in private life, public policy, and constitutional law.

From now on, whenever a right is asserted, we should immediately say, "That is an incomplete sentence. Where is the responsibility that goes with that right?" Just as every coin has two sides, a right cannot exist without responsibilities.

During this conversation, we should emphasize that rights and responsibilities are not like a teeter-totter, where one goes up and the other goes down. They are reciprocal. The relationship is like the oriental symbols, *yin and yang*. If one shrinks, the other will inevitably shrink as well.

People can experience freedom only within the security of a community whose members take responsibility for one another. Only then are people able to exercise their rights and share in the common experience of having rights that they themselves have rights. To live in a community where people do not exercise their responsibilities toward you is to live constrained and unfree.

An extreme example is a public housing development in Washington, D.C. The mothers do not allow their children to go out at night for fear of the drug dealers who rule the street. They put their children to sleep in the bathtub to protect them from random gunfire. Some pile mattresses against doors and windows for protection from gunfire. These mothers do not experience freedom. No matter what it says in the Constitution, no matter how much money is spent on lawyers to protect them against police and housing authority managers, these women are not free, because they are not embedded in a healthy community where people are exercising their responsibilities to one another.

Anytime we talk about rights in political conversations, we need to acknowledge that rights are not individual, absolute, and disconnected from social obligation. Quite the opposite, every right is conditional, limited, and embedded in a social context. Thus, when someone wishes to assert a right, whether it is the right to health care, the right to smoke, the right to choose one's own doctor, whatever, the statement is not complete. The person must also talk about the limitations upon the exercise of that right, the social relations required in order for that right to exist, and finally, who is going to pay for it. Furthermore, a critical notion must be reintroduced into the discussion of what it means to be a successful person. The capacity for responsibility for self and to others is not only part of a successful life, but rather, it is what living a successful life means.

In New York, there is a job-training program called "Vehicles" for people outside the economic mainstream. Janet Avery Barrett, the founder, worked her way up from being a child in a single-parent household in public housing to head of personnel for a major New York bank. She argues that much job training today is not designed to help clients deal with the problems of their lives. When people come into her office, they are greeted by a sign on the wall that says "Step One--No Whining." Her philosophy is this: if you have a problem, it does not make any difference who caused it, you are the only one who can get you out of your plight. She has been criticized by people in the job-referral and job-training community in New York, yet she has a much higher record of placement than these other programs. She starts with faith in the capacity of each person; she makes demands on them, stressing that this is not an entitlement. "You are entitled to an opportunity to get up in the morning, to breathe the air, and that is where entitlements stop. After that, your life is your responsibility." The power of her convictions has infused in her clients the crucial idea that self-reliance is always better than dependency.

Another vital element of the conversation about responsibility is the assertion that service to the community through action is a part of what it means to be a citizen. Everyone ought to consider it his or her duty as a citizen to vote, but the obligations of citizenship only begin there. It must also be expected of everyone to answer, "What roles have you chosen in service to your community?" William James said action precedes feeling, and the feelings of community and connection develop through action, not just through talk. Service is perhaps the best way to restore those feelings of connection. Thanks to a bill passed by Congress in 1993, thousands of young people will be engaged in community service for the next two years. It is up to local communities, however, to assure the success of the program by providing young people with the opportunity to work together in diverse groups and contribute to the common good. Local initiative and support, not government mandate, will enable this to be a true service-learning experience by which young people can gain understanding of social interdependence and the democratic arts.

This new conversation about responsibility must infuse discussions of private life, public policy, and constitutional law. As we rediscover a new language of responsibility we can take up the second aim of the communitarian movement: strengthening community institutions as problem-solvers. Schools need to become safe places for students, and their central role must be moral education, not just the accumulation of information. Churches and other neighborhood institutions must again see themselves as primary problem-solvers within the community.

One Church--One Child, a program started by Father George Clements of Chicago, is an example of this kind of initiative. One Church--One Child asks each church in America to find within its congregation a family willing to adopt a child who is in foster care, and it asks the church community to provide support that the family will need to assume the responsibility of raising that child. A testament to the ability of local institutions to address national problems by engaging communities, One Church--One Child has lead to over 40,000 adoptions in the past ten years.

More community institutions need to be likewise strengthened by finding ways for the community to speak to its members with a moral voice. The barriers to this step will be formidable. For example, in 1992, the City of San Francisco proposed to locate a new multi-service facility for evaluation and referral of homeless persons in the downtown area immediately south of Market Street. The neighborhood was already struggling to overcome crime, disorder, and urban abandonment. People opposed the new facility out of fear that it would attract homeless people to camp on the grounds of nearby federal property, urinate on sidewalks, sell drugs, and panhandle.

A local United Way agency called the South of Market Problem Solving Council, with representatives of all sides, negotiated a compromise. The local police officers would issue tickets to people sleeping in public places overnight, engaging in public elimination, aggressive panhandling, loitering for prostitution or drug dealing. They would also notify the counsellors at the multi-service center. The staff at the center agreed to counsel their clients, saying, "We're trying to be good neighbors. You can't do that around here. That's part of your problem, and let's deal with what causes you to be in that situation." The facility managers agreed that repeat offenders would be denied services.

Shortly after the agreement was signed and the facility was built, the

ACLU threatened to sue, alleging that the proposed cooperation was unconstitutional. For police to inform the managers before a guilty verdict, they maintained, would violate the privacy rights of the alleged violators. To deny service to repeat violators was placing an unconstitutional condition on a public benefit. As a result, the cooperative agreement was discarded. Similar facilities will be harder to locate in the residential neighborhoods of San Francisco in the future.

When we have gotten so far down the line that the people running a homeless shelter are disabled from learning of the antisocial conduct of their patrons in the surrounding neighborhood, we have disabled our community's capacity to speak with a moral voice to its members.

The third theme of the communitarian movement is to identify and defend public policies that strike a balance between individual rights and community responsibility. Communitarians maintain that the values associated with individualism and community are of equal moral weight. They are in constant tension, and to allow one to dominate over the other can only produce bad social results.

We need to stop taking good, pragmatic solutions off the table before we have a chance to try them. The San Francisco experiment mentioned above is a perfect example. We must permit and support public policies that restore the link between entitlements and rights on the one hand and duties and obligations on the other. For example, in Alexandria, Virginia, after drugs and crime had become rampant in public housing, folks instituted a policy that the leaseholder was responsible for anything that was done in their unit by family members and guests. Therefore, if a boyfriend or child was dealing drugs, the entire family would be evicted. The leaseholder could no longer say, "Well, I didn't do it, I didn't know, therefore I get to stay."

Jim Moran, the liberal Democratic Mayor of Alexandria, insisted that the people being harmed by the drug dealing and crime were the majority of public housing residents who were not involved in the drug dealing and criminal behavior. Moran wanted to restore the link between the opportunity to live in public housing and the responsibility to control your household. He was challenged by critics who argued that evicted families would be thrown into homeless shelters. He answered that his first responsibility is to the health of the community, in making it a safe place for the law-abiding residents to live and raise children, not to mention the long waiting lines of people anxious to move into public housing.

Interestingly, under Moran's policy there have been very few evictions, but the rates of drug dealing and crime have gone down. It turned out that a clear rule linking the right to housing with obligations to protect your neighbors resulted in strengthening the hand of some mothers who were having trouble with teenagers, relatives, and friends.

Similarly, in Chicago, the Chicago Housing Authority began requiring that every person in public housing who is going to reside in the unit be on the lease because every person entering the building would have to carry an ID card or sign in on a daily basis. The first thing that happened was a flurry of marriages. The second result was lower crime, because it was hard to sell drugs out of an apartment if all guests had to identify themselves and sign in. Subsequently the ACLU sued the Housing Authority, claiming that metal detectors at entrances and a sign-in requirement for visitors violated rights secured by the Fourth Amendment and the Due Process Clause. The case is not yet resolved.

Until recently the State of Maryland did not have a mandatory helmet law for motorcycle riders. In the last legislative session, frustrated sponsors of the helmet law introduced two bills. Bill number one required motorcycle riders to wear helmets. That was defeated. On the same day, there was a vote in a separate committee on Bill number two that would have required motorcycle riders to carry major medical insurance before they could have a license to drive a motorcycle. You can guess what happened to that piece of legislation. It was defeated. In other words, motorcycle riders have a right to go down the freeway on a motorcycle with the wind blowing in their hair, and no responsibility is necessary to insure against serious accidents. The community is going to be responsible if someone without a helmet needs long term care after slamming into a tree.

REVERSING THE TRENDS

The collapse of responsibility is not an irresistible trend. America has an enormous capacity for self-renewal as a nation. The emergence of this communitarian movement is a reaction, a response, a recognition by parents and children and teachers and ministers that things have gone awry and that we need to figure out a way to respond. Happily, the leaders of this movement recognize that overreaction is just as bad as the original problem. What we are searching for is balance.

One of the highlights of 1993 for me was the testimony of five citizens who tried to protect the white truck driver pulled from his truck and beaten by a vicious mob during the Los Angeles riots. These citizens saw the event unfolding on television and recognized the intersection. They got up from their sofas, got in their cars, and drove to the site to defend a man they had never met. Asked the obvious question by the prosecutor, one of the citizens answered, "I felt like they were hitting me."

What we need to regain in this country is the feeling--feeling is the key word--the feeling that when a problem exists within our communities, we "feel like they are hitting me," that we feel impelled to go forward to be part of finding a solution to the problems which beset our communities instead of sitting on the sidelines in a self-contained, self-absorbed stew. If five people in Los Angeles are willing to put their lives in jeopardy in order to protect a man who is being beaten on the street, there must be five million or 50 million who are willing to come back toward a very old and traditional American idea: that when there is a problem in this country, that we, the people, working together in little squadrons as citizens, respond. That is the core of the communitarian idea, one that may well turn this country around.

Chapter 21

Libertarian: Building Civil Society Through Virtue and Freedom

Doug Bandow

INTRODUCTION

Ours is a secular age. But faith has not disappeared. Rather, the deities have changed. Today the reigning theology is statism: government, not God, is charged with the people's salvation.

Indeed, this century was rightly termed "the age of politics" by historian Paul Johnson. It has given us the great collectivist experiment, the lengthy, global test of the proposition that the state can and should be the institution through which we organize our lives. The results are now evident to all and, alas, have proved disastrous. Writes Johnson:

> But whereas, at the time of the Versailles Treaty, most intelligent people believed that an enlarged state could increase the sum total of human happiness, by the 1980s the view was held by no one outside of a small, diminishing and dispirited band of zealots. The experiment had been tried in innumerable ways; and it had failed in nearly all of them. The state had

---

The editor wishes to inform the reader that Doug Bandow identifies himself as a "classical liberal." In the current vernacular, Libertarian is usually used to denote a person who consistently defends liberty and opposes statism, but the term can be misleading.

proved itself an insatiable spender, an unrivalled waster. Indeed, in the twentieth century it had also proved itself the great killer of all time.

So, too, it has been in America. Although the results of the age of politics have been a bit "kinder and gentler" in the United States than in Germany and the Soviet Union, the state has had no more success in solving mankind's most vexing problems, such as crime and poverty. To the contrary, all too often it is government policy, usually inadvertently, but sometimes intentionally, that has created and then exacerbated social problems. And it is politics that continues to thwart serious efforts to solve these same problems.

Yet politicians of all ideological stripes all over the world refuse to accept the verdict of history that their time is drawing to a calamitous close. Instead, they continue to fight to preserve their positions. The worst do it by diverting attention from their past failures by causing new crises--demanding national aggrandizement, inflaming ancient ethnic passions, and demonizing traditional scapegoats, such as immigrants and Jews, for instance. The more subtle seek a different sort of diversion, claiming that they are "new" politicians. They troll for popular support by endorsing "change," proposing to "reinvent" public institutions, and pledging to offer "meaning" to people's lives.

It is difficult to predict whether these stratagems will succeed. In the short-term they have worked for men as different as Slobodan Milosevic and Bill Clinton, but the positions of these officials, and of the raft of thugs and mediocrities who run the vast majority of governments around the globe, are hardly secure. In the long-term most of these people will be consigned to the ash-heap of history. The only question is whether they will be alive to see their memories execrated and their monuments desecrated.

TODAY'S PROBLEMS

But, as Lord Keynes said, in the long-run we are all dead. Today we have to contend with an age of politics that has not yet fully wound down. If the United States has never suffered from the sort of totalitarian rule that long characterized the Soviet Union, even the West suffers from decades worth of veritable deification of the state. While political authority has been exposed for the dangerous and deadly temptation that it is, its manifold bureaucracies and operatives remain in place, refusing to yield their power. Between 1950 and 1990 government spending in America rose 3,163 percent, and that growth shows no signs of abating.

Today the state consumes roughly 43 percent of national income, and even that incredible number understates the government's influence: the average person works from January 1 to May 5 to pay his taxes, to May 18 to cover government spending, and to *July 10* and after including the cost of regulation. Virtually no human activity today is outside the jurisdiction of politics. Where you work, how much you earn, how you manage your family, with whom you associate, what car you buy, from whom you receive medical care, what you ingest, how you have sex, whether you visit other lands--all of these and more are now matters of grave concern to government at one and often several levels.

As a result, our freedom, prosperity, and morality remain very much at risk. America's reliance on politics as the solution to most every problem and alleged problem has turned envy into official public policy, stripped individuals and communities of their traditional social responsibilities, destroyed economic opportunities for the disadvantaged, promoted unjust foreign intervention, and undermined private moral and spiritual values. The solution to so pervasive a crisis will not come from a little tinkering here or there--whether a reduction in the rate of government spending, the devolution of one program or another from the federal to state governments, the creation of a few tax loopholes, or something equally modest.

Instead, what is required is a redefinition of the relationship of the individual to the state. The purpose of government should not be to rearrange economic and social relationships to fit the selfish preferences of influential minorities or even majorities. Not only is there no moral justification for systematic income redistribution, but the process inevitably breaks down, enriching not the poor but a "new class" of politicians, bureaucrats, lobbyists, and interest groups. Attempts to enforce "social justice," an empty phrase that has been used to rationalize all manner of social engineering schemes, usually end up even more tyrannical, remolding private consensual conduct based on the whimsical desires of whoever happens to hold political power. In both economic and social life, government involvement should require not only the presence of some pressing need that genuinely concerns the "general welfare," a constitutional phrase that has been tortured to justify every new federal program, but also a reasonable, indeed, compelling, expectation that public sector failure will not exceed the private sector shortcomings to be addressed.

In short, the age of politics must be brought to a close. Statism has failed so badly in so many ways. This century has proved--in a far more costly manner than was imaginable before man demonstrated how destructive could be the power of modern technology in the hands of the all-powerful state--that politics does not offer the solution for the human condition. And though the ruling elites that once treated politics as religion have now abandoned their faiths, they are not yet prepared to yield power voluntarily. Thus, if the first nine decades of this century have been devoted to the rise and fall of collectivist ideologies, the final one is likely to involve the fight to bring political systems around the globe into conformity with a new, freer intellectual paradigm.

WHAT NEXT? CIVIL SOCIETY

Still, simply making the case against government is not enough. Recapturing Americans' traditional caution about turning to politics--based on a recognition of the fallibility of human beings, the inefficiency of human institutions, and people's tendency to abuse power--tells us much about what government should no longer do. But what should replace the state as the organizing center of life? Civil society. The institution that was always intended by those who founded the nation to act as the framework for economic and social activity. Indeed, 200 years ago virtually everyone looked first to civil society, or the "private sector," in today's parlance, to provide the forum through which citizens would work through their problems. Government was to be called in only in extraordinary circumstances, when private discourse and action was not possible or would likely prove inadequate.

A similar approach would work today. A strong, vibrant, creative civil society, supported by the citizenry and unhindered by government, could deal with the vast majority of problems now thrust into the hands of public officials, eliminating or alleviating the alleged crises that now seem to arise with disturbing regularity. The state would obviously not disappear, and the transition to increased reliance on civil society would be difficult, even painful, at times. It remains, however, eminently possible.

The outlines of such a system are relatively simple. (Much has been written elsewhere as to potential private solutions to today's social problems; such detail is not possible here.) For instance, were government to perform its basic duty of maintaining a stable, noninflationary economic environment, eschewing the almost constant political manipulation evident today, there would be few boom/bust cycles with the accompanying interest rate gyrations and unemployment swings. Business could better plan for the future, hire more workers, offer steadier jobs. If the state cut the cost of employment, now inflated through mandatory benefit laws, excessive regulatory burdens, and hefty tax levies, employers could add more and new jobs. And if government dropped its raft of protectionist labor legislation--minimum wage, Davis-Bacon Act, National Labor Relations Board, occupational licensing, and the like--it would allow more people, particularly minorities, to find and fill those extra jobs.

Expanding employment opportunities is obviously a critical piece necessary for solving the poverty puzzle, which today seems so intractable. So too is improving education, which has largely become a government monopoly. Competition through increased reliance on private institutions and home-schooling, backed with vouchers, tax credits, and "choice" programs, offers a far greater chance of preparing young people for productive and responsible futures than does dumping more money into the existing public system.

Reforming welfare to reduce its counterproductive impact on behavior--particularly decisions to marry, have children, attain schooling, and work--would help ensure that the poor faced the same incentives and standards as everyone else. It is also critical to reduce the overall level of public subsidy, by, for instance, cutting so-called general assistance for the able-bodied and extra benefits for additional children, in order to reemphasize the role of individual responsibility to avoid poverty and of private community institutions, such as churches, to assist the poor in becoming independent.

Dropping restrictions on low-cost housing, such as antiquated building codes and exclusionary zoning ordinances, as well as destructive measures such as rent control, would naturally, and privately, improve poorer Americans' shelter options. Groups like Habitat for Humanity could then step in to help meet the problems of poverty, and not of government policy. Ending local transit regulations and taxicab licensing would allow the development of a diverse private transportation marketplace serving all parts of urban areas, and not just the wealthy sections, such as lower-to-mid Manhattan in New York City. Decontrol of child care would end government's attempt to push kids into larger, commercial centers. The list as to where civil society, freed from the restraints of politics, could better meet human needs goes on and on.

Indeed, simply shrinking both the government's regulatory reach and financial take would leave space for civil society to again expand. People who cared about the arts, for instance, would themselves have to act in the absence of a federal National Endowment for the Arts. And, freed from subsidizing everyone from farmers to exporters to academics, they would have the resources necessary to support the arts and many other things.

This, in fact, would be one of the most important impacts of rolling back the state: to allow a diverse flowering of individual and community activism throughout society. It was this voluntarism that so impressed Alexis de Tocqueville more than a century ago and which continues to set this nation apart from most other countries around the world. Yet, so much more could and should be done. Indeed, the virtue of such civic activism is two-fold. First, it tends to be more effective: for instance, a church or other community organization is more likely than a distant bureaucracy to understand the needs of a poor family, which may be as much spiritual and moral as economic. Private institutions will also be far freer to respond, adjusting their response to meet individual circumstances.

Second, this sort of personal involvement, in contrast to simply writing a check, or, even worse, having the government write a check, helps transform the giver as well as the recipient. As Marvin Olasky, author of *The Tragedy of American Compassion*, has observed, "compassion" once meant to suffer with. The exercise of compassion, then, required one to get involved in another person's or family's life. It thereby strengthened, rather than severed (as welfare does today), the sinews of community. Such an approach obviously is not easy to implement. But it is necessary for a good society.

THE IMPORTANCE OF COMMUNITY

It is community that underlies civil society and therefore must be reconstituted if we are to escape the ravages of the age of politics. The vision of "atomistic individualism" attacked by some critics of market economics exists only on the pages of an Ayn Rand novel or the discussions of a university philosophy class. We naturally exist in community with one another; there are few individual "islands" in any social system. After all, we grow up and form families. We work with other people. We play games with one another and gather to watch others play. We worship our creator in varying ways but almost always collectively. And we come together to try to solve the many, diverse problems that are an inevitable outgrowth of human sin and imperfection.

The real question, then, is what kind of community?

A Virtuous Community

First, a virtuous community is vital. While a liberal, in the classical sense, economic and political system is the best one available under any circumstances, it will operate well only if nestled in a moral social environment. This point may seem obvious, even trivial, but deserves emphasis. For instance, a market system will function more effectively if people are honest and voluntarily fulfill their contracts. People who believe in working hard, exercising thrift, and observing temperance will be more productive. Economic life will function more smoothly if employers treat their workers fairly. Fewer social problems will emerge if families, churches, and communities organize to forestall them in the first place. Greater personal responsibility will reduce welfare expenditures and tort litigation, and so on. A lush lawn of a compassionate, cooperative, and virtuous society will make it harder for weeds of social breakdown and ensuing government encroachment to flourish.

Indeed, consider the social implications for our society of the declining belief in the moral precepts against murder/theft and teenage sex/illegitimacy. For instance, crime can only be understood fundamentally as a moral problem of stunning dimensions. Those who murder, rape, and steal are committing evil acts--and committing a lot of them. One of every four households is affected by crime every year. There are almost 34 million "victimizations," as the government puts it, a year. According to the Justice Department, "you are more likely to become the victim of a violent crime than to be injured in a motor vehicle accident." Moreover, violent crimes are increasingly premeditated, callous, and committed for no purpose other than to harm others. Indeed, some older criminals profess shock at the seeming irrational brutality of today's killers, where murder has increasingly become sport.

Nor is crime an equal opportunity scourge. Although violence affects everyone, it disproportionately harms the least advantaged, those with the fewest options. Explains the Justice Department, "Black households, Hispanic households, and urban households were the most likely to experience crime." Blacks are 50 percent more likely than others to be victimized by a violent crime. Someone earning less than $7,500 a year is three times as likely to suffer from a violent crime as someone earning more than $50,000.

Attitudes towards human life are not the only moral values that have changed in recent years, so, too, have beliefs in the importance of family.

The disintegration of the family has been frightening to behold. Over the last 30 years the black illegitimacy rate has jumped from 25 percent to 68 percent, and even more, on the order of 80 percent, in the inner-city. (It is now 22 percent for whites.) Particularly grievous is the problem of children having children. Just between 1986 and 1991, birth rates for 15-to-19-year-olds rose by 24 percent. In 1960 there were five times as many births to married teens as unmarried teens; in 1991 there were more than twice as many to unmarried teens.

This lack of family formation, joined with a rise in family break-up, has had severe economic and social consequences, especially when combined with a lower proclivity to work. It is, first, the leading cause of poverty. As of 1990, the official poverty rate for two-parent households with one fulltime worker was just two percent. For all two-parent households it was 5.6 percent. For female-headed households it was 32.2 percent, almost one in three. For single women who do not work, the rate was 67 percent. Second, by crippling the mechanisms that are most effective in transmitting values--families, and family-based community activities--the decline in family values has left too many youngsters without a moral compass, leading to both self-destruction and crime against others.

Indeed, the consequences of this phenomenon are truly catastrophic. Children from broken homes are more likely to do poorly in school, use drugs, require psychiatric attention, and commit crimes than those in equally low-income homes where a father is present. The latter point is particularly important: former Education Secretary William Bennett points out that since 1960 illegitimacy rates have jumped 400 percent, while those for violent crime have risen 560 percent. The 34 million "victimizations now occurring annually are perhaps the most obvious social cost of a valueless, rootless generation." But that generation itself is paying a very high price. By the early 1990s, 42 percent of young black males in Washington, D.C. and an incredible 56 percent in Baltimore, Maryland were enmeshed in the criminal justice system--in prison or jail, on probation or parole, or being sought on an arrest warrant. Most African-Americans obviously are law-abiding citizens, but the amoral few are enough to terrorize all of us: roughly 1.7 percent of black males account for *45 percent of all arrests.*

We obviously need a moral community.

A Free Community

We also need a free community, however. Perhaps the most important debate today is not whether we should have virtue--after all, who can really disagree--but how we should generate it? Through voluntary or involuntary means? How do we achieve the best society that is possible?

With virtue losing ground daily, the temptation to turn to the state is strong. If civil society is too weak to generate the right moral values, so goes the argument, then the government must step in. And if that means some loss of liberty, then so be it. This temptation is particularly strong when confronting a Left that seems to believe in "choice" if it means moral relativism and escape from responsibility, but abhors "choice" if it means private individuals making informed decisions about their children, kids' educations, jobs, and other aspects of their lives.

Freedom and virtue, however, are not antagonists; it is a mistake to assume that one must be sacrificed for the other. To the contrary, they are complementary. That is, as argued earlier, virtue is necessary for a free society to flourish. In turn, liberty--the right to exercise choice, free from coercive state regulation--is a necessary precondition for virtue.

Virtue cannot exist without freedom, without the right to make moral choices. Coerced acts of conformity with some moral norm, however good, do not represent virtue; rather, the compliance with that moral norm must be voluntary. There are times, of course, when coercion is absolutely necessary--most importantly, to protect the rights of others by enforcing an *inter*-personal moral code governing the relations of one to another. The criminal law is an obvious example, as is the enforcement of contracts and property rights. But quite different is the use of coercion to promote virtue, that is, to impose a standard of *intra*-personal morality.

Of course, drug use, pornography, homosexuality, and similar "self-victim" crimes all have some larger social impact, which some people contend justifies state intervention. I would argue, and have done so extensively elsewhere, that most of the ill consequences, such as drug-related crime, are primarily a product of legal prohibition rather than the activity itself. If, in fact, government regulation makes the social problems worse, then the argument for intervention is really to promote virtue.

NATION'S MORAL TONE

Our nation's moral tone is not good and seems to have gotten worse in recent years, though, of course, one should have no illusions that a perfect age ever existed. Still, if things have gotten worse, one has to ask two questions: Is that because we have become more free? Would becoming less free make America more virtuous? The answer to both questions is "no."

First, did our society become virtuous *because* government no longer tried so hard to mold souls? Blaming moral shifts on legal changes mistakes correlation for causation. In fact, America's onetime cultural consensus eroded even during an era of strict laws against homosexuality, pornography, and even fornication. Only cracks in this consensus led to changes in the law. In short, as more people viewed sexual mores as a matter of taste rather than a question of right or wrong, the moral underpinnings of the laws collapsed, followed by the laws. Only a renewed consensus could allow the reestablishment of the laws. But such a renewed consensus would obviate the need for such legislation.

Second, government is not a particularly good teacher of virtue. The state tends to be effective at simple, blunt tasks, like killing and jailing people. It has been far less successful at reshaping individual consciences. Even if one could pass the new, stricter laws in today's American current moral ethic, the result would not be a more virtuous nation. True, there might be fewer overt acts of immorality, but there would be no change in people's hearts. Forcibly preventing people from victimizing themselves does not automatically make them more virtuous, righteous, or good. The rest of us may feel better, but we should not confuse uplifting society's moral core with improving society's superficial appearance.

Attempting to forcibly make people moral would make civil society itself less virtuous in three important ways. First, individuals would lose the opportunity to exercise virtue. They would not face the same set of temptations and be forced to choose between good and evil. In this dilemma we see the paradox of Christianity: a God of love creates man and provides a means for his redemption, but allows him to choose to do evil. While true Christian liberty means freedom from sin, God gives us a different sort of freedom to choose not to respond to His grace.

Second, to vest government with primary responsibility for promoting virtue shortchanges other institutions, or "governments" in Puritan thought, like the family and church, sapping their vitality. Private social institutions find it easier to lean on the power of coercion than to lead by example, to persuade, and to act to solve problems. Moreover, the law is better at driving immorality underground than eliminating it. As a result, moral problems seem less acute, and we are less uncomfortable. We are therefore less likely to work as hard to promote virtue.

Third, making government a moral enforcer encourages abuse by majorities or influential minorities that gain power. If one thing is certain in life, it is that man is sinful. The effect of sin is magnified by the possession and exercise of coercive power. Its possessors can, of course, do good, but history--especially the age of politics this century--suggests that they are far more likely to do harm. Even in our democratic system, majorities are as ready to enact their personal predilections, such as okaying the use of such dangerous substances as alcohol and tobacco while outlawing marijuana, as uphold real morality.

And as America's traditional Judeo-Christian consensus crumbles, we are more likely to see government promoting alternative moral views. Consider the activities of Surgeon General Joycelyn Elders, the condom queen and publicist for the benefits of gay sex. Even the easy issues are tough for her. For instance, when asked about the moral appropriateness of having a child out-of-wedlock, she responded, "Everyone has different moral standards... . You can't impose your standards on someone else." It will prove increasingly dangerous to give government the authority to coercively mold souls and manipulate civil society in order to "promote virtue." Despite the best intentions of advocates of statecraft as soulcraft, government is more likely to end up enshrining immorality as morality. All told, an unfree society is not likely to be a virtuous one.

RECONSTRUCTING A VIRTUOUS AND FREE CIVIL SOCIETY

There is no higher priority today than to reconstruct a civil society that is both free and virtuous. The first, and necessary, step is to roll back political society, the ever-extending reach of the state into virtually every human home, business, and other endeavor. Government should continue to act where civil society has broken down--to punish the wrongdoer, in the words of the Apostle Paul, for instance. This is a very limited role, however, the vast range of human life should be freed from government's control. Although at the margins there will be many disagreements over exactly what public authority should do, its central role in the organization of life should be ended.

And in the limited instances where the state continues to act, officials should adopt as their maxim "First, do no harm." For instance, although the community-wide moral breakdown most evident in the inner-city has many causes, government has greatly exacerbated the problem through the perversities of the welfare system. Tax policies punish both marriage and thrift. The state has spent years attempting to expunge religious values from the public square. And so on.

Second, people need to recognize and act on their increased responsibilities in place of government. No longer can citizens excuse inaction with the excuse, "I gave at the office." Civil society arose originally as a natural outgrowth of people's desire to solve the problems around them. Civil society can be repaired and reinvigorated today only when people act on that same desire.

While rebuilding community, people should remember two overriding considerations. One is that values matter. Thus, families, through their upbringing of their children; churches, through their emphasis on a transcendent moral code of conduct; and other community organizations, through their promulgation and enforcement of communal standards, need to teach morality. They need to preach against crime, irrespective of the hardship of the family or social circumstance a person suffered. They need to work to forestall and alleviate destructive social problems, opposing promiscuity, illegitimacy, and divorce, and to emphasize the overriding responsibility of parents, particularly now absent fathers, to provide safe, stable, and secure homes for their children. And they need to point to the importance of work to improve self-respect and living standards. The role of churches is particularly important since only they offer the perspective of ultimate accountability for moral failing.

The government, too, has a duty in this area, though of a different kind than that of private institutions. There is little that the state can do directly to improve the moral tone of society: public officials possess no special qualification to lecture others about morality. The best that we can hope for--and, indeed, which we should expect--is that political leaders will maintain a modicum of moral rectitude in the conduct of their personal and public lives, thereby acting as good role models.

Beyond that, public institutions can perform an educative function, but the moral discourse needs to be carried on at the broadest level of consensus possible. There is, for instance, general agreement from across the philosophical spectrum that teens should not be having children; therefore, abstinence can be promoted in public schools for reasons other than adherence to traditional Jewish and Christian moral teachings. However, advocates of virtue must be careful in using the state in even this modest fashion lest they abdicate their own essential roles through the private institutions of civil society. Moreover, while the government may help buttress private instruction, it remains a very imperfect tool and subject to misuse by officials and influential special interest groups with their own, usually very political, agendas. Indeed, what goes around tends to come around. Once advocates of virtue use the state to politicize the process, they lose their strongest argument, on principle, to prevent other forces from using government for immoral ends.

The second principle of rebuilding civil society is that freedom is as important as virtue. People should never hesitate to speak to moral issues, but they should be willing to tolerate the quirks and failings, even serious moral lapses, of their neighbors, so long as such actions have only limited effect on others. Society does not become more virtuous by filling the jails with fornicators and homosexuals. The punishment of most sins should be left to God.

For this reason, moral-minded citizens should turn to the state only as a last resort. The issue needs to be important enough to warrant government intervention; the activity involved also needs to have a significant impact on nonconsenting parties. And *private alternatives should be clearly inadequate.* For example, religious believers should lead their children in prayer at home rather than foisting that duty onto unbelieving teachers in the public schools. Opponents of pornography should organize boycotts before demanding the arrest of buyers and sellers. And, perhaps most importantly, vocal supporters of the importance of virtue need to exhibit morality in their own lives before suggesting that government place cops in other people's bedrooms.

CONCLUSION

The age of politics has failed; it is time to recover an older tradition, one that recognizes that a free people should rely on cooperation through the manifold institutions of civil society rather than coercion through the monopoly state of political society to organize their lives. Although we have not wholly lost the sense of community necessary to bind us together, the moral consensus that we once shared has badly frayed and many of the institutions necessary to enforce that consensus have fallen into disarray. Restoration and revitalization are therefore desperately needed.

As we embark on that repair mission, we should keep in mind the importance of preserving a free *and* virtuous society. Both facets of our system of ordered liberty are likely to face increasing challenges in the coming years. We need to respond by strengthening both, for neither is likely to survive without the other. And without them we cannot rebuild civil society--or bring to a close the age of politics.

Chapter 22

Populist: Citizenship as Public Work and Public Freedom

Harry C. Boyte

INTRODUCTION

Nineteen eighty-eight was a watershed moment in the changing language of American politics. "Community" emerged as an idea that spoke powerfully to the collapse of liberalism in the Dukakis presidential campaign. But community as a theme needs to be reframed by a populist view of citizenship, understood as the ongoing problem-solving work of citizens. Otherwise, the language of community slides easily into moralism and exhortation. Moreover, citizenship provides more than a pragmatic elaboration of communitarian ideas. In its deepest resonances, citizenship also suggests public freedom, the self-directed engagement of citizens in contributing to and rebuilding the society we hold in common. In this sense, citizenship has possibilities to regenerate the political hopefulness that is urgently needed in America today.

After 1988, the idea of community enjoyed great success as a political concept. It shaped the 1992 election. It formed a touchstone for the Clinton administration. Community's appeal derived not simply from flaws in liberalism but also from the fact that it addressed general problems of politics, economics, and social life. Yet the banner of community, called communitarianism, has lumped together two distinct, opposed strands of politics, one mainly local in focus, the other national.

On the one hand, public intellectuals like Amitai Etzioni, 1995-96

President of the American Sociology Association, and William A. Galston, a political theorist who became Deputy Director for Domestic Policy in the Clinton White House, have drawn together a decade's scholarship and activism to give a pluralist, democratic twist to themes like neighborhood, small business, family, and voluntary association that conservatives effectively championed against big government for more than two decades. Etzioni and Galston's "Communitarian Platform" document recruited many public officials, while their stress on local community and civil society influenced Clinton policies on issues such as community development and democracy promotion abroad.

On the other hand, "communitarianism" also took the form of a call for a national community of compassion, love, and caring. The arguments of Michael Lerner, editor of the progressive Jewish magazine *Tikkun*, for a "politics of meaning" based on love and care were emblematic. Designated "prophet of the year" in 1993 by the *New York Times*, Lerner's ideal of a national community of caring had wide appeal. It purported to serve as an antidote for racial and social fragmentation, the anomie of modern life, and the destructiveness of the marketplace. While it recalled older Progressive Era calls for "the Great Community," the vision of a national community of love and care also elaborated important themes from the new left and the late 1960s counterculture.

Both local and national versions of communitarianism are in part strategic and political responses to large dilemmas. Communitarians have sought to redress the growing disengagement of Americans from public affairs. The stance of innocent outsider produces a debilitating fickleness and irresponsibility in American politics, represented by everything from "talk show democracy" and the popularity of Rush Limbaugh to the man on the radio show who declared, "Taxpayers shouldn't have to pay for the S&L mess; government should pay for it."[1]

Communitarians have addressed the growing fragmentation of our society into a myriad of cultural, economic, lifestyle, and political groups who see themselves as besieged and often at war with each other. Finally, communitarians tried to bridge the chasm that has opened as a result of the process that Robert Reich described, the imaginative and even physical secession of America's governing class of symbolic analysts--scientists, managers, financial analysts, service professionals, journalists, academics, and others--from the rest of society. This class, with its own self-referential universe of symbols, educational institutions and communities, is more connected in some respects to a global context than to local institutions and America's social problems.[2]

Yet communitarianism's local and national emphases pull in opposite directions. On the one hand, communitarianism as a local concept has a populist flavor, drawing attention to rooted, richly articulated, local, and voluntary institutions too often taken for granted or even dismissed as parochial and unjust by a state-centered liberalism. In this sense it resurrects a vernacular sense of civic life that challenges the reductionist, modernist, and technocratic tendencies of our time.

On the other hand, the idea of a national community of love and caring has the opposite effect. It is too hortatory to bring together groups with widely varying histories and concepts of justice. Moreover, its solicitude for "the people" contributes all too easily to the process that has turned citizens into clients. National community here becomes a new clothing for the therapeutic interventions of a service society.

Anomie, cultural fragmentation, and the professional middle class emerge from features of our large-scale mobile world that seem unlikely to disappear in the foreseeable future. Yet the civic viability of the nation itself depends upon renewal of a robust citizenship: wide public involvement in solving our problems and an expansive sense of public possibility.

THE COMMUNITARIAN CRITIQUE

In mainstream liberal thought, by the 1980s "politics" was centered in government. The chief function of "private citizens," beyond choosing representatives through elections, was to press their case for what they considered to be legitimate rights and resources. Yet this version of politics also generated mounting problems. In the rhetoric of the presidential campaign of Michael Dukakis, the citizen was largely presented as an individual with certain rights, on the one hand, or as the *client* of government, on the other. The task of officeholders was to distribute fairly rights, opportunities, and resources. In a time of widespread unease about economic prospects, the erosion of community life, the corruption of public values, and the seemingly intractable problems facing the nation, such a focus was far too thin to stir most voters' deeper passions. Americans also voiced unease at conservatism's economic individualism and laissez faire attitude about social problems. Dilemmas on both left and right opened space for three communitarian criticisms.

Forgotten Foundations

First, communitarians argued that liberals advance a narrowly individualist, rights-centered, thin conception of the citizen. In conventional liberal approaches, the human self is "disembodied," in the phrasing of Michael Sandel, uprooted from the meanings, attachments, and life stories that make up the full identities of actual human beings.[3]

Such communitarian arguments found wide resonance. Thus, books that diagnosed Americans' "rampant individualism" and self-absorption like *Habits of the Heart*, by Robert Bellah and a team of researchers, or *Culture of Narcissism* by Christopher Lasch, had sales in the hundreds of thousands, remarkable success for relatively scholarly work. Religious leaders such as the Catholic bishops, civic organizations like Common Cause, and progressive populist politicians argued that the 1980s were characterized by an excess of greed, radical individualism, and the neglect of the common good.[4]

Moving from critique of individualism to prescription, communitarians in academia joined with community practioners, community-oriented analysts of social policy, and theorists of local community action to stress governmental policy that provides to local communities tools and resources but does not presume to solve community problems through one-way intervention. Borrowing in part from the work of conservatives such as Peter Berger, Robert Woodson, and William Schambra, "New Democrats" like Will Marshall and Elaine Kamarck argued that government-centered social policy has systematically neglected the role of what are called "mediating institutions" like family, voluntary association, religious congregation, and informal networks. They proposed that mediating institutions are essential in developing and implementing successful social policy across a range of issues, from crime control to welfare reform or maintenance of health.

The communitarian point also emphasized the implicit but crucial wellsprings of liberal politics itself, those experiences through which democratic values are cultivated and character is developed. In 1988, William Galston, who, as Issues Director of Walter Mondale's 1984 campaign had seemed an exemplar of state-centered social policy, made this argument in "Liberal Virtues," an article that signaled a sea change in liberalism. Galston challenged liberalism's singular focus on government and its neglect of the ways citizens *become* civic:

> The operation of liberal institutions is affected in important ways by the character of citizens (and leaders). . . at some point the attenuation of

individual virtue will create pathologies with which liberal political contrivances, however technically perfect their design, simply cannot cope.[5]

Elite Politics

Secondly, communitarians like Michael Walzer, Jane Mansbridge, Cornel West, and Benjamin Barber proposed that liberals stand apart, ivory-tower-like, separated from the give-and-take civic world of democratic politics. This insulation has meant a neglect of recent widespread forms of political activism, what I described as "the backyard revolution" of thousands of neighborhood groups, community-based economic development corporations, community-focused social services, self-help groups, community housing projects and the like that developed out of sight of the political mainstream in the 1970s and 1980s. These have nonetheless involved perhaps a quarter of the adult population. As *The Christian Science Monitor* observed, grassroots community activism was arguably the "invisible story of the decade" during the 1970s.[6]

Conservatives, drawing on the mediating structures argument, were far more adroit in speaking to this new development than were liberals. Thus, Ronald Reagan, declaring that "the revitalization of neighborhoods is the heart and soul of rebuilding America" in the 1980 campaign, sensed the shifting landscape and new political constituencies. Ironically, his administration also soon set about dismantling every program that local groups had found useful in self-help and self-organization, from VISTA and community-based anti-crime efforts to housing rehab and energy conservation initiatives.[7]

Liberals by the 1980s had come to rely increasingly upon the courts, the *least* democratic institutions of government. In his book, *Speaking American*, former Mondale and Dukakis and now Clinton speechwriter David Kusnet observed that liberalism was largely the cultural and linguistic property of professionals, managers and other well-educated upper middle class groups who tend to be social liberals or radicals but economic conservatives. As a result, it was increasingly dependent on judicial review. "Victorious in the courts, liberals have rarely had to make a public case for these positions [affirmative action, busing, criminal defendants' rights and others] or try to assemble majorities in their behalf. They've ended up speaking 'legalese,' not plain English."[8]

Impoverished Vision

Finally, communitarians charged that liberal, institutional politics has an impoverished vocabulary of public purposes. It fails to speak to the erosion of a sense of common purpose and common tasks in the nation, on the one hand, or the centrifugal forces that increasingly fragment the society, on the other.

Hannah Arendt wrote decades ago that "What makes mass society so difficult to bear is not the number of people involved, or at least not primarily, but the fact that the world between them has lost its power to gather them together, to relate and separate them." By the 1990s, there was little, indeed, in the nation's civic life that "gathered people together."[9]

In electoral campaigns, communitarians have sought to address this fragmentation through more moderate, complex positions on a variety of social issues that balance questions of rights with responsibilities. They have also worked to articulate an integrative language for the nation as a whole. Such a focus allowed moderate Democrats in 1992 to reconnect with value concerns of most Americans on issues ranging from crime or the lyrics of rock music to welfare. In its more expansive aspects, communitarianism gave a lilt to Bill Clinton's campaign, surfacing in his calls for national service and for a new convenant among Americans and government.

Yet the range of problems that communitarians identified cannot be solved by the concept of community. Attention to community as a local and participatory theme redresses flaws that have long plagued American liberalism and welfare-state politics generally. But calls for a national community of common moral values--while they may have an immediate utility during elections--do not work well in the actual practice of governance. They fail, on the one hand, to reengage a population that sees itself as outsiders and clients. And they are unable to bridge the gap between groups with widely varying perspectives on justice and history, on the other. Finally, at their worst, summons to national community can feed therapeutic interventions which erode local community.

COMMUNITIES AND CIVIC LIFE

It is a commonplace of recent historical scholarship to observe that citizen-centered ideas of politics came under assault in the world of large institutions and transcontinental communications of the 20th century. The Progressive period of the early 20th century sought a radical relocation of politics to the state. Progressives spoke in democratic accents to rhetorically confront "the mighty forces" of commerce and industry that dominated the American economy. But they also envisioned "control" over commercial interests in a sense far different than had earlier democratic movements of the 19th century. While Progressive reformers took aim at corrupt urban machine politics, they also saw officials and professionals as the significant public agents. Herbert Croly, *New Republic* editor who redefined democracy away from any local, civic activity to what he called the "great community" of the state, argued that democracy no longer could mean that citizens "assemble after the manner of a New England town-meeting." Instead of the communal experience of towns, the nation as a whole must be bound together by "a comprehensive social ideal," arbitrated by modern media. Direct civic encounter was not necessary since "the active citizenship of the country meets every morning and evening and discusses the affairs of the nation with the newspaper as an impersonal interlocutor," providing "abundant opportunities of communications and consultation without any meeting" at all.[10]

As Walter Lippmann, another architect of mainstream progressive thought put it, the growth of citizens, large scale industry, communications, transportation and so forth "had upset the old life on the prairies, made new demands upon democracy, introduced specialization and science . . . destroyed village loyalties . . . and created the impersonal relationships of the modern world."[11]

Yet historians who take such rhetoric at face value have also neglected a more complex side to 20th century history. More active understandings of politics continued to flourish in what might be best called mediating political institutions like parties, ethnic groups, local business organizations, active unions, neighborhood schools, settlement houses, publicly minded churches or synagogues, and local press. These had local, community dimensions, but also connected people's everyday lives to larger arenas of public action and policy.

Women's suffrage organizations and their offspring, for example, not only fought for expansion of rights of formal citizenship through enfranchisement of women voters. They also sought to teach an understanding of politics and citizenship as "civic housekeeping" on a range of problems. Thus, the *Woman Citizen's Library*, a 12 volume collection of practical and theoretical material on "the larger citizenship" included among its authors leading suffragists such as Jane Addams and Cary Chapman Catt. In its 1913 inaugural edition, it declared that "the

State is as real as the people who compose it. The duties of citizenship are as definite as the duties of housekeeping. Only as these self-evident facts are fully appreciated will women be able to share in those many and splendid reforms which we can see must come in our social life." The volumes included topics that ranged from the mechanics of political parties to questions of "the larger citizenship," like "the liquor traffic," "child labor," "equal pay for equal work," "schools," and "safeguarding the women immigrant."   Such a view of citizenship inspired lasting organizations like the League of Women Voters, direct successor to the National American Women's Suffrage Association.[12]

Ethnic and machine political organizations continued as a strong presence in many large cities until the 1950s or 1960s. In Chicago, Mike Royko has described how precinct captains and ward bosses of the political machine created the connections between immigrants and larger society:

> The immigrant family looked to [the captain] as more than a link with a new and strange government: he was the government. He could tell them how to fill out their papers, how to pay their taxes, how to get a license. He was the welfare agency, with a basket of food and some coal when things got tough, an entree to the crowded charity hospital. He could take care of it when one of the kids got in trouble with the police.[13]

None of this should be romanticized; it had strong personal and parochial dimensions. Middle class suffrage organizations which called for a "new citizenship" had racist and nativist features. They justified women's voting in part by arguing it would reduce the influence of undesirable foreigners and blacks.   Ethnic political bosses created organizations that resembled feudal strongholds. Neighborhoods like Bridgeport, the Irish enclave that produced Richard Daley and two previous mayors of Chicago, was a parochial small town within the city, as quick to threaten an errant black as are the Howard Beaches of our day. Daley's boyhood club known as the Hamburgs was found by a Chicago commission to have played a major role in instigating the race riot of 1919, which left 15 whites and 23 blacks dead, after a black youth crossed the line separating the 27th Street beach from the 29th Street beach.

For all their limitations, however, political institutions like the suffrage organizations and the urban party machines created an everyday public scaffolding for politics, a kind of civic capital, that the nation could draw upon in times of challenge and crisis. Under the umbrella of urban machines, for instance, immigrants became involved in a range of civic initiatives, from building churches, synagogues, native-language newspapers, and ethnic organizations to launching reform efforts. All these could be considered a form of everyday politics that helped widen people's particular identities to include a larger understanding of their role and stake in the nation. Boundaries between formal institutions like the local school and union were not nearly as distinct as they were to become.

Back of the Yards, the larger community for Daley's Bridgeport, was a major center of trade union organizing which helped to fuel the New Deal. During World War II, each Chicago neighborhood had block captains and air-raid wardens. People saved their bacon grease and chicken fat and faithfully used rationing coupons.

The civil rights movement of the late 1950s and early 1960s was a powerful extension of these traditions of citizen-centered politics. When Martin Luther King stressed the need to "make real the promise of democracy" and to "bring our nation back to those great wells of democracy which were dug deep by the founding fathers," he meant considerably more than simply winning for blacks an end to segregation or the right to vote in elections. He also meant recovering a strong practice and understanding of citizenship and democratic politics.

The theme of public participation became a central motif in the movement. Indeed it formed the heart of efforts like the Citizenship Schools of the Southern Christian Leadership Conference and the Freedom Schools of the Student Nonviolent Coordinating Committee, adapted from Highlander Folk School. These schools, while registering voters, also taught thousands of local leaders new approaches to citizen problem-solving in communities. They focused not only on the evils of segregation but also on practical problems of community life. "Teachers" and "students" were peers. Methods drew directly on the stories and experiences of participants. The formal political process was concretely connected to issues in people's daily lives. Such experience could create a transformative sense of public life. Unita Blackwell, involved with the Mississippi Freedom Democratic Party, who later was elected mayor of Mayersville, Mississippi, described her experience: "We found ourselves involved in working in political work, and we still ain't figured all of it out yet, but it's been just wonderful."[14]

Despite civil rights, however, our civic capital began to erode significantly with World War II. A view of the professional, manager, and expert as the significant problem-solver spread through European and American politics alike. In the 1950s, the Swedish sociologist Gunnar Myrdal could argue that "increasing political harmony . . . [is emerging] between all citizens in the advanced welfare state. The internal political debate in those countries is becoming increasingly technical in character." Social policy in countries like Sweden--long a model for progressively-inclined Americans--was if anything further advanced toward a professionalized view.[15]

In America, McCarthyism and the atmosphere of the Cold War further contributed to a depoliticized, professional-dominated public environment. The citizen was reinvented as the oxymoron, "private citizen." Home ownership, seen by community activists like Mary Follett earlier in the 20th century as analogous to Jeffersonian small freeholds, foundation for involvement in the public life of the community, had changed its meaning. The house was a "castle," a fortress from the world. The ideal became isolated suburban families tied together by the consumer culture.

Television and the increasingly media-centered nature of election campaigns furthered the distance between citizens and politics. Candidate packaging reworked the link between citizens and candidates into a connection between audience and spectacle, with periodic moments of consumption when voters got to select the best "package." Simultaneously, the growth of professional services in every field--from education to trade unions to voluntary organizations like the Red Cross and the YMCA--more and more rendered citizens as clients, not problem solvers, and detached professional knowledge from any larger civic meaning or context. Unions switched from centers of community life to service organizations providing packaged benefits to members. Schools became suffused with professional jargon, which made them seem foreign territory to many parents. Organizations like the YMCA deemphasized citizenship and stressed sports facilities and programs to enhance self-esteem. At the center of this, people came to see government less as their instrument--"of and by the people"--than as service provider.

POLITICS AFTER CITIZENSHIP

The professionalization of mediating political institutions and the spread everywhere of the professional-client pattern created a vacuum that had disastrous consequences for both officeholders and the general citizenry. The vacuum has been filled over the last generation by the rise of an insular, professionalized politics, on the one hand, often accompanied by a therapeutic language of caring and concern. On the other hand, it is populated by utopian, personalized, and righteous strands of activism.

In a process that Robert Reich has well described, over the last generation global economic changes have meshed with a middle class restlessness--what could be well termed a new utopianism--to fuel a continuous process of occupational and psychological, as well as geographic, suburbanization. A class of conceptualizers and problem solvers has become increasingly removed from the lives and social problems of most Americans. Today there are more private security forces than public police.

The active understanding of politics that emerged in the civil rights movement inspired a generation of young radicals on college campuses and helped to spark important social movements such as contemporary feminism. At its heart, the new left appeal was grounded in the articulation of a wide-ranging hope that democracy could be far richer, more dynamic and more engaging of people's energies and passions than was understood in conventional terms. "The very isolation of the individual--from power and community and ability to aspire--means the rise of a democracy without publics," declared *The Port Huron Statement*, a 1963 manifesto of the Students for a Democratic Society drafted largely by Tom Hayden which became the touchstone for 1960s social movements on the left. Despite characteristically gendered language of the early sixties, the manifesto nonetheless captured well the democratic wish to move beyond the given, everyday, and conventional view of politics to a larger possibility which animated a wide variety of later protests, from women's liberation to other ethnic, sexual, and racial movements:

We would replace power rooted in possession, privilege or circumstance by power and uniqueness rooted in love, reflectiveness, reason and creativity. As a *social system* we seek the establishment of a democracy of individual participation, governed by two central aims: that the individual share in those decisions determining the quality and direction of his life; that society be organized to encourage independence in men and provide the media for their common participation.[16]

Yet for all its poetic edge, the new left also positioned itself as a critic on the outside of American institutional life and culture. This was in sharp contrast with the southern civil rights movement. SCLC citizenship schools aimed at helping blacks become "first class citizens." Martin Luther King's Letter from a Birmingham Jail framed the black struggle for freedom as the embodiment of America's diverse traditions and institutional aspirations, and invoked a rich array of national, patriotic and religious images. In contrast, *The Port Huron Statement* included an unrelenting attack on virtually every American institution.

Despite democratic energy, youthful protests thus also generated a personalized, moralistic, and utopian politics that advocated *for* the dispossessed and powerless even while activists sought to bypass the compromises and ambiguities of existing communal and institutional life. Such a radicalism was fundamentally at odds with populism, which articulates a sense of public life grounded in the messy, ironic, even tragic complexities of the vernacular. The tension filled balance between the vibrancy of a public world in which ordinary people claim and develop their authority, power, and creativity, on the one hand, and the necessary rootedness of public life in the particular, everyday, and down-home, on the other, is at the heart of any serious populism.

In consequence, the new left counterculturalism belied its democratic aspirations. Such a posture found all too easy accommodation with patterns of expert-client relationships in which professionals present themselves as benevolent outsiders who rescue the unfortunate from depraved environments. With eerie kinship to Leninist notions of the vanguard, college educated radicals slipped into the growing professional class which viewed itself as the source of social redemption.

Formal politics has embodied this pattern. A new generation of politicians and officials came of age at every level motivated by the idealism of the 1960s. Concerned about issues such as civil rights, feminism, or environmental activism, they took on local power structures and backroom maneuvering across the country with sometimes striking successes. Yet they also faced the paradox of growing isolation from their constituencies and gridlock in decision making as they dismantled ties between officials and the citizenry at large that they saw as corrupt. Today, writes Alan Ehrenhalt, the "political system . . . is going professional and full-time" in an unprecedented fashion. It is also filled with political leaders like Rick Knobe, the insurgent liberal who won a victory over the entrenched establishment of Sioux Falls, South Dakota, in 1983, only to find "I was carrying the whole city on my back. I was an island unto myself."[17]

Patterns of distanced, professionalized advocacy tied to service delivery are widespread today, not only in government but also in the range of human service arenas. Service systems address problems in terms of individual deficiencies and needs, using a language of deviance with terms like at-risk, culturally deprived, or culturally disadvantaged. Professionals have agency, but their work is narrowly cast, defined in terms of one-directional interactions in which they have singular authority. Experts present themselves not as civic actors with power and their own specific interests, but rather simply as altruistic and objective specialists whose interest is only in serving the client. Indeed, Ross Perot's offer to present himself selflessly as a disinterested fix-it man for the nation's problems is a perfect embodiment of a service society's politics.

In the wake of the sixties, weekend therapy sessions and television talk shows, self-help groups, the total quality management movement, the language of self-esteem and personal development in K-12 education and varieties of New Age phenomena all have helped to generate a radically personalized culture of public encounter that provide a background for the new political ideology of care in the 1990s. Such public interactions expand a language of private experience and shared vulnerabilities into a personalized utopianism writ large. The ultimate logic of intimate politics is to refashion the nation as a limitless encounter group where everyone is expected to share with everyone things that they would rarely discuss in the privacy of their own homes.

Today, a politics of professionalized, intimate care structures large sections of the economy, while it also is advanced as the solution for America's fragmentation and civic disengagement. In health care, for instance, the intense focus on individualized care makes cross-disciplinary public problem-solving difficult, as the Pew Health Professions Commission has observed. In public policy, the intensely personal, individual language of health care greatly erodes public capacities to make tough choices about issues such as the trade-offs between expensive technology and primary care.

In another instance, the language of care suffuses the community service movement as often structured. Educators and politicians advance community service as the most promising method for reconnecting the younger generation with the duties, values, and practices of citizenship. Yet in fact the use of a personal development approach in community service often turns programs into apprenticeships for professional service delivery, not environments in which young people learn the civic and political skills of public leadership.

One recent study of high school community service programs found that educational objectives typically include such aims as "learning to care for others," "developing self-esteem," "a sense of personal worth," "self-understanding," and "capacity to persevere in difficult tasks." Learning "politics" through political themes like interest, power, and strategic thinking was absent. In settings like this, students may become "politicized" about the larger social problems and policies of issues they confront in individual terms, but their resulting activism is moralistic, personalized and anti-institutional, not informed by any deep understanding of problems. Moreover, their view of the people whom they "help" emphasizes deficiencies with little attention to the rich communal resources and possibilities to be found within even the poorest communities. In these terms service reproduces the pattern of middle class solicitude for the poor and the unfortunate which erodes citizen capacity in the name of change.[18]

The result of the moralized, intimate, and sentimental quality of citizen activism at every point on the political spectrum is that people see themselves as aggrieved, righteous, and misunderstood outsiders. Countless variations on the theme of "send them a message" have, in consequence, become the main way in which many people are connected to the larger world. People ask to be heard in politics and to receive things from government. They rarely imagine themselves as creators or producers *of* politics. As John Brandl, an economics professor who served several terms in the Minnesota Senate puts it, today government largely means the delivery of benefits to the appreciative, paid for by the oblivious.

CITIZENSHIP AS PUBLIC WORK AND PUBLIC FREEDOM

The language of community is simply not sufficient to move beyond fragmented purposes and rights-based political activism. Differences in moral perspectives cannot be understood in terms of the success or failure of communal institutions in inculcating virtue. Often dramatic power dynamics are involved: "moral conversation" is neither appropriate nor effective for relationship-building between an inner city youth and a suburban businessman. Moreover, the dynamics of specific histories are crucial, even among groups with roughly similar status and power.

The problem in America is often not so much the *lack* of moral speech or deliberation as it is *contending* moralities. Blacks in South Chicago and white ethnics in Cicero, for instance, likely have different views of racial justice, based on different experiences. Seeking moral consensus is liable to deepen the divide, without any way to bridge it.

The politics of working on common problems always has a normative dimension--it raises the question of "what we should do." Moreover, at moments issues can become occasions for moral crusades that reshape the social and political landscape. This was the case with the movement for black civil rights in the 1960s, for instance, and with modern feminism's assertion of women's entitlement to equal public roles.

But politics does not simply revolve around questions of justice. Public life also has strong pragmatic, problem-solving dimensions that bring together people with very different conceptions of what is just and right. Thus, politics is different than ethics. For good reason, Aristotle wrote different books on the topics. On most pressing issues public values are not given *a priori*; they are rather *created* in practice through the ongoing, multi-dimensional work of people with different interests and perspectives who address problems they find they have in common.

A sense of public affairs and politics as common work was the peculiar genius of America's political culture that emerged from the revolutionary period. As new scholarship has begun to emphasize, the distinctive feature of the American Revolution was neither a liberal focus on rights nor a classical republican concern with civic virtue. Rather, America's revolution produced a political culture that was practical, down-to-earth, work-centered, and energetic. As Gordon Wood put it in his recent book, *The Radicalism of the American Revolution*, "when [classical ideals of disinterested civic virtue] proved too idealistic and visionary, [Americans] found new democratic adhesives in the actual behavior of plain ordinary people."[19]

Thus, for America's founders, education was aimed at practical citizenship, focused on the development of people's capacities for work together through civic problem-solving. Such education was seen as the foundation for democracy. Thomas Jefferson put the matter clearly when he argued:

> I know of no safe repository of the ultimate powers of the society but the people themselves; and if we think them not enlightened enough to exercise control with a wholesome discretion, the remedy is not to take it from them, but to inform their discretion by education.[20]

Education for citizenship entailed especially practical, generalist training. Thus, Benjamin Franklin argued that any man might have to do anything in an open, fluid society; the point of his model school, the Philadelphia Academy, was to train male children to deal with unanticipated situations. It was to be a school out of which boys "will come . . . fitted for learning any Business, Calling, or Profession."[21]

Moreover, the Jeffersonian, populist faith in "the people themselves" as repository of the powers of the society combined practical work with a powerful vision of public freedom. Again, in our recent history the civil rights movement has most vividly articulated this sensibility.

In the civil rights movement, freedom conveyed the common meaning of freedom *from* repressive conditions: release from the degradation of segregation (in conventional terms, freedom or liberty today continues to entail mainly this negative sense, freedom *from* overweening control).

Yet freedom's most powerful resonances came from its positive *public* dimensions. Freedom suggested the freedom *to* participate as full, independent and powerful citizens in public affairs on an ongoing basis. Precisely this public participation--in the movement's rallies, sit-ins, demonstrations, voter registration drives, Freedom Schools, and more practical day-to-day practices of community problem-solving--generated the movement spirit, despite violent opposition and situations of great danger. Freedom language here entailed a new and strengthened sense of "citizenship," through which people came to experience themselves as participators in governance.

Such a vision of freedom had old roots in the African American tradition. Charles Gomillion had described earlier efforts to bring about political equality in Tuskegee, for instance, as "civic democracy . . . a way of life in which all citizens have the opportunity to participate in societal affairs." In Ralph Ellison's great novel on the black experience, *Invisible Man*, the protagonist has such an experience as he breaks loose of the Communist Party's orthodoxies and speaks directly from his experience to an audience in Harlem:

> I feel suddenly that I have become *more human*. Do you understand? . . . Not that I have become a man, for I was born a man. But that I am more human. I feel strong. I feel able to get things done! I feel that I can see sharp and clear and far down the dim corridor of history . . . I feel that here, after a long and desperate and uncommonly blind journey, I have come home . . . I am a new citizen of the country of your vision . . . I feel that here tonight, in this old arena, the new is being born and the vital old revived. In each of you, in me, in all of us. SISTERS! BROTHERS! WE ARE THE TRUE PATRIOTS! THE CITIZENS OF TOMORROW'S WORLD! WE'LL BE DISPOSSESSED NO MORE![22]

Despite the technocratic, therapeutic, moralized temper of our age, a sense of citizenship that combines the practical work of problem solving with a larger vision of public freedom has a renewed relevance.

Today the inability of a narrowly specialized and expert approach to solve virtually any serious public problem has increasingly become apparent. In response, a populist, practical politics has begun to reemerge on a wide scale, especially in recent community organizations. Thus, for instance, the lesson of much community organizing experience over the last two decades is that when groups with different views on issues like affirmative action, gay rights, or abortion find ways to work together on issues like housing or teen pregnancy, the experience can improve relationships, and also lessen moral polarization.

Moreover, since the 1960s the most effective community organizing networks have added to practical citizen-led problem solving through developing an expanded concept of a *public arena* that carries resonances of positive freedom. In these terms, the public arena is a diverse, challenging realm in which citizens reclaim responsibility and develop the power and learn the skills and knowledge to seriously address public issues and to become "co-creators of history." In the language of Ernesto Cortes, one of the chief architects of this approach, such community groups call themselves "universities for public life, where people learn the arts of public discourse and public action." Ed Chambers, director of Industrial Areas Foundation (IAF) network describes the shift toward political education as the major development in the network's 50 year history. "We began to see every action as an opportunity for education and training," said Maribeth Larkin, an organizer with the IAF group, United Neighborhoods Organization, in Los Angeles.[23]

Civic education in this vein results in a pragmatic rendering of the theme of "commonwealth" or common good. Classically, community organizing opposed any language of the common good. Yet IAF groups and others redefine "commonwealth" by changing the static idea of the common good into a dynamic, practical notion. In IAF terms, the commons, or basic public goods, cannot exist outside of politics. They are those things like schools, roads, parks, the local economy and so forth that politics identifies as occasions for pragmatic civic collaboration. Developing such collaboration means the shift from "protest to participation in governance," in the phrasing of Gerald Taylor, on the IAF national staff.[24]

Building on such lessons, the challenge in politics is not so much to generate larger numbers of experts, to find moral consensus, or to develop capacities for emotional self-revelation. Rather it is to translate the practical, public, citizen-centered politics that has developed in community groups into an approach to public problem-solving and an articulation of public life that can revitalize America's civic spirit.

This means cultivating the political skills and capacities that allow people--both professionals and clients--to work productively with others, whether or not they like or agree with each other. It also means framing problem solving in a language of citizenship that draws attention to the broader significance of local and particular efforts.

Robust citizenship means understanding public action as the everyday, demanding craft of addressing the problems of our common existence. This means acknowledging differences in interest and power (if not accepting them as static or absolute), and often working alongside people with whom we may disagree about moral issues and with whom we may not wish to "live in community," for the sake of broader objectives.

Project Public Life, a grassroots civic education and action initiative of the Center for Democracy and Citizenship, based at the University of Minnesota's Humphrey Institute, has found it possible to develop the lessons from successful grassroots community efforts in many institutional environments, from schools and low income parent groups to 4-H clubs, nursing homes, hospitals, and large public bureaucracies like Minnesota Extension Services. We have discovered that teaching civic concepts can help considerably in reembedding professional practice in public life, with a resulting shift from a service provision-model of problem-solving to a more horizontal, interactive approach that leads to collaborative action on problems among many interests. We have also found that a citizen-centered politics has wide general appeal.

For example, Communities Mobilized for Change on Alcohol (CMCA) a joint project on teen age alcohol use in seven counties of Minnesota and Wisconsin, undertaken with the Department of Epidemiology at the University of Minnesota, differs from customary patterns of campaigns on such issues that mainly target individuals for "education" about the deleterious consequences of drinking. It also differs from a newer approach in public health, which seeks to mobilize communities around policy changes that professionals have determined produce beneficial results. In CMCA, strategy teams represent a wide array of community interests, including young people, who spend considerable time in defining what "the problem" of underage drinking is in the context of their specific communities. CMCA has found that citizens are eager to be challenged to see their own roles in broad and multi-dimensional ways. Marie Klinghagen, an organizer for CMCA in Hutchinson, Minnesota, observes that "people feel very left out of government and public problem-solving today. Though they may have answers and insights, no one has asked them. So the usual coffee shop talk is about the stupidity of government, school, police, courts and so forth." A citizen-centered approach to politics, in Klinghagen's observation, not only allows people to do something practical about politics but also puts them back into the equation. "Citizen politics confronts their inaction because it gives them a way to do something, and helps them appreciate having experts available rather than making fun of them."[25]

A language of "publicness" gives people a way to see themselves as serious public actors while it also draws attention to larger, common civic projects. Citizenship as public work recognizes the appropriate roles of professionals but is not overawed by professional expertise; in the phrase from community organizing, it puts experts "on tap, not on top." Public spaces are open, accessible, and involve a mix of different people and groups. Private and personal interests often draw people into public arenas (an insight of modern feminism that is expressed in a dynamic concept of self-interest). But principles of action are different in public. The aim of politics is action on significant problems--not bonding, or intimacy, or communal consensus. This means people must be able to work with a variety of others, whether or not they like each other. In private, we want love and loyalty. In public, principles such as recognition, respect, and accountability are appropriate bases for action.

Public work which develops people's sense of themselves as contributors on a larger stage can generate new confidence and strategic capacity. Thus, community service projects viewed as public leadership education-- ways for young people to learn strategic political skills and concepts of civic engagement--equip youth to address creatively "the mess" they believe they are inheriting from prior generations. Over the last several years Project Public Life has helped Community Pride, a large service project of Minnesota 4-H which involves more than 20,000 young people each year, to integrate political and civic concepts into their training. Many projects youth take on have dramatically changed as a result, with a new seriousness and depth evident in their work across the state. Teens have moved from projects like sending Valentines Day cards to seniors in nursing homes to efforts to reconnect residents with the life of communities. They have switched from clean-up days to campaigns to save wetlands and build treelines that preserve topsoil.[26]

To renew a public and democratic politics will require not only widespread civic education and examples of citizen problem-solving. It will also mean political leadership ready to acknowledge that government cannot alone solve the nation's problems. The new generation of democratic public leadership--whether in office or not--will need to claim an identity as fellow citizen, rather than posing as savior or fount of wisdom. Acknowledgment of common civic identity also means a challenge to all Americans to become involved in civic problem-solving. Finally, political vision for our future needs to call us from singularly private pursuits into the liberty of public life. We become free, in the largest sense, as we work together to build and pass on the society that we share in common.

ENDNOTES

1.   Amitai Etzioni, *The Spirit of Community* (New York: Crown Publishers, 1993), 3.

2.   Robert Reich, *The Work of Nations* (New York: Vintage, 1992).

3.   Michel Sandel, *Liberalism and the Limits of Justice* (Cambridge: Cambridge University Press, 1982).

4.   See for instance, Robert Bellah et al., *Habits of the Heart* (Berkeley, CA: University of California, 1985); Christopher Lasch, *Culture of Narcissism (New York: W. W. Norton, 1979);* National Conference of Catholic Bishops, *Pastoral Letter on Catholic Social Teaching and the U.S. Economy* (Washington, D.C.: National Conference, 1985); Congressional Populist Caucus, "Statement of Principles" (including members such as Lane Evans (D-IL), Barbara Boxer (D-CA), John Bryant (D-TX), Tom Daschle (D-SD), Sen. Tom Harkin (D-IA), Sen. Barbara Milkulski (D-MD), and Sen. Albert Gore (D-TN); quoted in Harry C. Boyte, *Citizen Action and the New American Populism* (Philadelphia: Temple University Press, 1986).

5.   William Galston, "Liberal Virtues," *American Political Science Review* 82, (1988): 1279.

6.   *Christian Science Monitor* poll, 23 December 1977; see also Renee Berger, *Against All Odds: The Achievements of Community-Based Development Organizations* (Washington: NCCED, 1989).

7.   For a rich description of the difference in language, see William Schambra, *The Quest for Community and the Quest for a New Public Philosophy* (Washington: American Enterprise Institute, 1983), 30.

8.   David Kusnet, *Speaking American: How the Democrats Can Win in the Nineties* (New York: Thunders Mouth Press, 1992), 7.

9.   Hannah Arendt, quoted from Michel Sandel, ed. Introduction to *Liberalism and its Critics* (New York: New York University Press, 1984), 7.

10.   Herbert Croly, *The Promise of American Life* (New York: Macmillan,

1909), 139, 453.

11.   Walter Lippmann, quoted in Schambra, *The Quest for Community and the Quest for a New Public Philosophy*, 5.

12.   Harry C. Boyte, "Reinventing Citizenship," *Kettering Review* (Winter 1994): 78-87. See also Sara M. Evans, *Born for Liberty: A History of Women in America* (New York: Free Press, 1989), Chapter 7.

13.   Mike Royko, *Boss* (New York: Penguine, 1971), 68.

14.   Unita Blackwell, quoted in Richard King, "Citizenship and Self-Respect: The Experience of Politics in the Civil Rights Movement," *Journal of American Studies* 22 (1988): 22.

15.   Gunnar Myrdal, quoted in Jeffrey Galper, *The Politics of Social Services* (Englewood Cliffs, NJ: Prentice Hall, 1975), 113.

16.   *Port Huron Statement*, quoted from James Miller, *Democracy Is in the Streets* (New York: Simon & Schuster), 330, 333, 336.

17.   Alan Ehrenhalt, *The United States of Ambition: Politicians, Power and the Pursuit of Office* (New York: Times Books, 1991), 40, 37.

18.   Dan Conrad, "Learner Outcomes for Community Service," *The Generator* (January 1988): 1-2.

19.   Gordon S. Wood, *The Radicalism of the American Revolution* (New York: Vintage, 1991), ix.

20.   Paul Leichester Ford, ed., Thomas Jefferson, *The Works of Thomas Jefferson* (New York: Knickerbocker Press, 1903), 278.

21.   Benjamin Franklin, quoted from Colin Greer, *The Great School Legend* (New York: Basic Books, 1972), 15.

22.   Charles Gomillion, quoted in Robert J. Norrell, *Reaping the Whirlwind: The Civil Rights Movement in Tuskegee* (New York: Alfred Knopf, 1985), 41; Ralph Ellison, *Invisible Man* (New York: Vintage, 1989), 346.

23.   Ed Chambers, interviewed by author, Baltimore, 7 November 1987; Maribeth Larkin, interviewed by author, Los Angeles, 17 May 1977.

24.   Gerald Taylor, interviewed by author, Baltimore, 11 November 1987.

25.   Marie Klinghagen, memo to author, 13 January 1994.

26.   Carol Shields, interviewed by author, Minneapolis, 27 February 1994.

Chapter 23

The Expanding Role of the Center: Affirming American Ideals

Elizabeth B. Lurie

INTRODUCTION

Superficially, the Center is a political metaphor, often described as "moderate," technically described as either Center-Left or Center-Right, and sometimes described as "undecided" or without strong convictions and therefore fickle, easily led or misled. Generally, we view the Center as "the broad middle" whose votes will determine the outcome of an election. In national debates, we continually attempt to define the sentiments of the Center through the use of "scientific" public opinion polls.

Here I use the term Center in a broader context, in the sense of *heart*. In a society of empowered citizens whose governmental system is representative democracy, the Center is at the core, advancing toward and affirming the ideals to which the society generally aspires. That is the Center's cultural role, and that role shapes the Center's subsidiary political role. In the United States, because of the unique diversity of her people, the Center is truly an amalgamation: it defies arrangement by class, color, sex, age, ethnicity, religiosity, heritage, or political affiliation. The Center is larger than any of these, and it goes its own way. Hence, even the most complex of polls presents but an approximation of public opinion.

THE CENTER'S IDEALS

The Center, as heart, is defined by its ideals, by what it aspires to achieve as the good, the beneficial--for one, and for all.   In the Declaration of Independence, the Founders cited the ideals of "life, liberty and the pursuit of happiness" as "certain unalienable rights" premised upon the equality of men and "endowed, by their Creator." In the Constitution, "we, the people" cited certain other ideals as its purpose: "to form a more perfect union, establish justice, insure domestic tranquility, provide for the common defence, promote the general welfare, and secure the blessings of liberty to ourselves and our posterity." In an officially secular society, such ideals substitute for the establishment of religion: they constitute the substance of our consensual creed, the objects of our civil aspirations. They define what one dare not challenge unless one wishes to decamp to the precincts of extremism.

The ideals defining the vision and purposes of American civilization have not changed a great deal in the time since their articulation. We are engaged in an argument about the right to life, but that argument is largely about what life *is*, and therefore under what circumstances the state must affirm the right. It is also true that we are having certain arguments about liberty, but those arguments are actually focused on what is libertine. They are not about freedom, but about license. We are also having an argument about happiness--whether it is therapeutically conferred or, instead, achieved--and that is not an argument about happiness itself. Similarly, we do not seek to form a more imperfect union, establish injustice, insure domestic discord, provide for the common subjugation, promote the general ill-being, or secure the fruits of oppression to ourselves and our posterity. These are not among our ideals, and those who might argue openly for such are hardly to be found, even at the extremes.

The Center has other broadly writ ideals. Like our civil ideals, many of them are religiously derived. Like all ideals, they inspire a profound allegiance akin to religious faith. One is fairness, the principle of the Golden Rule expressed in the notion of human equality before the law, and by extension, embodied in our notions of civility and manners in private and public behavior. Fairness encompasses the principle that we judge each other within the capacity of volition, attempting to exclude consideration of such immutable accidents as color; the aspiration to fairness spawns both tolerance and forgiveness, and undergirds our view of justice.

Another such ideal is virtue, the aspiration to "do what is right," to be trustworthy and reliably so.   Undergirding our ideal of virtue is the presumption of knowledge, not only the capacity but also the capability to discriminate between right and wrong, and hence to be responsible for one's actions. Implicit in the presumption of capability is the presumption of learning: we educate our children to the ideal of virtue.   The Center does not aspire to unfairness, prejudice, intolerance, condemnation, amorality, ignorance, indifference, or irresponsibility.

A third such ideal, actually a component of virtue but deserving of separate mention, is what we call "trying." In the American Center there is a spirit of innovation, an openness to the effort and experimentation that, while not foreign to others, receives unique emphasis in the United States. The old adage, "If at first you don't succeed, try, try again!" is perhaps the quintessential expression of this ideal, a reflection of our faith that human beings can achieve when they expend the required effort. A willingness to invest in the experimentation that mastering a skill or exploring a better way requires, the ideal of trying gives us a particular receptivity to what is inventive or innovative, to what is "new and improved," to the activity we call progress. Our trying is so pronounced an ideal that we do not even view the unable as without capacity; we view such among our fellows as having potential to develop capability, if only we will help them to try.

It is worth noting that the Center's ideals do not include the acquisition of *things* by fiat, *i.e.* an entitlement to property. Rather, the focus is on the ideal of self-sufficiency, achieved through the opportunity to produce those things which are needed to serve necessity, first, and desire, second. The concept of earned ownership, our version of material success, governs wealth accumulation and distribution; for the ideal of the Center is that every citizen exercise the (not "an") opportunity to create wealth sufficient to support himself and his children. This ideal spawns charity, respect, and pity: charity toward those unable to succeed due to incapacity; respect for those who aspire to success (regardless of any number of false but trustworthy starts); and pity toward those unwilling to aspire. We hear much of "compassion" today, but compassion is not one of the Center's ideals; it is a responsive behavior, part charity and part pity, and so it is better understood in its separate components.

The Center's ideals are exactly that--ideals. There is an expectation to "do better, go forward, make progress," but there is no expectation to achieve the ideal states. Because ideals are states of imagined perfection-- not actualities--to which the Center aspires, and because in the American experience their pursuit is seen as within the voluntary capacity of individuals, progress is the Center's general activity in any sphere. While we are accustomed to discussing the activities of the Center in political terms, the American Center is not primarily, or even specifically from time to time, a political phenomenon. It is instead a broadly diverse associational phenomenon, and its primary concern is not public governance, but private initiative spanning the entire spectrum of American culture.

The Center does not act--or vote--unless it believes it can achieve progress against some impediment or evil that is preventing forward movement. Though an activity, progress is often presented as an ideal--a kind of abstraction subsuming all other ideals. When used in this sense, progress is so ill-defined as to have no meaning, but calls for progress are nevertheless heard. During the 1992 presidential campaign, for example, progress *qua* change was presented by the Democratic Party as a unifying--and meaningless--theme. When one hears calls for progress as an ideal, one hears a call to confuse effort with result, to confuse trying with success.

The American "can-do" spirit is pervasive, so nearly omnipresent that it is impossible for politicians of any stripe to successfully campaign absent a platform of progress. It is similarly difficult for any party that is out of touch with the Center to win national elections; that party will be seen as failing to present a platform of progress. That both the Republican and Democratic Parties are noticeably out of touch with the Center explains why, in 1992, President Bush lost his bid for reelection, President Clinton won by a narrow plurality, and candidate Perot sparked a noisy protest movement from significant numbers of the Center who voted "none of the above."

That the Center did not really like *any* of the above explains why an election among three highly visible candidates did not excite (as was predicted by many) an unusually high level of voter turnout. The issue is more than one of candidates, or even of parties. The failure of either established political party to garner a majority in the presidential elections of 1992 is but one manifestation of elites out of touch with the Center. The Center does not see the institution of government as relevant to addressing its most salient concerns.

THE CHANGING NATURE OF ELITES

From the viewpoint of the Center, our political and cultural elites are dysfunctional.[1] They are irrelevant to the Center because they do not speak to the ideals of the Center: they write and speak a great deal, but they have nothing to say.

In this context it is useful to note the unusual nature of elites in the United States. Their most significant feature is that they number in the thousands, because even the most formal system of elite designation--election to public office--is temporary. While there are those who have promoted the attainment of semi-permanent elite status through licensure or other rules of admission such as the granting of tenure, elite populations remain fluid--particularly with regard to openness of entry--because admission does not depend upon such accidental characteristics as heritage. Rather, elite status in America is rooted in qualification by achievement, and that qualification is not necessarily (or universally) material in character.

Not infrequently, an elite individual is abruptly reassigned from the elite to the non-elite: recall Richard Nixon's "resignation" from the presidency. Many such reassignments occur; not many are so noticeable. As I write, President and Mrs. Clinton are enmeshed in a public debate about his elite status (and hers, derivatively), due to actions they may have taken regarding the conduct of their marriage as well as the conduct of their business affairs.

Complementary to the absence of permanence is a second source of elite fluidity, geographic dispersion. The president of the local chamber of commerce may be an elite person, as may be the person who leads a litter clean-up campaign, as may be the secretary of a community's public employee union. All three of these people might find themselves members of another elite, say, the local parish church council. Among our thousands of elites, some have national definition and character. Members of professional sports teams generally constitute a broad national elite, as do members of particular prongs of the entertainment industry. There are also national elites who occupy niches of society: among such elites are those involved in the visual and performing arts, the writers and speakers constituting "the intelligentsia," and those elected to national public office.

The diversity and fluidity of elites given, there is evidence of pronounced dysfunctionality among our highly visible elites today, manifest in both the cultural and the narrower political arenas. What is dysfunctional is what does not work and is rejected by the Center because

it does not work.   What does not work is what fails the test of
transcendence--of hope for betterment, the affirmation of the Center's
ideals. The problem among our most visible elites is that the conditions
they promote as the best available approximations of our ideals are
dysfunctional, and so found wanting by a Center quite aware of their
insufficiency. The Center is constructing new elites to serve its ideals, and
the process of realignment underscores the inadequacies of those who
would prefer not to be reassigned. Theirs are the shrill voices raised in
defense of a status quo that is, already, no longer the status quo, although
new elites have not yet fully emerged.

DYSFUNCTIONAL ELITES: THE CULTURAL ARENA

In what claims to be high culture, as distinguished from what is called
popular entertainment, we see a virtually universal abandonment of the
integration of intellect and imagination in pursuit of any ideal.[2] Nearly
still--and very few--voices aside, progress has ceased. What is advertised
as "new" is not "new"--not an advance.   What is "new" is falsely
advertised, and the Center knows it, intuitively perceiving the worthless.
What is missing is the transcendence that inspires us to consider our
aspirations. At one extreme we see, we hear, and we read an art of
nihilism, an iconoclastic desecration of what can be known and
communicated, an art that in its very production reflects a premise of
denial born of despair. The "ideal" of such elite art is that there can be no
hope. Little wonder that the Center rejects such expressions.
    At the other extreme, we see an elite that has disengaged itself from the
contemporary altogether, an elite that condemns the nihilist but neither
seeks nor cultivates anything in its place. In mourning for the great art,
this group can be said to aspire to the "ideal" that art is no longer possible,
the creative spirit being dormant, if not dead. Of course exhibitions and
performances of the great art of the past continue to be well attended and
otherwise supported by the Center. This support is indirectly encouraged
by the elite who assert that in this "modern" era, great art is no longer
possible.   Such encouragement, however valuable as a matter of
conservation, discourages the emergence of contemporary genius, in favor
of uninspired imitation of the past.
    Paradoxically, the "ideals" of these elites are not too far apart--neither
affirms the possibility of progress. The Center properly rejects both the
revolting and the vacant as empty. With good reason, the Center is
reassigning these elites to the ranks of the marginal.

Not surprisingly, in what is called popular entertainment, which is to say the virtually ubiquitously available, there are parallel trends, though the situation is not nearly so bleak. At one extreme, and because in elite culture the preponderance of "new" expression is nihilist in character, the natural haven of today's more demanding popular audience is self-indulgent narcissism: an overabundance of explicitly sexual and/or violent expression constituting a voyeur's tour of immorality, frequently accompanied by the promotion of amorality. Here, there is a loss of drama--an absence of the tensions involved in the aspiration to transcendence--substituted for by a titillation that invites permission to be seduced, to wallow in unadorned passion. What is asserted here as popular is not imaginative: it is easy, coarse, and indecent. Temptations aside, the Center knows these things, which is why we hear so many complaints about gratuitous sex and violence on television and in films.

Fortunately, much of what is called popular culture is not so determinedly marginal. For example, the film industry has long known that the purely prurient will be permitted, but not broadly endorsed, by the Center. So there remains a lively market for works that affirm the human capacity for integrity. Put simply, there are good guys and bad guys--and the good guys win! It is irrelevant that such work is sneered at by the dysfunctional elites as "popular," tainted by having mass appeal, or "sentimental," tainted by addressing allegedly anachronistic notions of right and wrong. The Center goes its own way, and it will continue to insist upon offerings that reflect, to one degree or another, its ideals.

The situation in television is also encouraging. Though for decades government regulations promoted the maintenance of a communications oligopoly by restricting the use of readily available frequencies, and thus encouraged what amounts to censorship in programming via access restrictions, the advent of satellite/cable transmission systems enabled the Center to bypass the artificial elites created by license privileges. These developments have fostered a healthy, voluntary censorship: in a society whose sense of civility accepts the opportunity for individuals to indulge in narcissism as a matter of free speech, it is also possible to "lockout" such options in favor of literally dozens of channels offering the work of those who address the Center's ideals, its aspirational heart.

The "communications revolution" given, popular culture will exhibit an increasingly aspirational character, so long as citizens do not allow government to repeat its past mistakes by adopting censorial policies, however otherwise promoted. There are also elite efforts to promote "fairness" policies oriented toward censorship. Despite these impediments, the communications revolution will prove to be quintessentially Centrist in character.

There are two other quite encouraging signs, not often discussed in the context of culture. One is sports--at all levels of competition broad brush strokes across the American cultural landscape. The healthy American addiction to sports in all seasons is fundamentally Centrist. Our nearly universal American devotion to following the ball--be it golf, foot, basket, base, tennis, or volley--reflects both the fluidity of elite formation known as equal opportunity, and the ideals of fairness and achievement, or honorable success. In sports there is no question of following the rules, of self-indulgent flouting: if you commit a foul or some other violation, that is wrong and you are penalized and can even find yourself removed from the game. The entire emphasis is on doing what is right: on improving one's qualifications to play and keep score, on cooperating in the competition by learning and playing by the rules, on grace and dignity whether the contest is won or lost, and on the chance to compete, to try again another day. From the little leagues to the big leagues, and for both players and spectators, the high excitement generated by sports contests derives from their affirmative character.

Sports are about what we "can do" rather than what cannot be done. The ideals of our games parallel those of our political system to a remarkable degree. And, primarily because they are voluntary, our sports organizations function better than our governmental organizations; it is no surprise that many of us devote more attention to sports than to governance. Our dysfunctional elites, especially "the intelligentsia," sneer at this phenomenon because they think it reflects both ignorance and inattention. The Center knows better: nothing succeeds like success. And one of our ideals is to try for it.

The second encouraging sign is another American addiction--we are a nation of volunteers. In this sphere we practice progress, and we practice constantly. We form parent-teacher associations, we become Rotarians, we teach Sunday school, we have United Way campaigns, we organize Special Olympics, we become Big Brothers and Big Sisters. In short, we identify community concerns, and that "can-do" aspiration to make "it" better kicks in, motivating us to join up and take action, get a move on the situation. At these activities, too, our dysfunctional elites often sneer, labeling them as "unprofessional" and therefore inexpert, paltry. Here again, the Center knows better, and it goes its own way.

It would be helpful if the dysfunctional elite that is disengaged would emerge from its self-imposed hermitage to engage progress. That, however, is unlikely to happen. This dysfunctional elite is enamored of complaint, and I suspect that it has become too lazy to do anything much but talk to itself. Its most frequently observed public activity is whining about its opposite number. This elite dislikes trying, and it does not really want to engage a Center that it assesses as both corrupt and ignorant, entirely too vulnerable to temptation and lacking the capacity to discriminate to boot. Never mind. This elite is going the way of dinosaurs; it is producing nothing of interest to the Center because it is incapable of cultivating its own garden.

As to the nihilist elite of the "anything goes because nobody *can* know anything" school,[3] its influence is also increasingly marginal. What this elite is promoting is dysfunctional, and so disengaged from the Center. A cultural "ideal" rooted in despair--the idea that we cannot know anything and that therefore there can be no hope for betterment--does invite self-indulgent *anomie*, but denies the dignity born of hope. The Center recognizes that the "If it feels good, do it!" rubric, usually dressed up in the language of value neutrality (as a good), is both dispiriting and destructive, the province of the foolish. And so the Center is moving to dismiss this dysfunctional elite as irrelevant, even harmful.

DYSFUNCTIONAL ELITES: THE POLITICAL ARENA

Functioning as a subset of our cultural elites are our political elites, taken here as Left and Right, without regard to the two established political parties. Since both parties' memberships and leaders encompass the spectrum from Right to Left, the distinctions can be more clearly drawn without reference to the parties. In this arena there are again two broadly dysfunctional groups, both markedly out of touch with the Center. Two issues are not understood by either elite. First, the Center cares far more about right and wrong than it does about Right and Left. Second, the Center cares about right and wrong within the context of freedom to act. Put succinctly, the point of life is to lead a decent life, and to enable and guide one's children toward that goal.

In its central activity--progress--the Center is more concerned about cultural matters than political matters, and it views government as a necessary but recalcitrant servant of its ideals. Hence the concept of citizenship is accepted warily: to cede one's authority to an abstraction called government is to relinquish not only a corner of freedom, but also a corner of the responsibility to prevent anarchy that makes freedom possible. Whether the institution of government can promote freedom by fostering the continuing development of a common culture is open to question, because while freedom is natural, responsibility is voluntary--and government is coercive.

Thus the relation between the individual and government called citizenship is dangerous, a notion that involves "giving away" freedom by "giving up" responsibility. On the one hand, there is the possibility that order may be better preserved, and the range of individual choice enhanced, if certain elements of common culture are established at law as universal: If I "give away" a piece of my freedom, I will no longer have responsibility for X myself, someone else will take charge of X for me. On the other hand, there is risk: If I "give up" too much responsibility, then I will have given away most of my freedom; I will be bound to rules beyond my control, I will have made myself subject to coercion. If things don't turn out right, then the situation will be very difficult to change.

Seen in this light, citizenship actually involves two negatives: giving away freedom and giving up responsibility. To turn the famous phrase of a famous president, we citizens are always being asked what we can do for our country, in the context of what our country can take from us. That is the reason that no politician in this country can win an election without a platform of progress, a platform that addresses the Center's ideals. Our fail-safe mechanism is that even if we have given away and given up too much, we can require those to whom we have given away and given up to return their takings: we vote. It is in this context that the dysfunctionality of today's political elites manifests itself.

In the first case there is a Left that has been expert in promoting the idea that progress can best be achieved if the two components of citizenship are divorced, the idea that "giving away" freedom and "giving up" responsibility are not necessarily connected. The idea became merchantable precisely because it is idealistic, and therefore extremely attractive, amenable to discussion in the most positive of terms. It promises that our ideals can be achieved, not in approximation, but in actuality: to dream is to be.

The programmatic expressions of this idea have been many and pervasive, but the most salient demonstration of its falsehood has been the rise of a public, symbiotic, and parasitic poverty that has little to do with material well-being. The principal victims of this poverty are the underclass and the therapeutic class. In reconfiguring the nature of citizenship, an elite Left persuaded us to reintroduce slavery absent the color bar.

The reconfiguration of citizenship involved belief in two complementary myths. The first is that if you give up responsibility you will not give away your freedom, and the second is that if you give away your freedom, you will not give up your responsibility. The two myths are equally prevalent among the underclass and the therapeutic class. If, for example, you accept or award an assignment to public housing, the action is seen as enabling freedom. One is either liberated from an impediment preventing progress, or fostering progress by meeting a need. Never mind that the individual receiving shelter is not free to seek *any* shelter, and never mind that the individual awarding shelter is not free to seek *any* awardee, as would be the case in a voluntary contract between tenant and landlord.

Conversely, if you accept or award an assignment to public housing, the action is seen as enabling responsibility. One is either seeking to protect oneself or one is fostering such protection. Never mind that the individual receiving protection does not determine its suitability, and never mind that the individual awarding protection does not warrant its suitability, as would also be the case in a voluntary contract between tenant and landlord. Neither party to the transaction has acted freely or responsibly; each has accepted a degree of coercion that creates a symbiotic dependency. The dependency is also parasitic because the physical and moral capital required to sustain it is produced by and obtained from others.

As a result of the structures built upon these myths--and at a cost in human potential that is incalculable--millions of people have been condemned to bondage, however unshackled and enfranchised. They live apart, consigned to public housing and school plantations far worse than any other plantations that ever existed in this country--far worse because the new slaves are told that they are free. They live apart, bonded to masters who issue "welfare" checks, Medicaid authorization forms, food stamps and "surplus" food, and who administer a host of "therapeutic intervention" programs purporting to impart "living skills" ranging from "work readiness" to "parenting." Many of the new slaves are mentally ill and, tragically, they receive no care whatsoever.[4] Their masters are slaves of a different kind; feeding upon the bondage, they depend upon its perpetuation. Since the relationship between the new slaves and their masters is symbiotic, it is as difficult as the old slavery to dissolve. However, it is dissolving.

That the new slaves know the truth--instinctively, which is to say as a matter of common sense--is becoming increasingly apparent. The rise of vigilante patrols in areas liberated from police, the movement toward chastity until marriage, the demand that parents be empowered to escape assignment of their children to "schools" of violence and impropriety masquerading as tolerance, the increasing role of church-based independence programs, the resurgence of commitment to fatherhood in partnership with motherhood--all of these things bespeak a movement toward emancipation and the reuniting of freedom and responsibility, toward progress.

The creation of a professionally parasitic ministerial and therapeutic class, in both social work and education, arose directly from the American "can-do" ideal of progress. The idea of assuring opportunity by providing assistance to the less fortunate--and that in a spiritual rather than in any specific economic sense--is a part of our consensual creed. It is for the "can-do" reason that the ministrations of the therapeutic community are being rechanneled--by its membership. They are challenging the gospel of self-esteem that supplants the achievement of self-respect when freedom and responsibility are divorced. They are demonstrating that feeling good, as distinguished from doing well, does not constitute accomplishment. Many recognize the architecture of failure and are disengaging themselves from the machinery of the new slavery. Some are forming partnerships with others also in the process of reclaiming their citizenship.

That these strivings are still accorded little attention speaks to the tenacity as well as to the obsolescence of a dysfunctional elite Left. There was a time when it was possible for the Center to say--and it did say--that the idea of dreaming as being deserved a chance. That idea had not been tried under the particular--some would say peculiar--American rubric of progress. It is no great mystery that the Center gave away, and gave up, too much. That Center, however, is now reasserting itself, and those of the dysfunctional elite Left are being reassigned.

What of the Right? What of a political elite that has generally failed, in recent decades, to engage the Center's ideals altogether? It, too, is dysfunctional. In the first case, the Right has flirted openly with a fascism so wholly inimical to the American creed that it would be thought ludicrous were it not so menacing. The enterprise of this Right is not developing, but overturning, the American system of opportunity. This Right promotes the introduction of rank and hierarchy, conferred rather than earned, as meritorious. In constructing its proposed aristocracy, it threatens to accept accidents such as color or heritage as determinative of admission and status. The entirety of American experience rejects such constructions, though their menace is real: we fought a long civil war and adopted more than one Amendment to our Constitution in order to enshrine our ideals in this regard. While movements espousing prejudicial admission to opportunity remain on both Right and Left--and indeed we are practicing one Leftist variety now in our engagement of purposive discrimination known as affirmative action--our Centrist ideal is equal opportunity. Arbitrary hierarchies are alien to the American heart, and indeed their permanent establishment is viewed as morally wrong.

In the second case, there is an elite of the Right that simply refuses to engage progress *qua* political process. Matters of national security aside, this Right refuses to give a positive answer to what citizens can do without "giving away" or "giving up" too much. This elite answers the challenge of citizenship's double negative with further negatives: do nothing, do not try anything.

These purveyors of gloom are of three kinds. Some argue for retrogression, the return to a past described as idyllic--never mind that the workday ran from sunrise to sunset, the washing machine had not been invented, and not every adult could vote. Others specialize in tearing down the present, offering nothing in its place. They tell us that welfare is terrible, the tax system is terrible, public works projects are terrible, everything is terrible. Just tear it all down and--abracadabra!--see how much better life will become. Still others broadcast failure, neglecting success. Their message is: If we try X or Y, disaster will result, so do not try anything. This collection of whiners, complainers, and naysayers has nothing to say to a Center looking for "what works" so that progress can continue.

On the Right also, however, change is afoot. I have described two distinct elites of the Right because the Right as an elite is no longer monolithic. The elite that wishes to overturn the American system of opportunity was reassigned to non-elite status some time ago, by both the Center and by a majority on the Right; its extremist voice is now heard primarily under the auspices of a Left seeking to camouflage its own Marxist extremists by promoting the Right as extremist. The Center has taken note. And while the voices of the whiners, complainers, and naysayers are still being heard, new voices are addressing the need to affirm the Center's ideals by articulating an agenda of progress. As with the Left, the Center is reasserting itself with the Right, and reforming both elites in the process.

As in the cultural arena, in the political arena our dysfunctional elites are remarkably similar. The Center properly views both Left and Right as promoting and protecting their own elite status, rather than the opportunity to become elite. It is not, after all, that we object to elites. We know that leadership and the elite status that goes with it are necessary, even helpful. What we prefer--and indeed insist upon--are temporary elites, leaders whom we can reassign as progress dictates. If the failure of the Left can be summed up as elite dictation, then the failure of the Right can be summed up as a failure of elite invitation. In either case, those who continue to advocate what is dysfunctional will find themselves talking only to their mirrors.

THE VOICE OF THE CENTER

One of the reasons that the Center is reasserting itself--both pulling and pushing at the dysfunctional elites--is that our political parties are currently in complete disarray, inconsistent and even incoherent. It is not possible to delineate the structure of Left and Right by reference to the political parties, because both parties span the spectrum. This structure given, party coherence is impossible, and the result is more gridlock than progress. There are some who blame gridlock on a fickle Center, a Center that cannot make up its mind. It seems more likely that the Center has organized gridlock, so that the risk of additional damage by dysfunctional political elites is minimized while the Center conducts its business of realignment by reassignment.

Occasionally, we form a new political party, generally when some public evil is seen as so widespread that progress against it cannot be made absent radical change. At present, there is the possibility that a new party will form, for the new slavery is precisely such an evil. (Recall that the Republican Party was founded in 1854 as an anti-slavery party.) Certainly, a realignment is well underway. Politically, it is reflected in the progress of term limit measures across the states. To the extent that our dysfunctional political elites ignore the Center's pulling and pushing, they will increase their opportunities to be reassigned to non-elite status. The speed and direction of their response to the Center's dissatisfaction will determine whether "the Perot phenomenon" was a fluke, or the first breath of a new party.

The orientation of our society toward progress and the continuing development of capacity for citizenly well-being, or the pursuit of happiness, is in the hands of a Center determined to assert and pursue its ideals. In this project the Center will continue to formulate an enhanced, more visible and more public citizenship that involves claiming both freedom and responsibility for self-governance rather than the giving away of freedom and the giving up of responsibility involved in coercive governance.

Those on the political Left decry this movement as a shift toward the political Right; they express considerable fear, for example, of an evangelical Christian revival movement that is active politically. Not infrequently, one hears hysterical denunciations of a "religious right" determined to "impose their values" on the society as a whole. In some quarters of the Right also, this movement is being taken as a sign of political "victory." Neither the Left nor the Right understand fully that the shift underway is first, a phenomenon of the Center, and second, a cultural rather than a political phenomenon. What is occurring is more easily understood in the context of the Center as *heart*.

There is no question that the Center's project of realignment has political consequences. A great deal of what is being addressed involves restructuring the role of public governance in the culture, freeing the culture from enslaving influences and coercive, intrusive laws that have proved to be impediments to progress precisely because they limit citizens' freedom to experiment, to change course when a particular approach to solving a problem proves dysfunctional. Coercive inhibitions to the teaching of religious faith are, for example, under scrutiny by a Center interested in experimenting with parental selection and control of their children's schools. That this movement is national in scope but local in character is but one indication of the Center's direction. A wholesale rejection of public programs is highly unlikely, but the movement toward local control and supervision of such programs is clear.

The trend is toward simplification, toward making such activities as are assigned to the public sphere accessible and comprehensible. In the area of "law and order," for example, the trend is to require clearly understood and enforced penalties for felonious crimes. The broad appeal of the sports metaphor, "three strikes and you're out" is one reflection of the trend toward simplification.

Perhaps the most salient feature of the Center's new assertiveness is its insistence upon a larger and more public role for functional families, families with two parents caring for the children. In this area there is the likelihood that we will see a trend away from policies that discourage complete family formation and in favor of policies that encourage active fatherhood by discouraging (though not prohibiting) both divorce and bastardy. Indeed, one of the factors influencing the school choice trend is the sexualization of childhood resulting from educational efforts that have proven to encourage illegitimacy. As this trend develops, we are likely to see revisions to the tax code that assign more freedom and responsibility for self-governance to families, both those that are intact and those led by single parents.

In all of these cases, the Center is addressing areas of the culture to which it assigned a share of public governance now seen as dysfunctional in that it is unwieldy, inflexible, coercive, difficult to change, and failing to serve the Center's ideals. Thus the broad consequence of the Center's realignment will be a refinement, and something of a narrowing, of the role that politics and public policy play in the culture. Concurrently, the roles of self-governance and voluntary action will expand to conduct such activities as are removed from public governance. We can therefore be hopeful about the emergence of an embryonic but visible elite of the Center that promotes an expanded citizenship whose range of activity involves far more than voting. This citizenship is oriented to self-governance of communities through local involvement, experimentation and supervision, and its elite will be very broad indeed. The emergence of this elite is an indication that American civilization is approaching maturity, having passed through a long and tumultuous adolescence.

ENDNOTES

1. I am indebted to Paul M. Weyrich of the Free Congress Foundation for introducing me to the concept of "defective" elites.

2. I accept the notion that an appreciation of "high" culture requires at least autodidactic cultivation. I reject the idea that "popular" culture neither invites nor encourages such discerning endeavors. The distinction between the "high" and the "popular" is increasingly irrelevant in this era of universal audience self-selection.

3. I am grateful to sculptor H. Reed Armstrong for many discussions exploring the nature of nihilist influences in American culture.

4. Myron Magnet masterfully documents the plight of the homeless mentally ill in *The Dream and the Nightmare: The Sixties Legacy to the Underclass* (New York: William Morrow, 1992).

5. Notable accomplishments are reflected in the work of the Institute for American Values (New York, NY), the National Fatherhood Initiative (Lancaster, PA), the National Center for Neighborhood Enterprise (Washington, DC), and *Project 21* at the National Center for Public Policy Research (Washington, DC). New publications have also emerged; examples include *Urban Family, Diversity and Division*, and *Destiny Magazine*.

ABOUT THE EDITOR

DON E. EBERLY is the President and Co-Founder of the Commonwealth Foundation in Harrisburg, Pennsylvania, an institute committed to civic, democratic and economic renewal. He is also the founder of the National Fatherhood Initiative, a new national civic group seeking to restore fatherhood in culture. Mr. Eberly has held key staff positions in both the U.S. Congress and the White House. He has written extensively on economics and social policy issues. Mr. Eberly is the author of *Restoring the Good Society: A New Vision for Politics and Culture* (Baker Books, 1994). He received his M.A. from George Washington University and his M.P.A. from Harvard University. In addition he has done doctoral studies at the Pennsylvania State University

ABOUT THE CONTRIBUTORS

DOUG BANDOW is a senior fellow at the Cato Institute in Washington, D.C. He is a nationally syndicated columnist with the Copley News Service and the former editor of *Inquiry* magazine. Mr. Bandow has written and edited many books including *The Politics of Envy: Statism as Theology* (Transaction), *Perpetuating Poverty: The World Bank, the IMF, and the Developing World* (Cato Institute), and *The Politics of Plunder: Misgovernment in Washington* (Transaction). He received his B.S. from the Florida State University and his J.D. from Stanford University

DAVID G. BLANKENHORN is the founder and President of the Institute for American Values in New York City. The Institute for American Values is a private, nonpartisan organization devoted to research, publication, and public education on major issues of family well-being, family policy, and civic values. Mr. Blankenhorn was appointed by the president in 1992 to serve on the National Commission on America's Urban Families. He received his M.A. from the University of Warwick in Coventry, England and his B.A. from Harvard University.

T. WILLIAM BOXX manages the Philip M. McKenna Foundation in Latrobe, Pennsylvania. The Foundation concentrates on public policy and education. He is also a Fellow in Culture and Policy with the Center for Economic and Policy Education at Saint Vincent College in Latrobe. Mr. Boxx is co-editor of *The Cultural Context of Economics and Politics*, which is to be published in the fall of 1994 by the University Press of America and the Center for Economic and Policy Education at Saint Vincent College. He received a M.A. from Duquesne University in

Pittsburgh and his B.A. from Arkansas State University. In addition, Mr. Boxx is a Ph.D. candidate in theology at Duquesne University in Pittsburgh.

HARRY C. BOYTE is the founder and Co-Director of Project Public Life, a national civic education initiative based at the Hubert H. Humphrey Institute of Public Affairs. He is also the Co-Director of the Center for Democracy and Citizenship at the University of Minnesota, a Senior Fellow at the Humphrey Institute and a graduate faculty member of the College of Liberal Arts at the University of Minnesota. He has written extensively on community organizing, citizen action and citizenship, including *CommonWealth: A Return to Citizen Politics.* Dr. Boyte received his doctorate from the Union Institute.

ALLAN C. CARLSON is the President of the Rockford Institute in Illinois. He has written several books on the family in America including, *From Cottage to Work Station: The Family's Search for Social Harmony in the Industrial Age* (Ignatius, 1993). Appointed by President Reagan, Mr. Carlson was a member of the National Commission on Children from 1988 to 1993. He received his Ph.D. from Ohio University.

A. LAWRENCE CHICKERING is the founder and Associate Director of the International Center for Economic Growth. He also helped found the Institute for Contemporary Studies. He has worked as an associate for *National Review* and is a regular columnist for the *San Francisco Chronicle.* Mr. Chickering served on the National Council on the Humanities from 1981 to 1987. He received degrees from Stanford University and the Yale Law School.

ROGER L. CONNER is a lawyer and founder of national nonprofit organizations working in the field of immigration reform and civil liberties. He is now the Executive Director of the American Alliance for Rights and Responsibilities in Washington, D.C. Mr. Conner is a frequent commentator on U.S. drug policy. He is a former Scholar in Residence at the Brookings Institution. Mr. Conner is a graduate of Oberlin College in Ohio and the University of Michigan Law School.

JOHN W. COOPER is the former president of the James Madison Institute for Public Policy Studies, located in Florida. Dr. Cooper has served as research fellow for the Ethics and Public Policy Center and the

American Enterprise Institute, both in Washington, D.C. He has written extensively in the area of religion and politics. Dr. Cooper received his B.A. and M.A. from Florida State University and his Ph.D. from Syracuse University.

DENNIS DENENBERG is a graduate level professor and Director of the Student Teaching Program at Millersville University in Millersville, Pennsylvania. He is a writer, lecturer, and teacher in the area of curriculum innovation. Dr. Denenberg received his doctorate and masters from the Pennsylvania State University and his B.A. from William and Mary College.

DENIS P. DOYLE is a Senior Fellow at the Hudson Institute. He is a former director of Education Policy Studies and Human Capital Studies at the American Enterprise Institute and a former Fellow at the Brookings Institution. He is also the former director of the National Institute for Education. Mr. Doyle works as a consultant, policy analyst, and a writer on education. He received his M.A. and B.A. degrees from the University of California at Berkeley.

ERIC R. EBELING is an assistant professor in the College of Education at Texas Tech University where he teaches graduate courses in the history and philosophy of education. He holds his Ph.D. from the University of Maryland, College Park. His research interests include the role of families and communities in education, school reform, and the history and future of American education.

JEFFREY A. EISENACH is the President of the Progress and Freedom Foundation in Washington, D.C. Dr. Eisenach is a former research associate at the American Enterprise Institute, former visiting fellow at the Heritage Foundation, and former senior scholar at the Hudson Institute. In 1985 and 1986, he served in the White House as chief of staff to the Director of the Office of Management and Budget. Dr. Eisenach has held teaching appointments at the University of Virginia, George Mason University and Virginia Polytechnic Institute. He received his B.A. from Claremont McKenna College and his Ph.D. from the University of Virginia.

OS GUINNESS is an author and speaker who lives in Fairfax County, Virginia. An Englishman, he has been a Visiting Fellow at the Brookings

Institution and is currently the Executive Director of the Trinity Forum in Burke, Virginia. He is the author of several books, including *The American Hour* (Free Press, 1993). Dr. Guinness received his D.Phil. from Oxford University.

EUGENE W. HICKOK, JR. is associate professor of political science at Dickinson College and adjunct professor of law at the Dickinson School of Law. He is also the Director of the Clarke Center for Contemporary Issues at Dickinson College. He is the author of numerous books and articles on American politics, law and the Constitution, most recently *Justice versus Law: The Courts and Politics in American Society* (The Free Press, 1993; with Gary McDowell). Dr. Hickok received his Ph.D. from the University of Virginia.

HEATHER RICHARDSON HIGGINS is the Executive Director of the Council on Culture and Community in New York City. This organization focuses on the examination and promotion of those attitudes and values necessary to democratic capitalism and American civilization. She is also a senior fellow at the Progress and Freedom Foundation. Mrs. Higgins has served as an editorial writer for *The Wall Street Journal*. She co-hosts, *The Progress Report*, a live weekly hour-long program on public policy issues. Mrs. Higgins received her B.A. from Wellesley College and her M.B.A. from New York University.

NEIL HOWE is a writer, historian, economist and demographer. He is currently senior advisor to the Blackstone Group on Public Policy, and the chief economist for the Competitiveness Policy Institute. Mr. Howe has written extensively on budget policy and aging, on attitudes toward economic growth and social progress, on the collective personalities of generations, and on how different generations succeed or fail in creating endowments for their heirs. He received his B.A. at the University of California at Berkeley and his M.A. in economics and M.Phil. in history from Yale University.

MICHAEL S. JOYCE is President and Chief Executive Officer of the Bradley Foundation in Milwaukee. Prior to his position with the Bradley Foundation, he was Executive Director and a trustee of the John M. Olin Foundation, Executive Director of the Goldseker Foundation, and a Research Associate at the Educational Research Council of America. He has also been a teacher of history and political science at the secondary and college levels. Dr. Joyce has been an advisor to two presidents. He was a member of the Presidential Transition Team in 1980 and has served on two presidential commissions. He received his B.A. from Cleveland State University and his Ph.D. from Walden University.

GLENN C. LOURY is a professor of economics at Boston University. He previously taught economics and public policy at Harvard, Northwestern, and the University of Michigan. Dr. Loury has written extensively in the fields of microeconomic theory, industrial organization, natural resource economics, and the economics of income distribution. He has been an advisor and consultant with state and federal government agencies and private business organizations in his fields of expertise. Dr. Loury received his B.A. from Northwestern University and his Ph.D. from the Massachusetts Institute of Technology.

ELIZABETH B. LURIE is the Director and President of the W.H. Brady Foundation in Maggie Valley, North Carolina. Formed in 1956, the Brady Foundation currently concentrates on the enhancement of the institutional foundations of a free society: morality and public life, family and community; and competitive educational structures affecting the preservation and continuing development of western civilization. Mrs. Lurie is a successful businesswoman in Maggie Valley, North Carolina. She received her A.B. from the College of William and Mary.

EDWARD A. SCHWARTZ is the President of the Institute for the Study of Civic Values in Philadelphia. He founded the institute in 1973 to develop education, research, and action programs that relate contemporary issues to America's historic ideals. Dr. Schwartz has served on the Philadelphia City Council and directed Philadelphia's Office of Housing and Community Development between 1987 and 1991. He is a visiting lecturer in the Urban Studies Department at the University of Pennsylvania and has taught at Haverford College and Temple University. Dr. Schwartz received his B.A. from Oberlin College and his Ph.D. from Rutgers University.

COLLEEN SHEEHAN is on the faculty of political science at Villanova University. She is currently compiling a volume of essays on the practical wisdom of Jane Austen. Her articles on the American Founding have appeared in journals such as *Interpretation: A Journal of Political Philosophy* and *The William and Mary Quarterly*. She received her B.A.

from Eisenhower College and her M.A. and Ph.D. from the Claremont Graduate School.

WILLIAM A. STRAUSS is a writer, historian, theatrical director, and entertainer. Mr. Strauss's research and writings have focused on U.S. generational history, including a complete history of America told from a generational perspective. He has held several staff positions in the U.S. Congress. Mr. Strauss cofounded the Capitol Steps, a professional satirical troupe. He holds degrees in economics, law, and public policy from Harvard University.

BARBARA DAFOE WHITEHEAD is a social historian and research associate at the Institute for American Values in New York City. She directs the Institute's project on The Family in American Culture, a program of scholarly and field research on the family as an institution of civil society. Dr. Whitehead also serves as the Associate Director of the newly formed Council on Families in America. She holds her Ph.D. and M.A. from the University of Chicago and her B.A. from the University of Wisconsin.

WILLIAM VAN DUSEN WISHARD is the President of WorldTrends Research in Reston, Virginia. He has analyzed global trends for over three decades, including a nationally televised address to members of Congress, outlining patterns of world change. He has served the U.S. government in four administrations. During his career, Mr. Van Wishard has worked in over 30 countries in the areas of public information and education programs.